True Relations

A true
RELATION
OF
The late great Mutiny which was in the City and County of NORWICH, April 24. 1648.
WITH

That accident that befell thofe Mutiniers that day:
there being as is thought, above 200. flaine by the fireing of 98.
Barrels of Powder;being truly related in a Letter from the
City of *Norwich* , to an honourable Perfon of the honourable Houfe of Commons , with the Votes of
the Houfe concerning the fame, and ordered
to be printed,to prevent mifinformation.

In fove m quam foderunt ,&c.

LONDON. *Printed for* George Whittington, 1648.

TRUE
RELATIONS

Reading, Literature, and Evidence
in Seventeenth-Century England

FRANCES E. DOLAN

PENN

UNIVERSITY OF PENNSYLVANIA PRESS

PHILADELPHIA

Published by
University of Pennsylvania Press
Philadelphia, Pennsylvania 19104-4112
www.upenn.edu/pennpress

Printed in the United States of America on acid-free paper
10 9 8 7 6 5 4 3 2 1

Library of Congress Cataloging-in-Publication Data
Dolan, Frances E. (Frances Elizxabeth), 1960–
    True relations : reading, literature, and evidence in
seventeenth-century England / Frances E. Dolan. — 1st ed.
    p. cm.
    Includes bibliographic references and index
    ISBN 978-0-8122-4485-4 (hardcover : alk. paper)
    1. English literature—Early modern, 1500–1700—
Criticism, textual. 2. Law and literature—England—
History—17th century. 3. Evidence—History—17th
century. 4. Knowledge, Theory of, in literature. 5.
Reality in literature. 6. Truth in literature. 7. England—
Intellectual life—17th century. I. Title.
PR438.42   2013   2012031342

Frontispiece. Title page of *A True Relation* of an explosion. The attempt to "prevent misinformation" is typical of texts that present themselves as true relations. The flying body parts of the mutineers might stand for the fragmentary, dynamic nature of evidence, and the demand it places on readers to collect and relate scattered remains. Reproduced by permission of The Huntington Library, San Marino, California.

Contents

Note on Spelling

I have largely retained original spellings and punctuation in quotations from early modern texts except when I am quoting from modern editions. However, in the interests of granting access to as many readers as possible, I have also followed the standard practice of silently expanding contractions, distinguishing i/j and u/v, and altering the long s.

Introduction

Shakespeare's tragic heroes often attempt to control how they will be remembered. Hamlet famously enjoins Horatio to forego the felicity of death "To tell my story" (5.2.291). Othello instructs Lodovico on exactly how to describe his tragedy: "I pray you in your letters / When you shall these unlucky deeds relate, / Speak of me as I am. Nothing extenuate, / Nor set down aught in malice" (5.2.349-52). The play's last lines are Lodovico's: "Myself will straight aboard, and to the state / This heavy act with heavy heart relate" (380-81).[1] What interests me here is the word Othello and Lodovico use to describe the activity of transmitting information—"relate." This verb signals a transaction between Othello and Lodovico in anticipation of a transaction between Lodovico and posterity, in which Lodovico will have to recount these unlucky deeds. The story itself is, of course, about relations fraught with conflicts around status, gender, sexuality, race, and ethnicity. And the project of relating is tinged with concerns about veracity. Othello attempts to control how he will be spoken of and how those who receive this relation will perceive him. But, as in *Hamlet*, the play draws our attention to how unpredictable and contingent this process of narrative transmission is.

The connotations of the words "relate" and "relation" are at the center of my project. According to the *Oxford English Dictionary*, the term relation may mean variously (1) An account, narration, or report of something; (2) An attribute denoting or concept expressing a connection, correspondence, or contrast between different things; a particular way in which one thing or idea is connected or associated with another or others; (3) The position which one or more persons hold with regard to others by means of social, political, or other mutual connections; the connection of people by circumstances, blood, association, marriage, or feeling. For my purposes here, "true relations" connote supposedly true textual relations or accounts; the way such texts intervene in, depend on, supplement, or substitute for social relations; the central role of figures of relation, such as simile and metaphor, in the period's vexed attempts to relate truth through words; and the sometimes occluded relations between our methodological debates now and debates in the period. The words relate and relation are just as ubiquitous and freighted in scholarly discussions of seventeenth-century texts as they are in the texts themselves. Perhaps for that very reason, their meaning and functions have not been scrutinized. It is my purpose to draw them to the center of attention in order to explore their richly varied meanings.

Seventeenth Century True Relations

In the motley ranks of seventeenth-century print, we find narratives, accounts, discourses, and news, as well as relations. We also, occasionally, find relations that pronounce themselves strange or do not opine on their own truth. But the most common title is the "true relation," sometimes intensified as the true and perfect or true and exact. I do not offer a survey of true relations or restrict myself to texts with that title. Instead, I take that ubiquitous phrase as a provocation for thinking about truth in and as relation.

While, in the chapters that follow, I will not limit myself to texts whose titles identify them as true relations, that group of large and various texts should offer a useful starting point. In the English Short Title Catalogue, one finds hundreds of titles that purport to offer relations of important events and discoveries, relations that often proclaim themselves true. They offer their readers access to information of interest; announcing their own status as mediated relations, they also make bids to veracity. According to Barbara Shapiro, "stories or tales" were considered to be distinct from "relations," which made greater claims to accuracy.[2] While my investigations will muddy rather than clarify the distinction between stories and relations, I agree with Shapiro that the designation of a text as a relation, especially a true one, announced its particular claim on the reader's trust or belief. Such a text might be as short as a single-sided broadside or hundreds of pages long. It is almost always in prose. True relations describe monsters, miracles, natural disasters, murders, shipwrecks, battles, executions, live burials and resurrections, apparitions, prophetic infants, and the treatment of prisoners of war. True relations also convey discoveries achieved through exploration or experiment and solicit investment in ventures such as plantations in Virginia and Maryland. The title, shape, documentation, and vocabulary of the true relation of a recent battle might differ very little from that of a miracle or an experiment. Often such texts present themselves as credible accounts of happenings they worry readers may find incredible. Sometimes they attempt to interpret the meaning of the occurrences they describe, and sometimes they do not, leaving the reader to evaluate it for him- or herself.

Many true relations respond to other relations they disparage as inaccurate, aiming to set the record straight. While they relate events, then, they also relate themselves to other accounts of those events. For example, *A True Relation of the Unjust, Cruell, and Barbarous Proceedings against the English at Amboyna In the East-Indies* (London, 1624) responds to a Dutch pamphlet that was translated into English and distributed in England "to brave and disgrace us at our own dores, and in our owne language. This, no English patience can bear." It also reprints this unbearable text that has forced the English East-India Company, "contrary to their desire and custome, to have recourse also to the Presse . . . to acquaint the world with the naked truth of this cause, hitherto masked, muffled, and obscured in a fog of fictions, concealments, and crafty conveiances."[3]

"True Relations" often support their truth claims with documentation. Sometimes authors refer the reader to living witnesses. For example, Richard Sutton, "an Eye-Witness, and a Fellow Sufferer," assures readers of his *True Relation* of the mistreatment of prisoners of war that "I am able to produce the Testimony of at least twenty Men, in a short time, if occasion required, that are able to make Oath, that I have not writ any thing in this whole Work that is contrary to Truth."[4] Some texts shore up such promises with lists of names or addresses where witnesses can be found. William Davies explains to readers of his *True Relation* of his own *Travailes and most miserable Captivitie* (1614) that he has expended considerable effort securing the signatures of six masters of ships of London "who . . . relieved me often during my thraldome." While he "might easily have procured" the "hands" of many others who "did see, and can witnesse my slavery," he "held it needlesse to trouble either them or my-selfe any further" because "these present witnesses are sufficient."[5] But they are present to the reader only as a printed list of names; only Davies's description of his process avows that living persons stand behind their subscriptions.[6] Or at least that they once did.

Many texts reproduce documents rather than directing the reader to eyewitnesses. *A True Relation of the Poysoning of a whole Family in Plymouth* (1676) provides its reader with "an Authentick Relation" of the examination of those convicted as well as "other persons depositions concerning it, as they were transcribed from the day Book of the Town"; *A True Relation of the*

Wonderful Cure of Mary Maillard (1694) reproduces "the Affidavits and Certificates of the Girl, and several other Credible and Worthy Persons, who knew her both before and since her being Cured" of lameness and assures the reader that the originals of these documents "are in the Hands of Richard Baldwin [the printer], which any Inquisitive Person may see and peruse whenever he pleases."[7] For the reader at a remove of space or time, such avowals usually cannot be verified. They stand in for the proofs toward which they gesture, whether original documents or witnesses. Listing witnesses or reproducing documents, these authors assemble a kind of archive to substantiate truth claims, challenge rival narratives, and win readers' trust. They also open access to this archive, in an impulse similar to that of later editorial projects like the Historical Manuscripts Commission or the Calendar of State Papers, first in print and recently in electronic form. Yet even as they relate their true relations to evidence that stands beyond or behind them, that alternative to the textual recedes, leaving us only with printed versions of "originals" we usually cannot check. Since we cannot, their existence becomes a matter of faith, faith in the truth of the relation.

Although texts were not the only form of evidence in the early modern period, even what we might consider the vividly corporeal circulated through verbal accounts—of a severed head that did not decay, a coroner's discovery, or an accusing apparition.[8] "Pen portraits" or verbal descriptions of suspects served as early modern police sketches.[9] Physicians asked patients for verbal reports on their condition, even by post. According to Roy Porter, "it was not believed that physical examination was a necessary or a sufficient procedure for diagnosing internal conditions. Rather the *sine qua non* of traditional diagnostics was the relating by the patient of his own 'history'."[10] The patient's relation of his case, and his relation to his physician, served as bodily proof. Increasingly, law courts valued written texts above other forms of evidence, and the document or "primary source" became central to historiography.[11] In all these cases, verbal relations both authorize themselves through their relation to what they describe and substitute for it. The way that printed relations reproduce their own documentation can best be understood in this context.

While there are sixteenth- and eighteenth-century printed texts whose title pages identify them as "true relations," the majority of such texts are from the seventeenth century. More broadly, the century seems to be particularly concerned with the contested nature of truth claims. Why should that be the case? The ongoing aftershocks of the Reformation and the political conflicts that led to revolution, regicide, and Restoration created both an urgent need to persuade and a nagging awareness that truth claims vary by party. A Catholic interpretation of a prodigy competes with a Church of England one;[12] the true relation of a priest's martyrdom counters the true relation of his treason; the Royalist true relation of a battle positions itself against the Parliamentary version. Historians have tracked dramatic changes in evidentiary standards and practices in this century, including the origins of an adversarial criminal trial before a jury, the emergence of coroners' autopsies, the supposed decline of magic, changing attitudes toward miracles and prodigies, the rise of experimental science, and the expansion of global exploration and conquest.[13] These changes all incited a need to share new knowledge, whether the results of experiments or the procedures and outcomes of trials, as well as a hunger for this hot-off-the-presses intelligence. Travel discourse, for instance, worked as a vehicle for "the primal act of witnessing," which was also its organizing principle and motive.[14] Many who had financial and intellectual stakes in new worlds had access to them largely through relations, oral and more often written. This became increasingly the case as the documentation of colonial expansion boomed.[15] Investors in overseas explorations and armchair naturalists relied on accounts of new world discoveries.[16] Even as contemporaries relied on purportedly true relations, they routinely disputed truth claims and the evidence on which they were based.

Despite dramatic conflict and change in the course of the century, it did not end with the codification of stable canons of evidence that have since been handed down to us unquestioned. Instead, what emerged in the course of the seventeenth century was a clearer sense of what was under debate regarding evidence and what was at stake. What one interpreter valued as credible, another dismissed as incredible. What was credited in one venue would be challenged in another. The debates that interest me here are those surrounding the interpretation of textual evidence. These debates did not originate in 1600 or conclude in 1700. Rather, we find in the seventeenth century an intensification of an inquiry that was already underway when the century began and continued in its wake. I focus on that heightened sense of urgency and self-consciousness regarding the contingency of truth claims because it was a defining feature of the period. But I am also interested in the seventeenth century because contemporaries' struggles remind us that our own uncertainty about how to achieve historical understanding is not just a function of postmodern theory or the simple passage of time. Uncertainty has not only been produced by missing documents, forgotten lore, or lost faith. It was a crucial part of how the seventeenth-century understood itself. Furthermore, some of the kinds of documents and evidence we long for never existed or were not particularly valued as repositories of truth.

It has sometimes been argued that the early modern period did not distinguish between fact and fiction in quite the way that we do now and that the boundary between the two thickened in the eighteenth century.[17] Many historians agree that a sea change occurred. Barbara Shapiro argues for a "growing breach between 'fact' and fiction" by the end of the seventeenth century, particularly in terms of the historian's practice: "By the end of the seventeenth century the 'facts' of history were 'real,' not imagined, and both history and fact were contrasted with the fictions of poetry and romance."[18] Malcolm Gaskill asserts that what he calls "fictionalized testimony" lost its "potency" after 1700.[19] In contrast, I argue that the boundary between true relation and fiction in the seventeenth century was not as fuzzy as such narratives suggest. If it had been, contemporaries would not have devoted so much energy to negotiating it. Nor is the boundary now as clear as this narrative of change asserts. Given the way that the courtroom and the press continue to function as arenas of contestation, it is hard to accept this insistence on a decisive paradigm shift. I focus on what is, for some scholars, the "before" picture, precisely because of the ways in which we have not moved beyond it yet. In many seventeenth-century texts, we find the supposedly postmodern claim that truth is a product or effect of narrative, that the story is not the opposite of reality, or the trope the opposite of truth, but the only means by which truth can be *related* both in terms of "conveyed to another" and in terms of "engaged with."[20]

The events that define the century and generate conflicts over truth claims are inseparable from the technologies that conveyed them to and constituted them for increasing numbers of people. While the printing press as "an agent of change" and a disseminator of information was hardly new, its output increased dramatically during this period. Print expanded textual access and, according to Elizabeth Eisenstein, made it easier for readers to compare one text to others. As a result, "contradictions became more visible; divergent traditions more difficult to reconcile."[21] With new genres, such as the newsletter, emerging, print also threatened "information overload" as Ann Blair has shown.[22] While print was certainly a revolutionary technology, it did not wholly supplant either manuscript or oral transmission.[23] The reader often had to think across evidentiary registers, comparing an oral report to a manuscript newsletter, printed newsbook, or trial account. As Adrian Johns argues, the new technology did not immediately promote confidence in the stability of the printed text, in part because of variants across a given print run.[24] Indeed, it might be argued that print has never achieved "fixity."

That places an onus on the reader, who must decide whether a relation is true for him- or herself. Many people depended on print for their access to information. Steven Shapin and Simon Schaffer argue that readers participated in experimental science by reading printed accounts, "literary technologies" of "truth and assurance," through which they stood as "virtual witnesses."[25] The virtual witness did not simply read a description of an experiment. He or she reproduced it in the mind's eye so as to participate imaginatively, thus obviating the need "for either direct witness or replication" and closing the opposition between reading and doing.[26] Affording access, true relations such as experimental reports also required both imaginative reenactment and critical engagement.

Since contemporaries were acutely aware that truth was interested and therefore contested, that there were multiple perspectives from which one might present "a" rather than "the one and only" true relation, texts had to reflect on and defend their own claims to veracity. The prophet Anna Trapnel justifies her autobiographical narrative *Anna Trapnel's Report and Plea* (London, 1654) as a true relation by contrasting it to what the title page calls "reproachful, vile, horrid, abusive, and scandalous reports, raised out of the bottomless pit against her":

> the Lord my God knows, had there not been so many severall reports passed far and near, I would not have set pen to paper in this kind, but it is that truth may silence falsity; and though I fail in an orderly penning down these things, yet not in a true Relation, of as much as I remember, and what is expedient to be written; I could not have related so much from the shallow memory I have naturally, but through often relating these things, they become as a written book, spread open before me, and after which I write.[27]

The meanings of "relate" are almost dizzying here. Trapnel distinguishes a true relation of what she remembers and is "expedient" from "an orderly penning down." Her memory would not have allowed her to relate all she does if it were not for the fact that "through often relating" her experiences she has fixed her memory into "a written book" she can follow as she writes her book. Her access to her experience is, then, inseparable from relating it, through which she shapes as well as records her memory. Relation is thus the cause, effect, and process of her text.

Since Trapnel claimed that she was not present during her own trances, she needed others to record and convey what she said during them. In other words, she needed the services of a "relator." Those who presented true relations of one kind or another were routinely called relators, that is, a person who relates something, a narrator or reporter, an informant. For example, *A True and Perfect Relation* of a poisoning assures the reader that "the Relater was an eye and ear witness" of the "sad, doleful spectacle."[28]

A text about Trapnel's prophecies compiled by a male "relator" elaborates on the multiple meanings of *relation*. The title page announces the text as "a relation" and describes what it "relates to": *The Cry of a Stone: Or a Relation of Something Spoken in Whitehall by Anna Trapnel, being in the Visions of God. Relating to the Governors, Army, Churches, Ministry, Universities: And the Whole Nation.* Before the reader gets "to the Relation itself," the relator offers an account of Trapnel's "condition in her Relations, her acquaintance, her conversation" presented in the first person "taken from her own mouth." The relator explains that he undertook to "present to publick view a true and faithful Relation of" what he could "take" from Trapnel over seven or eight days "by a very slow and unready hand" so as to counter those "various reports" that present her words "deformed and disguised with the pervertings and depravings of the Reporters." Even though this text, like Trapnel's *Report and Plea*, is presented as a corrective to inadequate reports, the relator consistently emphasizes the inadequacy of his transcription. The text offers only "some taste" of "the things that were spoken, as they could be taken by a slow and imperfect hand." She "uttered much more in Prayer, which the Relator, because of the press of people in the Chamber, could not take." In Trapnel's trances, then, there are some things no one could have grasped and others that the relator simply could not get down: "She sung of the glory of the New *Jerusalem*, which escaped the Relators pen, by reason of the lownesse of her voice, and the noise of the people; onely some pieces were taken here and there, but too broken and imperfect here to relate."[29] Trapnel's relator bids for the reader's confidence by drawing our attention to his struggles to capture the experience of being in Trapnel's presence when she was in a trance. But other than that, he tells us nothing about himself, keeping our focus on Trapnel and the vexed process by which he struggles to "take" and "relate" what she said.

What, then, is the relationship between the relator's credibility and that of his account? Since, like so many relators, this one is anonymous, he defies some claims about credibility in the early modern period. Steven Shapin, for example, has argued that credibility was a function of social status and that, as a consequence, only some people "embodied" credibility; he argues that Protestant gentlemen were most likely to be found credible.[30] When knowledge is a function of the knower, the knower is not an obstacle to objectivity but a source of authority.[31] While Shapin has been influential, his claim that credibility was restricted by gender, status, and religious affiliation has been challenged.[32] Like Trapnel's nameless relator, many outside the very privileged circle on which Shapin focuses made claims to credibility, albeit contested ones, on the basis of their access to information, that is, their status as eye- and earwitnesses. Sometimes, one's relation to the events described—what one did—qualified one as a reliable eyewitness more than social status—who one was. As Peter Dear puts it, "Located, explicitly or implicitly, at a precise point in space and time, the observer's reported experience of a singular phenomenon constituted his authority."[33] "Reported" is a crucial word in Dear's formulation since the issue is not the observer's experience as much as his ability to compose a compelling relation of that experience. The relator's credibility was not the source of his text as much as its product or consequence. An observer becomes a witness by relating what he or she has seen to others and thus fostering a relation between relator and reader/listener.

As one seventeenth-century relator explains, he determined that he could place his "historical faith" in eyewitness true relations if the witness was someone "whose Candor and Truth" he had "no reason to doubt," if, on "wary inspection," he was convinced that the witness "can have no interest to lead him to impose upon" him, and if multiple witnesses "unknowing to each other" produced consistent accounts.[34] These carefully explained criteria are brought to bear on a case that, on the face of it, might seem improbable to many readers today: the miraculous preservation of the corpse of a Christian slave who was executed for beheading a Turk who had attempted to rape him. Especially in such cases, other writers remind us, we must be able to trust witnesses "whom we can have no suspicion of, for joining in a Conspiracy to carry on a Lye . . . as if we had seen it with our own Eyes; for there is the foundation of the most part of our knowledge." That is, most of what we know is on the report of other people.[35]

The value placed on having "no interest" and being "uninterested" might suggest the possibility of what Peter Burke calls the "innocent eye," a "gaze which is totally objective, free from expectations or prejudices of any kind."[36] But if such an eye is ever possible, it does not seem even to have been an aspiration in the early modern period. Some relators were authorized precisely by their interest in a topic at hand, their partisanship. This is one way in which

a true relation was a function of other social relations; what a reader apprehended as true depended on his or her relation to the perspective espoused
by the text in question—the signals, for instance, that this was a Catholic or
Protestant true relation. Still, many true relations supply information about
the relator's relation to the events described rather than the details of his or her
social status. In fact, he or she often remains anonymous. Furthermore, he or
she often relates and authorizes another witness's account to readers. In many
cases, then, credibility is lodged in a text as much as a person.

Early Modern Methods: The Reader as Relator

The proliferation of true relations raised the question, as Adrian Johns points
out, not only of whom to believe but of "how readers decided *what* to believe."[37] As the assumption that a person's character or credit guaranteed credibility began to erode, new criteria had to be developed for assessing testimony
itself and not just its source, that is, the authority of witnesses.[38] Increasingly,
texts appealed to readers to adjudicate among rival truth claims.[39] While we
cannot know what texts meant to their early readers, I investigate the way that
extant texts present themselves as true and relate themselves to the events they
depict, to other texts, and to their readers, especially the ways in which they
appeal to readers to find or make the truth using the materials they supply,
but only in part, so that their truth resides not with the relator or even in the
text but in the reader's relation to both. The reading practice that interests
me is a practice of positing relations. This relational reading practice does
not just grasp the relations a text implies nor does it join texts only to other
texts. As it is imagined in a range of texts I study, this practice unpredictably
but robustly relates texts to events and persons and feelings, prescription to
practice, fiction to fact, description to experience, thus muddying distinctions
that structure many of our assumptions about early modern texts. Building
on recent scholarship on active, appropriative reading, I consider the reader
as a relator, creating networks or collages of meaning. This reading practice is
not confined to the early modern period; indeed, I am arguing that we take it
as our own model. But it emerges out of the particular circumstances of that
time and place.

The extraordinary scholarship on the history of reading in the last few
decades has painted a picture of the early modern reader as active, creative,
impertinent, opportunistic, and unpredictable. While I am interested in an

interpretive practice that does not leave the kinds of material traces on which most historians of reading depend, I draw on their work in support of my conjuration of a reader equipped to act as a relator. In an influential essay, Anthony Grafton and Lisa Jardine argue that "humanistically trained" readers were "goal oriented," reading classical texts selectively and purposefully to equip themselves or those they advised for action in the world. A reader's own goals thus shaped his or her reading, so that "a given text could give rise to a variety of readings, depending on the initial brief," and to a variety of outcomes or practices. Such readers also read in relation to others, who might include colleagues, friends, students, or a spouse, scribe, or secretary. Grafton and Jardine call this a "transactional model of reading."[40] Subsequent scholars have built on and extended their idea of a transactional model of reading—focused on relations among persons and texts, between thought and action, the past and the present—arguing that active reading stretches from the sixteenth century across the seventeenth and down the social scale; it includes women as well as men.[41] Presumably, readers' purposes varied, and many readers might not have articulated their purposes, even to themselves.

The detailed case studies that have transformed the history of reading have focused, understandably, on those readers who documented their practices and for whom that documentation survives. Marginalia have offered one form of evidence; such annotations are also called *adversaria* because they document a reading practice that is "adversarial: the text is the site of an active and biased appropriation of the author's material."[42] This is the kind of consumption that is also production.[43] While some readers' marginal marks engaged directly with the text at hand, linking it to other texts or contemporary events, other users, according to William Sherman, left marks that "had no obvious connection with the text they accompanied—but nonetheless testified to the place of that book in the reader's social life, family history, professional practices, political commitments, and devotional rituals."[44] Such readers extended the terrain of the transactional. Another important source has been the commonplace book, a personal record of quotations from and comments on reading. Once considered little more than a record of sententiae, the commonplace book is now recognized as taking many forms, including miscellanies of transcriptions, translations, clippings, and wildly various compositions and notes.[45]

Close attention to marginalia and commonplace books has transformed our understanding of the history of reading. But, as has been much discussed, this evidence is also rare and biased toward certain kinds of readers: elite, self-documenting men whose self-documentation survives. To discuss readers whose practices remain off the record, historians of reading often have to resort to speculation. I join in that speculation here, reflecting on a reading practice in which seventeenth-century texts instruct their readers but for which we do not necessarily have material traces. I examine cases not of particular readers or the reception of particular texts as much as moments and genres that invite readers to posit relations. Thus, although I draw on the conclusions of historians of reading, I use different evidence to discuss interpretive possibilities rather than material reading practices.

One of the most useful insights I have taken from histories of reading is that reading is not only active but what I am calling here relational. Commonplace books might include fragments of print pasted onto pages or print pages bound into a manuscript.[46] Some readers, eager for more space than margins provided, had blank pages bound into books to accommodate their comments. The reader who makes space for himself in a printed book or disassembles printed texts to use pieces in his own scrapbook focuses not on the text's origin but on its place in his composition. The reader makes meaning by materially asserting the relations he or she sees or creates among texts. This practice resembles that of Grafton and Jardine's readers in that it is about the process of positing relations, not only among texts but between texts and their readers, texts and experience. Comments in different hands in the margins or in a commonplace book open up another dimension to these transactions as well, as one reader adds to or critiques what another has written. Those who wrote in the margins or assembled commonplace books, notebooks, and diaries signaled that, for them, print was an interactive technology through which they could forge relations among texts and ideas and among people.[47] All these remarkable material traces of reading practices open up the more elusive possibility that readers who were not necessarily scholars might read not only with "authorities" in mind but mindful of people they knew, problems they were trying to solve, issues that worried them. They too were creating networks or maps of meaning with themselves or their family at the center, forging relations among texts, between texts and their experiences, and with other people.

Pursuing his or her own interests rather than cracking an authorial code, the reader was a rover as well as a collector and relator. He or she was not confined to the library or to what we would recognize as a book. The unhoused and freewheeling reading practice that interests me might take place anywhere. Many early modern people related to the built environment itself as a collection of texts.[48] The urban perambulator, as a result, constantly apprehended texts and made connections among them, just as the consumer of print might render a book into fragments that could then be reassembled in new ways. If reading was a relation to the material world and not just to the text, it was also an active process of positing relationships among the many textual fragments one found, clipped, or ripped, a creative act of assembly like collage or quilting.

In *Areopagitica*, John Milton argues that the body of truth has been dismembered and its parts scattered. My frontispiece, the title page from a true relation of an explosion, offers a vivid image of scattering body parts. I take this as a fitting image of the farflung and frayed pieces of various, intermingled bodies of truth. As a consequence of truth's dismemberment, according to Milton, the reader must wander and inquire after the fragments of "the torn body of our martyred saint," gathering them and figuring out how the parts relate to the whole.[49] In this image, the reader is a relator in a somewhat different sense than the relator who conveys a true relation. I juxtapose research into material practices of collaging and text-quilting with Milton's figuration of the reader collecting relics of truth and reassembling them into a kind of Frankenstein so as to suggest that the idea of a reader as a weaver or piecer together—a relator—might extend beyond those rare texts that record such practices. The relator constitutes from existing texts his or her own, whether or not he or she produces that new text in the form of a commonplace book that survives.

The reader stands at the center of an ever-reconfiguring web, constituted through his or her practice of selecting and connecting. As one seventeenth-century writer put it, the reader must choose what to cull out that was "fittest for your pleasure or profit" because "the laborious Bee gathereth her cordiall Honey, and the venomous Spider her corroding poison (many times) from the same Flower."[50] It is, thus, the culler's purpose that distinguishes honey from poison. Such a practice is associative and unpredictable. If different readers find different substances in the same book or flower, then poison or honey is something readers make as much as gather.

The active role of the reader—what the reader is doing when he or she "culls"—is not only an issue of how a reader posits relations between texts but how figuration itself, as it operates within a text, requires readers to grasp relations. In *The Art of Rhetorick Concisely and Completely Handled* (1634), John Barton defines the tropes of simile and metaphor, synecdoche and metonymy as figures of relation—relations that the author draws on but that the reader must not only grasp but help create. These are not only relations of likeness and difference: "Relation is, when a thing in any respect hath reference to another." Metonymy, for instance, is an "accidentall Relation" because it posits a relation between two things that "continues onely while they are Tropes, or otherwise they are not necessarily considered together." Barton gives as an example the description of a language as a "tongue" since animals have tongues without language. In contrast, he identifies synecdoche as describing a "naturall Relation" and a "true Relation" which exists inside and outside a trope: "the Genus must have his Species, and the whole his parts, and contrarily. These do subsist one in another." While metonymic relations temporarily substitute one thing for another with which it has affinity—"So the Lawyers speak in the cause of their Client, as if it were their own, though meer relation make them a part"—those things that are more naturally or truly related "subsist in one another" and have "consanguinitie."[51] This quickly becomes bewildering. But my point here is that Barton describes the art of rhetoric as an art of drawing upon as well as distinguishing "meer" relations from true ones and an art in which writers rely on readers to apprehend the relations they propose. Just as an author establishes figural relations for a reader to engage, so extended systems of figuration direct the reader's interpretation, thus making the writer the hider or planter of meaning and the reader the finder or decoder.[52] Typology, for example, required the reader to see England as a new Jerusalem or the New Testament as a redemption of the Old. It was possible for a reader to get metaphor, typology, allegory, or analogy right or wrong, from an author's point of view.

But other early modern reading practices were somewhat less predictable. In application, for example, the reader applies what she reads to her own experience or circumstances. The "goal-oriented" reading Grafton and Jardine describe is a form of application in that the goals are the readers' rather than the author's. Readers might apply what they read to circumstances the author could not anticipate. As Roger Chartier reminds us, "reading is a creative practice, which invents singular meanings and significations that are not reducible to the intentions of authors of texts or producers of books."[53] For Michel de Certeau, the reader "invents in texts something different from what they 'intended.' . . . He combines their fragments and creates something un-known" and unforeseen.[54] While de Certeau calls such a reader a poacher, she brings to the text as much as she purloins. Building on such emphases on unintended effects, I consider a relational reading practice that is invited rather than prescribed, but also errant rather than obedient.

This relational reading practice is indebted to what Philip Sidney describes as the "predicament of relation" by which one can know some things only in their relation to other things.[55] In a similar formulation, Francis Bacon marks as an error the belief that there is nothing new under the sun. There is new knowledge, he claims, but we resist it until we can relate it to what we already know: "as may be seen in most of the propositions of Euclid, which till they be demonstrated, they seem strange to our assent; but being demonstrated, our mind accepteth of them *by a kind of relation*, as the lawyers speak, as if we had known them before."[56] Lorraine Daston and Katharine Park argue that visual and verbal representations of unfamiliar phenomena operated through just this process of relating the strange to the familiar: "Descriptions of strange facts strained the resources of language and tended toward multiple analogies that decomposed the oddity into a mosaic of features, each to be mapped piecemeal onto a familiar element of experience."[57] The knower thus needed to bring existing knowledge to this interpretive practice, to break the strange phenomenon into pieces that could be related to the already known, and then to stitch those familiar pieces into a new assemblage, such as the chimera. The knower is then a relator, who supplies as much as she derives.

Linguistic cues signaled the reader to engage the conceptual operation of relating. William Gouge, whom I will study at length in chapter 5, identifies "so" as the "particle of relation"; "so" signals the simile, that figure of relation. But it also works more broadly to help the reader mark relations: as in one case, so in another. For example, in his marginalia, Sir William Drake used this particle of relation to point the relationship he saw between history and his present moment, writing in the margins of Henri de Rohan's *Treatise of the Interests of the Princes and States of Christendom* (1646): "so King James" or "so England."[58] This relational reading practice was not specific to the seventeenth century, and those who employed it would have read in other ways as well. The word relation is so ubiquitous that it is easy to miss how it connects figuration, knowledge production, interpretation, and social connection. Precisely in its capacious and slippery multi-valence, relation can, I will argue, provide a new way to think about our own practices even as it offers a keyhole into seventeenth-century methods.

Early Modernists' Methods

If contemporaries often depended on true relations for information, so, of course, do we. As has been much remarked, we too suffer from information overload, with electronic resources intensifying the process print began.

These resources too are changing reading practices. Online databases such as
Early English Books Online (EEBO), to name just one, have increased early
modernists' access to early printed texts; other databases, such as the Perdita
Project, are beginning to open up access to manuscripts as well. No matter
the discipline, those studying this period draw on an ever-widening range
of materials without any agreement, or even self-awareness, about how we
use these texts. There has been surprisingly little reflection on principles for
selecting evidence and standards for privileging some forms of evidence over
others or sorting evidence in terms of the kinds of claims one is trying to support. As access to early printed texts and manuscripts expands, so that what
once required a trip to an archive can now often be downloaded onto a home
computer, perhaps our emphasis can shift to what we do with textual evidence
once it is in front of us.

Although databases have sometimes been disparaged for stripping away
crucial layers of historical information from the reading experience, some ar-
chitects of "second generation" databases, that is, those that are both more
narrowly focused and more searchable than first generation behemoths like
EEBO, argue that such databases might actually enable us to reproduce something like contemporaries' fragmentary reading practices. According to Patricia Fumerton, "They allow us to remember the early modern period as it
encountered itself: by and through dismembering."[59] Thus, even the newest
resources require us to attend to the relations between early modern methods
and early modernists' methods.

The mediated and textual nature of our access to historical knowledge has
been much noted in recent decades and can now stand as a kind of given, as
likely to be rehearsed by historians as by literary critics. It's useful to return
to the nuances of Fredric Jameson's influential articulations. For Jameson, the
text

> articulates its own situation and textualizes it, thereby encourag-
> ing and perpetuating the illusion that the situation itself did not
> exist before it, that there is nothing but a text, that there never was
> any extra- or con-textual reality before the text itself generated it
> in the form of a mirage. One does not have to argue the reality of
> history: necessity, like Dr. Johnson's stone, does that for us. That
> history—Althusser's "absent cause," Lacan's "Real"—is *not* a text, for
> it is fundamentally non-narrative and nonrepresentational; what can
> be added, however, is the proviso that history is inaccessible to us

except in textual form, or, in other words, that it can be approached only by way of prior (re)textualization.[60]

As Jameson makes clear, he does not contend that "there is nothing but a text" or that there is no "extra- or con-textual reality;" he argues, instead, that texts encourage this illusion.

Many literary critics share Jameson's insistence that our access to history is mediated through texts. In a review essay on what was then called "new historicism," Louis Montrose defined the approach through its emphasis on the historical situatedness of texts and "the textuality of history"—that is, our textually mediated access to "a lived material existence."[61] Some historians and literary critics balked at what they viewed as eroding distinctions between representation and reality, literature and documents. In the mid-1990s, Patrick Collinson warned that, among literary critics, "even so-called new historicists are ultimately indifferent to what actually happened in history" and advised historians to draw the line amid all this loose talk about texts: "If documents, many of them, have a certain textuality, historians need to know they can put their trust in texts as documents." One must not, he suggests, concede too much to "the textuality of both historical sources and historical compositions."[62] Some literary critics share Collinson's longing for historical certainty and disciplinary distinctions, for what Catherine Gallagher and Stephen Greenblatt call "traces that seemed to be close to actual experience" and a sure sense of the kinds of documents in which such traces might be found.[63]

Yet it is also true that, in the wake of "the linguistic turn," many historians assume "the textuality of history" in all its complexity.[64] Carlo Ginzburg, for instance, argues that evidence is neither an "open window that gives us direct access to reality" nor "a wall, which by definition precludes any access to reality." Both views "take for granted the relationship between evidence and reality" rather than recognizing its complexity.[65] Many historians are making just the concessions that worried Collinson. For example, Stuart Clark, in his introduction to a collection of essays on the "languages of witchcraft," points out that, with regard to witchcraft, "historical investigation is increasingly being treated, in conceptual terms, as a kind of reading . . . approaching the past in much the same manner as a reader confronts a text—that is, by exploring patterns of meaning rather than causal relationships." As a consequence, historians of witchcraft must now be "readers of plots and tropes—experts in 'cultural narratives'."[66] Mary Fissell says of sensational pamphlets: "I would not venture to hazard any opinion about their veracity. Historians have tended

to employ some of these pamphlets as if they were truthful witnesses to real
events, and to dismiss others as fiction. Instead of emphasizing these texts'
production in relation to some real events, I understand them as stories whose
value to the historian lies in their popularity."[67] In yet another example, Peter
Lake and Steven Pincus assert that "We take the first task of the historian to
be to situate socially and politically the stories contemporaries told about their
circumstances rather than to evaluate immediately the truth-value of those
stories."[68]

Obviously, Clark, Fissell, Lake and Pincus do not speak for the discipline of history or for all historians. Nor would all literary critics embrace
the historically situated reading practice that they describe. But these quotations point to some shared terrain. Despite frequent reassertions of the divide
between literature and history, these are statements by historians that might
have been made by literary critics, especially in the wake of the no longer
"new" historicism. Perhaps we have moved beyond an opposition between literary analysis and the creation of historical knowledge in part by identifying a
shared object of analysis: the relation, the story, the fiction. While identifying
a text as a fiction might seem to let us off the hook of determining its vexed
"relation to real events," I will argue that is far from the case.

Considering the implications of recategorizing a document or evidence
as fiction helps explain why some might resist. Kevin Sharpe explains that the
word document "owes its origins to that which instructs, teaches, 'furnishes
evidence,' as if demanding no action from its historical pupil but to listen" and
that evidence "has as its first meaning 'clearness,' 'obviousness,' and derives
from the Latin *videre*, a word which means to see, to perceive. What both
terms *imply* is the availability of the past to communicate to and be seen by
the historian as a clear object or lesson unmediated by representations—or
time." Rejecting the claims both words make to offering unmediated access,
Sharpe prefers the word "text" because it draws our attention to its own manufacture as "something woven, artfully compiled."[69] Similarly, Gallagher and
Greenblatt emphasize that many texts are "fictions, in the root sense of things
made, composed, fashioned."[70] Many historians refer to "stories" or "fictions" to
draw our attention to texts' made-ness, to the process of their production. We
must then take their fabrication and provenance into account as part of the
story we use these texts to tell. Attentive to the artfulness of texts, stories, and
fictions, one might say that all "true relations" from the seventeenth century
are necessarily fictions without assuming them to be untrue. Of the possible
relations of a given event, a text presents itself as a true one, defined by its

ability to transact a relation between event and representation, between relator and reader.

For many early modernists interested both in the past and our mediated access to it, the problem remains how to conceptualize the true relation between representation and reality. As Jean Howard put it in a justly famous review essay on new historicism, undertaking "serious historical criticism . . . raises the question of some relationship between literature and what may be considered external to itself. The key question is: what is the nature of that relationship? Does the text absorb history into itself? Does it reflect an external reality? Does it produce the real?"[71] This is also, it has emerged, a key question for serious histories of "stories." As Ginzburg pointed out, the issue is not only a representation's relation to the real but its relation to other texts. Meaning must be grasped "relationally," Howard argues. "Relation" in its multiple meanings is a key word in many attempts to understand a reading practice that attends to a text's embeddedness and evidentiary value. To offer another example, in *Marvelous Possessions*, Stephen Greenblatt treats representation as "a social *relation* of production," so that a given text is "not only the reflection or product of social *relations* but that it is itself a social *relation*, linked to the group understandings, status hierarchies, resistances, and conflicts that exist in other spheres of the culture in which it circulates." This is especially the case in narratives of contact, which exist to record and manage new social relations, and are, for Greenblatt, "engaged representations, representations that are *relational*, local, and historically contingent."[72] Considering Greenblatt and Howard together, we see that representation is a social relation and that it must be grasped relationally. The word *relation* is so ubiquitous and multivalent that it is easy to ignore. We can agree across generations and disciplines that the key question and the key word is *relation* without being able to determine what that relation is. Furthermore, the relations at issue are not just ones we apprehend but relations we are in.[73] As scholars of the early modern period, we think in relation to one another, to our training, to the period we study, and to the object or issue under analysis.

At this juncture, there is nothing remarkable about pointing out that we can achieve access to knowledge of the early modern past largely through texts and that the extant body of textual evidence is one historians and literary critics share. The question remains, however, how to evaluate the textual form in which history is accessible to us and how to understand the meanings of texts as documents *and* as literature. On that, after much productive discussion, we have reached something of an impasse. Despite long discussion of the textuality of history, we are still negotiating the relationship between literature and evidence. On the one hand, terms such as "texts," "documents," or "discourses" both evade the distinction between what is literature and what is not and leave the category of literature unchallenged. On the other hand, many of the historians who describe legal depositions as "stories" or "fictions" do so in order to acknowledge their limitations as evidence. From this angle, I take the protestation of literariness as a provocation rather than a conclusion so as to argue for the usefulness of literary techniques of analysis, techniques many seventeenth-century readers both employed and distrusted, in the creation of historical knowledge. Ignoring a distinction between literature and document so as to broaden the range of objects available for my analysis, I then reintroduce the literary as a method rather than a taxonomy. In my usage, literature is embedded rather than transcendent, hard to localize but impossible to ignore, dispersed and mercurial. It is a grab bag of tactics of expression and interpretation that we can find in many places and that we can bring with us into an archive. While I include the words "literature" and "evidence" in my title, then, my purpose is to muddy the distinction, arguing that what is usually called literature can and does serve as evidence, depending on the claim, and that many texts confidently accepted as evidence can and should be read in ways we think of as literary.

The Plan

The book is divided into two sections of three chapters each. The first three chapters address early modern crises of evidence, including the Gunpowder Plot, witchcraft prosecutions, and the London Fire; these crises hinged on the contingency of truth claims, particularly how "true relations" depended on social relations. Each chapter in this first section examines how accounts of a particular traumatic event became the occasion for contesting standards of evidence. In most of the crises I consider, a process of inquiry ended in the discovery of the "fact" of Catholic, particularly Jesuit, lying and treachery. But that "fact" was also contested even at the time.

It could be argued that evidence is always a crisis. But even if that is so, in the seventeenth century there are moments of heightened awareness of truth claims' contingency. Furthermore, in the cases on which I focus, the archive against which we might want to check print relations is missing or spotty. I look at the official account of Henry Garnet's trial, which comments on all the ways in which it is both published by authority and exceeds the record, including things that were not said in court but should have been; the London Fire in which the parliamentary report on the fire's causes was rejected by Charles II and "leaked" to the press and exists largely in its printed forms; and witchcraft, in which printed accounts are usually much fuller than whatever terse legal records survive. Thus, whatever evidence we would like to believe subtends print or can provide a standard against which we can measure it is missing. When Hayden White disparaged "grubbing in the archives" and Dominick LaCapra diagnosed it as "archival fetishism," they questioned the idea that the archive facilitates unmediated access to the past or that its contents are prior to or outside interpretation.[74] Attention to the processes of selection and exclusion, loss and fabrication by which archives are formed has drawn our attention to the fact that, as Jacques Derrida puts it, the process of archivization "produces as much as it records."[75] More a process than a place, an archive creates a particular version of the truth by including some documents and excluding others and by positing relations among the materials archived. In *True Relations*, I have selected my crises of evidence precisely because they offer so little recourse to an archive and thus throw into question what it is we might have hoped to find there.[76] In cases in which we are forced to recognize the limits of the archival, historians and literary critics must share evidence in ways that many prefer to ignore. But that enforced collusion also requires us to think anew about how to make print yield bigger interpretive dividends—and what it means that we, like many contemporaries, depend on print for our access to information about seventeenth-century England. How do different scholars, in different disciplines, use the same materials? What assumptions seem to guide their selection and interpretation of evidence? Is discipline the most meaningful determinant of how a scholar will select and employ evidence?

The second half of the book explores the affinities between early modern and contemporary attempts to wrest meaning from texts. The final three chapters consider unlikely genres of evidence—legal depositions, advice literature, and drama—precisely because they are not the usual suspects; they are not what Barbara Shapiro identifies as "discourses of fact."[77] Hovering between fact and fiction, these are genres on which scholars rely heavily, even as doubts linger about their documentary and literary value. Confronting these doubts, and their roots in the seventeenth century, I read these texts as literature *and* as evidence. The issue is always: evidence of what?

I organize my first chapter around a detailed analysis of *A True and Perfect*

Relation of the Whole Proceedings against . . . Garnet a Jesuite (1606), the official account of the trial of Fr. Henry Garnet, supposed confessor to the Gunpowder Plot conspirators. In this 416-page text, I am especially interested in the way that the attorney general and members of the Privy Council present their ability to decipher Catholics' "dark figures" as the key to defeating Catholic treason even as they themselves rely on tropes to convey their prisoners' guilt. By concentrating on their figural turn, I show that their fascination with equivocation in part stems from their own reliance on "dark conceits." Interpretation is central to the trial and its representation, suggesting the disturbing ways in which the two sides are more alike than they are different. The competitions staged in Garnet's trial remain unresolved. Just as Garnet's "confessional identity" as a Catholic disabled him from speaking credibly at his trial, it also shapes how his case continues to be treated in reference works such as the *Oxford Dictionary of National Biography*. This chapter concludes with a discussion of how in the late 1670s, in the fevered aftermath of the Popish Plot, a single phrase, "as innocent as the child unborn," linked convicted murderer Leticia Wigington to Jesuits and traitors.

The relationships among confession, identity, tropes, and evidence lead me to an inquiry into how the purported truth value of "true relations" was often a function of other relations widely agreed to be under transformation in this period—among religion, magic, and science; between Protestant and Catholic, urban and rural, men and women, rich and poor, court and city. One's region, class, religion, and political affiliation often determined one's confidence in the procedures of evidence collection, as well as how one "read" the evidence itself. A reader's position in social relationships also shaped his or her response to a text. In *Hell Open'd . . . Being A True Relation of the Poysoning of a whole Family in Plymouth*, the relator, J. Q., enjoins the reader, at the end of his account, to grasp an appropriate lesson based on who he is, master or servant. "In what Relation standest thou? Inferior, or Superior?"[78] The truth of this relation is, then, a function of the relation in which one stands to it.

Chapter 2 explores the grounds on which some witchcraft accusations were accepted as probable and developed into prosecutions and convictions, while others were dismissed as "improbable." I focus on three cases that ended in acquittal: the copiously documented case of Anne Gunter, who accused three women of bewitching her and was ultimately tried, with her father, for malicious prosecution; Thomas Potts's account of the acquittal of the Samlesbury witches, an episode in his lengthy account of trials that largely ended in convictions, *The Wonderfull Discoverie of Witches in . . . Lancaster* (1613) and Thomas Heywood and Richard Brome's play *The Late Lancashire Witches* (1634), which was based on a later case of witchcraft in Lancashire that led to twenty convictions at the local level, but that Charles I reviewed, exposing the key witness's testimony as perjury. In all three instances, I am interested in the contingency of credibility, the ways in which similar stories can be adjudged credible or incredible. Witchcraft is a useful case study because the legal prosecution of this crime changed dramatically but unevenly in the course of the seventeenth century, leading ultimately to the end of prosecutions by the eighteenth century. Regarding witchcraft, then, changing beliefs, arresting stories, and disputed standards of proof had material but unpredictable consequences. As Shapiro argues, "Witchcraft provides an interesting example of a 'fact' whose general credibility eroded over time."[79] While the repeal of witchcraft statutes obviously spared lives, especially those of women, it also corresponded to increasing distrust of women's testimonies and of "ridiculous fictions" often associated with rural people and with Catholics.

In Chapter 3, I examine debates regarding the causes of the devastating London Fire of 1666 and how political and confessional affiliations shaped assessments of the evidence. I focus on two documents of the highly politicized process by which Catholics were blamed for setting the fire: the report leaked to the press by the parliamentary committee appointed to investigate the causes of the fire and Christopher Wren's monument, including the inscriptions that were written into the stone, then chiseled off, and then carved back on as political power shifted between city and court, "puritans" and Catholics. As solid as a widely disseminated parliamentary report and a still-standing 202-foot monument might seem, they are both the enduring traces of a process of investigation and commemoration that depended on rumor, missing documents, and contested authority.

In the second half of the book, I turn to chapters organized around particular kinds of texts. These chapters will fill a glaring gap in the field by offering an interdisciplinary assessment of strategies for reading a court deposition, a conduct book, or a play as a piece of evidence and probing the implications of various protocols of reading. I use the term "genre" broadly to suggest that texts can be grouped according to the expectations they invite from and the demands they impose on their readers. That is, I approach texts in part through their relations to other texts and through the relation they establish— or the contract they make—with readers.[80] Henry S. Turner describes form as "a constantly renewing, relational network" among elements whose value is not given but must rather be constantly reassessed. "In this view, 'form' should be understood as a verb rather than as a noun, as an *active relation* among significant parts that are apprehended through a transaction between that artifact and its readers, viewers, listeners, or speakers."[81] As I have shown throughout this introduction, and as we will continue to see throughout this book, "relation" frequently emerges as the key term both in attempts to return to form in a newly interdisciplinary way and in those to think about the relationships among literature and history, representation and reality, aesthetics and evidence.

In Chapter 4, I pursue Natalie Davis's now widely repeated insight that we find "fiction in the archives" by relating church court depositions, which most historians now call "stories" or "narratives," to other kinds of texts (including letters, rogue literature, and sonnets).[82] While many kinds of early modern legal records are terse, church court records are blabs. Their garrulity can disguise the vexed nature of the voices they seem to record. Furthermore, while many scholars seek in them evidence of historical presence, they always stood in its place, substituting a collaboratively composed, third-person text for the witness's presence in court. Indeed, law courts preferred witnesses' statements to the witnesses' presence. Placing pressure on both the evidentiary value of depositions and on the habit of calling depositions fictions, I explore the possibilities of applying to them the editorial practices and interpretive strategies that are usually reserved for "literature."

Chapter 5 considers what it would mean to read "how-to" manuals of advice on marriage and the family as literary texts. Although advice books are routinely disparaged as telling us how people were *supposed* to act and feel rather than how they did, these books are also constantly, if selectively, relied on by many students of early modern social life. More than any other genre, advice literature demonstrates how a textual relation can create, shape, or substitute for social relations. Heavily mined and widely quoted, these texts rarely command sustained, textured readings. After surveying how scholars from various disciplines describe (and often disparage) the evidentiary value of these texts, I explore the use of figuration and engagement with the reader in two of them: a "seminal" early text, Miles Coverdale's translation of Heinrich Bullinger's *The Christen State of Matrimonye* (1541) and what has been called "the most encyclopedic treatise of the kind," William Gouge's *Of Domesticall Duties* (1622).[83] In this chapter, Gouge emerges as an unlikely proponent of a relational reading practice that I suggest early modernists might learn from.

Chapter 6 examines how both historians and literary critics recruit Renaissance plays, especially those by Shakespeare, as evidence. I suggest here that we can move past the distinction between the literary and the historical by recognizing the dynamism within each rubric, the interplay between the two, and the particular opportunities drama offers for crafting relations. In a discussion of Shakespeare's and John Fletcher's *Henry VIII* or *All Is True* (1613), I argue that critical debates about the play suggest that the apprehension of historical truth requires the ability to grasp or posit relationships between a type and a particular individual, between a text or event and a familiar genre, between one historical figure and another, between playwrights, and between eras. As a consequence, the play pushes us to recognize the role of the reader or viewer as a relator, actively working to make those connections, and to supply information the play gestures to but does not contain. The same year that Shakespeare and Fletcher wrote *All Is True*, they may also have written *Cardenio*, a supposedly lost play that has recently been "discovered" embedded in Lewis Theobald's adaptation *Double Falsehood* (1728). What has constituted evidence of the play's authorship, from Theobald on, and how critics read the true relation between the Shakespearean original and Theobald's admitted "revision and adaptation" reveals that, in *The Double Falsehood* as in *All Is True*, truth emerges as a matter of relations, relations made as much as found.

This final chapter revisits the organizing principle of the first three chapters in that Henry's divorce was, like the events considered there, a crisis of evidence, produced in part by disparate standards employed across confessional and gender divides and the status divide between king and commoner. But I focus here on how literature can serve as evidence and what it would mean for scholarly readers to own their agency as relators, collecting and connecting fragments, taking away what they need but also bringing to bear what they already know.

True Relations is unique, then, in its project of tracing the particular ways that scholars of the early modern period devise a practice of reading in the wake of the consensus that the real is constructed and in its pairing of a methodological inquiry with an historical analysis of specific case histories connecting fact to fiction in the early modern period. Throughout, I try to read other scholars' work as carefully as I read seventeenth-century texts, and I often shadow them as they read key pieces of textual evidence. It is not my purpose to critique other scholars' uses of evidence; most of the maneuvers that interest me are ones I have used myself. Instead, I articulate and interrogate broadly shared interpretive practices that, at present, often go unremarked. For example, many scholars make disclaimers about their evidence—about the highly mediated nature of legal depositions, for instance, or the implausibility of a spectacular slander—and then promptly forget them in order to rely on the document in question in an unqualified way. That acknowledge-then-forget maneuver often begins with words such as "nevertheless" or "nonetheless." This sleight of hand, widely used, suggests that many of us feel that we must suppress our knowledge of evidentiary problems to get on with the work at hand. As a result, any reflection on sources and method is sometimes experienced as a "cease and desist order," a call to sit down and be quiet to which we must turn a deaf ear if we are to be able to write at all. Drawing attention to issues that many scholars prefer to ignore, I propose that self-consciousness might be generative rather than paralyzing, collaborative rather than isolating.

PART I

Crises of Evidence

Chapter 1

True and Perfect Relations

Henry Garnet, Confessional Identity, and Figuration

As provincial of the English Jesuits, Henry Garnet was a person of interest to the Jacobean state. But he became the target of an urgent and extended manhunt when Guy Fawkes, during interrogation, claimed the Gunpowder Plot conspirators had met in his house. When he was finally discovered hiding in a cramped priest hole on January 27, 1606, an intensive process of interrogation and evidence collection began. He was arraigned and tried on March 28, 1606—almost five months after the plot was discovered and two months after the condemnations of the six major conspirators. James I himself attended the trial in King's Bench, over which Sir Edward Coke presided. So many people attended that Coke complained that it was difficult to hear. A jury found Garnet guilty after a fifteen-minute deliberation. But then more than a month elapsed before his execution on May 3, 1606, in St. Paul's Churchyard. Fr. John Gerard claims that the execution was so crowded that spectators paid twelve pence apiece to stand on purpose-built bleachers, and "All windows were full, yea, the tops of houses full of people, so that it is not known the like hath been at any execution." Himself a hunted man who had escaped from the Tower, Gerard could not attend because he left England the very day of the execution. Instead, he depended on "a Priest of great credit and estimation" for information about "these particulars," a priest who had been "glad to give twelvepence only to stand upon a wall."[1]

His life and the Jesuit mission at stake, Gerard was an interested observer. Yet he had to rely on oral and printed accounts of the trial as well as the execution, even as he contested them. With Garnet's death, contests to evaluate his story intensified. Gerard and other Catholics entered the fray to spin Garnet's story in their own direction, defending him for making some disclosures in the process of the investigation and offering hagiographic descriptions of his martyrdom, including reports that his head, displayed on a pike, did not decay and that his face had appeared on a straw splashed with his blood.[2] The Crown, in turn, invested in a lengthy apology for its own actions, making its case to an international audience in *A True and Perfect Relation of the Whole Proceedings against the Late Most Barbarous Traitors, Garnet a Jesuite, and his Confederats* (London, 1606). Although the indefinite article concedes that there might be other true relations of these proceedings, this was the official account of Garnet's trial and execution, quickly translated into Latin and broadly distributed.[3] In this chapter, I will focus on this text. Whereas *A True and Perfect Relation* has often been cited as a context for more obviously literary works, especially *Macbeth*,[4] I argue that it offers us an entry point into a contestation in which all the key players were ambivalently but busily engaged in figuration and its interpretation. Trials such as Garnet's, and readers' "virtual" participation in them via written accounts, helped to motivate and popularize skeptical reading practices and to hone the skills this kind of reading requires. But they also spread doubt about these practices.

A *True and Perfect Relation* is not the best known or most frequently cited text about the Gunpowder Plot. That honor goes to *His Majesties Speech in This Last Session of Parliament* (1605), also known as "the King's Book" since it was the official government narrative of the plot and its discovery. The King's Book is 96 pages long. It remains widely cited by scholars. Assembled and printed very quickly, it seems to have been published at the end of November 1605, just weeks after the plot was first discovered; efforts were made to publish it even earlier, but new conspirators and confessions kept coming to light. For Mark Nicholls, an influential historian of the Gunpowder Plot, the King's Book documents "the slow, tentative way in which the investigators acquired their knowledge of the plot," presenting, albeit in simplified form, "as much as the government knew at that time."[5]

In contrast, *A True and Perfect Relation* is extremely long—416 pages—and belated. It was published as much as seven months after Garnet's execution. The text's girth and belatedness render its purpose less clear. If the King's Book rushed to place the case against the traitors before the public, *A True and Perfect Relation* tells a story most people probably knew. Its purpose is to elaborate on the issues at stake, although it also lays out a

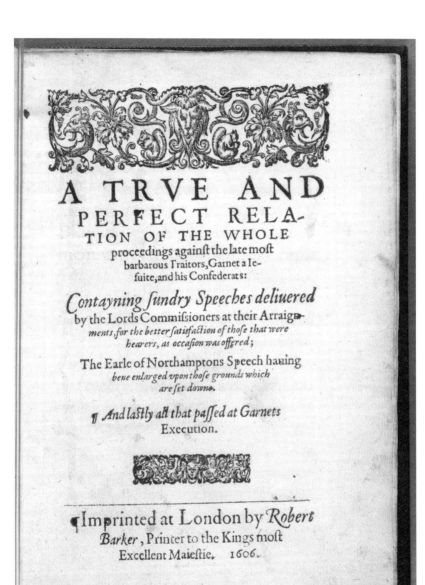

A TRVE AND
PERFECT RELA-
TION OF THE WHOLE
proceedings againſt the late moſt
barbarous Traitors, Garnet a Ie-
ſuite, and his Confederats:

Contayning ſundry Speeches deliuered
by the Lords Commiſsioners at their Arraign-
ments, for the better ſatisfaction of thoſe that were
hearers, as occaſion was offered;

The Earle of Northamptons Speech hauing
bene enlarged vpon thoſe grounds which
are ſet downe.

¶ *And laſtly all that paſſed at Garnets*
Execution.

¶Imprinted at London by *Robert*
Barker, Printer to the Kings moſt
Excellent Maieſtie. 1606.

Figure 1. Title page of *A True and Perfect Relation*. Reproduced by
permission of The Huntington Library, San Marino, California.

chronology of the plot and the prosecution's case. It is a rumination more than a procedural.

Ultimately, Garnet's trial focused on the fact that he had known of the plot, largely through a nested confession; fellow Jesuit Oswald Tesimond sought Garnet's advice about a confession *he* had heard, that of Robert Catesby. Although Garnet seems to have advised strongly against such a conspiracy, he was held accountable for not revealing what he had learned in these complexly privileged communications. Throughout the trial, we find a double attitude toward confession that is well expressed by Lewis Owen in his *The Unmasking of All Popish Monks, Friers, and Jesuits* (1628): "For in truth, there is nothing that openeth a wider gap, or way unto sinne, than *Auricular Confession*" wherein "under pretence of confessing their sinnes, they [Catholics] maliciously consult, how to effect and practice their sinfull purposes." Henry Garnet is Owen's prime example: "First, he heard their *Confession*, then he absolved them of all their sins, and afterwards ministred the *Sacrament* unto them. Where you may perceive how their *Sacrament* of *Confession* (or *Penance*, as they call it) served him for a cloake to cover his treacherie, or rather a net to catch such wicked Traytors; and the other *Sacrament* (which they affirme to be the very body of *Christ*) to be as it were a Signet, wherewith he sealed their mouthes up close . . . from ever revealing the same."[6] In this passage, Owen tellingly uses a figure that almost immediately slips out of his control: a cloak, which obscures and thus enables treachery, becomes, somewhat confusingly, a net, which enables the State to catch wicked traitors and, therefore, one might imagine, a good thing. Opening the mouth to confess and receive communion effectively shuts it. We could not find a clearer articulation of the view that what is wrong with the sacraments is that they stand in the way of the state's own ability to extract a confession. The judicial process is in competition with auricular confession, striving for the same goal of full disclosure and repentance. What stands as confessional identity in court, and in the subsequent print accounts that attempt to fix and disseminate this identity, is often marked by withholding confession or protesting innocence, that is, by attempting to resist an identity already thrust on one.

I am especially interested in the way the lord chief justice, members of the Privy Council, and the ordinary (or minister) of Newgate prison rely on tropes to weld confessions and identities together. Perhaps because the resulting ligature is figurative, it often unties itself within the very text that posits it. These men's fascination with equivocation has in part to do with their own reliance on manipulating meanings and resorting to tropes. In the end, it seems as if those who are not on trial, the winners who write the history of these trials, are the ones who feel compelled to speak so as to compensate for the silence or evasion of those at the bar. And in their speech, they, like Owen above, rely on figurations that slither out of their control and ally them with the dark figures and equivocations they decry.

At the end of the chapter, I look briefly at another moment in which, in the wake of a crisis, an attempt was made to secure a "true and perfect" relation between confession and identity. In this case, I consider the rhetorical aftershocks of the executions of the alleged Popish Plot traitors. Both of the moments I will discuss are a little after the most intense panic, when the broader consequences of crises began to manifest themselves. Although more than seventy years intervene, we can find in both 1606 and the early 1680s a concern regarding whether Catholics can or will speak the truth of their "confessional identities" in a way that will be credible to others.[7] Furthermore, through the recycling of titles, texts, and tropes, the later moment circles back onto the earlier one, suggesting the difficulty of resolving or moving beyond the problems entailed both in confessing one's own identity and in identifying the truth in others' confessions.[8] Throughout, I am interested in how scholars, too, circle back, restaging partisan debates in their attempts to secure a stable relation between confessions and identities.

Published by Authority

From the title page on, *A True and Perfect Relation* addresses "those that were hearers" at Garnet's trial but might have missed important details. In the proceedings themselves, Coke asks indulgence for "the necessary repetition of some things before spoken" and then argues that this is valuable: "Nay it may be thought justifiable to repeat in this case, for that in respect of the confluence & accesse of people, at the former araignment, many could not heare at that time" (O2v–O3r). So even those present in court require repetition during the proceedings, in case they have missed something, as well as the subsequent repetition provided by the printed account. *A True and Perfect Relation* is extremely self-conscious about its own status as a text and about the investigation's reliance on texts. It was not enough that the defendants confess: in court, "their severall examinations (subscribed by themselves) [were] shewed particularly unto them, and acknowledged by them to be their own & true." What is more, "for further satisfaction to so great a presence and audience, and their better memorie of the carriage of these Treasons, the voluntarie and free confessions of all the said several Traitors in writing subscribed with their owne proper hands, and acknowledged at the Barre by themselves to be true, were openly and distinctly read" (sig. K3). The reading aloud is explicitly described here as an instructive performance, satisfying the audience, inscribing the contents in memory, and disciplining the defendants by making them listen to what they have already confessed, subscribed, and acknowledged.[9] The text also addresses readers who will encounter the proceedings for the first time through print or who require a more exhaustive contextualization of the trial and its issues. In a preface "To the Reader," the editor acknowledges that some may wonder why it is necessary to publish the proceedings after the sentencing and executions. In the wake of the executions, what else is there to learn? He explains that the text is needed because "there do passe from hand to hand divers uncertaine, untrue, and incoherent reports, and relations of such Evidence, as was publiquely given upon the said severall Arraignments" (sig. A2v). This text aims to counter and correct those untrue relations and to offer a genealogy of the treason, for which there was not time in the urgency of its first discovery and prosecution.

Yet even this attempt to set the record straight acknowledges its own provisionality. Coke's remarks at the arraignment and trial are presented "as neere to his owne words, as the same could be taken" (O2v; cf. D2r).[10] In turn, Gerard admits the provisionality of his attempts to counter the official version. He presents Sir John Crooke's [the king's sergeant's] pleading "as near as it could be remembered by two or three sufficient men that were present and did carefully observe both that and all other speeches." Gerard explains that Coke "began his speech with a low voice, that so his words could not at the first be so distinctly heard; but it tended to this effect."[11] How are we to interpret the gap between what was actually said and what could be taken or gathered or remembered? This is especially interesting with regard to the earl of Northampton's speech, which appears in *A True and Perfect Relation* in a form in which it was never delivered "having been enlarged upon" (title page). Northampton makes numerous speeches in the text: at Sir Everard Digby's arraignment (which is presented "as it was taken . . . by T. S." [M1r]), at Garnet's arraignment, and after Garnet's conviction. This last speech is the longest. It begins on signature Dd1r. By signature Xx3r, Northampton refers to something about which "I need not at this time say much, when much cannot be said for want of time." He concludes on signature Eee4r, that is, 199 printed pages later.

The editor of the text explains to us at some length both why he presents the speech in this enlarged form and the process by which he secured this expanded version "exceeding the proportion wherin it was first uttered." While "others" had "overrun" or perused the "maimed copy" of their remarks and pointed out corrections, Northampton found the "fragment" he was given to review "so farre short not onely of that which should have bene, but of that also which was at the arraignment delivered" that he remedied both problems, offering a memorial reconstruction of what he thought he said "as neere as his Lordship could call to minde" as well as the "amplified and enriched" version that "should have been." He left it to the editor to choose between the two. Mindful of the "egernesse" with which a transcript of the speech "was desired by the Auditors after the delivery," the editor concluded that "it would better fit the motive in folio, then in decimo sexto, in the fruit then in the blossom, and the larger the better" (sigs. Eee4r–v).[12] The editor takes full responsibility for offering the expanded speech to the reader, although, as we shall see, Northampton seems to have framed the text largely as a vehicle for this speech. Garnet's whole trial is about the reliability of what Catholics say on the stand, yet the authorized version of Northampton's "enlarged" concluding speech is authorized precisely because it is not what he was able to say in court.

The fact that this text undoubtedly was a piece of propaganda occludes the fact that it also had a very particular author, one whose status reminds us that the Privy Council was internally divided—as were at least some of its members. In her biography of Henry Howard, earl of Northampton, Linda Levy Peck offers a detailed explanation of his contribution to the text's composition (or compilation), with the help of Sir Robert Cotton, who conducted research, edited, and prepared the manuscript for publication.[13] Cotton was, then, the editor to whom I have referred. Cotton often provided Northampton with the historical precedents and documentation he sought to shore up his political arguments.[14]

Northampton was a remarkable political survivor. He was jailed five times in the course of his life. He was arrested in conjunction with the attempt of his brother, the duke of Norfolk, to wed Mary, Queen of Scots (for which Norfolk was executed in 1572); closely associated with the earl of Essex, from whom he dissociated himself just in time to avoid complicity in his rebellion; in correspondence with Mary Stuart and later her son James over many years; and instrumental in facilitating James's succession. Northampton finally achieved wealth and power after that succession. He was a close ally of Robert Cecil, earl of Salisbury, another key player in Garnet's prosecution, and was also an influential and active member of the Privy Council. Thus, Garnet's trial took place just as Northampton reached the pinnacle of his career after years of struggle. The trial, and indeed the whole Gunpowder Plot, posed for him an opportunity—and a threat since Northampton was widely regarded as a Catholic, despite the fact that he consistently attended the Chapel Royal.[15] Shortly before his death, in 1614, he was received back into the Catholic Church by a priest sent by the Spanish ambassador; this was not known at the time of his funeral but was suspected.

In choosing Northampton to oversee *A True and Perfect Relation*, James chose someone whose position at court would reinforce the idea that those with Catholic sympathies could be successful and powerful courtiers. The Venetian ambassador wrote in December 1606, "The work is highly commended by all, by the king in particular, he has ordered it to be translated into French, Latin and Italian. The fact that the author has been and still is reckoned a Catholic is expected to lend the work a greater authority."[16] Northampton himself had a stake in arguing that conforming Catholics could be loyal subjects. While Northampton was a professional rhetorician, presenting the Crown's case in court and in print, he also had a personal interest in distinguishing himself and other loyal Catholics from traitors; scapegoating Jesuits in general and Garnet in particular served his purpose as well as the Crown's.

Yet suspicions about Northampton's affiliations seem to have undermined the text's avowed purposes. As Peck details, in 1612 Northampton learned of rumors that he had written to Cardinal Bellarmine, "an important Roman Catholic polemicist," advising him to ignore what Northampton had said in *A True and Perfect Relation* as written "only to placate the king." In response, Northampton brought a suit in Star Chamber in which the defendants, court officers and gentry, confessed to having spread the rumors. Six publishers of the libel were given heavy fines and imprisoned; at Northampton's request, five of the six were released after a month and their fines were remitted. His was thus a symbolic victory. As Alastair Bellany shows, numerous libels circulated about Northampton's confessional allegiances from 1612 to 1614. For example, Sir Steven Proctor was tried in Star Chamber in February 1614 for alleging (among other things) that "Northampton and others 'had suppressed and discountenanced some witnesses and proofs' during the Gunpowder Plot investigations."[17] Northampton was thus suspected of suppressing and manipulating evidence from both sides.

While one cannot understand *A True and Perfect Relation* without some awareness of Northampton's complicated status and the text's provenance and subsequent history, it is hard to know what to do with that awareness. Then as now, even those who distrust the text rely on it as a crucial piece of evidence. Garnet's contemporary, Fr. John Gerard, scoffed at the text as skewed but also depended on it. Gerard's own account proceeds as a detailed refutation of the text, which Gerard clearly consults throughout, comparing it against other sources, including "eye and ear witnesses," and enabling his readers to do the same. Calling the official print accounts "pestilent" and "malicious" books, he reads and engages them for that very reason. Sometimes he even uses them in support of his own claims. For instance, he points to other conspirators' "printed examinations" as proofs that they never accused Garnet.[18] In his biography of Garnet, Philip Caraman describes the text as "a propaganda document," yet he too takes all his citations of the indictment and prosecution from *A True Relation*, assuming it to be "the official account of the case for the prosecution, reported almost verbatim."[19] In a case such as this one in which we have no benchmark against which to compare an account, the determination that it is "almost verbatim" requires a leap of faith. Still, however much it is distrusted, *A True and Perfect Relation* remains a crucial piece of evidence for scholars like Caraman, just as it did for a hunted priest like Gerard.

In the nineteenth century, David Jardine, a magistrate who edited accounts of criminal trials and Garnet's *Treatise of Equivocation*, fulminated against *A True and Perfect Relation*'s claims to proof value:

> The "True and Perfect Relation of the whole Proceedings,"
> which . . . has become most generally known, is certainly not
> deserving of the character which its title imports. It is not *true*,
> because many occurrences on the trial are willfully misrepresented;
> and it is not *perfect*, because the whole evidence, and many facts and
> circumstances which must have happened are omitted, and inci-
> dents are inserted which could not by possibility have taken place
> on the occasion. It is obviously a false and imperfect relation of the
> proceedings; a tale artfully garbled and misrepresented.[20]

Given the inadequacies he found in this "false and imperfect relation," Jardine turned to manuscripts, only to discover that they posed their own problems. Jesuits' histories such as Fr. Gerard's "may tend to correct and qualify the gross partiality of the authorized report" but cannot quite do so because they "are themselves grossly partial in the relation of a transaction which might tarnish the character" of a man they wished to view as a martyr. Furthermore, these partial relations—both incomplete and interested—were "compiled by for-eigners from hearsay" and so are "more absurdly inaccurate, though perhaps less willfully false" than *A True and Perfect Relation*. To compensate for this, Jardine inserts as many documents as he can into his own account. Since "the dramatic interest, and the feeling of reality excited by a literal narrative of the proceedings in dialogue, as they occurred, which constitutes the principal charm of a criminal trial to the general reader is, in this case, entirely lost," he settles for a report that serves as "a vehicle for as many facts and as much useful and interesting knowledge as possible, consistently with a due regard to historical truth."[21] Recognizing that the reader wants a narrative with dramatic interest, he offers instead a supposedly artless collection of facts. While Jardine is particularly outspoken in defense of his own practice as an alternative to *A True and Perfect Relation*, his assumption that misrepresentation, willful-ness, and artfulness go together continues to inform assessments of this text. Whereas Coke and others attributed artfulness to Catholics, Catholics them-selves accused the state of artfulness.

Discussions of evidence regarding the Gunpowder Plot tend either to say that some kinds of alterations in the published versions were standard practice—intended to make the narrative more cohesive and comprehensible—or that any evidence that the published accounts were shaped proves that the whole conspiracy was fabricated. Mark Nicholls, for instance, defends the pro-cess by which the published version of the King's Book "replaced the original third-person account" in Fawkes's confession "with a more dramatically effec-tive first-person narrative, incorporating the names of his confederates into Fawkes's main confession" while omitting "some less significant parts of the original." For Nicholls, these changes amount to "alterations in style, made for the purpose of incorporating in one publishable confession all that Fawkes had to tell. Fawkes duly signed this amended version."[22] To produce what Jardine calls "a narrative of dramatic interest," the state, then, followed a strat-egy similar to that used by many historians when they quote depositions or examinations, shifting them from third to first person to create a more engag-ing narration, as I will discuss at greater length in chapter four. In contrast to Nicholls, Fr. Francis Edwards interprets any evidence of what he calls "tamper-ing"—missing originals, differences between originals and print versions—as evidence of conspiracy, not by the alleged traitors but by those attempting to frame them. [23] Staking out a reading position between the defense of "altera-tions" as standard practice and the anguished suspicion of sinister tampering requires us to put pressure on Jardine's dismissive use of the word "artful." All the contestants in this attempt to frame a true and perfect relation were suspicious of their opponents' artfulness and yet themselves artful as rhetoricians and interpreters. In reading what they have left behind, it behoves us to be a little artful too.

When we read these texts now, we read across a field determined, in part, by earlier efforts to winnow and shape what is available to us. The debate surrounding the Gunpowder Plot was always about how to interpret evidence: how to read faces, utterances, and documents. Garnet's ability to speak effectively—with no appearance of "art"— in his own defense was, of course, disabled by the fact that a manuscript copy of a *Treatise of Equivocation* annotated by Garnet had been found in Sir Francis Tresham's chambers at the Inner Chamber; Coke never seems to have guessed that it was probably written by Garnet. This treatise challenges the assumption that knowledge bears a nonnegotiable "relation unto the utteringe of the same knowledge" by claiming that there is truth and then there is truth to tell: "Some knowledge is not to be uttered; even so some actions and other veretyes are to be concealed." The strategy recommended is speaking part of a truthful statement and reserving the rest in silence so as not to incriminate oneself or others.[24] As he is presented in *A True and Perfect Relation*, Garnet is a theorist of and apologist for equivocation more than a practitioner of it. Yet Coke took the very existence of such a treatise as providing a rationale for distrusting all Catholic testimonies: "And surely let every good man take heede of such Jurors or witnesses, there being no faith, no bond of Religion or civilitie, no conscience of trueth in such men" (I2v). Before such a lord chief justice, it is simply impossible for Catholic witnesses to be heard as speaking the truth. Coke, Garnet's chief antagonist in the trial, insists that the plotted treason is unspeakable: unnameable, unprecedented, and immeasurable (D3v–D4); *A Treatise of Equivocation* concurs that some truths are untellable. Ultimately, *A True and Perfect Relation* suggests that what is unspeakable is not Catholic guilt but Catholic innocence.[25]

Torture, Confession, and Identity

Just as debate continues about whether documents were tampered with or destroyed, debate persists about the treatment of Catholic bodies, particularly the use of torture to pry information out of unwilling defendants. *A True and Perfect Relation* revolves around contradictions about the value of Catholic speech. On the one hand, we have the enigma of Garnet, censured for sealing the conspirators' mouths and himself keeping mum about the conspiracy. On the other hand, the proceedings seem less concerned with securing Garnet's speech than one might expect. The text is crammed with long speeches, histories—not just of this plot but of the papacy, papal deposing power, the sacrament of confession, and other conspiracies—and disquisitions on political theory. It is easy to lose track of the details of the alleged crime and the trial proceedings, even of who is talking. The text spends ninety-eight pages on earlier trials before it even gets to Garnet's arraignment (sig. N4r). At the center of this trial, we have the copious speech of Coke, the earl of Northampton, and others—and the reticence of Garnet both before and after capture. The proceedings make it almost impossible for Garnet to speak. According to Fr. John Gerard, Garnet was "so often interrupted in his own discourse, that it was misliked by divers of the standers-by; yea, the King himself, who was there in private, sent word at length to my Lord of Salisbury [Robert Cecil], he should give the prisoner leave to speak freely."[26]

In part because *A True and Perfect Relation* amplifies the prosecution and guts the defense, the text reads as an unsettling standoff between a withholding defendant and a garrulous group of commentators. Throughout the proceedings, various participants express their extreme frustration at Garnet's taciturnity. Northampton complains directly to Garnet: "I confesse that never any man in your state gave lesse hold or advantage to examiners, then you have done in the whole course of proceeding to us that were in Commission: sometime by forswearing . . . sometime by dissembling . . . sometimes by earnest expostulation: sometime by artificiall Equivocation: sometime by sophisticating [or adulterating] true substances: sometime by adding false qualities" (Z4r). Employing a range of verbs to describe Garnet's tactics of evasion, Northampton "confesses" that Garnet, implicated because of what he heard in confession, is trying Northampton's patience by refusing to cooperate with examiners in their attempt to secure his confession. The interrogator's frustration raises the question of torture and its dubious role in securing and verifying information.

James I issued a "royal directive" on November 6, what we might call a torture warrant, allowing the use of torture if necessary in the interrogation of Fawkes.[27] We cannot know for certain whether torture was used. On the one hand, the King's Book claims that Fawkes readily confessed and, in his two or three examinations in as many days, "the Racke [was] onely offred and shewed unto him when the maske of his Romaine fortitude did visibly begin to weare & slide off his face. And then did he begin to confesse part of the trueth, and thereafter to open the whole matter." In contrast, a pamphlet entitled *The Ara-ignement and Execution of the Late Traytors* describes a broken Fawkes on his way to the scaffold: "His body being weake with torture and sicknes, he was scarse able to goe up the ladder."[28] Fawkes's signatures infamously deteriorate in the course of the interrogation; many historians agree that Fawkes was, indeed, racked. Even Mark Nicholls, who tends to be skeptical about claims that the Crown tortured Gunpowder Plot suspects, concedes that Fawkes was tortured.

Nicholls uses the biographies of Gunpowder conspirators he wrote for the *Oxford Dictionary of National Biography* (*ODNB*) to offer a systematic defense of the Jacobean state against the charge that it tortured the conspirators. In his biography of Francis Tresham, he writes, "Like every other prisoner, with the early exception of Guy Fawkes, Tresham was well treated in the Tower." In his entry on Sir Everard Digby, he remarks, "The truth is that after the initial panic and confusion in the days immediately after 5 November the prisoners were well looked after in the Tower, to the extent that they wondered at the motives behind their treatment." He describes Fawkes's stoical endurance of interrogation as his "finest hour" and, while he concedes that "it seems almost certain that torture of some kind had been employed," he also insists that "Fawkes alone suffered in this way." Although Nicholls uses his own entries to comment obliquely on others outside his control, the writers of those entries, historians of recusancy, stake their own claims. Thomas M. McCoog's *ODNB* entry on Garnet (which he spells Garnett) claims that he was tortured in the course of his twenty-three interrogations in six weeks.[29] Thomas Cooper and McCoog's entry on Edward Oldcorne states that "he was tortured." McCoog's entry on John Gerard claims that, while imprisoned in the Tower in 1597, "he was often suspended by his wrists for hours on end." Nicholas Owen, Garnet's servant and a designer of priest holes, certainly died while in custody, either because he was tortured to death, having been weakened by a strangulated hernia, or because, as was officially but unconvincingly claimed, he disemboweled himself. Michael Hodgetts's *ODNB* entry on Owen states bluntly that "he was tortured" and "he died of the torture." Weaving through the *ODNB*, then, we find two old, competing stories about torture and the Jacobean state: distant echoes of *A True and Perfect Relation*, in Nicholls's entries; and the critiques of it offered by Jesuits such as Gerard and Tesimond, in entries by McCoog, Cooper, and Hodgetts. Both versions are interested. Together, they restage a seventeenth-century debate in the pages of a "new and improved" reference work. In the particular case of Garnet, the question of whether he was tortured pertains not only to assumptions about the Jacobean state but to evaluations of Garnet's own conduct. His Catholic apologists, then and now, struggle to explain the fact that he revealed some information during his interrogations, which they justify by saying that Catesby had freed Garnet to reveal the content of his confession if Garnet were threatened with torture. As a consequence, undergoing torture gave Garnet permission to break the seal of the confessional.[30]

For what it is worth, *A True and Perfect Relation* insists that torture was *not* used against Garnet. The earl of Salisbury urges Garnet to admit he has been "as well-attended for health or otherwise, as a nurse child" (Y2v). According to this text, the prosecution cleverly avoided torture by staging a scene in which Garnet would disclose his secrets. Garnet and Edward Oldcorne, a fellow Jesuit, were placed in adjoining cells in the Tower with a small hatch between through which they could communicate so that their conversations could be monitored. [31] If closed access spaces were "spaces of treason," then the Crown entrapped Garnet into just such a space and then observed what he would say, in utterances coded by their very privacy—a privacy in this case created by incarceration—as potentially treasonous.[32] It is hard to believe that the two men did not suspect that they were under surveillance or that they trusted the "kind" jailor who arranged this accommodation and smuggled letters out of the prison for them (and into Coke's hands). Fr. Gerard claims that the cell had been specially built to facilitate eavesdropping and to entrap Garnet but that Garnet revealed next to nothing in these staged confidences.[33] But *A True and Perfect Relation* presents Garnet's speech to Oldcorne as spontaneous and revealing. According to the earl of Salisbury, "Your former reservedness, being now encouraged and urged by the spurre of opportunitie, became so confident in running beyond it selfe through the chiefe points whereof the State was most eager and desirous to take certaine notice at that time, as they that could not reape, might gleane, and many shifts & subtill traverses were overwrought [which may mean overtaken or outdone] by this occasion, which could not bee extracted out of your brest either by intreaty or industry" (Bbb4v). Content to "gleane," Salisbury expresses gratitude that witnesses just happened to overhear this conversation, which just happened to cover exactly what the state most wanted to know. By so unburdening himself, Garnet spared the state the uncomfortable burden of having to torture him: "For thereby had the Lords some light, & proofe of matter against you, which must have bin discovered other wise by violence and coertion, a matter ordinary in other Kingdomes, though now forborne here" (Y2v–Y3r).

As presented in *A True and Perfect Relation*, Salisbury manages both to boast of and lament the decision not to torture Garnet: "I doe confidently assure my selfe, that you would as easily have confessed your self to be author of al the Action, as the Concealer, but that his Majestie, and my Lordes were well contented to draw all from you without racking, or any such bitter torments" (Y3r). Northampton too finds the eavesdropping a providential corrective to the lack of torture: "since the Lords of the Commission forbearing torture, dealt so tenderly" (Bbb4v). Although Coke avows at the trial that "against the stroke of providence, all counter-practices are vaine" (Ccc2r), *A True and Perfect Relation* demonstrates repeatedly that the prosecution relied on deception and artful practices rather than trusting to providence. It also shows that the prosecution equivocated about its use of torture.

Dark Figures

Even as the true and perfect elaboration on the proceedings against Garnet insisted on his association with the disturbing practice of equivocation—that is, speech that strategizes to withhold some of the truth—it failed to distinguish equivocation from other forms of figuration or restrict it to Catholic traitors. According to Margaret Ferguson, Garnet, in his insistence that equivocation "was authorized and illustrated by Christ himself in various New Testament passages of great hermeneutic difficulty," reminds readers that equivocation is not a Catholic practice and indeed may be unavoidable by any who attempt to employ "a 'literary' language of irony, indirection, and 'dark conceit'."[34] Both Catholic defendants, such as Garnet, and those who attempt to outwit and expose them, such as James I and Coke, rely on the equivocal literacy of dark conceits, sly evasions and insinuations, and wily interpretative strategies.[35]

For instance, the discovery of the plot, as narrated in the various official accounts, hinged on a cryptic letter, perhaps written by Sir Francis Tresham.[36] The letter, which has come to be called the Monteagle letter, warns the recipient not to attend Parliament: "For though there be no apparance of any stirre, yet I say, they shall receive a terrible Blow this Parliament, and yet they shall not see who hurts them."[37] According to the King's Book, the lord admiral, and the earls of Worcester and Northampton, determined to give this letter to the king in part because of "the expectation and experience they had of his Majesties fortunate Judgement in cleering and solving of obscure riddles & doubtfull mysteries."[38] And, indeed, according to the earl of Northampton, as quoted in *A True and Perfect Relation*, the whole plot was thus revealed through an astonishing act of interpretation on the king's part. James was able to decipher "an obscure Letter (more resembling the riddle of an *Oedipus* then the counsel of a friend) that hee should abstaine from the place prefixed at the time determined. The darke figure of the writing, the strange maner of delivering, the smal likelihood of any cloud at that time gathering, might have mooved many men rather to have neglected, then apprehended so blinde a figure of discovery" (Bbb1v–Bbb2r). James would later boast, "I did upon the instant interpret & apprehend some darke phrases therein, contrary to the ordinary Grammer construction of them, (and in another sort then I am sure any Divine, or Lawyer in any Universitie would have taken them) to be meant by this horrible forme of blowing us up all by Powder."[39] But how "darke" or "blinde" were the figures of discovery in the Monteagle letter? Fr. John Gerard assumes "His Majesty and divers of those Councillors also, who had the scanning of the letter, to be well able in shorter time and with fewer doubts to decipher a darker riddle and find out a greater secret than that matter was, after so plain a letter was delivered."[40] But whether commentators praise or disparage the act of interpreting the Monteagle letter, they agree that discovering the Gunpowder Plot depended on the ability to use figuration and to decipher it.

James and his councilors were not simply the interpreters of figures artfully employed by Catholics. *A True and Perfect Relation* presents privy councilors who are artful as well as voluble speakers. Arthur Marotti, for instance, describes Northampton's speeches as "polemically overblown": "Unlike the more economical speeches of Coke and Salisbury, Northampton's turgid and pedantic Ciceronian performance repeatedly waxes metaphoric" and "Northampton indulges in rhetorical overkill."[41] Especially in the expanded version of his closing speech, Northampton's rhetoric *is* bloated. But, because of his amphibious identity, what James I once called Northampton's "Asiatic style" attaches to his Catholicism; however much he castigates Garnet, he is still implicated in the slippery, dark conceits associated with the Jesuitical equivocation he condemns.

But he is not alone. Although Marotti distinguishes Northampton from Coke and Salisbury, they too "wax metaphoric." The two Jesuits who offer counternarratives to *A True and Perfect Relation* both focus on Coke's artfulness. Gerard remarks that "Mr. Attorney can add and diminish like a cunning orator." Tesimond accuses Coke of trying to discredit Garnet before the trial by putting about "slanderous tales," "fables," and "mendacious and extravagant inventions" and offering in court "nothing more than a few vain and airy conjectures" rather than "real evidence."[42] Indeed, Coke seems incapable of expressing himself without the dark and blind figures so often associated with his enemies. One of Coke's most famous figurations appears in *A True and Perfect Relation*:

> For these *Jesuites*, they indeede make no vow of speaking trueth, and yet even this Equivocating, and lying is a kinde of unchastitie, against which they vow and promise . . . The law and Sanction of Nature, hath (as it were) married the heart & tongue, by joining and knitting of them together in a certaine kinde of marriage; and therefore when there is discorde betweene them two, the speech that proceedes from them, is said to be conceived in Adulterie, & he that breedes such bastard children offends against Chastitie. (T2v–T3r)

Coke's figuration is both vivid and unstable. Phrases such as "a kinde of" "as it were" and "in a certain kinde of" signal the simile that morphs into a metaphor—by the end of the passage equivocation *is* bastard speech conceived in adultery. The comparison is fairly straightforward, and it draws on the venerable tradition of denouncing the supposedly celibate clergy for unchastity.[43] Here Jesuits put asunder what God intends and the trial process requires be bound together. They breed bastards.

Coke offers an example of the problems equivocation poses; this example makes the comparison to marriage even more troublesome. Sir Francis Tresham, on the brink of his death, apparently of natural causes, was "of charitie" permitted to have his wife visit him "for his comfort." His wife knew he had accused Garnet of involvement in "the Spanish treason." Fearing the spiritual consequences should he die with his betrayal of Garnet on his conscience, she urged him to recant. But his hand was so shaky that he had to dictate to his servant that he had not seen Garnet for sixteen years; he then "weakely, and dyingly subscribed" this paper and asked that it be given to the earl of Salisbury.

Tresham's scrupulously authorized statement seems to have included a pointless lie since there was considerable evidence, including from Garnet, that he and Tresham had often been together.[44] Coke concludes of this episode, "Thus were they stayned with their owne workes, and went a whoring with their owne inventions" (T3v). Coke prepares us for this deathbed equivocation by describing the needful marriage of heart and tongue. But in the ensuing example, marital solicitude leads Tresham's wife to make what is from Coke's perspective a misguided intervention. Coke presents her as attempting to rejoin a heart and tongue that she feels have been sundered by the pressures of the investigation, by the fear of torment and death, but also wrenching heart and tongue apart in a lie. In Coke's scenario, the state's "charitie" rejoins husband and wife "for his comfort" but should really have kept them asunder since their deathbed reunion breeds whorish invention and the bastard of equivocation. In Coke's view, marital solicitude promotes the adulterous breach between conscience and tongue, testimony and recantation. The wife's loving intervention achieves perjury.

Coke's figuration is irresistible—at least to literary critics—and has been much cited, perhaps more than any other passage from *A True and Perfect Relation*, with the possible exception of Coke's amazing reading of the semiotics of the treason punishment (K2r–v). Biographies of Garnet and Tresham question his motives in this deathbed equivocation. But the context that links Coke's trope and Tresham's lie has dropped out. This context focuses our attention on the triangle of Jesuit, wife, and husband. The wife divorces heart and tongue in Coke's account, although she does it out of concern for the Jesuit's survival and her husband's salvation. And the state plays a crucial role in facilitating and then lamenting this speech that is simultaneously uxorious and adulterous. This episode in *A True and Perfect Relation* suggests the impossibility of escaping or controlling figuration once it has been unleashed. By describing equivocation as adultery, Coke links Jesuits and women to discredit both and Catholicism more generally for throwing them together. But, like securing Northampton to write the true and perfect relation, Coke's trope blurs the division it aspires to sharpen—between Catholics and Anglicans, adultery and marriage, dark figures and plain speaking, adulterous and faithful relations.

I want to conclude by considering a text from the end of the seventeenth century in which a turn of phrase is taken as revealing a relation between an individual and Catholicism, a relation she herself does not claim. Here too we find both the power of figuration to impose a confessional identity and the very unstable parameters defining what counts as confessional identity at the bar, on the scaffold, and in print.

As Innocent as the Child Unborn

In January 1681, someone named Elizabeth or Alice or Latice or Leticia Wigenton or Wigington or Wiggens was convicted of whipping her thirteen-year-old apprentice girl to death; she was hanged at Tyburn in September. There are several pamphlet accounts of this case, as well as mentions of it in printed reports of Old Bailey trials and in newsheets.[45] The multiplicity of her names, while not wholly unusual in the period, signals the slippery evasiveness of identity not only at the bar, so to speak, but in our own attempts as researchers to track down and tie together all the references to a particular person. I will call her Wigington, however arbitrarily, since the other scholars who have assembled her surprisingly numerous print traces do so.[46] What I wish to focus on is the mystery of her confessional identity.

As Randall Martin has shown, references to Wigington and her accomplice and lodger, John Sadler, pop up in a variety of early newsheets. Many of these early newspapers were driven by partisan politics, especially in the hysteria surrounding the Popish Plot, as the prominence of "Protestant" in their titles might suggest.[47] Yet the *True Protestant Mercury* and other newspapers that mention Wigington's crime do not mention her religion. The sensationally sadistic nature of this crime might in itself have justified charting the progress of the trial, but it seems likely that it would also have prompted emphasis on any connection between Wigington and Catholicism.

The suggestion that Wigington had fallen in with Catholics in prison occurs only in the fullest printed account of her crime and punishment, *Confession and Execution of Leticia Wigington of Ratclif.* Not coincidentally, this text begins by casting doubt on Wigington's confession even as it presents it as "written by her own hand":

> We are fully satisfied, that the following Paper was written by this
> unhappy womans own hand, a while before her Death, and though
> at her Tryal for this horrid Fact, the Evidence against her, was full,
> clear and undeniable, yea which is more, though she was then so
> ingenious to confess herself really guilty thereof, having lain so
> many Months in *Newgate*, we have very great reason to judge she
> has been too well acquainted with that cursed crew of Popish Priests
> and Jesuites, who it is to be feared have debauched her with their
> own damnable Principles, whereby they have perswaded her to deny
> what she before had so fully confessed, which she does in the very
> words of those Jesuites who lately deservedly suffered for Treason
> against his Majesty, &c. who though they were tried and con-
> demned (as well as her self) upon the clearest Evidence imaginable,
> yet *Atheistically* even with their last Breath affirmed, *That they were
> as innocent as the Child unborn.* (1)

Thus, before we can read Wigington's confession we have been told that she is "too well acquainted" with priests, Jesuits, and traitors because of her insistence on her own innocence; her rejection of clear evidence, which is somehow also an "atheistical" denial of God; and particularly because of the phrase she uses to articulate her innocence.[48]

In the confession attributed to her—really a refusal to confess—Wigington repeats the phrase three times: she refers to herself as one who is "as innocent as concerning the Murder for which I suffer as the Child unborn" (1); she denounces "the Girl that Swore against me and was the cause of my dying this Shameful Death, though as innocent as the Child unborn" (4); and she announces on the scaffold that "I dye as innocent of the Crime for which my Body suffers, as the Child yet unborn" (4).

Wigington's use of the phrase "as innocent as the child unborn" had a particular, gendered valence in her case. In her purported confession, Wigington explains that she pled her belly on advice she received from others in prison but that this further estranged her from her husband, whom she had not seen in two years. He learned about her strategy, she claimed, from "Ballads and Books" in circulation after she was brought to Newgate, which "raised great scandal and ignominy, and added grief to my Afflictions" (4). To defend her virtue and to appease her husband—who withdrew his financial support for her reprieve in outrage—Wigington retracted her claim that she was pregnant.[49] Even if Wigington's attempt to plead her belly was particularly vexed, her claim on the scaffold that she dies as innocent "as the Child yet unborn" sounds very much as if she is still claiming to be pregnant and asserting her innocence within the logic of "benefit of belly," by which a pregnant woman's execution should be deferred because the quickening fetus she carries is innocent of her crime and so should not be punished.[50] While the unborn child's innocence might be a point of some theological dispute—since even the unborn might be tainted with original sin—the "privilege of the belly" focused on crime rather than sin, assuming that the child unborn was, indeed, innocent of its mother's crime. If we consider Wigington's statements within the context of the secular law, then she seems to say, "As innocent as the fetus you would spare am I." Thus, Wigington's repeated use of this phrase might be seen as particularly appropriate to her own case: (1) because she was accused of having murdered a child; (2) because she had pled her belly (as many female felons did); and (3) because she was demanding the same kind of legal immunity that would be conferred on a fetus and staking a parallel claim to the court's mercy.

The printed account frames her use of this phrase in a very different context, preparing us to be critical and politicized readers of her confession and to identify that phrase not with her history of pleading the belly but with the Popish Plot traitors and their protestations of innocence that were similarly read as refusals to confess. In the years after those convicted of treason for their involvement in the Popish Plot protested their innocence on the scaffold, this phrase accrued negative connotations, signaling the way that the sacrament of confession defeats the state's attempt to secure confessions and blocks access to the truth. This text presents Wigington as relating herself to the Popish Plot traitors by denying her guilt, presenting an opaque front to the court, and doing so through the repeated use of a particular phrase.

Samuel Smith, the ordinary of Newgate, who might have been the author of this account of Wigington's months in Newgate, had printed, two years earlier, *An Account of the Behaviour of the Fourteen Late Popish Malefactors*, a series of biographies and assessments of Popish Plot traitors. In his account of these popish malefactors, Smith speculates that Robert Green would not confess to his crime because he "had received a Popish Absolution from the Guilt" of the murder of Sir Edmudbury Godfrey "and so look't upon himself as Innocent as the Child Unborn." Note that Smith does not attribute the phrase to Green but rather imagines how Green "look't upon himself." The text says of Lawrence Hill that he affirmed "in the usual Canting Language, *That he was as Innocent of it, as the Child unborn.*" Smith argues that this equivocation either depends on an oath of secrecy to render a traitor as incapable "of committing or declaring the Heinousness of such a Crime" as an unborn child would be, or on a riddle, "I am as *Innocent* of the Fact, as there is Truth in this, That the *Child unborn* is here present, reserving this Supplement of the Assertion unto himself."[51] For a pregnant woman protesting her innocence, the unborn child might be the "supplement" who renders such an assertion true.

In the aftermath of the unsettlingly unsatisfying Popish Plot executions, references to the innocence of the child unborn were taken as indictments of confession and absolution, which free Catholic malefactors to assert their innocence no matter what they have done. Benjamin Harris's newspaper *Domestic Intelligence*, which claimed to "prevent false reports," asserts that a priest living with a person of honor had impregnated his lady's chambermaid and, when she demanded marriage, consulted with another priest who advised him to swear that he had been falsely accused "and to add Oaths and Execrations to it, that he was as clear as the Child unborn; which when he had done, the Priest promised to absolve and pardon him for the same."[52] The simile of the unborn child appears particularly unseemly as a denial of paternity. But the issue here, as in other dismissals of this protestation at around the same time, is the charge that Catholics believe they can erase any guilt and that, if they have received absolution, they *are* innocent, no matter what they have done. As one anti-Catholic satire in 1680 put it, Catholicism is the perfect religion for bawds because they "can *Whore* and *whore* again, and *Confess* and *fess*, and obtain *Pardon*, and be *pardoned* to all intents and purposes, and go out of the World after a whole life of *sinning*, as *Innocent as Children unborn*."[53]

Thus, when the confession printed as Wigington's assigns her an identity by simile—as innocent as the child unborn—condensed into the phrase is an identity Wigington does not seem to claim for herself but one that, for the author of her account, discredits her by association. So much about her is unclear—from her name to the nature and extent of her involvement in the murder—yet the author of *Confession and Execution of Leticia Wigington* thinks he knows something about her because of one phrase she uses. Whose "canting language" is this? Did Green, Hill, and Wigington use this phrase, so innocuous at first glance? Or did the ordinary of Newgate put that phrase in their mouths and then use it to link and condemn them? It is impossible to know. But what is interesting to me here is that one phrase works to identify or classify each one as distinctively Catholic in his or her inability to speak the truth.

Assigned a "confessional identity" as inculpatory as their alleged crimes, they are also assumed incapable of legally useful confessions. The author of the "true relation" of Wigington's crime and confession tells us how to read her use of this phrase she shares with the alleged Popish Plot traitors. But drawing a connection between Wigington and the Popish Plot traitors opens up more questions than it answers. In the immediate aftermath of the Popish Plot, there were repeated attempts to reassert the guilt of the traitors and the probity of their punishments. As time passed, however, many came to wonder whether those who were executed had been guilty and to question a legal system that denied counsel to those accused of treason.

In turning a skeptical eye on seventeenth-century testimonies, we are not achieving something contemporaries could not. Sir Matthew Hale posits a hermeneutic of suspicion as central to the jury trial: "the jury is not bound to believe; for the excellency of the trial by jury is in that they are the triers of the credit of the witnesses as well as the truth of the fact; it is one thing, whether a witness be admissible to be heard, another thing, whether they are to be believed when heard."[54] As we will see in the next chapter, judges presiding over witchcraft trials sometimes viewed testimonies more skeptically than juries did and instructed spectators, and, through print, readers to critique the narratives offered to them as evidence. In the seventeenth century, a suspicious reading practice is inseparable from religious conflict, as we will continue to see in subsequent chapters, and from the unending work of weaving confessional difference. On the one hand, many were poised to try the credit of Catholic witnesses. On the other hand, the bloody consequences of refusing to credit Catholic protestations of innocence ultimately led to greater efforts to ensure fairness in some kinds of criminal trials.

It is useful to undertake a similarly suspicious and relational reading practice not only for the texts I have considered here but for databases and reference works. Early English Books Online (EEBO) offers three different copies of *A True and Perfect Relation* but no information about the text's authorship, provenance, or afterlife; the *English Short Title Catalogue* offers no information about this either. Thus, just as Coke castigated Garnet as the arch-equivocator while failing to grasp that he might be the author of *A Treatise of Equivocation*, so Henry Howard, earl of Northampton, both is and is not positioned as the author of *A True and Perfect Relation*. To relate this text to him, the reader must bring to bear outside knowledge. Comparing the biographies of different Gunpowder Plot "conspirators" in the *ODNB* reveals that confessional identities of a sort still shape the spin on these figures. *The Confession . . . of Leticia Wigington* is not available on EEBO, and the relating reader must work hard to collect together and compare surviving accounts of the case because of the different spellings of her name, among other impediments.

I have employed here two different reading strategies. I have dwelt at some length on one text—a text about evidence and itself standing in evidence. And I have tracked a phrase across texts ignoring many of their complexities so as to focus on the resonance of that one phrase. I have attempted to synthesize the current state of knowledge about the authorship and context of *A True and Perfect Relation* and of *The Confession . . . . of Leticia Wigington*. But I have also argued that careful attention to the form and texture of these texts, as well as how each relates to other texts, can yield insight into events that were, at the time, understood or produced through "dark figures" and texts that are themselves engaged in what today goes by the name of literary analysis. My approach acknowledges how very suspicious and artful contemporaries were as readers and as writers and the role of their figural language in constituting the perceived threat of Catholicism and in attempting, from various points across the confessional spectrum, to fix a true and perfect relation between confessions and identity, a relation that was necessarily a fabrication.

Chapter 2

Sham Stories and Credible Relations

Witchcraft and Narrative Conventions

We have seen that, at moments of heightened anxiety about Catholic treason, in the wake of the Gunpowder Plot and then again in the wake of the Popish Plot, Catholics provoked evidentiary crises because it was feared that they might equivocate on the stand and might even plead innocence on the scaffold—and believe it—if they had confessed their sins. Witchcraft too posed an extended evidentiary crisis, with periods of heightened intensity, sometimes intersecting with anxiety about Catholic superstition, treachery, and unreliability. Like Catholics, witches were considered to be both credulous and incredible. The problem of witchcraft, like the problem of Catholic inscrutability and untrustworthiness, worked as a discursive engine, producing stories of accusation, self-defense, or confession and demanding interpretation. What remains to us are those stories; their dubious stature as evidence makes witchcraft a continuing subject of debate.

It might seem from our vantage now that all stories of witchcraft were improbable, that all who testified to witchcraft were lying, that convicted witches were executed for a crime they did not commit, and that the accused were always the "real" victims.[1] Yet many scholars now working on witchcraft are reluctant to dismiss testimony as deluded or malicious, trying instead to get inside what it meant to believe in witchcraft.[2]

Many historians agree that, in England, the prosecution of witches was neither "a spontaneous expression from below" nor a "lawyer-led campaign from above."[3] The formal prosecution of witches resulted instead from compromises, negotiations, and collaborations. Prosecutions were sporadic, occurring unevenly over time. For example, the 1542 Henrician statute against witchcraft was repealed by Edward VI in 1547 and not replaced until the Elizabethan statute of 1563. For prosecutions to happen, local people had to narrate their complaints and fears in a form that ministers and justices of the peace could recognize and affirm. According to James Sharpe, "There was no single view of witchcraft, no mindless intolerance. Some people were rabidly against it, some were very sceptical, but most people's thinking on the subject was somewhere in between: unable to reject the notion of witchcraft entirely, they were none the less ready to evaluate each supposed instance of it on its own merits."[4] This evaluation was likely to occur through reading.

While many people participated directly in witchcraft prosecutions, especially as witnesses, many more participated through print, which pulled them into the process of evaluating evidence to determine what they would accept as true. Accounts of many witchcraft trials were published—often proclaiming themselves to be true and indeed to be correctives of inaccurate reports in circulation. Pamphlets range from brief to long. Some were written or endorsed by legal personnel involved in the trials and purported to include documents from the trials such as depositions and confessions. Others were written by interested bystanders or even by participants. Sometimes we cannot determine the author's relation to the case. Printed accounts of witchcraft were so widely available that one writer could simply refer readers who wanted proof of his claims about witchcraft to "those manifold Treatises which have bin frequently published to this purpose, and are usually to be had upon the *Stationers Stalles*."[5] As a result, witchcraft discourses are difficult to categorize as "popular" or "elite."[6] At the "popular" extreme, one might place ballads and stories that circulated orally (although they also circulated among and were even collected or recorded by the literate, urbane, and "elite"). At the "elite" extreme, one might place lengthy, learned treatises on witchcraft, written by, and largely for, theologians, doctors, and jurists (although they often compiled and helped disseminate the beliefs and practices of villagers). Most witchcraft discourses flow between these unstable extremes along a continuum on which one cannot clearly mark the difference between popular and elite.

Henry Goodcole, minister of Newgate prison, expresses some nervousness about publishing his account of the confession and execution of Elizabeth Sawyer for witchcraft because of "the diversitie of opinions concerning things of this nature, and that not among the ignorant, but among some of the learned." Despite this reluctance to wade into controversy, he explains that he was driven to publish his own account in order

> to defend the truth of the cause, which in some measure, hath
> received a wound already, by most base and false Ballets, which were
> sung at the time of our returning from the Witches execution. In
> them I was ashamed to see and heare such ridiculous fictions of her
> bewitching Corne on the ground, of a Ferret and an Owle dayly
> sporting before her, of the bewitched woman brayning her selfe, of
> the Spirits attending in the Prison: all which I knew to be fitter for
> an Ale-bench then for a relation of proceeding in Court of Justice.
> And thereupon I wonder that such lewde Balletmongers should be
> suffered to creepe into the Printers presses and peoples earcs.[7]

In this much-discussed passage, Goodcole sharply distinguishes the "Ale-bench" from the "Court of Justice," ridiculous fictions from his own true "relation of proceeding in a Court of Justice." In Goodcole's text, what is "ridiculous" is whatever he himself does not believe (sigs. A4r, A4v). He marks his own account as reliable by appending a list of witnesses. Although Goodcole differentiates his text from other popular narratives, his pamphlet was itself "popular": cheaply produced, available to many of the same kinds of readers who purchased the "base and false ballets," and the source for a play, William Rowley, Thomas Dekker, and John Ford's *The Witch of Edmonton* (1621). His pamphlet's title page promises "the relation of the Divels accesse to her [Sawyer], and their conference together" in Newgate prison—that is, the ridiculous fiction of "spirits attending [her] in the Prison" that Goodcole claims he writes against. As the recently appointed minister of Newgate, Goodcole might have been motivated to defend the prison against the charge that it housed such goings on.[8] Goodcole's scrupulous marking of boundaries demonstrates the controversial, contested nature of the very distinctions on which he insists.[9] By insisting on a distinction he cannot sustain, Goodcole implicates his true relation as itself a ridiculous fiction, a fiction he hopes will be ridiculously popular.

Witchcraft continues to be an evidentiary crisis—a site of interdisciplinary negotiations about evidence—because historians and literary critics alike must rely on the same evidence, these very printed pamphlets. Detailed records of testimony from court proceedings rarely survive, sometimes by chance, sometimes because they were not particularly valued, and sometimes because they were deliberately destroyed (as in cases ending in acquittal).[10] The only extant court records tend to be indictments, which are relatively terse and which do not usually record the outcomes of cases. After comparing pamphlets to assize records, Alan Macfarlane concludes that pamphlets often supply new information: they are thus "a vital and reliable source, providing otherwise inaccessible material and correcting the somewhat narrow impression of witchcraft prosecutions provided by indictments."[11] In the absence of anything like transcripts of court proceedings, no source stands behind the testimonies as pamphlets present them. While few turn to pamphlets to find out what really happened between the accuser and the accused or even what a given witness actually said, historians and literary critics alike turn to pamphlets to discover what stories about witchcraft were "in circulation."[12] As a consequence, witchcraft pamphlets have received more sustained and textured readings as texts than have pamphlets on other topics.[13] The questions literary critics and historians bring to these texts are often more alike than different.

When we read these printed texts, we follow in the footsteps of those who evaluated these narratives with life-and-death stakes in the seventeenth century. Early modern scholars and judges, witnesses and pamphleteers labored to make fine distinctions between the sorts of narratives that should be admitted as "good evidence," either in court or in learned debates, and those that were "mere" or "ridiculous fictions." How was one to tell "sham-stories, and Mock-Relations" from "Credible Modern Relations"? According to Richard Bovet, who provided these contrasting terms in his 1684 treatise *Pandaemonium*, "credible modern relations" relate events "most of which have happened in these few years, and will be attested by persons of Unquestionable Worth and Reputation now alive amongst us."[14] If a relation's credibility was a function of its relator, that relator's "unquestionable reputation" depended on relations between men and women, domestic and foreign, Protestants and Catholics, court and country, judges and juries. These were all relations that were in tumultuous flux. As Peter Elmer argues, the decision to pursue witchcraft charges or for judges to take them seriously was contingent on "the broader political climate which prevailed at a particular time and place."[15] Content and form shaped the reception and effects of a given relation of witchcraft.

Examining early modern skirmishes over the indistinct boundary between evidence and story, probable and improbable, I will argue that the history of witchcraft prosecution and its decline can be told, in part, as the breakdown in shared expectations of what made a story ridiculous or plausible. Witchcraft offers an extreme test case for an historical inquiry into the role of stories as legal and historical evidence. Depending largely on discriminations among narratives, judges' and juries' decisions about innocence and guilt, acquittal or hanging, as well as the published accounts of and debates over witchcraft prosecutions, manifest the concrete and extreme material consequences representational conventions can have. I will focus here on three cases that have been much discussed: the Anne Gunter case in 1608, the Samlesbury witches tried as part of the massive trials of Lancashire witches in 1612, and the "late" Lancashire witches of 1634. Each of these cases disintegrated because of the determination that a key witness had lied. In two of them, a sovereign intervened. While these cases overlap with those in which demonic possession and its exorcism were exposed as impostures, I will focus on the distinct if related issue of perjury, which is at the heart of these three cases, particularly the question of how a supposedly fabricated narrative of accusation was distinguished from a persuasive or "true" one. But first I will consider the conventions shaping the story of witchcraft.

Proof and Plots

Witchcraft was very difficult to prove by means of physical evidence. The accusers, neighbors, justices of the peace, and jury members building a case against a suspect might search his or her house for "pictures of clay or wax, &c. haire cut, bones, powders, books of witchcrafts, charms; and for pots or places where their spirits may be kept."[16] By the seventeenth century, they might search the suspect's body for proofs of her guilt; juries of matrons routinely inspected suspects for witches' marks, that is, supernumerary teats for suckling familiars or the devil himself.[17] Although the pursuit of physical evidence became increasingly aggressive and inventive, while yet stopping short of the inquisitorial tortures disdained as un-English, even unscrupulous witch finders like the infamous Matthew Hopkins (that is, bounty hunters who got paid by the head for "discovering" witches) could not rely on physical evidence alone. Indeed, Hopkins's aggressive efforts to solicit or manufacture physical evidence such as witch marks might have generated suspicion of such evidence and placed greater weight than ever on narratives.[18] For suspicions and accusations to develop into indictments, and indictments into trials, victims and suspects had to tell their stories. Victims' accusatory narratives and suspects' confessions provided the primary evidence against suspected witches; learned authors who debated the existence of witches also depended on stories as their evidence both for and against.[19]

Since witchcraft trials depended on witnesses, legal practice suspended many of the usual restrictions on who might give evidence. For instance, the accused's children could testify against him or her; women also took on increasingly significant roles as witnesses against other women.[20] As long as witchcraft prosecutions continued in England, virtually no one was turned away as unsuitable to testify against a witch. Yet the suspension of usual standards of evidence occasioned uneasiness, even in those who were committed to the legal prosecution of witches. Of course, there were witches, such writers argued, but how could one *prove* it in a court of law? They therefore advised caution in building cases. In 1608, William Perkins urged potential jurors to be as diligent as possible in detecting witches "by all sufficient and lawfull meanes" yet to be careful not to convict on presumptions rather than proofs, lest they be guilty "through their owne rashnesse of shedding innocent blood."[21] John Cotta argued in 1616 that "many cases justly necessarily and unavoidably stand perpetually inscrutable undecided and never determined, as certaine proofes and evidences of the limitation and annihilation of mans knowledge in many things of this life."[22] Many legal theorists particularly worried that the disregard for usual procedures of investigation and standards of evidence in witchcraft trials would undermine due process, as well as subjects' confidence in and respect for the legal system as a whole. By 1646, John Gaule argued that punishing the innocent on mere suspicions endangered social order more than allowing the guilty to go unpunished. Real witches deserve the most ignominious deaths, "but God forbid they should be thus punished for witches; that indeed are no Witches."[23]

This caution probably contributed to the relatively high acquittal rate in England. It is hard to quantify the rates of conviction or acquittal because the records on which such quantification would depend are so spotty. Based on the surviving assize court records for the best-documented courts, the home circuit assizes, historians have calculated that less than 50 percent, even as few as 22 percent, of those indicted were convicted and punished.[24] While these statistics suggest greater certainty than uneven record survival warrants, all historians agree that there were acquittals, and many of them, in England. The significance of acquittals can elude us when we focus on print evidence, which tends to emphasize particularly newsworthy cases ending in convictions. As Keith Thomas points out, "contemporaries, like some modern historians, were dependent for their knowledge of the subject upon the chance appearance of a pamphlet account of a notable trial, and unacquainted with the routine prosecution disclosed by the assize records," routine prosecution that often ended in acquittal. But even big trials like those in 1612 in Lancashire included some acquittals, and some trials ending in acquittals were described in print.[25] In many proceedings, the judge and jury determined that the charges were not reliable. How did they make those determinations? As Thomas suggests, print might be a poor archive for answering that question. But it must suffice.

According to some early modern commentators on witchcraft, accusers in villages and the legal personnel who gave credence to their charges shared a striking agreement on what constituted a credible narrative of witchcraft. Learned writers who questioned the existence of witches, or the possibility of proving their existence in court, most clearly articulated the features common to what they took to be the most familiar, convincing narratives of witchcraft. As early as 1584, Reginald Scot identified witches as, typically, "women which be commonly old, lame, bleare-eied, pale, fowle, and full of wrinkles; poore, sullen, superstitious, and papists; or such as knowe no religion."[26] Almost a century later, John Gaule similarly described the vulnerability of those women who conformed to the "type" of the witch as we still know it: "every old woman with a wrinkled face, a furr'd brow, a hairy lip, a gobber tooth, a squint eye, a squeaking voyce, or a scolding tongue, having a rugged coate on her back, a skull cap on her head, a spindle in her hand, and a Dog or Cat by her side; is not only suspected, but pronounced for a witch."[27] Although both Scot and Gaule acknowledge that there was a type of the witch and that women whose appearance and social position fit the type were vulnerable to suspicion and persecution, their insight did not prevent prosecutions. Gaule himself includes among "infallible and certain" signs of witchcraft "semblable Gestures and demeanures of Witches, with Comparable expressions of passions and affections which in all Witches (of all Times and Places) have been observed and found to be very much alike."[28] In short, he argues that a person can tell a witch because she looks and acts like a witch, thus demonstrating that the conventions he questions also shape his own expectations. Even as resolute a skeptic as Scot helped codify and sustain such conventions, however inadvertently, by cataloguing them.

If widely circulated conventions influenced those who were suspected, accused, and successfully prosecuted for witchcraft, convention sometimes governed the plot according to which neighborly tensions spiraled into witchcraft trials, at least as this process was narrated by those who brought accusations and then disseminated through print. As early as 1587, George Gifford, who questioned the legal and theological justifications for executing witches, described the formula:

Some woman doth fal out bitterly with her neighbour: there fol-
loweth some great hurt. . . . There is a suspicion conceived. Within
fewe yeares after shee is in some jarre with an other. Hee is also
plagued. This is noted of all. Great fame is spread of the matter. Mother W. is a witch. [Other examples accrue; someone she
curses falls ill.] Every body sayth now that mother W. is a witch
indeede. . . . It is out of all doubt: for there were [some] which saw
a weasil runne from her housward into his yard even a little before
hee fell sicke. The sicke man dieth, and taketh it upon his death
that he is bewitched: then is mother W. apprehended, and sent to
prison, shee is arrayned and condemned, and being at the gallows,
taketh it upon her death that shee is not gylty: and doubtles some
are put to death not beyng gylty.[29]

As Gifford describes it, the standard plot always entails a dispute, followed by
suffering, followed by suspicion and blame. An accusation of witchcraft depends, then, on a presumption about the causal relationship between a griev-
ance incurred and harm inflicted.

This was so much the case that Richard Bernard, in his *A Guide to Grand
Jury Men* (1627), argued that this sequence of events might be taken as imply-
ing a witch's malign intent as its cause. Bernard carefully distinguishes proofs
sufficient to secure a conviction for witchcraft from probabilities and presumptions, which are less reliable and more open to dispute. For instance,
neighbors' "common report" that one is a witch, while grounds for suspicion,
might be cause to investigate but not sufficient to convict because "a common report may arise, though not upon no grounds, yet upon very weake
grounds, being duely examined." Yet Bernard includes among his compelling
proofs a damning sequence of speech acts: if suspects "have been heard telling
of the killing of some man or beast, or of the hurting of them, or when they
have not onely threatned revenge upon any, or their cattell, but have foretold
particularly what shall happen to such an one, and the same found true, and
their boasting afterwards thereof." In this case, the accuracy of prediction joins
with hearsay accounts of the witch's words to constitute sufficient proof of a
witch's compact with the devil.[30] Cunning women and men practiced various
forms of prognostication that did not necessarily lead to criminal prosecution.
In witchcraft trials, the presumption to foretell, as retrospectively related, is
sometimes taken as criminal; in other cases, any negative outcome can be
viewed as the consequence of any prior action—be it a gift or a curse—so that

the accused accrues blame as the origin of a sequence of unfortunate incidents and therefore their cause. The sequence itself, a plot, serves as proof of the accused's initial agency and therefore her culpability.

This plot was so conventional that it is intelligible in the compressed form in which the first witch in *Macbeth* recounts it. Asked where she has been, she replies:

> A sailor's wife had chestnuts in her lap,
> And munched, and munched, and munched. "Give me," quoth I.
> "Aroint thee, witch," the rump-fed runnion cries.
> Her husband's to Aleppo gone, master o'th'Tiger.
> But in a sieve I'll thither sail,
> And like a rat without a tail,
> I'll do, I'll do, and I'll do. (1.3.3–9)

She vows to make the sailor "dwindle, peak, and pine" and to make his boat "tempest-tossed" (22, 24).[31] The only thing missing from this rehearsal of the standard plot is her cursing when the sailor's wife refuses her the chestnuts and calls her a witch.

Some historians have argued that indictments, depositions, and pamphlets all reveal how consistently witchcraft prosecutions actually conformed to this plot.[32] The crucial episode in this frequently replayed narrative is the opening one, the initial rebuff of a request from the person who will ultimately be charged with witchcraft. The person who refuses the request, it is argued, then feels guilty; this guilt causes his or her suffering, which s/he then manages by blaming the witch. The guilty person, in other words, transforms him or herself into the victim.

Others have argued that this narrative of charity refused does not really describe how prosecutions began and progressed. For example, detailed case studies have indicated that an accuser sometimes bore a grudge against the suspected witch or her family rather than feeling guilty about denying her charity.[33] Malcolm Gaskill emphasizes the "disregard many paid to popular typologies when it came to the practical business of accusation," although he also admits that "stereotypes may well have influenced accusers and jurors in certain cases."[34] Just as prosecutions unfolded differently across time and place, case by case, so stories changed over time and depending on who was doing the telling.[35]

While witchcraft prosecutions had many motives and played out in a variety of unpredictable ways, the paucity of evidence other than pamphlet accounts makes it very difficult to distinguish cleanly between how cases actually unfolded and how witnesses or pamphleteers chose to tell that story. Whether or not it described each sequence of events experienced as witchcraft, the plot contemporaries schematized is important because it shaped how many contemporaries told the story of witchcraft in the texts that survive. Learned skeptics' recognition of narrative conventions did not prevent the reproduction of those narratives in villages and courts, speech and print, at the expense of accused women and men.

How do we evaluate the relationship between the conventional and the outlandish in these stories, and where does the probable reside? Just as this is a challenge for readers now, it was a challenge for readers then. On the one hand, as I have argued, stories of witchcraft compelled belief in part by conforming to a well-known plot. Narratives of witchcraft, however terrifying, simultaneously offered the reassurance that even the most incredible, preternatural events might unfold according to predictable plots.[36] On the other hand, narratives grabbed attention through extraordinary occurrences and distinctive details. In *Pandaemonium*, Bovet argues that one should not be put off by descriptions of "unaccountable" events and improbable transactions: "for such as endeavour to impose strange Fictions upon the Credulous, use to adapt them as near as they can to a supposal of Truth in the management; tho attended with very strange, and seemingly Prodigious circumstances."[37] In other words, since those who want to gull you make their stories seem as probable as possible, it is the improbable that is more likely to be true. From a more skeptical position, an account of the possession at Loudun similarly argues that the strange compels belief more than the familiar: "strange circumstances stand not idle in miraculous stories, but are very effectuall to perswade beliefe."[38] It might seem impossible to make distinctions between strange and familiar, credible and incredible in stories about witchcraft, all of which might be seen as outlandish. Where do we locate the eruption of what feels like evidence in the midst of a narrative? Is it when a pamphlet undermines its own moralizing project by sympathizing with the accused?[39] Is it in the conventional or the extraordinary, the familiar outline or the arresting detail? How can we know where to draw the line between questioner and witness, between convention and some content that we might see as exceptional and therefore somehow closer to the truth? Like jury members and pamphlet readers in the seventeenth century, those who now read these pamphlets as evidence must try to decide.

There has been much discussion of what we are to make of those witches who confessed to crimes that, as some state bluntly, they cannot "really" have committed. Peter Brooks asks us to question the assumption that confession is "the prime mark of authenticity, par excellence the kind of speech in which the individual authenticates his inner truth" and reminds us that "there is probably something true in most confessions, but the kind and nature of that truth is not always evident—and not always evidence."[40] If all confessions are suspect, then perhaps alleged witches' confessions are especially so. Just as isolation, entrapment, and at the very least the threat of torture were used to secure a confession from Henry Garnet, witches' confessions resulted from a complex process of coercion, dialogue, and ventriloquism. Fear, shame, sleeplessness, hunger, and, in some cases, old age, illness, or dementia might compel suspects either to confess, drawing on familiar tropes, or to collaborate with their interrogators to shape the kind of story the court was prepared to hear and to believe. Even those who defended the judicial use of confessions address the various reasons for suspecting an imprisoned old woman's statements. John Gaule, for instance, argues that a witch's

> owne mouth can speake her owne guilt best, and may not amisse
> be taken for a right discovery of her own Conscience. Nor doth her
> Sexe any whit invalid her own testimonie against her self. Never-
> theless it would be wel considered whether she was forced to it,
> terrified, allured, or otherwise deluded. And withall, if in her owne
> mind and perfect senses; If not out of some Melancholy humour or
> discontentment working to say anything through tediousnesse of
> life.[41]

Gaule's acknowledgment of the pressures that might induce someone to confess does not, for him, necessarily vitiate the value of those confessions as evidence.

Some commentators on the witchcraft phenomenon questioned the work of witch finders such as Hopkins precisely because of their aggressive pursuit and manipulation of evidence to support their accusations. Hopkins, who "discovered" numerous witches and secured their convictions, defended himself against the charge that he coerced confessions out of suspected witches and justified his high rate of conviction by insisting that he could distinguish between the probable and the improbable. Answering the challenge that he had "wrung" confessions out of "these stupified, ignorant, uni[n]telligible, poore silly creatures," he insisted that "he utterly denye[d] that confession of a Wit[c]h, when she confesseth any improbability, or impossibility, *as flying in the ayre, riding on a broom, &c.*"[42] That Hopkins dismisses as improbable or impossible the image of the witch now most widely recognized in English and American popular culture suggests that threats that cease to warrant legal regulation and stories that cease to compel belief in court can tenaciously maintain symbolic currency. Grounding his adjudication among confessions in his contempt for old women, Hopkins also maximizes women's account-ability while minimizing their power. Hopkins assumes that, through ill will and harsh words, a woman might cause property damage, disease, and death; he assumes, that is, that a woman can commit a felony. But he scorns the pos-sibility that even the supernaturally empowered might fly.

Usually, however, the coherence and conventionality of an accused witch's confession, its neat fit with her examiners' and accusers' expectations, made it more, rather than less, credible. On the one hand, Reginald Scot insisted that witches' confessions were invariably either coerced or delusional; and, almost a century later, John Wagstaffe's *The Question of Witchcraft Debated* warned that "The wisest men in the world, may by imprisonment and torture be brought to confess anything, whether it be true or false; as many miser-able Creatures, confessing themselves Witches, have had their Confessions extorted from them by such cursed means."[43] Perhaps they believe in their own guilt, Wagstaffe suggests, simply because their social betters do. On the other hand, throughout this period, many assert that "the voluntarie confes-sion and examination of a Witch, doth exceede all other evidence" and put that assertion into practice.[44] For example, Henry Goodcole confides to his readers that Elizabeth Sawyer's confession was "with great labour . . . extorted from her" but does not see this as vitiating the value of her confession, which he extracted from her after her trial and as part of the process of preparing her to die, read to her at the place of execution, and required her to affirm.[45]

Scholars working with these confessions restage the seventeenth-century debates regarding whether they can be valued as evidence and, if so, of what. Everyone agrees that there were pressures on the accused to confess. The ques-tion becomes whether one can ascribe any agency to those who confess and how one might locate traces of the accused's interiority or expressions in the surviving texts. Carlo Ginzburg argues that scholars should take seriously the often "hostile testimonies, originating from or filtered by" the legal sys-tem that prosecuted suspected witches because they are the only testimonies that survive.[46] Many students of English witchcraft, especially those with an interest in women, who were the majority of both accused and victims, have sought some trace of women's agency in these hostile testimonies.[47] Defining agency as "the power to shape one's own life and story," Diane Purkiss argues that women who confessed to witchcraft were cultural producers, exercising some version of this agency by actively seeking the identity of witch or accepting it when thrust on them or taking the occasion of prosecution to tell "their own stories." According to Purkiss, then, "witches were women who scripted their own stories, at least in part"; the accused "struggled to incorporate some fragment of what she was to herself, what her own fantasy of herself as witch was, into her official confession."[48] It is satisfying to imagine the accused witch as agent as well as victim. And it is plausible that, since surviving texts describe some witches who did not confess, some did and that the reasons they did were more complicated than simple coercion. Surely some of those who confessed gained something from doing so. Some may have engaged in occult practices or recognized some of their beliefs as heterodox. Accused of wishing another ill, one might acknowledge having done so and even relish the thought that malice could be effective, that bad thoughts made bad things happen.

While I find the emphasis on the confessors' agency compelling and even necessary, I also think that it requires us to trust the texts through which that confession is conveyed to us, texts that are not only hostile but hectic, cluttered with the tropes and plots through which one might construct a story to call one's own but through which it is hard to identify the fragment or fantasy of a self. It might be there. And it is provocative to insist on its possible presence. But how could we know? We have the stories, but we cannot know who contributed what to the texts that survive to us or why. Nor should we discount the agency of silence. A collection of documents from the London ecclesiastical courts includes the 1566 proceeding against Alicia Gardiner for counseling a woman "who was a witche, that she shulde confesse nothinge, for yf thow dost, thow wolt dyve [die or dive] for hit; and thowe wilt turne thy neighbowrs to troble."[49] Since our game here is evaluating stories, it seems churlish to draw attention to a story blocker, assiduously trying to silence another woman. But in "counselling not to confess," Alicia Gardiner spoke against speech in a way that marked it as destructive rather than expressive.

Contemporaries acknowledged the power of speech to destroy in trials in which they identified perjury. What evidence survives of testimony that was discovered or asserted to be perjured suggests that testimonies might attract attention as unpersuasive because they were too obviously "by the book," or because they were conned from the wrong book, or because they exceeded the parameters for credible fictions of witchcraft, marking themselves as ridiculous. In each case, the fit between the story and the conventions for such stories was at issue. Of course, context was crucial to how a particular story played. But the story itself, and its ability to compel belief, mattered as well.

The Reading of Anne Gunter

In their detailed accounts of Anne Gunter's supposed bewitching, Brian Levack and James Sharpe have documented the complex process by which Gunter's case became the subject of intensive scrutiny and unprecedented documentation. In 1604, Anne Gunter fell ill and eventually began to show classic symptoms of demonic possession, such as going into fits and trances. She accused three women of bewitching her: a woman with a long-standing reputation as a witch, her illegitimate daughter, and a married woman who had a reputation for being difficult but who was also the kinswoman of two men whom Anne's father, Brian, had been accused of killing in a fight following a football match several years earlier. Because of family connections at Oxford, the case was widely discussed there, and Oxford dons interviewed Anne, supported her father's claim that she was bewitched, and encouraged a trial. In 1605, assize judges in Abingdon heard the case against the three women Anne accused but ultimately acquitted them. In part because the case had become so widely discussed and in part because Anne's father Brian was so dogged, it did not end there. On a visit to Oxford, James I interviewed Anne. Ultimately, he met with her a total of four times and referred her case to Richard Bancroft, archbishop of Canterbury, and his chaplain, Samuel Harsnett, who is now best known for his exposés of possession cases and exorcisms. Anne was removed from her father's house, and she lived in Bancroft's residence for some of the time that she was under surveillance. During this time, she was examined by Edward Jorden, a physician known to many students of early modern witchcraft for the text he wrote attributing one Mary Glover's symptoms not to bewitchment but to hysteria or "fits of the mother." The appearance of both Harsnett and Jorden in the story bears out Sharpe's contention that one of the fascinating things about this case is how many minor players in early Jacobean culture pop up in it.

The story of Anne Gunter's bewitchment reached its climax when, as a result of the king's interest and Harsnett's scrutiny, proceedings were brought against Anne and Brian in the Court of Star Chamber for falsely accusing the three women. Thus, the Gunters' claims were not just revealed as "ridiculous fictions" but as a criminal act; it was the government itself, not the falsely accused, who initiated this proceeding. According to Levack, "The Gunter trial was the first attempt by an English government, using the one central criminal court in which it could initiate criminal prosecutions, to bring the *accusers* of witches to trial."[50] The trial took place before Star Chamber, which was, as both Sharpe and Levack remind us, the Privy Council "acting in a judicial capacity."[51] It was not a common law court and so had no jury and no judge; all the councilors rendered the verdict. Although it became notorious as a venue in which sovereigns from Henry VII to Charles I disciplined their opponents, it focused largely on suits between parties. The most severe punishment the Star Chamber could impose was mutilation; William Prynne is one of the better-known victims of such treatment. Most often, the Star Chamber imposed fines. Unfortunately, we do not know what verdict the councilors reached regarding the charges against Brian and Anne Gunter.[52] But we do have a remarkable record of the testimony collected for the case. The testimony of over sixty witnesses, amounting to several hundred pages, makes this case, according to Sharpe, "quite simply the best-documented English witchcraft case."[53] While we have a level of documentation no other witchcraft case can rival, we lack the kind of source we often turn to in its absence, that is, a printed narrative of the case. To understand how witnesses' statements fit together into a story, I must rely on the archival research and storytelling skills of Sharpe and Levack. Thus I take as my object of study both their reading of the case and their account of Anne and Brian Gunter's reading.

While there is much of interest in this case, my focus here is the tantalizing suggestion that the Gunters learned how to perform possession by reading pamphlet accounts. Anne Gunter testified that her father consulted books about other bewitchment cases, including *The Most Strange and Admirable Discoverie of the Three Witches of Warboys* (1593), which other people brought him so that "he 'should see in what manner the parties named in those books were tormented & afflicted,'" and she testified that he did indeed 'read & consider them'." As a result, according to Anne, her fits were heavily influenced by the descriptions in the pamphlet about the Warboys case.[54] Brian Gunter also seems to have gotten the idea of giving Anne a mixture of "sack and sallet oil," which made her sick and supposedly provoked fits, from Samuel Harsnett's *Declaration of Egregious Popish Impostures* (1603). This knowledge from books helped provide a kind of script for how to act like a possessed person. So did feedback from her audiences. According to Levack, Anne's symptoms may have become "more pronounced as she became the main theatrical attraction in Oxford, sometimes commanding an audience of forty people at one time." Even as she may have played to these spectators and their expectations, they also acted as skeptics who tested her and her consistency.[55]

What are we to make of the role of pamphlets in shaping the performance of witchcraft? The historians who have uncovered this evidence of print's influence in manuscript records are reluctant to make too much of it. As Sharpe points out, "It has long been suspected that trial pamphlets and similar literature helped spread ideas on witchcraft, but such striking evidence of so direct a connection between a printed account of one case and what happened in another is very rare."[56] Malcolm Gaskill cites a case of mimicking the Warboys pamphlet two years later, but he too insists that "such examples are rare."[57] Although Gaskill introduces this example by cautioning that "it remains difficult to demonstrate either that print affected popular thinking directly, or that it faithfully reflects that thinking," his evidence suggests that, whatever the relation between print and thinking, there is a more demonstrable relation between print and social performance. Since there are at least two cases in which the bewitched confess to using the Warboys pamphlet as a prompt book, we can at least speculate that accusers may have conducted backstage research in cases in which it was not caught or confessed. If, as Gaskill argues, many of those who wrote about witchcraft were largely informed by other writings on witchcraft—so that discourse perpetuated itself—we might see victims and accusers in trials as shaped by available stories about witchcraft, "sources" that enabled as much as entrapped them.[58] Just as pamphlets constitute a crucial form of evidence after the fact, so they were a crucial form of evidence for contemporaries, not only as they made sense of particular cases but as they prepared, wittingly or unwittingly, to participate in others.

Sharpe's formulation that "people 'knew' what happened in cases of demonic possession, and demoniacs 'knew' how to behave if they thought they were possessed" in part because they read about it in books suggests that representations helped people "know" the conventions of a plausible story of demonic possession or witchcraft and then to perform within those parameters and/or to offer a narrative that conformed to those expectations.[59] To say that people know a story is not to say that their conformity to that plot is intentional and, in the legal context, a willful attempt to deceive. But without assuming that conformity is necessarily "knowing" in the sense of self-consciously doing or saying what is expected, one can say that possession, however disorderly, had meaning only as it was legible or scripted as such.

Some historians, including Sharpe and Gaskill, avoid going this far, in part because it is impossible to prove the link between stories and conduct, stories and belief. But others, such as Peter Rushton, suggest that storytellers across decades and a broad social spectrum shared a set of expectations with readers in studies or listeners in court or quarrelers in a village about the plots of witchcraft and possession. "Whether it was memory alone or possession of printed accounts which perpetuated this culture, it is impossible to establish, but clearly narrators were providing what they already knew their local listeners would believe."[60] Although some scholars of witchcraft prosecutions and discourses emphasize variety more than consistency, Anne Gunter's case offers an especially good opportunity to consider the complicated relation between print and conduct, not just because of the tantalizing prospect of knowing deception but because of the revelation that there was no *not* knowing, no way to be possessed except by the book.

In the particular case of pamphlet accounts of possession, Michael Witmore draws on actor-network theory to argue that, if print helped shape and disseminate a script for how to play possession, then pamphlets themselves became "virtual actors in the process."[61] As actors, Witmore suggests, printed texts worked in disturbingly remote ways. Many scholars of witchcraft have pointed out that witchcraft belief focuses on the fear that witches could make mischief beyond the limits of their own bodies and from a remove, spanning distance and penetrating barriers by means of skulking and insinuating familiars, unwelcome gifts, lingering curses. Potential victims were vulnerable through their own still-animate bodily detritus—fingernails, hair clippings, and worn clothing—or through images witches made of them. Thus, witches and their victims alike could become powerful or vulnerable through animate objects that served as subject-extensions.[62] Witmore argues that print too has this almost magical power to be a subject-extension, an agential object: "it could preserve, transmit, and perhaps even magnify the power of witches and devils by disseminating their exploits to a larger audience."[63] As Witmore acknowledges, print was not the only carrier of "the mobile repertoires of behavior associated with witchcraft or possession" that "could also circulate via rumor, personal memory or the lore proper to a particular place or community." But he emphasizes that, through all these means, the most conventional fictions of witchcraft and possession, those most likely to be deemed persuasive rather than ridiculous, in a way perpetuated themselves.[64] While the well-documented Gunter case, as narrated by Sharpe and Levack, focuses on Brian and Anne's intentions, thinking about print itself as an actor suggests that, whatever the Gunters' motives, whichever Gunter we view as the prime mover in this case, stories also played a role in breeding the stories Anne Gunter told.

The capacity of stories to be actors, and to reassert or perpetuate themselves, is visible not only in the confessions of a witness such as Anne Gunter but in the stories we tell about her, in turn. James Sharpe's wonderfully detailed and engrossing account of "the bewitching of Anne Gunter" must come to terms with how to emplot female agency, as well as how to bring an indeterminate story to an end. Eager to position Anne Gunter as an agent, which he associates with the benefits she accrues through imposture, including dancing before the king and falling in love, Sharpe seems unable to consider other ways in which we might view Anne as an agent rather than a victim. As Lena Orlin points out in a probing review, Sharpe "neglects to remind us of Anne Gunter's high level of literacy, discussed elsewhere, and her own access" to the books that supposedly influenced her fits. As a consequence, for Orlin, "it is richly apparent that Sharpe could also have made a case for Anne Gunter's leading role as deviser and perpetrator of the hoax."[65] The story of Anne's role as her father's puppet or instrument is, as Witmore's work suggests, as conventional in its own way as the story of her as victim of possession.[66]

Sharpe's rather conventional story of female desire and agency, in which Anne, while not a victim, is also not a literate perpetrator, is defined by its ending: it is "a story that had concluded with her meeting King James, falling in love and dancing before the court."[67] As the stories of Anne Boleyn and Catherine Howard suggest, this is not necessarily a recipe for a happy ending. Anne may have married Archbishop Bancroft's servant, whom she met in London, and James may even have granted her both a pardon and a dowry. She may also have married someone else entirely or no one at all. As Sharpe explains after detailing his assiduous efforts to discover Anne's fate, "We come . . . to a complete impasse when attempting to reconstruct what happened to Anne Gunter."[68] If she did marry Bancroft's servant, the romance is tarnished by the possibility that Anne was entrapped into the liaison for intelligence purposes. As Levack puts it, "Harsnett had apparently encouraged this romance in order to obtain Anne's unsuspecting admission to her deceptive behavior."[69] Those the Gunters accused faired better than some women who were acquitted of witchcraft in that they were free to return home. But, as Sharpe points out, "we can only imagine what it must have been like for an accused witch to go back to her community and attempt to reconstruct her life after such a trial."[70] However well-documented this case is, it has no conclusion.

Sharpe's attempt to challenge one conventional story—of a young woman who is a victim, of witches or of her father—leads him to produce another equally conventional story, of a woman whose self-expression and fulfillment take the form of dancing, attracting the king's attention, and falling in love. Perhaps the least conventional story would be the one toward which Orlin gestures, of a woman who reads, plots, and deceives. At any rate, the challenge of telling Anne Gunter's story reveals how hard it is to think outside the available conventions. The Gunter case, from this perspective, demonstrates how Brian and Anne Gunter learned how to put on a possession act by mastering narrative and performative conventions they learned from pamphlet accounts of cases. In narrating their case, Sharpe has to act as a relator, sorting through the many texts that survive from the Gunter case and deciding how to weave them into a compelling narrative. But the story he tells is, inevitably, as indebted to other stories and to inherited narrative conventions as were the Gunters themselves. And it depends as much on what we do not know—what happened to Anne—as it does on what we do; the absence of evidence of her later life frees Sharpe to relate her story as a true romance.

The Wonderfull Discoverie of Jesuits in Samlesbury

Assembling legal materials into a compelling narrative is a job the historian today shares with those who produced pamphlet accounts at the time. Legal clerk Thomas Potts claims that the judges in the 1612 trials of witches in Lancashire asked him to compile a lengthy and detailed pamphlet account of the trials because "there doe passe divers uncertaine reportes and relations of such Evidences, as was publiquely given."[71] Like *A True and Perfect Relation*, the subject of chapter one, Potts's true relation of a court proceeding claims to counter less true relations—but also to expand on what happened in court so as to heroize the person who appears to have commissioned the account, in this case Judge Edward Bromley. Stephen Pumfrey has called Potts's *The Wonderfull Discoverie of Witches in the Countie of Lancashire* "the first tract overtly commissioned by the presiding judge." Noting some rather lengthy and idealized speeches assigned to Bromley, Marion Gibson suggests "Possibly Bromley wrote down what he would like to have said"—as Northampton certainly did in *A True and Perfect Relation*.[72] Throughout his text, Potts praises Bromley and other judges for their ability to discriminate between sham stories and credible relations.

How reliable is Potts's account taken to be? Potts's first editor, James Crossley, concludes in his 1854 edition:

> With all his habitual tautology and grave absurdity, Master Potts is, *nevertheless*, a faithful and accurate chronicler, and we owe his memory somewhat for furnishing us with so elaborate a report of what took place on this trial, and giving us, "in their own country terms," the examinations of the witnesses, which contain much which throws light on the manners and language of the times, and nearly all that is necessary to enable us to form a judgment on the proceedings. It will be observed that he follows with great exactness the course pursued in court, in opening the case and recapitulating the evidence separately against each prisoner, so as most graphically to place before us the whole scene as it occurred.[73]

Despite Crossley's confidence that Potts is "faithful and accurate," it is hard to come to a determination on this since we have nothing with which to compare Potts's account; his account remains the crucial piece of evidence about these trials. Knowledge of how prosecutions usually unfolded in the seventeenth century, as well as close attention to Potts's text, has enabled more recent critics to cast doubt on whether Potts "follows with great exactness the course pursued in court." While Potts's relation of "the whole scene as it occurred" anticipates later expectations for courtroom drama, it obscures the fragmented and textualized nature of seventeenth-century assize trials. Since courts did not normally consider the evidence against each prisoner "separately," it is likely that Potts rearranges his materials so that each accused person seems to have an individual proceeding; he leaves out the involvement of the petty jury to keep his focus on the judges; and he presents testimony that was taken down before the trial as if it were delivered orally during the trial, thus erasing the collaborative process through which written statements were shaped and recorded and giving the impression that witnesses gave their statements in court rather than having them read aloud by someone else.[74] Thus, precisely to the extent that Potts tells a story that anticipates later conventions for a good courtroom drama, he may compromise his claims to accuracy.

Whether or not Potts was accurate, he was influential. His *Wonderfull Discoverie* is frequently cited as a precedent for prosecutions in both England and colonial America. For example, in his much reprinted and widely circulated manual for justices of the peace, *The Countrey Justice*, Michael Dalton draws his "observations" on what can substitute for "direct evidence" of witchcraft, "seeing all their workes are the workes of darkenesse, and no witnesses present with them to accuse them," in part out of Potts's *Wonderfull Discoverie of Witches*; thus, Potts's narrative constitutes precedent and dictates procedure.[75]

One particular informant's story motivates my return to this much discussed text. Most of the Lancashire witches were convicted and executed, leading to the remarkable hanging of ten at once; but five were acquitted, and one person was convicted for misdemeanor witchcraft and sentenced to the pillory rather than hanging.[76] I am particularly interested here in a separate trial Potts recounts of accused witches from Samlesbury in August 1612; the same judge, Sir Edward Bromley, dismissed the central witness's testimony as a "strange devised accusation" (sig. L3v). As a narrative, how did it differ from those Bromley found persuasive?

The treatment of the Samlesbury case is another example of how Potts manipulates the chronology of "the course pursued in court." Potts explains that he places the trial out of chronological order "by special order and commandement" (sig. N3r). But why? Perhaps Potts places the story between convictions of those who had confessed and more problematic cases of those who pled not guilty to prepare the reader to trust Judge Bromley's judgments in those tougher cases.[77] Yet if the story is retold at this point to emphasize Bromley's ability to distinguish true from false testimony, it is not clear that it does so. While Potts scoffs at the evidence brought in the Samlesbury case as obviously ridiculous, it closely resembles that accepted in the other trials as true.[78] Whereas Anne Gunter provoked suspicion by enacting possession too much by the book, the key witness in the Samlesbury case provokes suspicion, according to Potts, by revealing her reliance on outside sources.

"Upon her Oath," the delightfully named Grace Sowerbutts accused several other women—her grandmother Jennet Bierley, her aunt Ellen Bierley, and one Jane Southworth—of bewitching her. Her accusatory narrative invited suspicion in its sensational details, rather than in its familiar outlines: Sowerbutts described herself as participating with the accused in witches' sabbaths that included bloodsucking, cannibalism, exhuming corpses, and dancing and having sex with devils.[79] To demonstrate "what impossibilities are in this accusation," Potts assesses Sowerbutts's evidence point by point, dwelling on the alleged dancing and fornicating as especially improbable: "Here is good Evidence to take away their lives. This is more proper for the Legend of Lyes, then the Evidence of a witnesse upon Oath, before a reverend and learned Judge, able to conceive this Villanie, and finde out the practise" (sigs.

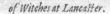

THE WITCHES OF
SALMESBVRY.

The Arraignement and Triall of IEN-
NET BIERLEY ELLEN BIERLEY, *and* IANE
SOVTHVVORTH *of Salmesbury, in the County of
Lancaster ; for Witchcraft vpon the bodie of* GRACE
SOVVERBVTTS, *vpon Wednesday the nineteenth of
August: At the Assises and generall Gaole-deliuery,
holden at Lancaster.*

Before

Sir EDVVARD BROMLEY *Knight, one of his Ma-
iesties Iustices of Assize at Lancaster: as hereafter fol-
loweth.* viz.

Iennet Bierley.
Ellen Bierley.
Iane Southworth.

 Hus haue we for a time left the Graund
Witches of the Forrest of Pendle, to the
good consideration of a verie sufficient
Iury of worthy Gentlemen of their Countrey. We are now come to the famous
Witches of Salmesbury, as the Countrey called them,
who

Figure 2. First page of the Thomas Potts's coverage of the trial of the
Samlesbury witches from his *Wonderfull Discoverie of Witches in the Countie
of Lancaster* (1613). Reproduced by permission of The Huntington Library,
San Marino, California.

M1v, M2v). In the early seventeenth century, descriptions of sexual orgies and feasts—of witches' sabbaths—were, in fact, rare in English witchcraft prosecutions, although fairly common in Continental witch lore.[80] The Lancashire case has been called unique because, according to Pumfrey, "For the first time an English jury heard sworn evidence, including four confessions, of pacts made with the Devil and of witches' sabbats."[81] Yet in Samlesbury, the judge dismissed a story of a witches' sabbath as implausible. While the witches convicted by Bromley in Lancaster had also been accused of attending a sabbath, theirs was a tamer affair than the one Sowerbutts described, a lunch party rather than an orgy.

What marks Sowerbutts's narrative as suspect is her description of the demonic lovers as "foure black things, going upright, and yet not like men in the face" (sig. L2v). As many scholars have demonstrated, early modern English culture habitually associated blackness with evil, sexuality, and the occult.[82] In *Othello*, for example, Brabantio and Iago insist that a white woman cannot be attracted to a black man—a "sooty bosom[ed] . . . *thing*"—unless she is the victim of "foul charms . . . drugs or minerals": "For nature so prepost'rously to err / . . . / Sans witchcraft could not."[83] Although the Duke advises Brabantio that "to vouch this is no proof," witchcraft prosecutions generally suggest that such pervasive cultural assumptions and patterns of association can, indeed, constitute proof.[84] Yet the Samlesbury case also suggests that miscegenation was so "improbable" that it set the limits even for witches' desire.

Although witches supposedly suckled weasels and relished the devils' freezing cold semen, those few suspects who confess to sexual relations with the devil describe him not only as "man-like" but as "proper," that is, gentle and English.[85] Descriptions of the devil as consort codify in the course of the seventeenth century. By the 1630s, when there was another round of prosecutions in Lancashire, Margaret Johnson confessed that the devil appeared to her as "a man in black attire, with black points," who called himself Mamilion, "and most commonly at his coming had the use of her body."[86] The witch finder Matthew Hopkins and his assistant John Stearne seem to have been particularly adept at soliciting or provoking statements from witches about their demon lovers. For instance, according to a "true and exact relation" of Hopkins's interrogation of Elizabeth Clarke, she told him that for six or seven years she regularly copulated with a devil "in the shape of a proper Gentleman, with a laced band, having the whole proportion of a man."[87] In Stearne's account of this interrogation, Clarke clarifies that "proper" means gentle, English, white—and not only more like authorities and accusers than unlike them but, indeed, of higher social standing and more attractive; she informs Hopkins that the devil came to her "like a tall, proper, black haired gentleman, a properer man then your selfe, and being asked which she had rather lie withall, shee said the Devill."[88] Hopkins's assistant presents this statement to prove Clarke's depravity, but the testimony these "witchfinders" attribute to Clarke conceives and articulates a devil and a witch's desire more familiar than "other."

Contrasting this text to Potts's account of the Samlesbury case suggests that, paradoxically, the recognizable form of Clarke's desire facilitates her prosecution by making her confession seem "probable." The confession Hopkins and Stearne assign to Clarke, even if it includes some defiance, works within the conventional parameters not only of witchcraft narratives but also of scripts for English female desire. Similarly, in Huntingdonshire, Hopkins and Stearne secured the conviction of one Joane Wallis of Keyston, "a very ignorant, sottish woman," on the basis of her confession that she kept imps and that "the Devill came to her in the likenesse of a man, in blackish cloathing, but had cloven feet, which she called Blackman, who used to lie with her, and have the use of her body, yet she confessed he was more uglier then man, and not as her husband."[89] Even this confession, which more closely resembles Grace Sowerbutts's testimony, dwells on the interplay of familiar and strange that seems to characterize successful evidentiary narratives: "Blackman" is "in the likenesse of a man" but "not as her husband"; he wears clothing, but he has cloven feet; although his garments are described as "blackish," his skin is not. All these narratives of witches' congress with the devil assume that even depraved, diabolical white English women would not choose to couple with "black things."

Potts also dismisses Sowerbutts's claims that the witches engaged in other outrageous practices such as sucking an infant's blood and later exhuming, boiling, and eating its corpse. Potts contrasts the witches Sowerbutts describes to the "Witches of the Forrest of Pendle"—those, that is, recently convicted in Lancaster—"who were never so cruell nor barbarous" (sig. M2v). Potts presents the accused in Samlesbury as vulnerable because they conform to the type of the witch: "the wrinckles of an old wives face is good evidence to the Jurie against a Witch." Even if a jury would fall for such "presumptions" rather than "proofs," the judge, Potts insists, makes needful distinctions. Those witches he convicts, for instance, have not only "withered face[s]" to incriminate them but familiars, or small animals who act as their agents, which Keith Thomas calls a "peculiarly English" feature of witch lore.[90] Grace Sowerbutts neglects to assign familiars to those she accuses (sig. M2r, M3r). Sowerbutts's testimony was rendered implausible, then, both by what it included—too foreign a version of the sabbath that was admitted as evidence in the main trial—and by what it excluded—the reassuringly familiar story of the witch's familiar.

On the one hand, Potts juxtaposes the two cases, Lancaster and Samlesbury, to demonstrate the perspicuous judge's ability to distinguish probable from improbable accusations: "*as* his Lordships care and paines was great to discover the practises of these odious Witches of the Forrest of Pendle, and other places, now upon their triall before him: *So* was he desirous to discover this damnable practise, to accuse these poore Women, and bring their lives in danger, and thereby to deliver the innocent" (sig. M3v, emphases mine). On the other hand, Potts contrasts witches who "really" haunt English forests and courtrooms to the exaggeratedly predatory and promiscuous phantoms of legends and lies. While "odious," the witches who lived around Pendle Hill and were convicted are not so "cruel or barbarous" as those Grace Sowerbutts describes; they may be witches, but they're "our" witches. Whether comparing the judge's wisdom in the two trials or contrasting the narratives offered in evidence in each, Potts invites his reader to grasp relations between one case and another. What makes the accusatory narratives presented in Lancaster so convincing is their regard for the parameters of probability; the evidence succeeds in hanging the witches because it presents them as English, familiar, and therefore plausibly demonic. The contrast between the convictions in Lancaster and the acquittals in Samlesbury suggests that successful prosecutions occurred at an intersection of the familiar and the outrageous, the credible and the incredible. Both the accused and the narratives about her or him first had to attract attention as disturbing. Yet that disturbance had to take recognizable forms; the story had to be told in terms that judges and juries could apprehend by what Francis Bacon calls "the principle of relation" by which we can accommodate new knowledge only when it has become familiar, apprehending new concepts "*by a kind of relation*, as the lawyers speak, as if we had known them before."[91]

Although Potts cavils with Grace Sowerbutts's testimony as he presents it, the turning point in his narrative is the moment when the accused fall to their knees before the judge, beseeching him "for Gods cause to examine *Grace Sowerbutts*, who set her on, or by whose meanes this accusation came against them" (M3v). By raising the question of a behind-the-scenes conspiracy, the accused put the judge on the alert and Grace out of countenance, so that she stands "strangely amazed." Soliciting counternarratives from the accused,

Bromley creates the kind of "narrative competition" one rarely finds in the published accounts of witchcraft trials.[92] Early modern trial procedures did not generally encourage the articulation of opposing views. The accused in criminal trials did not have defense attorneys and so relied on the presiding judge to defend their interests; the convictions of those accused in the Popish Plot would ultimately reveal the inadequacies of this system. Witnesses rarely testified on behalf of the accused, nor did accuser and accused usually confront one another in court. Furthermore, in witchcraft prosecutions, the accused sometimes confessed, confirming rather than contesting the charges against her. If "narrative competitions" did arise, they were more likely to take place among the various condemnatory narratives or within a single witness's fragmented and contradictory testimony, rather than between those narratives in accusation and those in defense.

What the judge discovers on inquiry is what Potts has presented as the truth of the matter from the start of his account: Grace was "prepared and instructed to give Evidence against" those she accused by the "subtill practise and conspiracie of a Seminarie Priest, or, as the best in this Honorable Assembly thinke, a Jesuite" (K3v). Potts explains, and laments, that the county of Lancashire has "good store" of Jesuits because the large population of Catholic families there affords them "generall entertainment" and "great maintenance," allowing them to flourish "farre from the Eye of Justice" (sig. K3v). This particular priest, one Christopher Southworth, who was related to one of the accused, Jane Southworth, "had instructed and taught her [Grace] this accusation against them, because they were once obstinate Papists, and now came to Church" (sig. M4r). Potts reminds his readers that "very seldome hath any mischievous attempt beene under-taken without the direction or assistance of a Jesuit, or Seminarie Priest" (sig. M3v). As we saw in chapter one, the official "true relation" of Garnet's trial dwelt on the responsibility of Jesuits for promoting equivocation. In 1624, John Gee enlisted Potts's account of the Samlesbury case as evidence of Jesuits' "practices and impostures." Gee claims Southworth "comploted this, to gaine to himselfe some credit by exorcising, or unwitching" Grace.[93] By the time of the London Fire of 1666, as we will see in the next chapter, Jesuits were assumed to be incendiaries; during the Popish Plot, Jesuits were widely assumed to run "swearing schools" in which they instructed witnesses how to equivocate and perjure themselves so that they could swear themselves "as innocent as the child unborn" no matter what they had done. Perhaps it is not surprising, then, that, in Lancashire in 1612, the most likely suspect in coaching a witness should be a Jesuit.

When Potts thus relocates the threat, substituting a Jesuit for witches, he reveals the connections between the two. Dependable scapegoats, both are oddly reassuring in their consistent malice and predictable methods, in their contemptible reverence for magical objects and tall tales, while yet deeply threatening as members of the local and national communities working to undermine order from within.[94]

The rather predictable slide from witch to Jesuit should lead us to question whether the conniving backstage Jesuit is the "truth." Many students of Potts's text seem to accept that the second story is the true one.[95] Since a Jesuit coach is so very conventional, and so useful to Potts's project of heroizing Judge Bromley and flattering James I, it is also possible that the Jesuit's relation to Grace as her coach and instigator is not the true one, but yet another story particularly suited to the occasion as Potts understood it.

Although Potts insists on the improbability of Grace Sowerbutts's accusation, its evident difference from the convincing accusations made in Lancaster, he also suggests that not everyone would be able to discriminate between the two kinds of narratives. The jury found Sowerbutts's story convincing, especially because "the Priest by the helpe of the Devill, had provided false witnesses to accuse them [the suspects]": "Who did not condemne these Women upon this evidence, and hold them guiltie of this so foule and horrible murder?" (sig. M3v). Potts's praise for the judge and his doubts about the verdict a jury might have reached unassisted remind us that juries and judges did not invariably agree on what constituted admissible evidence of witchcraft. A case like that of the Samlesbury witches, in which the same narrative was interpreted differently by different people, suggests that class, education, profession, confessional allegiance, political moment, even geographical location shaped how various seventeenth-century persons distinguished between the probable and the improbable. The outlandish details in Grace's narrative either alerted suspicion or justified it retroactively. In either case, the content of her depositions mattered.

Potts provides a happy ending for the Samlesbury case. "These poore Innocent creatures" were "delivered from the danger of this conspiracie; this bloudie practise of the Priest laid open" by "the great care and paines of this honorable Judge" (sig. N2v). As in the Gunter case, outside intervention was required to ensure this deliverance; our uncertainty about what exactly happened to the principals next also helps keep the focus on the judge's insight rather than its consequences. Like Anne Gunter, Grace Sowerbutts disappears from the historical record with the discovery of her imposture, and we can only imagine what it was like for her or for those she accused to go on with their lives in close proximity.

The Late Late Lancashire Witches

The 1633 trials in Lancashire were a kind of sequel to those in 1612. Witmore points to "cast overlap" between the two episodes—one of the accused, Jennet Device, had, as a child, testified against her mother in the earlier prosecution; Edmund Robinson, the father of the key witness in the later trial, had served on the earlier jury that heard her testimony.[96] There was so much interest in the 1633 case that one of the accused, Mary Spencer, later claimed that "the throng [was] so great that she could not hear the evidence against her."[97] Although the jury found seventeen of the accused guilty, the judge did not sentence them to death and remained uneasy about the trial and its outcome, especially about the evidence provided by young Edmund Robinson, on which the whole prosecution depended. The judge informed Charles I and his Privy Council of his reservations, and they appointed the bishop of Chester to examine seven of those who had been convicted. In the course of the investigation, three of the seven died of fever or old age. The remaining four—Margaret Johnson, Frances Dicconson, Mary Spencer, and Jennet Hargreaves—were sent to London to be examined by the king's physicians. Although incriminating marks had been "found" on these women in Lancaster, the seven physicians and ten midwives who then searched the women in London "under directions" of William Harvey "and in his presence," described different marks entirely and evaluated them as "nothing unnatural nor anything like a teat or mark," thus suggesting that bodies were as subject to reinterpretation as were stories.[98]

The young witness and his father were also summoned to London. Once separated from his father, young Robinson "confessed that he was taught and suborned to devise, and feign those things against them, and had persevered in that wickedness by the counsel of his Father, and some others, whom envy, revenge and hope of gain had prompted on to that devillish design and villany."[99] A witness who claimed to have overheard conversations between the senior Robinson and the accused as they awaited the arraignment reported that Robinson told Frances Dicconson that if she paid him neither he nor his son would speak against her.[100] Such evidence presents young Robinson as a pawn in his father's schemes, just as Sharpe presented Anne Gunter as the pawn of her father and Potts presented Grace Sowerbutts as the pawn of

Christopher Southworth. But the account of the boy's examination once he was in London presents him as confessing that he had "framed his tale out of his own invention" and that "all that tale is false and feigned, and has no truth at all, but only as he has heard tales and reports made by women." A "reexamination" taken about a week later elaborates that young Robinson got his cue from "hearing the neighbours talk of a witch feast that was kept at Mocking Tower in Pendle Forest about twenty years since, to which feast divers witches came," that is, the key story in the earlier Lancaster trials, and then decided to "make the like tale." This reexamination insists "Nobody was ever acquainted with any part of his fiction or invention, nor did any body ever advise him, but it merely proceeded out of his own brain."[101] Thus, the testimony attributed to him assigns him ownership for the accusatory tale—it is a fiction spun out of "his own invention" and "framed" from the matrix of neighbors' talk and old wives' tales, that repository and generator of stories available to all, perhaps even inescapable, rather than imposed on him by his father.

While Robinson was the chief storyteller, he was not the only one. The situation was complicated by the fact that Margaret Johnson, one of the accused who was brought to London, had confessed. The bishop of Chester, John Bridgeman, criticized Johnson as "having a strong imagination" that she was a witch but "too weak a memory to retain or relate" the crucial "particulars of her actions."[102] One might view Johnson as working within the available parameters for a story many wanted to hear and some were still willing to believe, a story so familiar from overheard "tales and reports made by women" that it rolled trippingly off the tongue, filled theaters and pulled fee-paying visitors into the prison. While the witches were in London, "great sums [were] gotten at the Fleet to shew them, and publick Plays acted thereupon."[103] The story circulated in various forms, including a puppet show, ballads, newsletters, and the touring performances of young Robinson himself.[104] But the bishop also required Johnson to "relate particulars" and to harness her imagination so as to compel belief.

Johnson's confession made the skeptical scrutiny of the case hard for some to understand. In early July of 1634, George Leyburn, in newsletters to other Catholics abroad, commented that the king "will not believe that they are witches, although one did confesse herselfe a witch, and haith dismissed them, and given them money to beare their charges into the country. This proceeding will make many more witches in Lancheshire and in other places. King James would never believe that there could be any witches, and many curtyers are of that opinion and some that ther are noe divels."[105] For Leyburn, then, skepticism is a refusal to believe, and the stakes are high. Dismissing the charges against these four witches, despite the fact that one of them has confessed, will, he fears, breed witches.

Although Leyburn complains that the matter has been settled in early July and that the accused have been "dismissed," they awaited a final judgment in jail more than a month later. The fact that their status was unclear and attitudes toward this case and witchcraft more generally under debate created a theatrical opportunity. Thomas Heywood and Richard Brome's *The Witches of Lancashire* opened at the Globe Theatre while the case was unresolved and in the news and the witches were incarcerated in London. Andrew Gurr links *The Witches of Lancashire* to Thomas Middleton's *A Game at Chess* as "the two most scandalous Globe plays" and as strong draws for the gentry.[106] The play's prologue presents it as homely news to supply a lack of "Newes of forraine State": "No accidents abroad worthy Relation / Arriving here, we are forc'd from our owne Nation / To ground the Scene that's now in agitation." The play is, then, what Grace Sowerbutt's narrative was not—recognizably our own, even as it is also newsy and thus worthy of relation.

In an August 1634 letter that has become central to discussions of the play, one spectator, Nathaniel Tomkyns, claims that the play was "acted by reason of the great concourse of people 3 dayes togither"; comments on the many "fine folke gentmen and gentweomen" he sees when he attends on the third day; and describes in detail key actions of the plot. He is disappointed not to find any "judgement to state our tenet of witches (which I expected)," finding instead that the play is "full of ribaldrie and of things improbable and impossible." The improbabilities include flying, taking on different shapes, and creating disorder and delusion. For instance, the witches turn the Seely household upside down, so that servants direct their masters and children chastise their parents; and they make a bridegroom impotent on his wedding night, leading his wife to beat him, which, in turn, prompts a shaming ritual.[107] Yet the play "passeth for a merrie and excellent new play" because of "the newnesse of ye subject (the witches being still visible and in prison here)" and because it provokes laughter and includes songs and dances.[108] Despite the play's emphasis on the witches' harmless and improbable pranks—" 'Tis all for mirth, we mean no hurt"—its newsiness depends on the awareness that something is at stake, at least for the accused. To the extent that the play suspends judgment, it is enabled to do so because a comedy will need to defer or avoid the scaffold, because the witches await the king's determination, and because witchcraft was a highly contentious and politicized debate in which everyone in the audience would have his or her own opinion. The playwrights can just leave them to it. But does the play suspend judgment, as Tomkyns claims?

Herbert Berry argues that, in exchange for inside information, the playwrights dramatized "the case for the prosecution alone." By the conclusion, he argues, all those characters "who have had doubts about the existence or seriousness of witchcraft are convinced that they have been wrong."[109] Purkiss takes this a step further to argue that the play "wants to punish the scepticism that its own theatricality encourages, while separating itself from the popular. Although popular superstition is constantly stigmatized as low or base, it is also shown to be the only correct way to interpret events."[110] There is a certain brutal concreteness, for example, in the process by which Squire Generous must learn that his wife really is a witch through a trick that leaves him holding her severed hand with a wedding ring on its finger.

The play excludes what is arguably the highest drama surrounding the case, that is, the doubts surrounding the key witness and his testimony. As Alison Findlay points out, if the playwrights gained access to information, that information was both dated and not all that "inside" in that it was based on the examinations that were already in question before the principals came to London. Although Findlay argues that "The Epilogue assumed that the women were guilty" she goes on to say that the epilogue also "recognised the provisional nature" of the judgment for which the accused waited.[111] The playwrights could not, after all, predict the king's decision. The epilogue does, indeed, emphasize uncertainty: "what their crime / May bring upon 'em, ripenes yet of time / Has not reveal'd." Leaving the witches to "expect their due," the epilogue also suggests that this might be "great Mercy . . . After just condemnation." The epilogue insists that the playmakers "dare not hold it fit, / That we for Justices and Judges sit." As a consequence, the playwrights, players, and spectators alike cannot know "What of their storie, further shall ensue."[112] For Heather Hirschfeld, this indeterminacy is Heywood and Brome's achievement. For Hirschfeld, the play is not the case for the prosecution as much as it is an attempt to forestall "any predetermined or unequivocal reading of" the playwrights' own attitudes toward witchcraft.[113] It is even possible to see the witch as a figure for the playwright, conjuring spectacles out of thin air.[114]

There is certainly no doubt that the play refrains from giving the story an ending. Like the cases of Anne Gunter and of Grace Sowerbutts and the Samlesbury three, the story has a loose end. Since this case, like theirs, is an episode in the history of witchcraft as well as of theater and popular festivity, this indeterminacy is problematic. For one thing, the play's refusal to make a decision might simply be a matter of its timing, rather than any particularly heroic resistance on the part of the playwrights. Although Hirschfeld argues that the witches' "witty resistance" blunts "the spectacle of the law that seizes them in the end" and that the playwrights' depiction of the witches' wit "protect[s] them from judgment," it is not clear that Heywood and Brome could protect them—either at the level of narrative or in the legal proceeding that subtends and animates this play, the case whose true relation to its dramatization is at issue for every critic.[115]

What did indeterminacy mean for the accused? No one knows for sure. After they were portrayed on the Globe stage and "still visible and in prison" at the Fleet, they were consigned to oblivion. Although the charges against the Lancashire witches were dismissed as "mere fictions," the women do not seem to have been released. However we decide the play slants, however its varied spectators took it, the accused and pardoned remained in jail. That fate is more indeterminate than hanging, I suppose. But it places pressure on how we think about their comic depiction and its social functions. Reprieved from hanging, they may have languished in prison—as did others whom justices chose neither to execute nor to release. William Ffarington, sheriff of Lancaster, listed ten witches "remaining in his Matys Gaole" in 1636, including Frances Dicconson, Mary Spencer, and Jennett Hargreaves.[116] When Henry Burton, who was sentenced to have his ears cropped at the same time that William Prynne was, began his prison sentence at Lancaster Castle in 1637, he complained that five witches and one of their children, who "had continued a long time there," were lodged in a single "dark roome" under his, and made "a hellish noise night and day." Several scholars of the play assume that these witches probably included those who survived of the four Lancashire witches who had been pardoned.[117] Many conclude that they died in prison;[118] while this seems likely, we do not know for sure.

The witches of Lancashire were "late" in that they were the 1630s witches rather than their 1612 progenitors; they were late in that, once the play was published, they were recent rather than now; the option of leaving their meaning and status in question was a relatively late development in the history of English witchcraft, very much of its time and place; and, for us, the accused are late as in dead, even if we do not know precisely when or how, so we can take their deaths as a given, a footnote rather than the main narrative. Even though we know their stories ended in death, wherever and whenever that occurred, the uncertainty surrounding their fates is a reminder that indeterminacy might not have been liberatory for them.

The Witches of Lancashire draws our attention to the relationship between law courts and the stage, a relationship that has been much discussed. In this instance, the question becomes how a play such as this one participates in the process of changing witchcraft beliefs. As I will discuss further in chapter six, the verb "participates" hedges on the mechanisms of cause and effect. Hirschfeld argues that Heywood and Brome identify with the witches as wits, celebrating them as figures for theatricality itself. Other critics have argued that dramatizations of witchcraft helped mark it as popular in ways that made it both less threatening and less important.[119] By the eighteenth century, Thomas Shadwell's *The lancashire witches, and Tegue O Divelly the Irish priest. A comedy* (1718) presents witches as safely silly and, predictably, couples them with a priest.[120] What the drama helped do, in this view, was to mark witchcraft as a fiction and as entertainment in ways that contributed to acquittals and ultimately the end of prosecutions, but that also contributed to sharper divisions between popular and elite. Since the accused were both presented as entertainment and, perhaps, kept in jail until they died, they offer an unsettling example both of the drama's political and social engagement and of its irrelevance.[121] Historians of witchcraft who are less concerned with the particular operations of dramatic form also argue for a widening division between popular and elite. As Barbara Shapiro puts it, "the educated classes . . . became increasingly reluctant to credit the wild accusations of ignorant countrymen."[122]

By drawing our attention to the central role of evaluating stories in witchcraft prosecutions and the high stakes but unpredictable consequences of those evaluations, *The Witches of Lancashire* suggests that what changed was not the relation of popular to elite as much as the relation between stories and evidence. In the second half of the seventeenth century, it became increasingly difficult for stories about witchcraft to convince judges, juries, ministers, or physicians. As witchcraft narratives lost their capacity to motivate and sustain legal prosecutions or to support scholarly assertions, they continued to circulate as stories. Although those texts that promoted belief in witches, and thus legal prosecution, continued to defend the use of stories as evidence, skeptics dismissed storytelling as an "unscholar-like way of arguing." In 1656, Thomas Ady complained of those who would "ingage me to answer to a story" as if it were a true relation, "in which manner of disputes I have heard sometimes such monstrous impossibilities reported and affirmed to be true, (for they had it by credible report) as would make the Angells in Heaven blush to hear them."[123] In 1677, when John Webster wrote to expose witchcraft as deceit and imposture, he claimed to present facts rather than "rhapsodies, and confused heaps of stories and relations, shuffled together."[124] In 1681, Joseph Glanvil, assuming that skepticism had become the common view, defended his use of stories as evidence that witches do exist and should be legally prosecuted:

> I have no humour nor delight in telling Stories, and do not pub-
> lish *these* for the gratification of those that have; but I record them
> as *Arguments* for the *confirmation* of a Truth which hath indeed
> been attested by multitudes of the like Evidences in all places and
> times.[125]

Insisting that telling carefully selected stories remains the best way to convince unbelievers, Glanvil defends his ability to distinguish between "near" and "remote," credible and incredible stories. But his project is motivated by the concern that, by the late seventeenth century, any story about witchcraft might be dismissed as a ridiculous fiction. As the seventeenth century progressed, even those among the learned who continued to believe in witchcraft questioned whether one could prove it in court. Accusations less frequently led to prosecutions; prosecutions less frequently ended in convictions.

Yet divergent opinions persisted, as is evident in the early eighteenth-century case of Jane Wenham. Like the Lancashire witches, Wenham was a celebrity: many people visited her in jail and attended her trial. Eight pamphlets about her case, some in multiple printings, appealed to "a large audience ready to read on both sides of the issue, and even to debate it."[126] With its coexistence of belief and skepticism, widespread curiosity and well-placed doubt, Wenham's trial, which ended with a jury convicting her but a judge reprieving her, seems to have marked "the definitive end to the possibility of witchcraft prosecution in England; and an end to any idea that witchcraft belief could inhabit some sort of politically neutral and abstract realm."[127] Two decades later, in 1736, a witchcraft act was passed that made it a crime to claim that anyone practiced magic or witchcraft, subject to one year's imprisonment.[128] Ultimately, the growing gap between stories and evidence meant that lives were spared—and that tale bearing itself became the crime.

The process of separating stories from evidence, like the other processes of distinction in which it participated, is not a simple story of progress, however. As an urban, learned elite increasingly found representations of witchcraft entertaining rather than threatening, amusing rather than persuasive, or scary rather than actionable, these representations lost their ability to justify the violent persecution of women. Yet these stories' depiction of old, poor women as supernaturally empowered determined, in part, their improbability; misogyny accompanied and aided skepticism. As one 1669 commentator concludes, "Witches now adayes are poor, silly, contemptible people . . . this old Gammer and that old Goodwife."[129] These narratives' association with rural folk, the untutored, and Catholics also compromised them. For instance, John Gaule recounts endless tales of the supernatural, only to conclude that "Fryarly Authors" and "the Tradition of the vulgar" simply "make . . . up" these stories "like a Tale or Legend." Working through these stories, according to Gaule, one is likely to discover "amongst some probabilities . . . manifold Impossibilities, & absurdities, among some truths, . . . manifold superstitions."[130] Gaule holds these stories in contempt at the same time that he tells them at great length.

If stories had a harder time standing as evidence, at least in the eyes of judges, they began to develop a life of their own. It has been argued that people in villages continued to tell and believe stories of witchcraft even if they could not get judges to believe them; they may even have resorted to vigilante justice to secure the endings they thought such stories required.[131] For the most privileged readers and listeners, stories that no longer served as proof might still command attention and inspire pleasurable terror. True relations of witchcraft gradually evolved into tales of the supernatural that remained compelling even as they became dissociated from evidence. Furthermore, after the witchcraft statutes were repealed and prosecutions faded into local lore, a fuzzy grasp of history meant that stories, rejected as evidence on one front, might stand in for it on another. By the time that *The history of the Lancashire witches. Containing the manner of their becoming such; their enchantments, Spels, Revels, Merry Pranks* appeared (c. 1785), its hodgepodge of funny stories made no reference to the specifics of seventeenth-century trials. According to Malcolm Gaskill, "confusion evidently set in as to what had actually happened during the era of the witch trials." For Gaskill, this suggests that "historical fact evolved into historical fiction."[132] But the two had never been clearly separate. Shaping how people remembered their own history, witchcraft stories simply took on yet another function. This was not progress, evolution, or decline. It was simply another instance in which a relation came to constitute the truth of witchcraft.

Chapter 3

A True and Faithful Account?

The London Fire, Blame, and Partisan Proof

There is little disagreement about the timing or extent of the "Great Fire," which was distinguished from the many other, smaller fires that plagued London by its scale.[1] It began on September 2, 1666; by some accounts, debris was still smoking in March 1667. Although it is possible to quibble about the precise tallies of damage, the fire laid waste to about 400 streets, 89 parish churches, and 13,200 houses, covering as much as 436 acres in ash.[2] The fire does not, however, seem to have caused many deaths.[3] It finally burned itself out after the houses in its path were blown up. By this time it had transformed the lives of everyone who lived in the greater metropolitan area; since it devastated the capital, it affected the lives of many across the country, as well as England's relation to other countries. This fire was, indisputably, news.

The fire and its carnage can certainly stand as "the real," since no one disputed that *something* happened. Considerable ink was spilled, however, about why and how the fire started. Our mediated access to that real event is not a consequence only of the passage of time. Even as the smoke cleared, no one was sure about the fire's causes. What one finds in whatever "archive" survives is rumor, disputation, missing documents, and contested authority. I will focus here on the fire's discursive documentation (the report leaked to the press by the parliamentary committee appointed to investigate the causes of the fire) and the fire's material commemoration (Christopher Wren's monument). That the monument is encrusted with inscriptions reveals the overlap of the discursive and the material. As we will see, the printed "informations" and the still-standing monument are readily accessible proofs of a considerably less accessible history, a history not only of fire but of equally incendiary conflicts about which "true relation" of a highly charged event achieves the widest circulation, which party's interpretation is written in stone. Considered together, this printed text and stone column suggest that the debates about standards of proof taking shape in late seventeenth-century England are inseparable from the highly factionalized matrix from which they spring. What constituted a true relation of the fire's cause was contingent on fraught relations between Catholics and Protestants, court and city.

The Secret of Causation

Responses to the fire ranged from catalogues of lost property and accounts of damage to lamentations, lyrics, and sermons. As Cynthia Wall has argued, the fire, erasing and rewriting the familiar topography of the city, and thereby challenging urban ways of defining and experiencing identity, inspired a prolific literature of loss.[4] Other critics too have argued that the fire became an important occasion of and incentive to textual production and visual representation.[5] The great diarists of the age, Samuel Pepys and John Evelyn, discuss the fire at some length; Gilbert Burnet and Edward Hyde, earl of Clarendon, grant it prominence in their histories; countless sermons and pamphlets dilate upon it. As Burnet explains, "many books are full of" the destruction the fire caused; "That which is still a great secret is, whether it was casual, or raised on design."[6]

"Many books" were as full of speculations about this "secret" as they were of descriptions of the damage. Indeed, the difficulty of establishing any one answer made this a more controversial topic than the relatively straightforward assessment of the ruins. According to Pepys, "Our discourse, as every thing else, was confused."[7] The conundrum of a disaster without cause, without agent, seems to have provoked ingenious efforts to assign purpose to the fire or to associate the fire with designing humans. Many works responding to the fire urged Londoners to look within themselves and not to avert an opportunity for reflection by hunting after other culprits.[8] Yet a great deal of effort went into the search for a person or group to blame for this catastrophe. This was the easiest way to make sense of the chaos the fire created: to tell a familiar story, even if a disturbing one, with a villain who acts as an agent but who also gives meaning to the mayhem and who can be rooted out and punished.

The most obvious suspects were the usual ones, Catholics or foreigners or a conspiracy between local and foreign Catholics. Like many other alleged conspiracies, "the Fire in *London* might be the effect of desperate designs and complotments from abroad, shrouded under and seconded by some male-contents at home."[9] According to Bernard Capp, arson was often blamed on "individuals viewed as suspicious on account of their uncivil language and be-haviour, or marginal status, such as servants, foreigners, and vagrants."[10] In the particular case of the 1666 fire, the search for scapegoats was directed toward Catholics and foreigners not just by habit but by the fact that the fire began in a neighborhood crowded with French and Dutch tradespeople, some of whom were Catholic. Those first suspected were, as a result, "strangers." Pepys records in his diary that many were seized as the suspicion of a plot spread, "and it hath been dangerous for any stranger to walk in the streets." The earl of Clarendon marvels that "in this general rage of the people no mischief was done to the strangers, that no one of them was assassinated outright, though many were sorely beaten and bruised."[11] This process of blaming foreigners issued in the rapid trial and execution of one Hubert, a confused, possibly insane Frenchman.[12]

Peter Stallybrass and Allon White describe as "displaced abjection" the process "whereby 'low' social groups turn their figurative and actual power, *not* against those in authority, but against those who are even 'lower' (women, Jews, animals, particularly cats and pigs)."[13] But the attempts to blame the fire on Catholics suggest that, in this particular case, scapegoating did not work in quite this way. Given that Charles II was suspected to be a Catholic, his brother James was known to be, and both were accused of not working hard enough to contain the fire, Catholics were not all "lower" than their fellow Londoners. Nor were they clearly foreign or strange.[14] As a consequence, the ritual of displacement never quite worked and was never complete: not with the death of Hubert, not when strangers were off the street, not when the fire was finally out.

Like Catholics, fire itself was widely viewed as simultaneously domesti-cated and necessary—"home is where the hearth is," after all—and unpredict-able and dangerous. As the "sad relation" of one fire warned, "How tyrannical a Master Fire is, when once it ceases to be a servant."[15] Contemporaries made the parallel between fires and Catholics explicit. According to one writer, the king of France employs Jesuits "with the same fear and circumspection the Common People do Fire, which though it be necessary to warm them, and boil or roast their Meat, yet are they loath to trust it out of sight, without a faithful Watch-man."[16] A country that tolerated Catholics was, thus, like a house or warehouse crammed with flammable goods. As Samuel Rolle says, spinning out this comparison at length,

> I cannot but thence think of the danger of Kingdoms and Coun-
> tries which are over-stocked with forraigners (especially if of a for-
> raign Religion as well as Nation) especially if men of fiery principles
> and spirits: for though such persons may lie still and make no noise
> for a time, so long as there are other parties to ballance and tie their
> hands (as the particles of Salt doth that of Fire) and whilst they are
> not suffered to imbody and flock together; yet let an enemy come
> (like water upon lime) presently they hiss, and smoak, and reak, and
> heard together, and are ready to burn up all that comes neer them.
> May the Popish party never verifie what I have now hinted from the
> nature of Lime.[17]

The incendiary combination, then, is that of the internal combustible and the external spark. In the leap from a metaphorical relation between Catholics and fire to a causal one, we can see the consequences of figuration. The widespread habit of linking the two slid into the assumption that Catholics had set the London Fire. This claim was revived again and again, especially at moments of crisis in Catholic/Protestant relations.

Catholics and the Burden of Proof

Whereas material evidence that there had been a fire abounded in the form of smoldering ruins, it was far more difficult to determine what might constitute proof of who had been responsible. In accounts of fire in the seventeenth century, proof of arson takes surprising forms. For example, a broadside about a small fire late in the century explains that, after the fire, a man was heard "speaking suspitious and reflecting Words; whereupon he was presently seized, and brought before Mr. Justice Evans, and upon Examination was found to be a Roman Catholick having Crucifixes, Beads, and other Trinkets about him, and therefore was committed Prisoner to the Marshalsea."[18] What is the logic of "therefore"? How does guilt of arson logically follow from the possession of "crucifixes, beads, and other trinkets"?

The cultural logic compressed into that "therefore" makes most sense in the context of a long-standing association of Catholicism with conflagration and arson. Fears of Catholic arson regarding the Great Fire hearken back to that earliest connection between Catholicism and fire: the burning of heretics. As J. P. Kenyon explains, "The association of Catholicism with combustion had been established, of course, by Mary I, who in her short reign (1553–58) had sent nearly three hundred men and women to the stake."[19] Kenyon's "of course" resembles the early modern "therefore" I cite just above; the association he points to was not logically inevitable but rather part of an anti-Catholic train of thought. The Gunpowder Plot, with its ambitious plan to explode the House of Parliament while in session, gave a particularly vivid focus to anxieties about Catholic incendiarism. Surely, "those, who could intentionally blow up King and Parliament by Gunpowder, might (without any scruple of their kinds of conscience) actually burn an heretical City (as they count it) into ashes" and, what is more, in a train of incriminating associations we have examined in chapter one, Catholics are assumed to "count such an action as this meritorious."[20] Many attempts to attribute the Great Fire to Catholics argue that they shifted their tactics from burning Protestant believers to burning Protestant homes. William Bedloe, for instance, argues that Catholics had decided "to ruine Protestants in a more oblique and clandestine way; since they had not (as is hop'd they never shall have) power to re-kindle the *Marian Bonfires*, and *consume* their Bodies: they resolv'd, and make it their business treacherously to *Fire their Houses*, to destroy their *Goods* and *Estates*, till they might be strong enough to venture on their *Persons*."[21] Another text remarks, "Certainly they who rejoyce to burn Protestants in *Smithfield*, would have been as glad to have burnt 'em in their own Houses."[22] Still another claims, "I had almost called it another *Smithfield* (alluding to the use that place was put to in the Marian dayes) for that every house was a kind of Martyr sacrificed to the flames: and that (as is vehemently suspected) by men of the same Religion, with those that burnt the Martyrs in Queen *Maries* dayes."[23] Thus, disputes about the causes of the fire attempt to confer significance and dignity on martyred property, to seize the moral high ground in mourning over goods, and to deny that Catholic Londoners also had something to lose.

These disputes also constantly negotiate the relationship between the discursive and the actual, between incendiary words and incendiary actions, between pen and ink and fireballs. For instance, *A True and Perfect Relation* of Fr. Henry Garnet's role in the "powder treason," the focus of my first chapter, describes the belief that the pope has the authority to judge the king or to relieve his subjects of their obligation to obey him, as "that Ball of Wildefire, which hath caused so great losse of lives & States by combustion in Monarchies."[24]

One text around the time of the Popish Plot cites as evidence of the dangers of papists "those swarms of Insolent and Audacious Papers, daily like their Fireballs flung amonst us, and which like Wild-fire take place with some persons, as in their houses formerly;" another, later, text warns of "a lurking *Jesuite* or *Priest*, whose Pen and Ink is now imploy'd to much the same Purposes as their Fire-balls of old."[25] Fire thus provided a model for how ideas, especially subversive ones, spread by circling back, scattering, starting up in unexpected places. According to Thomas Scott, even the Roman Church itself knows that the Word is fire: "For this cause the Romish Catholikes (a politique people) have taken order to stop the free passage thereof, lest men should burne their fingers with it."[26]

Other writers insisted that some Catholics, particularly Jesuits, were literally incendiaries, instructed in making fireballs and other explosive devices. In *Pyrotechnica Loyolana, Ignatian Fire-works. Or, the Fiery Jesuits Temper and Behaviour* (1667), the author couples this claim that Jesuit seminaries store gunpowder and teach the manufacture and use of explosives with an explanatory etymology of their founder's name as "*ab igne natus*," a firebrand born of fire and determined to "*send Fire*."[27] Especially after the "Great Fire," Jesuits were widely referred to as "*Master-Incendiaries*" and "those grand *Incendiaries* in all senses."[28]

The fire, then, and the attempts to assign and prove a cause of it enable us to consider the ways in which proof was partisan in this period. Disputes about method and evidence often assumed a connection between Protestantism and more rigorous standards, dismissing the superstition, obeisance to papal authority, and implausible stories that were associated with "popish" investigation, standards of evidence, and methods of argument.[29] At one level, these controversies and conflicts were headed in the direction of "progress"—clearer standards of evidence, more equitably and consistently applied. Yet the relation of these debates to religious controversy should remind us that this is not a simple matter of rigor triumphing over superstition, fact over fiction. The preferred standards earned their prestige in part because of their association with the winners of history; they were themselves always acknowledged as partisan—and as true precisely in their alliance with the "right" side. Proofs were dictated by and recruited in the service of truths already known but perhaps not always unwaveringly believed. This is borne out in the official proceedings to determine responsibility for the fire, as we will now see.

Figure 3. Frontispiece from *Pyrotechnica Loyolana, Ignatian Fireworks* (1667), showing Jesuits at work setting fires. Reproduced by permission of The Huntington Library, San Marino, California.

The Committee and the Official Story

Charles II appointed the Privy Council and the lord chief justice to look into the causes of the fire, but this body did not come to a resolution. Only Hubert was brought to trial, and the only evidence against him was his own confession. On September 25, 1666, after some debate, the Commons appointed its own committee (of seventy) to inquire into the causes of the fire.[30] One month later, the Commons joined with the House of Lords to petition "for the banishment of all Popish priests and Jesuits, . . . the enforcement of the laws against Papist recusants, and the disarming of all who refused the Oaths of Allegiance and Supremacy."[31] Charles II agreed to make a proclamation to this effect. Obviously, the inquiry took place in the context of profound anti-Catholic sentiment and the presumption of Catholic guilt.

The committee seems to have received testimony from a diverse range of informants; it collected reports of papist predictions, of papists throwing fireballs, and of papists bearing confiscated goods into Somerset House, the residence of the queen mother, Henrietta Maria. As the earl of Clarendon commented in retrospect, "Many who were produced as if their testimony would remove all doubts, made such senseless relations of what they had been told, without knowing the condition of the persons who told them, or where to find them, that it was a hard matter to forbear smiling at their evidence."[32] Clarendon here points to the characteristics that would mark a relation, for him, as true rather than senseless: a locatable, credible source. Those who purport to relate intelligence whose provenance they cannot explain engender doubt rather than removing it. Perhaps most damaging were suggestions that the duke of York, and to some extent the king, suppressed evidence, failed to pursue leads, and baffled attempts to stop the fire. This perception of complicity at the top contributed to the many dead ends and loose threads in witnesses' testimony. As Wall points out, "most accounts end with the witness admitting that the apprehended suspect was 'heard of no more,' or the witness 'could never hear nor learn' of his or her tale producing verifiable results."[33] In this, Wall suggests, these accounts anticipated the committee's inconclusive findings.

The committee began meeting on September 26; its chair, Sir Robert Brooke, reported to the House on January 22, read aloud some of the examinations gathered, and submitted his report to the Commons clerk.[34] Since the committee made no recommendation, its report seems to have been intended as an interim update on its findings. After hearing Brooke read the "many wicked and desperate expressions" his committee had collected, one member of the House of Commons concluded, "I cannot conceive that the House can make anything of the report from the committee."[35] According to Gilbert Burnet, Sir Thomas Littleton, a member of the committee, "often assured me that there was no clear presumption well made out about [whether the city was "burnt on design"], and that many stories that were published with great assurance came to nothing upon a strict examination." For his own part, Burnet concluded that "there was so great a diversity of opinions in the matter that I must leave it under the same uncertainty in which I found it."[36] Still, the report was slated for debate in the House the following day, then deferred to the next day, and then disappears from the business recorded in the journal of the House of Commons. Shortly thereafter, Charles II prorogued Parliament (February 8, 1667); Parliament was thus unable to give its judgment on the committee's report. The committee itself was disbanded. Although some citizens petitioned that the inquiry be reopened, it never was. Certainly, neither Charles nor the Privy Council was convinced; they concluded that "after many careful examinations by Council and His Majesty's ministers, nothing hath been found to argue the fire in London to have been caused by other than the hand of God, a great wind, and a very dry season."[37]

The official account of the cause of the fire appeared in the *London Gazette* (Sept. 3–10), the paper published by authority. This account emphasizes the efforts of the king and his brother to quell the fire and the continuing loyalty of their subjects. It is reproduced again and again, into the twentieth century, in accounts of the fire and its commemoration.[38] An eighteenth-century reprinting of this "official story" explains that, on weighing all the evidence, the king and his council concluded that it was impossible to make an exact determination and thus best to choose "the charitable, and perhaps probable Side"—that is, to decide to believe that the fire was God's judgment, not the result of human scheming. In this text, it is possible to distrust Catholics without abandoning standards of evidence: "tho' we account the *Papists* our bitter Enemies, 'tis highly wicked to bely and slander them; as has been too much the Practice of those who value themselves for being Protestants."[39]

Yet the matter was not closed. Nor were Catholics absolved of complicity in the fire. Quite the opposite. Although the committee never came to an official finding, its report was published as *A True and Faithful Account of the Several Informations Exhibited to the Honourable Committee appointed by the Parliament to Inquire into the late Dreadful Burning of the City of London.* That this text includes "a true account of what was represented to another Committee of Parliament touching the Insolency of Popish Priests and Jesuites, and the increase of Popery, &c." betrays its interestedness—the way it is faithful to Protestantism and thereby to a partisan version of the truth. Furthermore, this text contained not only the report that Robert Brooke made to the House of Commons on January 22, 1667, but also information "given into the committee but not by them reported to the House at that time."[40] Thus, *A True and Faithful Account* became its own original, standing for evidence that was otherwise inaccessible and, it was suspected, suppressed; the print version exceeds the "archival" version. It was both conclusive and inconclusive: "Your Committee have thought fit to give no opinion upon these Informations; But leave the matter of Fact to your Judgements" (sig. E1r). Yet *A True and Faithful Account* strongly suggests a perspective on events and a judgment other than that reported in the *London Gazette*. The last document it reproduces is a paper supposedly found in a pew in the temple church titled "A Warning to Protestants" (E1v–E2r).

The first print version "had the curious fate, for a Parliamentary document, of being burned at the hands of the common hangman in Westminster Palace Yard," perhaps because its very existence was a consequence of the discord between Parliament's assessment of the fire's origins and the king's.[41] As early as July 1667, the mayor of Bristol reported to the king that he had seized items from a woman bookseller, including "an account of the informations exhibited to the commissioners of Parliament appointed to enquire into the late dreadful firing of London"; in August, another source reported from Rydal the circulation of *A True and Faithful Account* and asked "whether to take any notice of a libel or not."[42] Neither confiscation nor burning successfully curtailed the circulation of this libel, which may mean simply a little book but may also carry the legal meaning of a complaint or the charge leading to a prosecution. Indeed, the news of suppression may have heightened interest in it. Samuel Pepys, for instance, responded to news of the order to burn "the printed account of the examinations" by planning to outwit it: "I will try to get one of them."[43] Published in many editions and versions, framed in many different ways, the report—at best a collection of witnesses' statements or "Relations (for substance) . . . delivered to Sir *Robert Brooks*, Chairman of the Committee, a little before the Prorogation of the Parliament" (sig. C2r)—took on a life of its own.[44] It earned authority through repetition and circulation: what is printed in *State Tracts: Being a Collection of Several Treatises Relating to the Government* (1693) is not the report Robert Brooke handed in to the clerk,

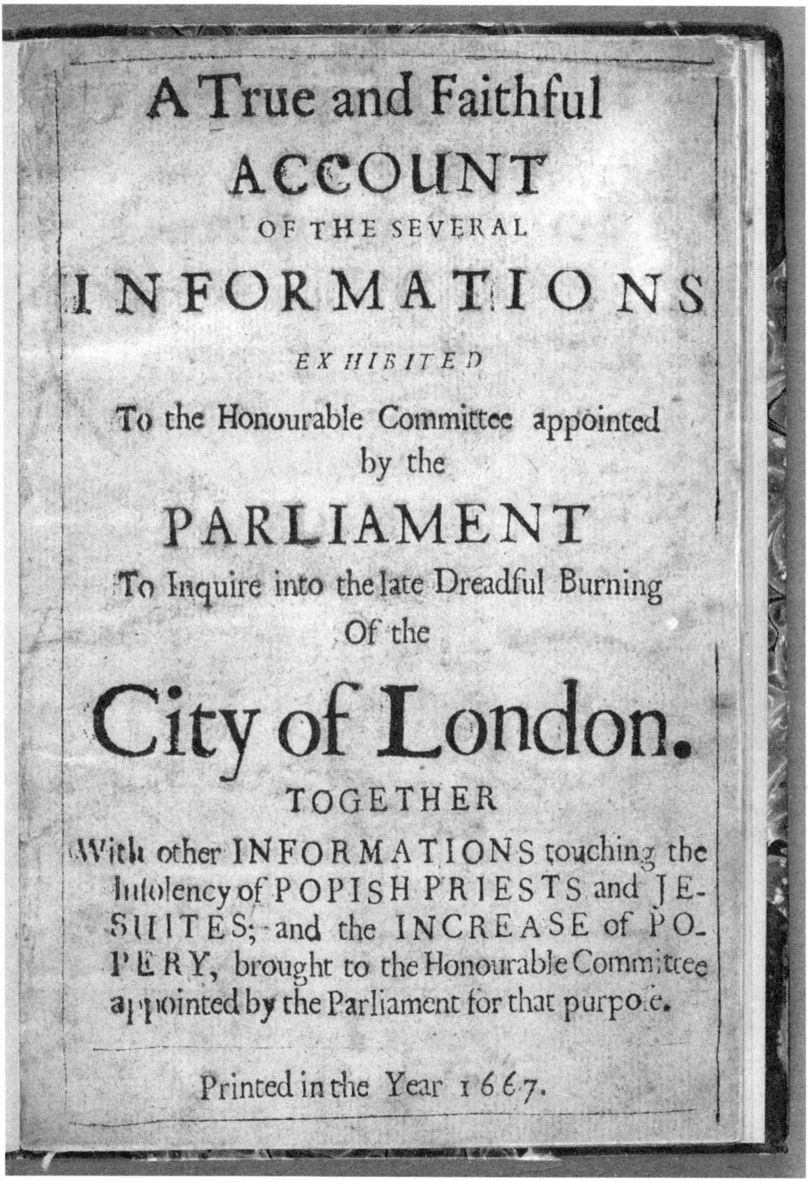

A True and Faithful

ACCOUNT

OF THE SEVERAL

INFORMATIONS

EXHIBITED

To the Honourable Committee appointed
by the

PARLIAMENT

To Inquire into the late Dreadful Burning
Of the

City of London.

TOGETHER

With other INFORMATIONS touching the
Insolency of POPISH PRIESTS and JE-
SUITES; and the INCREASE of PO-
PERY, brought to the Honourable Committee
appointed by the Parliament for that purpose.

Printed in the Year 1667.

Figure 4. Title page of the printed version of the parliamentary report.
Reproduced by permission of The Huntington Library, San Marino,
California.

but rather the expanded version printed as *London's Flames Reviv'd*; in the early nineteenth century, *State Trials* reprints *A True and Faithful Account* as "Examinations concerning the Firing of London" and consigns the *London Gazette*'s "official story" to the notes.[45]

One openly partisan account conveys some sense of just how much longevity the fire had as a focus for religio-political conflict and how this conflict always revolves around the partisan nature of evidence and its interpretation. *A True Protestant Account of the Burning of London* (1720) billed itself as *An Antidote, Against the Poyson and Malignity of a Late Lying Legend, Entituled, An Account of the Burning of London*, which was a reprinting of the "official" account of the fire and itself an antidote to Catholic bashing. Announcing its partisanship in its title, the *True Protestant Account* seeks to prove "from unexceptionable Evidence and Authority, that it was those Blood-thirsty Monsters the Papists, and none but they, who were the sole Authors of that most dismal Tragedy" (A2v). *A True Protestant Account* charges that the narrative published in the *London Gazette* and cited by *An Account* "doth no where say, either that the *Papists* did, or that they did not Fire the City; neither indeed could they insert such a Thing in favour of the *Papists* at that Time of the Day, when so many Thousands were Eye Witnesses that they did it; Neither if they had, would they have been proper Evidences for them, both the King and the Duke of *York* being *Papists*" (A4r).[46] As a result, "both because that Account published by Authority saith nothing of the *Papists*, and because the King (by whose Authority it was publish'd) was a *Papist*: It cannot in the least serve to clear the *Papists* of that heavy Charge of *Burning the City of London*" (A4v).[47] For this writer, the alliance between Catholicism and the court, particularly the control of the "Popish Court" over the press, compromises the proof value of the "official story." Of course, *A True Protestant Account* itself made it into print, but only much later, from which vantage it could reprint yet again the witnesses' statements first published as part of the committee's report and reveal that the official report on the fire is a false Catholic relation as opposed to a "true Protestant" one.

Texts that advertise both their Protestant bias and, therefore, their truthfulness also acknowledge that their own narratives are partial and interested. It is their "interest" that marks their stories as true. Mark Knights argues that, in the partisan political culture of the late Stuart period, in which "printed interventions became an intrinsic part of the political contest," readers had to adjudicate among competing truth claims and did so in part based on their own allegiances. While "disinterestedness" was sometimes valued as a sign of credibility, as we have seen in the introduction, "partisan allegiance could also confer credibility on what might otherwise seem highly implausible or even erroneous . . . truth could be something dependent on, even determined by, the authority of party." Truth was, then, "relative to partisan conviction." In such a culture, "imaginative fictions [were] embedded in partisan polemic, so that the political and the literary were fused."[48] This fusion is manifest in the many "informations" published as evidence regarding the responsibility of Catholics for the fire.

Versions of the committee's report were reprinted whenever the political climate warranted or required another denunciation of papists: not just in 1667, just following the fire, but in 1679, at the time of the Popish Plot, and in 1689, when the revolution was being justified in part through anti-Catholicism. All the versions of the Parliamentary examinations are roughly similar in content; to read the many reframings and reprintings of the "informations" supposedly collected by the Commons committee is to see again the fiercely partisan nature of what constitutes a true relation in this period. For many of these writers, the past—recent or remote—is a field on which one can mobilize old conflicts and conspiracies as proof of what one already knows, that is, who can be trusted and who cannot. To make the past politically useful, Protestant writers had to remember selectively. As Ernest Renan and others have argued, forgetting is as important a part of nation formation as remembering.[49] In the case of Catholics, past offenses were obsessively remembered and retold and sometimes invented. For all the durability of the claim that Catholics were responsible for the Great Fire of London, this claim never disguised its own interestedness or silenced the other explanatory narratives—even when this "true Protestant" relation was literally written in stone.

The Monument

In 1677, a monument commissioned by Parliament, designed by Christopher Wren and Robert Hooke, and begun in 1671, finally stood 202 feet to commemorate the fire. The monument, which still stands today, consists of a huge Doric column, topped by an urn of flames, a cheaper and less controversial choice than the fifteen-foot bronze statue of Charles II that Wren had first imagined. The vase is also more readily legible from a distance than the statue of a phoenix Wren also considered.[50] An allegorical bas-relief of Charles II coming to the aid of a female London, designed by Caius Gabriel Cibber, decorates the west side of the pedestal. The east side lists those who were lord mayor in the years during which the monument was begun, under construction, and, at last, completed. The north and south sides of the pedestal hold lengthy Latin inscriptions, one describing in detail the devastation wrought by the fire and the other praising Charles II's initiatives for rebuilding the city. Neither inscription blames a human agent for setting the fire. The Latin inscriptions simultaneously grant grandeur and permanence to the history they describe and withhold that history from wide circulation by limiting those who can decipher and thereby learn from it. Dr. Thomas Gale, head of St. Paul's school and later dean of York, seems to have composed them, in consultation with Wren and Hooke.[51]

The 1667 act for rebuilding the city stipulated that the inscription on the monument would be determined by the lord mayor and Court of Aldermen. The inscriptions that first appeared in 1677 seem to have been a compromise, praising both the lord mayor and the king. This compromise did not last long. In January 1681, in response to the anti-Catholic sentiment surrounding and fuelling both the Popish Plot and the Exclusion Crisis, the House of Commons voted unanimously both to thank the city of London for its vigilance in preserving the Protestant religion and to affirm "that the City of *London* was burnt in the Year One thousand Six hundred Sixty-and-six, by the Papists; designing thereby to introduce arbitrary Power and Popery into this Kingdom."[52] This assertion was not based on any new inquiry or new evidence. To the extent that Parliament heard any testimony at all, it heard key Popish Plot witnesses, Israel Tonge and William Bedloe, rehash the earlier "findings" of the Commons committee.[53]

But this pronouncement, so divorced from any forensic process, was soon to achieve a very public instantiation. The Court of Aldermen of the city of London, and their lord mayor, all decidedly Whiggish, ordered that this verdict be carved—in English—in a single line around the base of the monument's pedestal. This line was composed by City Comptroller Joseph Lane, who had also consulted with Wren, Hooke, and Gale on the original Latin inscriptions.[54] Here was an inscription that would be legible to a far larger number of Londoners. There are small discrepancies among the transcriptions of this inscription, but it seems to have said roughly this:

> This Pillar was set up in perpetual Remembrance of the most dreadful Burning of this Protestant City, begun and carried on by the Treachery and Malice of the POPISH FACTION in the beginning

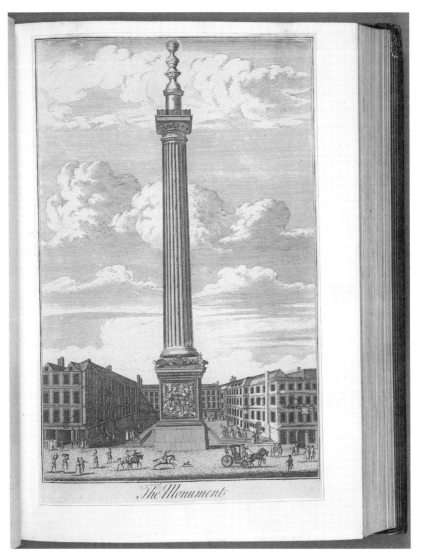

The Monument

Figure 5. Woodcut of the Monument from J. Heneage Jesse, *London: Its Celebrated Characters and Remarkable Places*, vol. ix (London: R. Bentley, 1873). Reproduced by permission of The Huntington Library, San Marino, California.

of September, in the year of our Lord 1666, in order to the carrying on that Horrid Plot for extirpating the Protestant Religion and old English Liberty, and the introducing Popery and Slavery.[55]

Guides to the monument printed in the eighteenth and nineteenth centuries explain: "And whereas, upon evidence, it was thought that this dreadful fire was contrived and carried on by the Popish faction, the same is expressed in English round the base of the pedestal."[56] This explanation erases the gap of fifteen years between, on the one hand, the fire and the Parliamentary inquiry into its cause and, on the other, the blunt assertion that Catholics did it. Furthermore, the phrase "upon evidence" begs the question of what this evidence was; the passive construction obscures who it was who thought that the fire was "contrived and carried on by the Popish faction." In 1681, a final sentence was also added to the Latin inscription on the north side: "Sed furor papisticus qui tam dira patravit, nondam restinguitur" (But Popish frenzy, which wrought such horrors, is not yet quenched).[57] This sentence bears no relation to the Latin passage it follows, which simply describes the devastation wrought by the fire. Presenting it in Latin grants it a certain credibility and blurs the difference between the sentiments and goals of 1677 and 1681. After the accession of James II (in 1685), the two inscriptions were effaced. With the accession of William III and Mary II (in 1689), the English inscription was restored, and perhaps the Latin one as well, in very deep characters, many explain. The inscriptions were not finally gouged out until 1831 (after Catholic Emancipation).[58]

The inscription on the monument so robustly pronounced the truth of Catholic conspiracy that, in itself, it became a kind of proof, not of belief or of desire, but of what had actually happened. For those who understood the inscriptions as true, attempts to erase them offered further proof of Catholic conspiracy and equivocation. As *The Burning of London by the Papists* asks in the early eighteenth century, "Who order'd the Inscription of it to be struck out of the Monument? And, Who put it in Again?"[59] For this writer, Catholics try to deny the truth, while Protestants bravely affirm it. *A True Protestant Account* adduces the monument's inscriptions as evidence as well as another inscription set up at 25 Pudding Lane, where the fire began, by Sir Patience Ward, lord mayor of London:

But yet further to Corroborate our Evidence, we will add the *Inscription*, Curiously Engraven on a Stone purposely affix'd to the

Wall of the House, that now stands on that very Spot of Ground, whereon that House stood, which was first set on Fire in *Pudding-lane*; which is this, *Verbatim: Here by the Permission of* Heaven, HELL *broke loose upon this* Protestant City, *from the malicious Hearts of Barbarous PAPISTS, by the Hand of their Agent HUBERT, who Confessed, and on the Ruins of this Place declared the Fact,* (for which he Hang'd) viz. *That he begun that Dreadful Fire which is describ'd & perpetuated on that neighbouring Pillar (the MONUMENT).*[60]

But what kind of proof is this?

While the appearing and disappearing inscriptions on the monument are usually read as markers of the shifts from one ruler to another—particularly James II to William III—and how these rulers reshaped national memory in their own interests,[61] this approach focuses too squarely on the sovereigns. The inscriptions emerged from a struggle between the Crown and the city, a city closely allied to the House of Commons and to political positions that have come to be called "Whig." By setting in stone one interpretation—the most aggressive and extreme Protestant one at that—Sir Patience Ward and his masons wrote onto their city the assessment of the fire's causes that was of greatest political use to them. Yet such unequivocal assertion could not suppress the controversy of which it was born. The monument became a site of struggle not just between Catholics and Protestants, but between Whigs and Tories, the city of London and the court. At the same time that Sir Patience Ward was presiding over the city's project of sententious graffiti, he and the Court of Aldermen were also engaged in conflict with Charles II, protesting his proroguing of Parliament and contesting the city charter and election of sheriffs, lord mayor, and aldermen. In 1682, Ward was indicted for perjury and sentenced to the pillory in relation to a conflict between the duke of York and several city aldermen regarding their claim that the duke had set the city on fire.[62]

The partisan inscriptions on the monument continued to pose problems for London boosters, long after these particular struggles had ended. While the inscriptions were still in place, guidebooks to London tended to present them as a blot on an otherwise impressive column, an embarrassing reminder of a less enlightened past. *A Critical Review of the Publick Buildings, Statues, and Ornaments in and about London* (1734) lavishes praise on the monument, insisting that "nothing material can be cavill'd with, but the inscriptions round about it."[63] *The Ambulator; or, A Pocket Companion for the Tour of London and*

its Environs (1811) proudly announces that "the inscription, imputing the calamity to the Papists, is now universally considered unjust."[64] *The Picture of
London for 1807; Being a Correct Guide* announces that "no rational being can
entertain the notion, that the Catholics, or any religious sect, could willfully
have perpetrated so horrible a deed as this pillar [imputes] to them."[65]

Most guidebooks across the centuries quote Alexander Pope's famous
couplet: "Where London's column, pointing at the skies, / Like a tall bully,
lifts the head, and lies." But if Pope could see it this way in the 1730s, why does
a "lie" retain the materiality of 28,126 feet of Portland stone? In his massive *The
Wards of London* (1828), Henry Thomas asks just this question. Like so many
others, he insists that there are no reasons to object to the monument "except
the tenor of the inscriptions. These were concocted by prejudice, penned with
spleen, and stand the bigotted evidence of party spirit, neither justified by
liberality, nor founded in fact." Of the Latin sentence he says, "It argues but
little for the liberality of the times" that it is still on the monument. "Why
does it now remain?"[66] Dismissing the inscriptions as an acknowledged lie,
such texts articulate a Whiggish sense of having moved beyond the prejudice
on which Whigs relied. In doing so, they remind us that what is still called a
"Whiggish" investment in progress was founded in a highly partisan construction of the past.

After the inscriptions were effaced, many guidebooks simply ignored
them. The Baedeker guides, for instance, do not refer to them. *Relics and
Memorials of London City* says exactly the same thing as the *Ambulator* had
earlier—the inscription was "universally considered unjust"—but can say,
with relief, "it has been erased for many years past."[67] But are the inscriptions
gone? In *Memories and Monuments in the Streets of the City of London*, A. K.
Bruce shows that the repudiation of Catholic bashing can also be the occasion
of keeping it in view: "The gross imputation cast upon Roman Catholics in
certain lines ("sed furor Papisticus qui tam dira patravit nondum restinguitur") of the original inscription need not be referred to, since the offensive
words were expunged by order of the Common Council on 26 January 1831."[68]
*A Description of the Monument, Erected in Commemoration of the Dreadful Fire
of London in the Year 1666* (1834) announces that it has been officially agreed
that the fire was not the work of papists, or at least that it is no longer politically expedient to insist that it was, yet also recounts the whole history of
attributing the fire to papists and records the "erased" inscription.[69] Thus, for
the readers of these guidebooks, the inscriptions are both absent and present.

Visiting the monument today, one similarly sees both the marks of the chisel and a plaque on the north side helpfully translating the Latin inscriptions, including the line that was removed. Those words, and that interpretation of events, are, thus, in no way gone. The monument itself now claims to commemorate an event without cause or perpetrator, yet it retains traces of a history of blame, a history inseparable from the history of the fire. The removed yet memorialized inscription at the Monument hints that this is the real story, marginalized only by squeamishness about boldly stating blame. Since the interpretation blaming Catholics is put into words, while alternatives are not, the version written in stone is still granted a weight and durability that alternatives cannot match.

Websites, the new guidebooks, help visitors make sense of the history of blame that is inseparable from the histories of London and of this disaster. The City of London's detailed and helpful website for the Monument includes,

Figure 6. Inscription on the North Panel of the London Monument. Note that the Latin inscription is both absent and present in the form of a translation. Image courtesy of the City of London and Harris Digital Productions.

under the heading History, translations of the inscriptions, including a brief
account of the process by which the "questionable addition" blaming Catholics on the north face came and went. But that account cannot explain, for
someone unfamiliar with the period, why such an addition would have been
made.[70] One can also find the stone from the house in Pudding Lane and a
reproduction of the English inscription on the Monument in the Museum
of London. The Pudding Lane plaque is reproduced on the Museum's detailed website, which offers some discussion of anti-Catholic prejudice and
"conspiracy theories of a Catholic plot."[71] Since I have been arguing that the
monument commemorates not only the fire but the whole process of making meaning out of that catastrophic event, the contestations over who set
the fire are as real as the fire itself. Thus, it is, in my view, quite appropriate
that evidence of this history of contested memory should be preserved. Like
contemporaries, we are faced with numerous pieces of evidence, numerous
assertions of truth. Indeed, the materials from which we can piece together a
history of blame are now more accessible than ever. Yet the surviving evidence
requires the reader or visitor to work as a relator, putting the pieces together.
It also requires the visitor to a website, monument, or museum to evaluate the
evidence critically and to resist the interpretation that is stated most boldly,
compels more interest as a story than alterative explanations ever did or could,
and answers to an interest in conspiracy and terrorism that is, if anything,
more robust now than ever.

The highly partisan, controversial nature of print culture in the seventeenth
century ensured that most readers could not take words printed on paper or
engraved into stone as inevitably true. A work needed other authorizations—
such as its own declaration that it was true and Protestant—to compel belief.
The story that Catholics were responsible for the Great Fire gained its status
as a memory of what really happened, as the "truth," first by reflecting what
many people were already prepared to believe and, second, by fixing this assumption into stable and durable texts; these representations, in turn, came
to stand, at least for some sympathetic readers at some moments, as the real.
These "true relations" still stand as evidence, listed by the Museum of London,
for instance, as the evidence of "eyewitnesses" and "officials."[72]

Thus, the Great Fire offers a reminder of what we do and do not have
when we find a rich piece of evidence. Relying largely on print evidence, much
of it available through Early English Books Online and Eighteenth-Century
Collections Online, and on a towering monument, I have not found anything
heretofore unknown. Both the print versions of the Parliamentary committee's

supposed findings and the monument are fascinating, highly visible, and apparently readily legible, proofs. But we can only begin to understand what they might mean by tracing their complicated provenance and the web of institutions, political struggles, and processes of transmission by which they have survived to us. To "find" them is no great victory. To begin to understand the history subtending what stands in plain view is challenging indeed. I have only begun to sketch out that history here. Neither of my central pieces of evidence is a smoking gun—definitive, irrefutable. Even a monument cannot stand alone, however much it may look as if it does. My project here is to emphasize not only the partisan nature of evidence—that is, the ways in which true relations are contingent on social relations—but the collectivity of the research process—the ways in which pieces of evidence accrue meaning in relation to other pieces of evidence and one scholar's necessary and unavoidable relation to, indeed dependence on, the efforts of others.

PART II

Genres of Evidence

Chapter 4

First-Person Relations

Reading Depositions

As we have seen, the Parliamentary Committee's report on its investigation of the London Fire offered its readers a collection of witnesses' statements. While its polemical purpose was clear, its deponents elusive, and its leads dead ends, the committee's report draws attention to the key role witnesses' statements played in legal proceedings with more conclusive outcomes. Felony trials in common law courts, such as Henry Garnet's trial for treason before the King's Bench and witchcraft trials in assize courts, relied on witnesses' statements transcribed and edited in advance. These documents, both produced and performed in court, formed the backbone of prosecutions. Church courts followed a similar procedure but with somewhat lower stakes. Church courts heard cases of intimate conflicts among family members and neighbors; since their purview was sin more than crime, they could impose punishments including public penance or excommunication, but they could not imprison or execute. The majority of their plaintiffs, defendants, and witnesses were women.[1] While testimony in these courts had consequences for defendants, especially in terms of their stature in their communities, it was not a matter of life and death. In this chapter, I shift my attention from criminal trials to church courts so as to consider why and how deponents' verbal relations became evidence and how we now evaluate the texts that result. I thus also shift from early modern crises of evidence to how scholars of the early modern make sense of certain evidentiary genres, in this case, church court depositions.

Depositions, also called examinations, were sworn statements taken in English in answer to questions. They were recorded in private (that is, not in the presence of other parties or their legal representatives) in the third person in the present tense ("This examinant sayeth") describing past actions ("that she saw . . ."). They were then read back to the deponent who, presumably, could correct the statement before swearing to its veracity.[2] In the deposition, the words are "taken down" by a relator as a king is taken down from his throne when he is deposed; the deposition derives its name from the connection between the act of taking or putting something from high to low and the act of putting oral speech into writing, putting testimony down on paper; the deposition was "taken down in writing to be read in court as a substitute for the production of the witness" (*OED*). After 1563 legislation that made it possible to compel witnesses to attend trials and made perjury a crime, "the process of trial," according to Peter Rushton, "increasingly became a *documentary* one of witnesses or victims and their statements in writing."[3] In other words, it was often the case that neither the accused nor witnesses against them spoke in court; their evidence was usually taken down in advance, as a series of responses to questions, edited into a narrative, and then read in court. The resulting narrative then had to be *taken as* accurately representing what the deponent had said.[4] The story stood in for the person to whom it was ascribed. The interrogation through which the statement took place and the contributions of the clerk who extracted that statement were usually obscured. Like the inquisitorial records John Arnold describes, the deposition "gained its authority, its claim to 'truth,' by virtue of its written-ness, its ability to fix the confession of the witness into a textual record."[5] As we have seen, in the Gunpowder Plot trials, even defendants who had confessed, reviewed, and signed their written confessions and were present in court had to listen as their confessions were read aloud. Church courts too depended on the collection and evaluation of written statements. In this arena, defendants might have a bit more leeway to contest depositions. In one well-documented church court case, according to Bernard Capp, "the principals held copies of the depositions, and showed them to their friends."[6]

It can be difficult to grasp how much criminal trials relied on documents because dramatizations of the adversarial trial for the last four hundred years—organized around a confrontation between the accused, the accuser, their lawyers, and witnesses subject to cross-examination—can get in the way, blocking recognition of a somewhat different procedure. What is more, in part because documents were heavily used and were valued as evidence toward an end rather than an archive to be preserved, surprisingly few documents from criminal trials survive. In the crises of evidence I discussed in my first three chapters, "originals" are almost always missing. Often only indictments survive for a criminal trial, especially if it was not a "state" trial. In contrast, the church court deposition is a blab when compared to the terse records that survive to us from other courts, such as assize courts. Paradoxically, the deposition's garrulity sometimes lures the reader into imagining presence rather than thinking about the fact that the deposition was always a textual account, not a person but a person's relation or representative. Popular dramatizations of criminal courts today can also distract us from how different were the proceedings and purposes of church courts, since no equivalent to the church court system now exists in Great Britain or North America.

Because of the complicated process by which depositions were composed and deployed, the scholars who rely on depositions invariably describe them as "mediated," although many also privilege them as providing especially valuable access to early modern "voices." I am interested here in the methodological challenge posed by the mediation of court records, a mediation that most scholars acknowledge and then ignore.[7] As we will see, this move is often signaled in sentences that take this shape: although these records are mediated, they grant us access to deponents nevertheless. My goal is not to catch scholars out in errors of one kind or another. Rather, it is to step back from whatever information is supposedly gleanable from these sources to reflect on how various scholars are reading them as texts and adducing them as evidence. The scholars I engage here are those whose work I most admire and who are most thoughtful and articulate about their use of evidence. I consider the methodological reflections of both historians and literary critics, arguing that there is more common methodological ground than disciplinary divisions might sometimes suggest and that, when we do find conflicts regarding evidentiary reading practices, they do not predictably fall out by discipline. Scholars with different training, investments, and questions share skepticism about what exactly the value of depositions is; a deep affection for them; and a habit of referring to them as stories as well as uncertainty about what that might mean, what limits this categorization as stories might place on readers or what license it might offer.

Whose Story Is This?
Mediation and Collaboration, Voices and Texts

As Natalie Davis pointed out in her pioneering work, what we find in archives is often "fiction" by which she means that those who wrote the pardon letters she studies were "authors" who "shape the events of a crime into a story" and through this strategic shaping created testimony calculated to strike their readers as "true" and thus to win them pardons.[8] Scholars now routinely refer to witnesses' statements as fictions. For instance, when David Cressy turns from polemical attacks on cross-dressing to the case of an "actual cross-dresser" he reminds us that "Since it comes from the archives it belongs to a genre traditionally labeled as 'evidence' but, given our awareness of the fictionality of court reporting, it may be better to call it a 'story'."[9]

To say that depositions are stories is usually to qualify their status as evidence. While they undoubtedly served as evidence in the proceedings in which they figured and scholars today turn to them as evidence, the question is: evidence of what? Among those working with court records, one can find a surprisingly wide consensus that these records cannot prove whether a given person was guilty of fornication or whether a remark was slanderous: according to Lena Orlin, "with multiple witnesses presenting competing accounts, what 'actually' happened on such occasions will almost always be a mystery"; as Alexandra Shepard puts it, "litigants' and witnesses' statements were shaped by and for their audience at court, and offer no more than a set of partial and contrived narratives rather than a re-creation of the events themselves."[10] Court records do not even include, most of the time, what the court's verdict was.

Surrendering the idea of depositions as evidence of one thing—what actually happened—can open the door to reading them as evidence of something else. One strategy is to talk about these records as evidence of "the social dynamics of the community" or "the underlying cultural values of the age." Depositions, then, offer us reliable access not to events or even to the specifics of individuals and their attitudes and actions but instead to the "values" and "assumptions" many held in "common."[11] Since the scholars who work most closely with depositions have shifted the terms of their interpretation this way, reevaluating the nature of the evidence depositions are seen to offer, the next step is to think about what literary critics might contribute to the analysis of these stories.

One contribution we might make is to chart some paths beyond the current consensus that church court depositions offer us "mediated" access to deponents. The questions posed to deponents shaped the responses they gave; the questions had been framed by the plaintiff's libel or charge, which was, in turn, informed by proctors, who served as ecclesiastical lawyers and who made decisions about what details would form the basis of the case and what version of the charge would make most sense to the court.[12] The questions usually do not survive because the clerks who recorded depositions wrote them down not as a dialogue between questions and answers but as a seamless narrative. The clerks also "added to the everyday speech of litigants the conventional legal usages of Latin and English that made up the court's language" and, according to Laura Gowing, imposed a clerkly "style that was virtually uniform across the country, and across several centuries."[13] For Lawrence Stone, repetition across depositions, which only becomes visible when we compare multiple depositions in a given case, should alert us to the role of clerks and proctors in coaching witnesses and/or shaping the narratives they took down: "What gives the game away is when a string of witnesses use exactly the same adjectives to describe a character, or exactly the same words to express admiration or dislike."[14] Like Gowing, Stone suggests that the style of a deposition is clerkly without going so far as to argue that the speech or voice of a deposition is more the clerk's than the deponent's.

Because of the clerk's role, we are often given the picture of male legal personnel standing between the reader today and the I who spoke then, particularly the female I whose voice is especially sought on the assumption that it is harder to hear. Scholars working with a range of courts and their records express this concern. Amy Erickson insists that historians cannot make generalizations about women's history unless they "ask the women themselves," but she also concedes that, even in the probate documents she interprets so effectively, "women's voices are muted not because they did not speak at the time, but because the probate court in which those documents were created was operated entirely by men."[15] Timothy Stretton advises that, "Given the obscuring filters created by male counsel, male scribes and male judges, it is unlikely that much survives in the records that could be labelled authentic female 'voices'."[16] Sara Mendelson and Patricia Crawford similarly warn that, "while female testimony appears to offer direct access to women's own voices, the historian must be constantly aware that every word spoken by a woman was recorded and edited by male officials."[17] The emphasis on these male gatekeepers sometimes intensifies the desire to get past them: Diane Purkiss, for instance, strains to hear the "faint, confused, pained voices of these women" whom they have drowned out.[18] "Voice" is usually the word for what depositions might not contain and for what readers hope to find there nevertheless.

The hunt for voice ignores the various ways in which early modern subjects and institutions questioned or distrusted speech. [19] Although legal authorities demanded articulate subjects, even to the point of pressing a plea out of those who stood mute, the courts did not always get the testimonies they required, as we saw in my first chapter. [20] Furthermore, they often preferred highly mediated texts to direct speech. Yet many students of the early modern period privilege legal testimony as especially valuable evidence of those who otherwise left little record. Of "records of the law," Stone advises that "here alone can the authentic voices of the poor be heard."[21] While Adam Fox concedes that the value of depositions is "seriously impaired" by the involvement of clerks, he also argues that they can provide "vivid insight into the spontaneous speech of ordinary men and women in this period": "Despite this heavy level of mediation between the actual words of the deponent and the resulting transcript, it is still possible in some cases to detect the popular voice sounding through the text."[22] Shepard stresses that court records are "not straightforwardly representative of everyday life" and that they "principally supply evidence of the ways in which stories were narrated in the context of a courtroom rather than direct statements of fact or fixed values." And yet, she insists, "the ideals and identities invoked by men and women in court are *nonetheless* suggestive, and depositions also contain a wealth of incidental detail pertaining to routine existence, thus providing the closest available point of contact with the lived experience of many early modern English men and women whose voices would not otherwise have entered the historical record."[23] Even as Shepard recasts the terms in which we understand the evidence depositions can offer, stressing their status as stories, she defends depositions as means for making contact with human actors, lived experience, and voices. Shepard's use of the term "nonetheless" is also typical of methodological statements as they move from qualification to justification. We will see "nonetheless" or "nevertheless" pop up again.[24]

We see the longing for voice in the titles of two useful sourcebooks, Valerie Frith's *Women and History: Voices of Early Modern England* (1995), to which I will return, and John N. King's *Voices of the English Reformation: A Sourcebook* (2004). In addition to signaling a focus on relatively anonymous historical subjects, the term "voices" also describes texts that are considered more as documents or contexts than as literary works in their own right; "voices" are often those of persons we might not recognize as authors or historical agents.[25] In these titles, the word "voice" advises us that we're about to gain intimate access to first-person perspectives on the past. Voice sometimes directs our attention away from genre, the vehicle through which we have access to that voice, presenting intelligence we are supposed to value in itself, not because of the beauty of its expression or the fame of its speaker. In so doing, the emphasis on voice can prevent us from engaging the ways in which voice, in sixteenth- and seventeenth-century England, is a function of venue and genre and is often produced collaboratively or conjecturally: the I who speaks is often someone else.

If legal records of women's voices were mediated by men, how different is this from the mediation that shapes all the texts that survive to us from the early modern period? As Purkiss reminds us, "*Any text* produced by an early modern woman was prone to male intervention, in the process of composition as well as at the point of transcription or printing."[26] The composition and transmission of early modern letters might pose a useful counterpoint to that of depositions. Women might, at first, seem to have more control over the letters sent out over their signatures than of the depositions submitted in evidence as theirs. But, in most cases, it is impossible to distinguish a woman's hand from that of her scribe, who was usually a man, or to disaggregate the various influences and interventions that might have shaped the composition of "her" letter. She might have dictated a letter word for word, or written out a first draft in her own hand, or presented a secretary with notes toward a letter. She might have consulted extensively with others before choosing her words, especially regarding legal matters. Often, we cannot know.[27] Nor is this particular to women letter writers; collaboration was part of the culture of letter writing. Monarchs and nobles regularly used secretaries to write their letters; illiterate people, too, hired others to write for them.[28] As a consequence, the "one who wield[ed] the pen" is not necessarily the one who was taken as a letter's author.[29] What Karen Newman calls "the scriptural I" is a collective achievement, an intersubject.[30]

Even if a letter survives in what appears to be a woman's own handwriting, James Daybell advises, "one cannot always rely on a letter's holograph status, safe in the belief that it was written by a woman unaided, or that it represents the unimpaired female 'voice' of a female signatory (if in fact this really existed, since forms of societal, cultural, and religious mediation are built into modes of expression)." Here, too, the signatory might have copied a letter composed by someone else or taken advice or dictation from others. But does this mean that the result is an "impaired voice"? Or, as Daybell also suggests, does it mean that women letter writers sometimes calculated, in consultation with others, an address best suited to the recipient and the rhetorical occasion?[31] Perhaps the most effective voice for the situation is the authentic one. The shaping of one's words to conform to others' expectations might begin before one opened one's mouth or picked up a pen. In church courts too, speakers would have left out what they thought they should not say, what they viewed as unimportant or what was unthinkable or inarticulable in the terms available.[32] They might have consulted about the right word to use.

As Lynne Magnusson says of letters in which women requested various kinds of redress or assistance, "Our conceptions of authorship may not easily accommodate verbal practices that are social not only in that they repeat set forms but also in that secretaries or family members were often collaborators in the composing process,"[33] collaborators whose contributions we cannot identify or isolate. Despite scholarship on collaborative writing practices, the author as possessive individual is far from dead in discussions of texts such as depositions when they are valued as traces of a speaking subject. But scholarship on collaborative literary production, whether of plays or of letters, can help us think more creatively about the collaborations that were required of women going to law.[34] Perhaps we might recast mediation as collaboration, a collaboration that facilitated women's expression as much as or rather than occluding it.

Collaboration need not silence, as we can see in the "works" of Elizabeth I. One of the editors of her collected works reminds us that she was an enormously prolific author: "As queen of England, she was responsible for thousands of letters, legal writs, ambassadorial instructions, and the like. . . . she was the official 'author' of most of the documents that were issued by officers of her court."[35] She was the author in the senses of the owner, the symbolic or authorizing origin, and the one held accountable for the content of these texts. Yet her textual production presents an extreme case of the collaboration that shaped both letters and depositions. Elizabeth often wrote "in collaboration or after consultation with" her advisors. Some of her most powerful first-person utterances were delivered by someone else.[36] The editors tell us that, especially in Elizabeth's letters, "it is impossible to separate the queen's 'authentic' voice from an official style that she developed in conjunction with her secretaries and principal ministers and that was used with equal facility by all of them."[37] Considering Elizabeth's writings in relation to depositions and letters, one might conclude that her authentic voice is as mediated, as inaccessible, as all of the others we strain to hear. As one reviewer asks, when, if ever, "do we hear Elizabeth's 'authentic' voice?"[38] The answer is, in part, no more often than we hear any authentic or unmediated voice in the period. The queen is not a subject otherwise absent from the historical record. She is not anonymous and certainly not marginalized. Still, the editors' point about the impossibility of disaggregating her authentic voice from the tapestry of a collaborative composition process advises us that her interiority remains, ultimately, largely unknowable—in part because it was not what she was communicating or contemporaries were seeking in her spoken and written relations to them.

Yet one of the editors' guiding principles of selection and editorial presentation depends on providing access to something that seems like presence. The editors tell us that they "have omitted letters that are routine and formulaic in nature." These letters are omitted not because they have an attenuated claim to Elizabeth as their author/owner but because they make an attenuated claim on our attention. The goal of gaining access to voice or presence clearly guides the edition's provocative hypothesis that auditors' memorial reconstructions of Elizabeth's speeches record them "as delivered" more accurately than do the published versions of her speeches: "While Elizabeth may sometimes have spoken from a prepared written text and did occasionally prepare written speeches to be read out by her principal ministers, in a large number of instances she spoke either extemporaneously or from memory, and only wrote the speech down afterward or had it transcribed from her dictation. Sometimes, the evidence clearly suggests, if she wanted a copy of a speech she had delivered, she acquired it from one of her auditors who had written down her words later from memory."[39] Here, as we see so often in this book, a manuscript origin eludes our grasp. A queen's foul papers are not the most true relation of what she had to say. She herself might rely on others' memories as the best record of her own utterances. Of the available versions of a given speech, the editors argue, memorial reconstructions—that is, texts that come after rather than before the performance—provide "more vivid and vigorous texts" and "more spontaneous rhetoric." This editorial approach requires us to discount "the queen's own hand" and, indeed, her wishes for how a speech might be disseminated, in the interests of a "more vivid" sense of her presence. The editors suggest that we gain access to Elizabeth's presence best through others' mediation rather than her own self-censorship. Our access to this most singular of speakers, they suggest, was facilitated by relators, as they were called at the time, that is, those who listened and tried to "take down" what they had heard, either in the moment or subsequently.[40] Even a queen's "voice" is as much a collaborative achievement as are the voices in church court records.

In arguing that we might view the clerks in church courts as collaborators, not unlike epistolary scribes or note takers at Elizabeth's speeches, I am not defending the accuracy of their transcriptions, as some do. According to Stone, whose work on divorce depends on the records of the Court of Arches (an ecclesiastical court), although "some of the conversations or details of events sound almost too good to be true," suggesting that they are not, "it would be a mistake . . . to exaggerate the unreliability of the evidence taken from these transcripts of court trials. They are not only the best evidence we have; they are also astonishing in their completeness and intimate detail." These "more-or-less verbatim" depositions allow us to "eavesdrop on the conversation of men and women of all sorts and conditions."[41] Garthine Walker uses this same odd phrase, "more or less verbatim": "My own view is that depositions were likely to have been transcribed by clerks more or less verbatim."[42] Gowing, too, presents these texts as both mediated and "more or less" accurate: "But at the same time, faithful reporting of words was both possible and important"; "clerks were well aware of the vital importance of establishing precisely which words were spoken and which were not."[43] Perhaps the most confident statement comes from Miranda Chaytor, who insists that although clerks made predictable changes to witnesses' statements, such as changing them into the third person, they otherwise "wrote at the plaintiffs' dictation, changing nothing and omitting nothing. Or so the internal evidence of these narratives suggests."[44] Yet we have no way of checking clerks' accuracy, and it must have varied from clerk to clerk.

Defending clerks as accurate places them after the act of storytelling, which they then record either accurately or inaccurately. But if we think of clerks as analogous to epistolary scribes, then we have to imagine them as participants in the process of storytelling rather than as the receivers, accurate or distorting, of stories that precede them. For depositions, as for letters, the presence of the scribe or clerk shapes the statement before and as it is solicited, dictated, and revised. But we should not imagine the clerk as imposing legal terms on an unwitting witness.[45] Legal terms were not alien to many litigants, imposed on them from above, but part of the vocabulary through which they understood the world and through which they apprehended themselves as aggrieved. Legal culture was popular culture and clerks, deponents, and plaintiffs shared language for order and disorder, probity and offense.

When we think about the mediation of testimonies, we often think in terms of locked-room interrogations that coerce confessions, either in cop shows on television or in depictions of torture. We might picture the interrogations of Henry Garnet and other Jesuits in those terms, as I have argued; we might also imagine the interrogations of suspected witches in terms of this model of coercion. Legal confessions are "troubling," as Peter Brooks argues, precisely because "the good interrogator maintains control of the storytelling, so that the suspect is put in a position of denying or affirming—often, affirming through denials that lead to entrapment—the unfolding narrative that, one notes, is largely of the interrogator's own making, his 'monologue'."[46] But the encounter between clerks and deponents in church courts did not work in quite this way. Even in common law courts, as Lorna Hutson reminds us, early modern English justice did not follow "an inquisitorial model."[47] In fact, as Cynthia Herrup and Barbara Shapiro, among others, have argued, early modern English law was broadly participatory rather than top-down; it depended on "common people" for its enforcement.[48] The relationship between deponent and clerk in church courts was probably less antagonistic than that between interrogator and suspect or even that between deponent and clerk in a common law proceeding. Many of the witnesses who gave testimony in church courts were neither plaintiffs nor defendants. They were simply neighbors with information and opinions they were eager to share. Many chose to be there, motivated in part by a desire to report on and regulate the conduct of others. The experience of having their words solicited and recorded, often against someone else, may have been empowering for some witnesses—at others' expense.[49] While they were hardly on equal terms with legal clerks, their relation to them might not have been antagonistic.

The deponents in church courts do not usually incriminate themselves. They were often telling, in effect, someone else's story, as we will see below, yet defining their own morality and credibility through their relation to that second person. When a deposition describes one person's account of what someone else did or said, as transcribed and shaped by yet another person, then, if the result might indeed be called a story, it is a collaborative one. It is not the deponent's or the defendant's or the clerk's; it is the church court's. What we have is the narrative produced by this process, but we cannot be sure who contributed what. If there is an agent we can identify here, it is not any of the individual participants but the institution of the church court itself, the system it put in place for soliciting, shaping, and recording testimony, and the narratives that result.

Scholars who quote from depositions routinely remove legal formulae, suggesting that they distract the modern reader.[50] This obscures the reader's awareness of the clerk, as it is intended to do. Formulaic repetitions alert us to the collaborative process of cobbling together depositions and the pressures placed on deponents by the demands of the legal system. Perhaps these formulae are more constitutive than they are extraneous. Furthermore, their apparent dispensability may prevent us from seeing that the effects of the exchange through which depositions were produced went much deeper than these formulae might suggest. The missing questions obviously shaped responses. But the relationships between clerks and deponents would have had subtler, harder to document effects. We can assume that the interactions that generate a deposition—before someone comes to court, as well as in the interview through which the deposition is produced—were deeply in the grain of the statement's structure and language. [51] Thus, removing the more obvious formulae, as if they are the veneer rather than the substance, might make it too easy for us to ignore the process through which this story was produced and the status of the story itself as our object of analysis rather than a window through which we can hear and see some other object, some person or action. To acknowledge the clerk is not to replace the deponent with the clerk; it is to start to think in a different way about the venue of the church court and the genre of the deposition.

Legal records have often been valued as an evidentiary bedrock. Malcolm Gaskill, for example, imagines archival material in three layers, through which the researcher must dig progressively down toward what he clearly privileges as the most reliable. As Gaskill imagines these layers, "normative" sources (such as statutes and sermons), representing "the way things were *supposed* to be," are on the top or surface; "beneath this we have more impressionistic sources," which would include broadsides, ballads, and pamphlets revealing "how things *seemed* to contemporaries;" and, at the bottom, we find "mainly administrative sources," in which he includes various legal records, which, according to Gaskill, "best reflect the input of ordinary people, and perhaps the way things really *were*."[52] In this schema, administrative sources afford the most reliable access to "the way things really were" because of their institutional context as well as "the input of ordinary people." They are simultaneously institutional and individual. While this archeological model is appealing, it is also illusory. As those who work with church court records sometimes concede, the ordinary people they seek therein are not quite there. If we give up the notion that administrative sources afford more direct access to the way things really were, we might be able to recover a notion of what it means to view some texts as produced by institutions more than persons. This means surrendering the ways in which depositions have come to be viewed as what Martha Howell and Walter Prevenier call "ego documents," which are not "reliable reports about an event" but rather "an index of what the author . . . considers his truth"; "ego documents record the author's perception of events, perhaps even his memory of how he experienced them."[53] It takes creative effort to install an ego in depositions, as we will now see. And that effort raises the question of whose ego it is.

The Editor and the First Person

The editorial impulse to remove legal formulae reveals that the holy grail of deposition reading remains the trace of a speaking self who can be seen as prior to and the origin of the deposition. Carolyn Sale finds a striking instance of a woman's voice, "a self-defining 'I'," in records of a Star Chamber Trial (*Hole v. White*). In her example, Thomasine White's third-person examination erupts into an "I" statement: "whereuppon this def*endant* used theis word*es* to the *s*aid Compl*ainan*t vizt M*aste*r Constable I am at my owne doore and here I will stand." Most of White's deposition is in the third person; but, for Sale, White's voice can only be heard when she speaks in the first person, asserting ownership of her house and, by extension, her self. Because the *Records of Early English Drama* volume in which Sale first found this statement includes only some of the depositions from the suit, "It is back to the archives, then, that we must go, prompted to do so by this single striking instance of her [Thomasine White's] voice."[54] Sale's goal is clear: finding evidence of women's agency and more particularly their authorship, broadly conceived. In pursuit of that goal, she reads assiduously and creatively. But she may overestimate what there is to be found in the archive when we traipse off there.

While "a self-defining 'I'" may occasionally erupt in a deposition, depositions were not designed to provoke or record it. Deponents sometimes attribute first-person speech to themselves, as in Sale's example. For instance, in the 1570s, William Pethie, in his personal answer to the charge that he had pledged to marry two different women, includes his first-person statements plighting his troth to each: "Here I, William, doo gyve you, Marian, my hand and my faith and treweth, that I will never marye other woman but you"; "Here, Grace, I gyve you my hand and my faith and my trewth, that I woll marye you and take you to my wyfe." "Trewth" here is both troth or faith and allegiance as in pledging one's troth and truth as in truthfulness to one's self and one's word, honesty (see *OED*). But, for the most part, the "I do" that remains a key example of verbal contract and of the linguistic performative appears in church court records in the examinations of witnesses rather than of the parties to the contract. For example, the aptly named William Storye's deposition in Thomas Manwell's matrimonial cause against Eleanor Colson includes the following:

> He saith, upon his othe, that at the said tyme, to this examinate's remembranc, the said Thomas asked first the said Helynor, talkinge of the matter, yf that she were the same woman she was at ther last being togither; and she the said Helinor annswerd, Yee, certainely, that she was. Then spoke the said Thomas to hir in this maner, and said "Yf ye be, Helinor, then I, Thomas, take you Elynor, to my wyf, and forsake all women for you, so longe as we 2 shall lyve togither; and thereto I plight you my faith and trewth to be your husband." And thereupon the said Elynor answerd and said, "I, Helinor, also do take you, Thomas, to my husband, forsaking all men for you, so long as we two shall lyve together; and thereto I plight you my faith and trewth to be your wyfe."[55]

Thomas's appeal to Helinor begins with the question of whether she is the same woman she was, the woman with whom he has an understanding and so can make a binding contract. The deposition reports her response in the third person, "that she was." The instability of her name, as recorded by the clerk, has a dizzying effect on the modern reader: "yf ye be Helinor . . . then I take you Elynor." I want to emphasize particularly that in this statement, as in most matrimonial disputes, the performative "I do" exists on the record only as testified to by others and only because it is in dispute. Many such contestations, which we might call breach of promise, appear in church courts. These cases also include arresting proclamations of devotion, usually, again, as remembered and reported by a third party. In 1576, John Casson says of Edward Johnson "that he harde the said Johnson saye that he had committed whoredom with Janet Slaiter; and, further, said that if there were a hundrethe harnessed men set betwixt him and hir, with drawen swerds in ther hands, that he wold run throughe them all to hir; and that, if ther were a hundrethe devels of hell betwixt him and hir, with fleshe croks in ther hands, that he wold run throughe them all to hir." This is an irresistibly vivid statement. But it comes to us as reported by Casson against Johnson.[56]

In depositions, then, we can find lots of "I" statements, but they are frequently as reported by someone else. We tend to assume that a witness is, of necessity, a "first person." Barbara Shapiro, for instance, argues that the authoritative and credible seventeenth-century witness, for the Royal Society or in court, is a "first person."[57] Yet in church court records, the deponent is not a first person but a third person. Since depositions were, for the most part, recorded in the third person, it takes "creative writing" to produce either an "I" or a "you" from them.

The insistence that, when we go to an archive, we will and should find a "self-defining I" guides the practice of intervening to restore the deponent to a first-person status that has supposedly been lost through transcription. Some historians who focus on patterns of litigation tend to quote sparingly from depositions, leaving them in the third person, as Susan Amussen and Martin Ingram, for instance, do.[58] But others amend the passages they quote. This approach appeals to those who wish to linger over juicy cases, and who seek to capture the interiority and experience of individual deponents. Lawrence Stone, for instance, describes his method this way:

> In recording the depositions and answers of witnesses, the clerks of the court, usually, but not always turned direct speech in the present tense into indirect speech in the past tense. For example, one record reads: "the deponent said that she was married to Mr Williams, and that he was her husband." In cases where a brisk exchange of dialogue is recorded, this indirect speech formula has sometimes been converted back into direct speech, but only when it seemed appropriate and when there is no possibility of ambiguity. Thus in telling the story the recorded statement has been adjusted to read: "I am married to Mr Williams and he is my husband." The purpose of the conversion is to recapture the immediacy and sharpness of the dialogue, much of which is so like that in a contemporary novel or play. It can be claimed with a very high degree of certainty that the statement as presented in the case-study now reads exactly as the witness spoke it before the clerk, and before he had turned it into indirect speech in the past tense.[59]

Stone presents his method as straightforward: through a conversion process, he can "recapture" exactly what a witness said. The transcriber now simply undoes a clerk's interventions, restoring the speech to its original form. An

interesting slippage arises in Stone's remark that the dialogue in its supposedly original form is "so like that in a contemporary novel or play." Even as he
claims that it is a more accurate representation of the statement "as the witness
spoke it before the clerk," he concedes that it also conforms better to his own
expectations of stories, expectations shaped through novels and plays. His use
of the word "contemporary" elides the distinction between now and then.
Contemporary to whom? In puzzling syntax, Stone also conflates the clerk's
agency in recording the "brisk exchange of dialogue" with his own in telling
the story.

This approach is not unique to Stone. While he has become the historian
one is supposed to know better than to cite uncritically, the gist of his confident and unguarded statements is not, in the end, that different from the more
carefully worded statements one finds from later generations of scholars—
usually buried in notes. Miranda Chaytor and Garthine Walker both say of
the depositions from which they quote that the "narratives have been returned
to the first person singular."[60] All these statements—Stone's, Chaytor's, and
Walker's—are in the passive voice, thus erasing the historian's own agency in
effecting this "return." By "returning" depositions to their imagined origin
as oral stories, Stone, Chaytor, and Walker can claim to resurrect an "I" who
speaks, a first person. In her work on depositions about rape, Walker builds
toward the rousing claim that

> the "I" that spoke in an early modern rape narrative was partially,
> but nevertheless emphatically, its own property. These stories reveal
> that the subjectivities of early modern women were not simply
> mediated through male discourses. Even patriarchal discourses
> were not the sole domain of men . . . . women engendered those
> same discourses which incriminated them with their own semantic
> and expressive intent. . . . . in choosing to tell her story, in decid-
> ing where to tell it, in describing it in one way and not another, a
> woman resisted annihilation.[61]

Yet this assertion of the self-owned, expressive, agential, and resistant female
speaking subject depends on fabrication. Erasing a disorienting distance in
the language of the depositions themselves, Walker makes the texts she quotes
much more engaging and compelling. The "I" here is an enabling and animat-
ing fiction, but it should be acknowledged that it is not a "return" to an origin
but a creation.

In her helpful sourcebook, *Women and History: Voices of Early Modern England*, Valerie Frith explains that she changes depositions to the first person "in order to facilitate reading the texts and to approximate more closely the way in which the evidence was originally given." She assures the reader that "The result is closer to the way deponents must actually have reported what they had heard or seen." Except for the elimination of legal formulae and the insertion of punctuation, "the texts are as they appear in the original, complete with grammatical errors."[62] In fact, the editorial practices in this rich volume are more various than this opening umbrella statement suggests. Some of the editors include the invented "I" in brackets, yielding pages peppered with bracketed Is. John Beattie leaves the documents he presents in the third person, substituting "she" for "this examinant."[63]

We can see a different editorial approach in *Reading Early Modern Women: An Anthology of Texts in Manuscript and Print, 1550–1700*. In the introduction, the editors, Helen Ostovich and Elizabeth Sauer, acknowledge the mediation of legal records and then, as we have seen elsewhere, proceed to defend the access they offer us to early modern experience:

> Legal accounts were shaped both by the questions put to the defendants and witnesses and by scribes who translated their "narratives" for the court; testimonies were mediated by male clerks who inevitably altered them. And women deponents participated in the art of testifying by censoring their words to conform with standards of female behavior. *Nevertheless*, evidence contained in the depositions could be presented with the expectation that it would be believed, and depositions do give us access to the representations of personal and social experiences of early modern lives.[64]

The phrasing "representations of . . . experiences of . . . lives" fudges the question of what exactly we are getting access to. The editors draw on methodological statements from the anthology's headnotes, in which experts including Lena Cowen Orlin, Laura Gowing, Loreen Giese, and Martin Ingram present facsimiles and transcriptions of selected depositions. The transcriptions do not alter the depositions in any way. While this is a scrupulous and thoughtful editorial policy, the result, I have to admit, is that the scholars who introduce the documents have to frame them so carefully that they strike me as less teachable than those that have been at least slightly altered. The presenter becomes the storyteller and interpreter. This is not very far from G.

R. Elton's "star chamber stories" in which the historian rather than the deposition tells the story.[65] Unaltered depositions can be a hard sell for students, while "narratives" presented in the first person are much more appealing.[66] Ideally, students should encounter both. Just as it has now become commonplace to invite students to think and talk about the process by which, say, their conflated text of *King Lear* was assembled, it would be useful to think with them about the process by which the I who appears to speak to them across time has been produced.[67] Perhaps our embrace of the idea of fiction in the archives might extend to admitting some of our own responsibility for putting it there.

Because Laura Gowing is highly self-conscious about her use of evidence, it is helpful to examine one incident in which she chooses to alter a deposition more dramatically than she usually does. In the sourcebook she edited with Patricia Crawford, *Women's Worlds in Seventeenth-Century England*, and in her quotations from depositions in her scholarship, Gowing usually restricts her editing to removing legal formulae and substituting third-person pronouns for "this examinant." She also scrupulously acknowledges every alteration she makes, including the one deposition that she "puts" in the first person in her book *Common Bodies*. In it, Elizabeth Page testifies against Mary Fox, her mistress's unmarried daughter, on the charge of fornication in 1685. Here is the deposition as Gowing presents it:

> Mary was wont several nights when she thought I was asleep to feel my belly, and then also to feel her own, and then she would fetch deep sighs, but one night above the rest I being awake Mary thought I had been asleep, [I] took . . . Mary's hand upon my belly, and demanding a reason what she meant and why she laid her hand there, . . . Mary asked me whether or no I ever had to do with any man and I replied No, why Mistress Mary have you had to do with any man?, and . . . Mary replied Yea, that I have; and being asked with whom she made answer with Mr. William Milward . . . who hath had twice the carnal knowledge of my body, and the first time he had to do with me he threw me violently upon a bed and then he gave me a ring, Whereupon I said, Mistress Mary I pray God he hath not begot you with child & she answered I hope not, for he promised me, he would not get me with child, and I further questioning her when it was that he had to do with her, the said Mary replied about the Whitsontide before. And being also asked by me

whether any other man had the carnal knowledge of her body, she replied, not any man in the world but he.[68]

Gowing signals with brackets the third "I" in this passage, but the deposition records "I" only inside the statements Page attributes to Mary Fox; the deposition refers to Page herself as "this deponent . . . . she." In the second transcription of the deposition you see here, I have marked the clerk's revisions, which are also visible in the facsimile (see Figure 7):

> This deponent . . . further saith That the sayd Mary was wont several nights when she thought this Deponent was asleepe to feel this Deponents belly, & then also to feele her owne, and then the sayd Mary would fetch deep sighes, but one night above the rest this Deponent being awake tho . . . Mary . . . thought shee had beene asleepe, tooke the sayd Marys hand upon this Deponents belly, & demanding a reason what she meant and why she lay'd her hand there, the sayd Mary asked this deponent whether or noe shee ever had to doe with any man and ~~the sayd Mary~~ this Deponent replied Noe, Why Mrs Mary have you had to doe with any man, & the sayd Mary replyed Yea that I have; and being asked with whome she made answer with Mr. William Millward then of the Burrough of Stafford, who hath had twice the Carnall Knowledge of ~~her~~ my body, & the first tyme he had to do with ~~her~~ me, he threw ~~her~~ me vyolently upon a Bedde & then he gave ~~her~~ me a Ringe, Whereupon this Deponent sayd, Mrs Mary I pray God he hath not begot you with Childe & she answered I hope not, for ~~she~~ he promised me, hee would not gett mee with Childe. And this Deponent further questioning her when it was that he had to doe with her, the sayd Mary replyed about the Whitsontyde before, And being also asked by this Deponent whether any other man had the Carnall Knowledge of her body, she replied, not any man in the world but for the sayd Mr. Milward. [69]

The first-person dialogue between the two women actually leaps out more when it is embedded in the third-person deposition. The deposition generally records Mary's indirect speech as Gowing presents it, except that the deposition includes in Mary's confession of her lover's identity the disconcerting specification that this was the Mr. William Milward "then of the Burrough

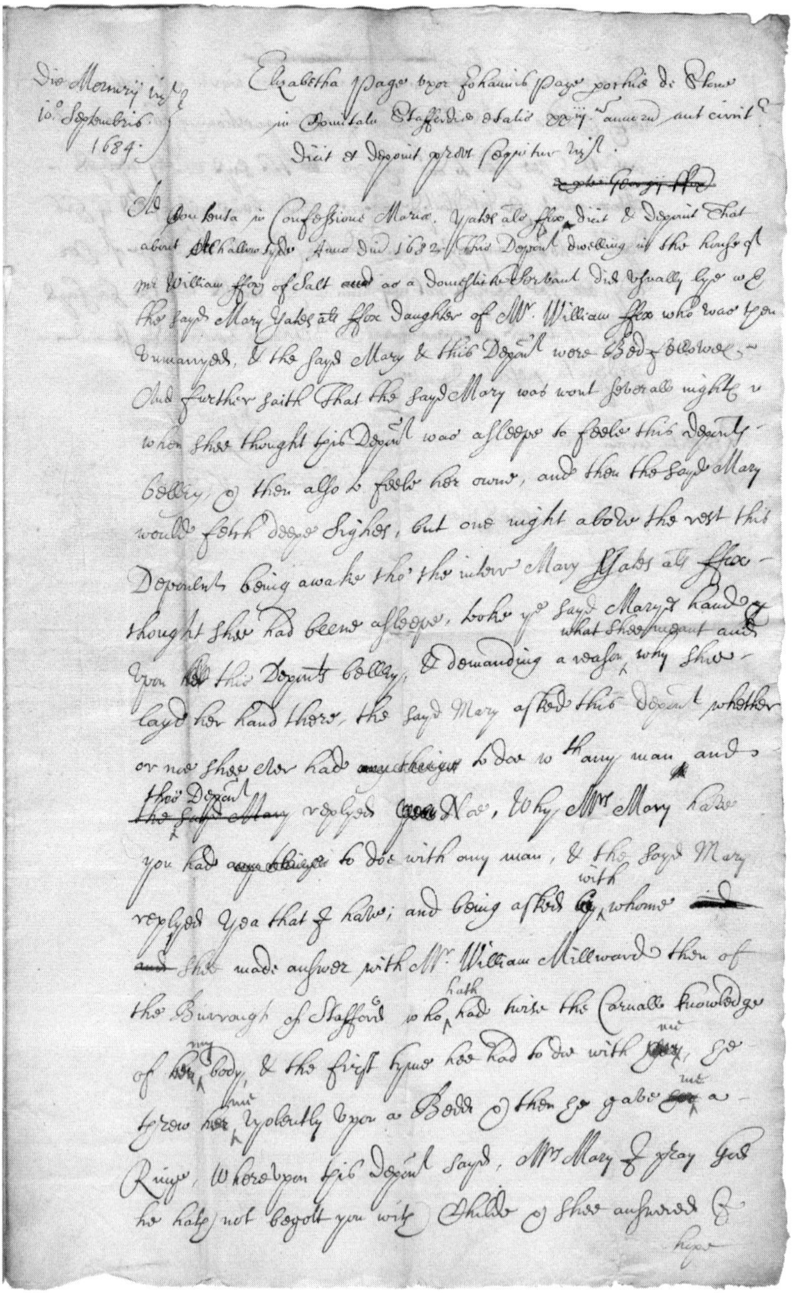

Figure 7. Elizabeth Page's deposition (1685), showing the clerk's attempts to clarify the relations among first, second, and third person statements. Lichfield B/C/5/1685/262. By permission of the Lichfield Record Office, Staffordshire County Council.

of Stafford" and records Mary's wonderful final assertion that she has not had sex with "any man in the world but for the sayd Mr. Milward," which has a little less punch than "not any man in the world but he." For our purposes here, what's interesting about the deposition in manuscript is that we can see evidence of the clerk reviewing and revising it in order to keep track of when Elizabeth Page is referring to herself and when she is attributing statements to Mary Fox, to distinguish between this deponent, Elizabeth, and the "sayd" Mary, and between Mary as a third person and as a first. Within the statements attributed to Mary, many "hers" have been crossed out and replaced with "me" so as to clarify that Page is describing what Mary says. So, in this case, the clerk himself appears to be "returning" the third person to the first, either because Page recounted Mary Fox's statements in the third person; or because the clerk, adroit at simultaneously translating first to third, overdid it; or because he could not keep track and had to revise the deposition. The distinction between Elizabeth and Mary, between she and I, is unclear in this account.

Of all the depositions Gowing quotes from in her book, it is interesting that this should be the only one she puts in the first person. Page's testimony goes to the heart of Gowing's concerns in *Common Bodies*: the way that the body is both a source of knowledge women have in common and an object of uncertainty; touch as a means of connection and as a means of distancing, controlling, and hurting others. There is, indeed, a "politics of touch" in this scene, in which the mistress presumes to touch her servant's body, looking for evidence "about how the chaste, virginal and not-pregnant female body ought to be," and the servant is presented as an authority on her mistress's body and conduct, even as a kind of representative for the court. As Gowing points out, the servant "turned the tables somewhat": "Her questioning of her mistress's daughter, who was very likely close to her own age, has echoes of the courtroom. 'When it was he had to do with her,' and 'whether any other man had the carnal knowledge of her body,' was precisely what magistrates would ask a woman pregnant outside marriage."[70] What we cannot know, of course, is whether Elizabeth Page asked these questions, or reported having done so, or if this echo of the courtroom is a product of her dialogue with a clerk who supplied these phrases. The first person amplifies what Gowing seeks throughout her book, an intimate if vexed moment between women. Emphasizing the clerk's presence and interventions changes our perspective on this exchange and qualifies the document's status as evidence of what happened between Elizabeth and Mary. Elizabeth is the antagonist of her mistress's daughter, with whom she shares a bed and against whom she testifies. But the deposition also suggests that, for the clerk, it is not all that easy to tell the two apart, to distinguish the censorious informant from the confiding fornicator.

If we place the deposition on a continuum with all the other seventeenth-century genres dedicated to the project of imagining voices, we find that in many of these genres there is a slippage between the first and third person because the narrator loses track of the distinction between his or her own voice and the one s/he is transcribing for or attributing to the speaker. For example, the ballad form allows the singer to give voice to an imagined subject's words and feelings: your voice can become that of the criminal or cuckold. Ballad subjects also often directly address and engage the second persons in the audience.[71] Goodnight ballads, describing criminals' deaths on the scaffold, attempt both to tell us of the transgressor's death and to allow the transgressor to speak. This requires some fancy footwork, as when "A Warning for All Desperate Women" brings Alice Davis's first-person account to a close by shifting to the third person for the two lines describing her death ("And then she shriek'd most pitifully, / before that she did dye") only to return to her first-person prayer that "I may be the last / that such a death did dye." In another ballad about Davis, "The Unnaturall Wife," she describes her own burning in first-person detail. The "Lamentation of John Musgrave" shifts from Musgrave's first-person voice, concluding with his hope that "with Christ I hope to lodge this night" in the penultimate stanza to a narrator's first-person conclusion, in which Musgrave is now referred to in the third person: "He is with Christ, as I dare say, / the Lord grant us that so we may."[72]

As Bruce Smith points out, in Shakespeare's sonnets, "forms of the first-person pronoun—'I,' 'me,' 'my,' 'mine'—constitute the single most frequently occurring word group," more frequent even than conjunctions or articles. Written in a confessional mode, "the Sonnets are set up as revelations of private experience. The reading 'you' is cast as a voyeur, a sharer of someone else's secrets." This voyeurism, so similar to that of the witness in a church court or the researcher delving into archives, provokes a sometimes uneasy identification between what Smith calls the "reading 'you'," or in the case of depositions, what I would call the peeping you, and "the speaking 'I'." And yet, he insists, "the 'I' who speaks Shakespeare's sonnets is much less *there* than 'he/she' appears to be." Even critics who know better, Smith argues, "seize upon the speaking 'I' and rush to identify with it as a universal 'we.' What they seize upon is an illusion." [73] This is an illusion first promoted by Edmund Malone, as Margreta de Grazia has shown, who identified the first person in the sonnets with Shakespeare himself and restricted the second- and third-person references to two individuals, a dark lady and a young man.[74] Identification of and with the speaking I can impede other kinds of identifications. Smith argues that an overinvestment in identifying with the speaking I of Shakespeare's sonnets has made some readers paradoxically resistant to the fluid sexuality of that I, an I defined in relation to both "he" and "she."[75] Smith's argument is specific to Shakespeare and to sonnets. But his focus on pronouns and reader identifications can be extended to depositions. In the rather different case of depositions, the critic's personal investment in an "I" can lead to identification with deponents. Research in church court records tends to invite the kind of personal investment Smith challenges: Miranda Chaytor's avowal, in response to a man's statement, that "I believe him"; Lynda Boose's claim that, in the narrative she "extracted" from depositions, "what seemed perfectly obvious" was that the female deponent "was telling the truth"; or Joanne Bailey's frank confession that she is "amused and even charmed" by the "eccentricities" of her "very own favourite wife-beater."[76] If one must be "wary" about identifying with the I of the sonnets, which constantly speak in the voice of I, then how much warier should one be in presuming to identify with an I that is even more illusory, allusive, and elusive?

In many early modern texts, we find an unstable relation between a narrator's voice and that of his character or informant, between the relator's first person and that of his witness. In his published account of the confession he "laboured" to "extort" from convicted witch Elizabeth Sawyer, Henry Goodcole, ordinary of Newgate prison, includes the questions he asked as well as her responses, thus exposing the process through which such extortion was achieved, a process that, as we have seen, was usually invisible in the documents that resulted. Goodcole makes a telling elision in his *True Relation of the Confession of Elizabeth Sawyer*, included in his pamphlet *The Wonderfull Discoverie of Elizabeth Sawyer, a Witch*. The answer to his question regarding how Sawyer became acquainted with the devil slides from Sawyer's first person ("The first time that the Divell came unto me was, when I was cursing, swearing and blaspheming") to the devil's first person as quoted by Sawyer ("Oh! Have I now found you cursing, swearing, and blaspheming? now you are mine") to Goodcole's first person ("I pray God, that this her terrible example may deter them [blasphemers], to leave and distaste them, to put their tongues to a more holy language, then the accursed language of hell").[77] Several critics have pointed to this slippage between narrator and subject, one I and another. Jonathan Gil Harris points out that Goodcole's role as "ordinary" or minister of Newgate, charged with preparing criminals for death, would have evoked another contemporary definition of *ordinary*: as a prompter in a theater, whispering lines and cues to players: "The impression that Goodcole has literally prompted her [Sawyer's] self-incriminations becomes most apparent when, probably due to a compositor's error, his words merge with Sawyer's own in answers to one of his questions."[78] This may well have been a compositor's error. But there is no clear place on the page for Goodcole's commentary on Sawyer's confession, especially since he has surrendered the margin to describing a bystander's interventions (see Figure 8). This error reveals, as Harris suggests, that Sawyer's words are Goodcole's, or at least that the distinction between them is unclear. The whole account is driven by Goodcole's goal of denouncing blasphemy, and he presents Sawyer in order to make that case. Diane Purkiss says of this passage that "once a gap opens up between the person speaking the words and the 'I' of the narrative, the authenticity of confession is lost; performance and authentic confession are opposites."[79] If a gap opens here, one might also argue that a gap closes between Sawyer's "I" and Goodcole's. Harris's reminder of the multiple meanings of an "ordinary" might also suggest that performance and authentic confession are not necessarily opposites. Where does authenticity lie? How can one access "the person speaking the words"?

A similar slippage occurs in the longest and most detailed tale in Thomas Harman's notoriously vexed relation of his interviews with vagrants, *A Caveat*

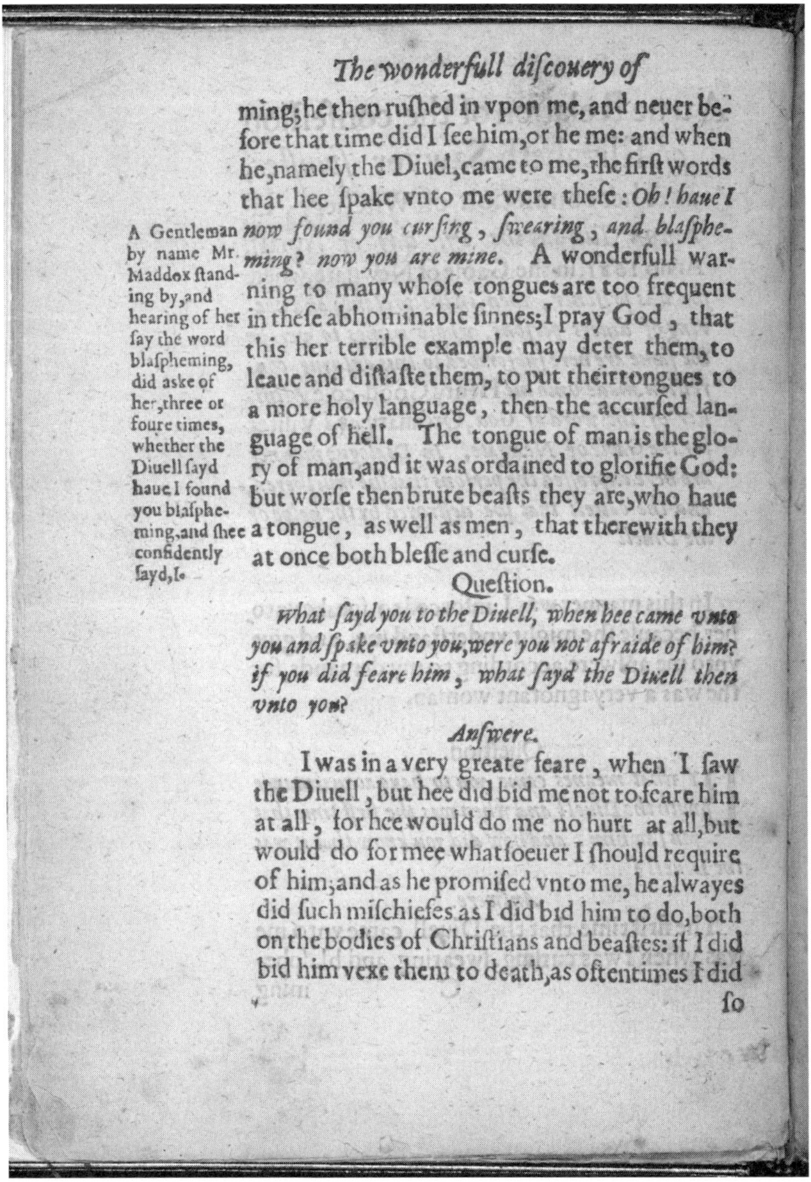

ming; he then rufhed in vpon me, and neuer before that time did I fee him, or he me: and when
he, namely the Diuel, came to me, the firft words
that hee fpake vnto me were thefe : *Oh ! haue I*
now found you curfing , fwearing , and blafphe-
ming? now you are mine. A wonderfull warning to many whofe tongues are too frequent
in thefe abhominable finnes; I pray God , that
this her terrible example may deter them, to
leaue and diftafte them, to put their tongues to
a more holy language , then the accurfed language of hell. The tongue of man is the glory of man, and it was ordained to glorifie God:
but worfe then brute beafts they are, who haue
a tongue , as well as men , that therewith they
at once both bleffe and curfe.

A Gentleman by name Mr. Maddox ftanding by, and hearing of her fay the word blafpheming, did aske of her, three or foure times, whether the Diuell fayd haue I found you blafpheming, and fhee confidently fayd, I.

Queftion.

What fayd you to the Diuell, when hee came vnto
you and fpake vnto you, were you not afraide of him?
if you did feare him , what fayd the Diuell then
vnto you?

Anfwere.

I was in a very greate feare , when I faw
the Diuell , but hee did bid me not to feare him
at all , for hee would do me no hurt at all, but
would do for mee whatfoeuer I fhould require
of him; and as he promifed vnto me, he alwayes
did fuch mifchiefes as I did bid him to do, both
on the bodies of Chriftians and beaftes: if I did
bid him vexe them to death, as oftentimes I did

fo

Figure 8. Page from Goodcole's *The Wonderfull Discovery of Elizabeth*
Sawyer, A Witch (1621), showing the shift from Sawyer's "I" to Goodcole's.
© The British Library Board. C.27.b.38.

for Common Cursitors. This is the much-discussed tale of the "walking mort." (Morts were itinerant female workers who often claimed to be widowed and whom Harman associates with occasional theft and prostitution.) What particularly interests me here is the way that the first person resides between Harman and the mort. It is a distributed, shifting, and shared first-person voice. In the story Harman attributes to the mort, she explains that, when she was hugely pregnant, reaching for oysters to quell a craving, she got stuck between rocks as the tide was rising and needed help to get out. A man who answered her cries for help would not assist her unless she promised to have sex with him, which she did so as not to drown. Ultimately, the mort collaborates with the man's wife and her friends, on whom he has also preyed sexually, to entrap and beat him.[80]

The mort describes her predicament as she contemplates her rescuer's demands as follows:

> And by my trouth I wist not what to answeare I was in such a perplexite, for I knewe that man well, he had a very honest woman to his wyfe and was of som welth and on the other syde if I weare not holpe out, I shoulde there have perished; and I graunted hym that I would obeye to hys wyll, then he plucked me out. And because there was no convenient place nere hande I required hym that I might go washe myselfe and make me somewhat clenly, and I would come to his house and lodge al night in hys barne, whether he myghte repaire to me and accomplyshe hys desire, but let it not be quoth shee before nine of the clocke at nighte for then there wylbe small styrring. And I may repayre to the town quoth she to warme and drye myselfe, for this was about two of the clocke in the afternoune do so quoth hee for I must be busye to loke oute my cattel hereby before I can come home. So I went awaye from him and glad was I, and why so quoth I, because quoth she hys wyfe my good dame is my very friend, and I am much beholdinge to her.[81]

The exchange goes on. But we can see just in this passage how Harman's "I" and the mort's "I" blur together in a single sentence: "So I went awaye from him and glad was I, and why so quoth I." The mort also oscillates between first person and third person. Harman suddenly reminds us that he is narrating her story at the moment he records how the mort collects herself after being "plucked out" and makes her assignation.

ſomewhat clenly,and I would come to his houſe and lodge al night in his barne,whether he might repayre to me and accompliſhe his deſire,but let it not be quoth ſhe befoꝛe nine of the clocke at nyght, foꝛ then there wilbe ſmall ſtyꝛring,And I may repayꝛe to the town ꝙ ſhe to warme & dꝛye my ſelf, foꝛ this was about two of the clocke in the after none,do ſo quoth he,foꝛ I muſt be buſie to looke out my cattell here by befoꝛe I can come home. So I went away from him and glad was I,and why ſo quoth I,becauſe quoth ſhe his wife my good dame is my very friend,and I am much beholding to hir.And ſhe had donne mee ſo muche good oꝛ this,that I were loth nowe to harme hir any way.Why ſo quoth I: what and it had ben any other man and not your good dames huſband.The matter hadd bene the leſſe quoth ſhe. Tell me I pꝛay thee quoth I,who was the father of the childe,ſhe ſtudied a whyle and ſayd that it had a father,but what was bee quoth I : Nowe by my troth I know not quoth ſhee,you bꝛing me out of my matter,ſo you do,well ſay on quoth I,then I departed ſtrayte to the towne and came to my dames houſe. And ſhe wed her of my misfoꝛtune,alſo of her huſbands vſage in al poin-tes and that I ſhowed her the ſame foꝛ good will and bydd her take better heed to her huſband and to her ſelfe,ſo ſhee gaue mee great thankes and made me good cheere,and byd me in anye caſe that I ſhould be redy at the barne at that time and houre we had apointed foꝛ I know well quoth this good wife my huſband will not bꝛeake with thee.And one thing I warne thee that thou giue me a watche woꝛd a lowde when he goeth about to haue his pleaſure of thee,and that ſhalbee ſye foꝛ ſhame ſye,and I will bee harde by you,wyth helpe.But I charge thee kepe this ſecret vntill all be finiſhed,and hold ſayth this good wyfe here is one of my petticotes I giue thee. I thanke you good dame quoth I,and I warrante you I will bee true and truſty vnto you. So my dame left me ſittinge by a good ſyer with meate and dꝛinke,and wyth the oyſters I bꝛought wyth me,I hadde great cheere,ſhe went ſtrayte and repayꝛed vnto her goſſipes dwelling thereby,and as I did after vnderſtand,ſhe made her mone to them, what a naughtye lewed lecherous huſband ſhee hadde,and how that ſhe could not haue his companye foꝛ harlottes, and that ſhe was in feare to take ſome filthy diſeaſe of him,he was ſo common a man,hauing little reſpect whom he hadde to do with all,and quoth ſhe now here is one at my houſe a pooꝛe woman that goeth about the countrey that he would haue hadde to doe with all, wherfoꝛe good neighboures and louinge goſſypes as you loue mee

and

Harman's relationship to his informants or characters and their "voices" has been much discussed. In his influential argument about subversion and its containment, Stephen Greenblatt dwells on the moments in which Harman admits that he has broken his promises to various vagrants. Harman, "so much cruder than Shakespeare," reminds us that betraying the trust of informants is a crucial part of affirming one's difference from and superiority to them. One might add that, when Harman invites us to think about his betrayal of his informants, they seem least his creatures even as, according to Greenblatt, they are most serving his purposes. In texts such as the *Caveat*, Greenblatt argues, "the subversive voices are produced by and within the affirmations of order; they are powerfully registered, but they do not undermine that order."[82] But *The Caveat* produces Harman's voice as well, and it is often difficult, as we have seen above, to distinguish his voice from those of his interlocutors, antagonists, and creations. As Elizabeth Hanson argues of the walking mort, "If the voice that tells the story and articulates principled resistance to Harman's moralizing is that of a subordinated, female Other—indeed, even if it records the actual availability to women of moral codes different than the one Harman propounds—that voice also speaks for Harman."[83] The shifting pronouns are one clue to an unstable distinction between Harman's story placed in the mort's mouth and the mort's story. Arthur Kinney argues that Harman "loses himself" in telling these stories.[84] But one might also argue that he loses his subjects, their supposed tellers, and perhaps even that he finds or creates himself by means of these stories.

Looking at the passage as it is presented in the 1573 edition also enables us to think about the difference adding punctuation might make. The minimal punctuation in the passage, especially the lack of the quotation marks a modern reader depends on, can be very confusing. When an editor punctuates this passage, as I have done myself for a textbook, inserting quotation marks is helpful except when one most wants assistance, when Harman's voice and the mort's blend together.

As Margreta de Grazia points out, it was not until the end of the eighteenth century that quotation marks assumed "their routine modern function of guaranteeing that the passage within quotes has been accurately reproduced and correctly ascribed."[85] Before the eighteenth century, there were some methods of marking off reported speech or borrowed text, such as setting it in italics or using quotation marks in the margin, but their use and meaning were haphazard. As de Grazia shows, when quotation marks began to be used consistently, they worked to fence off and protect the quoted speaker's ownership

of and responsibility for his or her words. They distinguish the narrator from
the speaker whose words he records, the first person from the second or third
person. In the absence of quotation marks, reporting clauses—"quoth shee,"
"quoth I"—do some of the work of attaching speech to speaker. But they leave
ambiguities, as Harman's *Caveat* demonstrates. The lack of quotation marks
in a church court deposition or in Harman's *Caveat* is not just a convention,
then. It signals the instability between the first and third persons, an instability that is central to these texts and that we would erase by inserting quotation marks. It is an apparently simple operation that proves more difficult in
practice.

For the modern reader or editor, it may make sense to add quotation
marks to Harman's *Caveat*. Given the fact that most scholars also "edit" depositions when they quote from them at length or reproduce them in anthologies, it might make sense to consider adding quotation marks around reported
speech in those depositions, as James Raine did in his 1845 collection of Durham depositions from which I quoted above, since that is no more intrusive
than other changes many routinely make. Doing so might acknowledge that
we are, in fact, altering these texts for readability in the same way we alter
other texts from the sixteenth and seventeenth centuries.

But this practice might complicate as well as clarify because, if quotation
marks function to assign ownership of speech, then trying to insert them into
depositions forces us to see that the ownership of statements in depositions is
often unclear. That uncertainty as to who is speaking is not a problem unique
to depositions but a feature of many sixteenth- and seventeenth-century texts.
Like these other texts, depositions blur the distinctions quotations marks try
to clarify. Depositions are not polyvocal as much as they are univocal: written
in a consistent clerical style that erases the prompts to which the deponent responds and casts the deponent as a third person. Although it is easy to see the
seams, it is impossible to dissect depositions so as to disaggregate the different
influences that combine to constitute them and the amorphous, dispersed yet
shared selves they reveal, the persons that cannot be neatly segregated into
first, second, or third.[86]

Word Choice in Depositions

The I who speaks, whether it erupts in a third-person deposition or we install it there, tends to provoke speculations about its motives and feelings.

Practicing what she calls "close and detailed textual analysis of church court records," Diana O'Hara points out that it is "difficult to know which of the conflicting accounts" to believe in a set of depositions and, as a consequence, "the actual truth . . . is not crucial." "What is more relevant is not the facts of an individual experience, but the structure within which it is incorporated." The structures that interest O'Hara are those that set limits on individual desire and action. As an example, she offers the following interpretation of a deposition in a marriage contract dispute between Edmund Coppyn and Katherine Richards, a servant in his uncle's house:

> In the Canterbury case of *Coppyn v. Richards*, Katherine Richards
> was offered a pair of gloves by Richard Dennys on behalf of one
> Edmund Coppyn. She refused them and, "at the refusal thereof
> [Dennys] declared unto her that she and Edmond should be suer
> together. And then she lamentted very sore howbeyt she wolde not
> declare any other cause of her lamentings saving that she said to
> [him] I pray you speake not for him for I will nev*er* have him nor
> I CANNOT love him." The emphasis is my own, but the rhetoric
> and Katherine's distraught condition suggest a tension arising from
> some prohibition other than personal inclination. Perhaps then,
> it is to this area of ambiguous meaning that attention needs to be
> drawn, in order for us to understand the problems which individu-
> als had in internalising family and social norms, and the way in
> which personal desire was suppressed or constrained. The justifica-
> tion which respondents gave for the breakdown in their marriage
> promises should not be taken at face value. Rather we should look
> for more subtle approaches to interpret their position, and to such
> emotions as "lamentation" which hint at less articulated consider-
> ations and feelings.[87]

While O'Hara is cautious about "sentimentalizing" evidence of individuals and their emotions, her emphasis on the structures that constrain courtships rather than the "fact of individual experience" leads her to assume that
Richards's "cannot" points to a prohibition imposed on her from outside. But,
following "I will never have him," Richards's claim that she "cannot love"
Dennys might as easily express her desire (in this case distaste) as its suppression by others. O'Hara's emphasis on CANNOT is a kind of stage direction,
encouraging us to imagine how Katherine Richards might have pointed the

statement attributed to her. Imagining how a speaker might have delivered a line or placing pressure on a particular word choice such as "lamentings" might appear to be a "literary" approach. But it also requires us to posit access to Katherine Richards's emotions in a way that belies most literary critics' doubts about our ability to understand motives, including our own.[88] O'Hara also strips this statement of its narrative context, emphasizing Katherine Richards's social position as a servant rather than her position as a character in a story told by someone else. "In the case," which must, as usual, be pieced together from several different examinations, Katherine Richards "was offered" a pair of gloves but according to whom? Whose deposition is this? Is this Richards's statement or a statement from one of the other deponents in the case? As it turns out, while there is a statement assigned to Katherine Richards, this is not it; this is Richard Dennys's deposition, so it is his account of what Richards said, his version of what she felt.[89] The fact that this is Dennys's deposition does not mean that Richards did not say these words, any more than we could be certain she did if her own deposition said so. It simply adds yet another layer of mediation, as does the context of the dispute, to which O'Hara is usually acutely sensitive.

Dennys's interest in the case appears to have been that he was acting as what O'Hara calls a go-between, representing Coppyn's suit to Richards and hoping for a reward for his services.[90] If Dennys's examination gives us access to Richards's "distraught condition," to almost inarticulable emotions, then the "speaking I" here is a three-way collaboration between Richards, Dennys, and a clerk. Coppyn might also be understood as a kind of party to this statement since Dennys worked on his behalf and speaks in a suit he brought. Perhaps it is only through someone else that Katherine Richards's resistance to Edmund Coppyn's suit could be articulated. Perhaps this statement has little to do with what Katherine Richards thought or felt or said. Dennys's depiction of her as "lamenting" places her in a long tradition of female lament, a tradition that even a bricklayer (like Dennys) or a servant (like Richards) or a clerk might know. Again, the issue is not that Katherine Richards did not lament but that that word was available to describe her feelings because lamentation is such a conventional female response to courtship. One might put pressure on "lamenting" without assuming that what it can tell us is what Katherine Richards felt.[91] In using word choice to lead us back to a speaking subject, who, it turns out, speaks at two removes in this deposition, O'Hara require us to forget what many studies of early modern language have taught us: that words tend to tell us more about webs of association and networks of meaning than about individual intention. A deponent is as likely to find other men's leaves in his heart as is the speaker in Philip Sidney's *Astrophel and Stella.* As Judith Butler puts it, "The 'I' has no story of its own that is not also the story of a relation—or set of realations—to a set of norms."[92]

When deponents and clerks conferred about their stories, they brought to that consultation their knowledge of narrative and linguistic conventions as well as of the law and of the events in dispute. Laura Gowing stresses that "the narratives people told at court reflected the stories they already knew," which included "the variety of strands in popular culture, a spectrum encompassing both oral and written sources."[93] Connecting her approach to court records to a defense of "fictional literature" as a source, Elizabeth Foyster looks to court records for "what insults and behaviour litigants and witnesses thought most damaging to male honour, and in the more detailed cases, what method of story-telling they believed needed to be employed to produce a convincing case to the court."[94] The best story would conform to well-established expectations for stories of marital conflict or sexual misconduct, adapting "familiar and meaningful *tropes*," "a common heritage of conventions and stereotypes."[95] These tropes and conventions achieved familiarity through repetition not only in legal proceedings but in the neighborhood squabbles they adjudicated, as well as in jests and ballads, pamphlets and sermons, talk and print. The discursive resources available to deponents and the clerks with whom they collaborated limited some possibilities, as has often been demonstrated, by, for instance, making it almost impossible for women to reveal sexual knowledge without incriminating themselves.[96] But they facilitated other possibilities by helping deponents and clerks apprehend and narrate sometimes traumatic experiences in intelligible terms.

To consider the options available for telling a story about sexual transgression or marital disorder, one must read across a wide discursive field, looking for what similar stories in different registers have in common. As Catherine Richardson explains, "Such a project makes meaning out of the relationships between different stories about similar subjects, whether those stories were produced as fact or fiction."[97] This approach of lateral rather than teleological analysis, whose proponents often refer back to Laura Gowing's explanations of her methodology, is now widely used by those who work with depositions from a variety of courts.[98] Focusing largely on assize court depositions, Malcolm Gaskill points to "striking similarities" between depositions and cheap print in terms of both form and function, perhaps because stories in both registers "sought to persuade rather than inform."[99] While I do not see so clear a distinction between persuading and informing in these texts, I agree that they are closely interrelated. Focusing on language rather than narrative, Paul Griffiths emphasizes the cross-pollination of street slang and legal language in Bridewell records: "People picked up this talk from pamphlets, conversations, or when they came to courts. Street speech was absorbed into legal cultures, vocabularies, and laws."[100] In turn, legal cultures, vocabularies, and laws filtered into street speech. All these models avoid pinning down a cause and effect relationship, with one genre or venue influencing the other. What they suggest, instead, is a two-way traffic between the "legal" and "popular." Gaskill argues, for instance, that "the common stylistic ground between the two genres" he studies, depositions and pamphlets, "stems from more than just the reliance of clerical or hack writers on depositions for source material, or, conversely, from witnesses' familiarity with the literary genre of the murder pamphlet"; as a result, it is "impossible to say which had the greatest effect on the other."[101] Even the phrase "two-way traffic" probably describes a neater process than occurred. As we saw with regard to witchcraft, the deposition that could be heard and recorded had to sound like the stories that had come before it; the right word to describe Katherine Richards had to be, in some ways, the conventional and familiar one: lamenting.

Sketching out the terms available to deponents and the forms into which stories were most readily cast, as well as the resemblances among stories, can lead us back, yet again, to the deponent, if not as origin, then as a transistor or a discourse jockey, choosing from a limited menu of story lines, calculating what will persuade, and combining available materials in creative ways. Suspicious of approaches that play up intertextuality and downplay the subject as source of a given deposition or defense strategy, Joanne Bailey argues that stress on mediation and the resulting "multi-vocal nature of court records" might lead us to "lose sight of the individuals who are represented in them" and directs our attention to other sources, including the letters plaintiffs wrote to proctors that "make it possible to hear separate voices" and also show the active roles plaintiffs and defendants took in shaping the course of litigation.[102] According to Garthine Walker, "Privileging the strategic nature of testimony may paradoxically imply that legal narratives are ultimately 'just stories'" and that "the system, rather than the narrator's experience, dictates the terms of the tale."[103] Like Bailey, Walker wishes to reinstall the importance of the narrator's experience and agency, and thereby the value of stories as evidence thereof. This desire to reanchor depositions to what we might call the real historical subject reemerges again and again in part as a way to redraw disciplinary boundaries and reestablish the value of depositions as evidence of events or experiences rather than discourses.

But while the return is predictable, it tends also to be unsustainable because the attempts to locate the I who speaks depend, necessarily, on close reading tactics that mire the reader in an interdisciplinary quagmire. As we have seen, the very "familiarity" of stories can be taken as evidence of the storytelling subject who apprehends his or her experience through available narrative forms and conventional moral judgments, or of a libel (in its meaning of a plea, complaint, or charge) that lays out the problem to be investigated, or of a collaboration with a clerk who, helpfully or obstructively, shapes the materials the deponent offers into the narrative most germane to the cause at hand or of the contours that stories about adultery or fornication tend to have in common whoever tells them in whatever form.

Many who read depositions most carefully seem to locate evidence of an elusive speaking subject when a deposition appears to *depart from* convention, to exceed legal formulae. Whether or not the devil is in the details, the deponent is seen to be. According to Gowing, although church court depositions "cannot be taken as a reliable transcription of oral narrative, many testimonies are notably individual and appear to be at least partly verbatim reports; in them, the formulaic phrases of the clerical style mingle with words and phrases that look as if they were remembered, and recorded, in their original detail."[104] Bailey argues that "Natural idioms, expletives and feelings frequently escaped the legalistic net, leaving some sense of the 'real' responses of speakers"; Gaskill suggests that "we should make a virtue of apparent 'distortions' present in the recorded words of our forebears as the very means by which to recover the true nature of their experiences, and even hear their angry and anxious voices rising from the shallows and silences of the past."[105] While Orlin reminds us that "some of the most arresting particulars were undoubtedly invented,"[106] these details capture readers' attention precisely to the extent that they "look as if" they exceed or erupt out of the restraints of convention. Just as Catherine Gallagher and Stephen Greenblatt describe their preference for "a vehement and cryptic particularity,"[107] so the unusual, even the bizarre, stands out as the marker of the historically authentic, the true because unpredictable and unconventional. Even as scholars have reappraised depositions, finding in them evidence of shared values rather than particular experiences, they have also dwelt on the idiosyncratic or individuated in their content.

Two of the depositions printed in the collection *Reading Early Modern Women* are presented as noteworthy precisely because of this eruption of the arresting and excessive detail. Loreen Giese selects a deposition in which George Ireland testifies that Joane Waters sucked on John Newton's neck to raise three spots by which she claimed she had "marcked him for her owne." According to Giese, "The accuracy of Ireland's account is impossible to determine; however, the unusual particularity with which he describes Waters's 'marcking' strongly suggests that he gave an accurate account."[108] In the Star Chamber deposition of Lady Elizabeth Vaux, Mary Blackstone particularly values "the sense of her voice that may be gained from her choice of descriptors (e.g., 'buslinge,' 'hurliburlie') or signs of independence and agency that qualify her self-characterization . . . as being 'fearefull'."[109] In such instances, the research process puts us in the oddly uncomfortable position of legal personnel and, in common law courts, juries; like them, we assess these narratives, looking for just the right balance of the conventional and the peculiar. The "heads-up" effect of the odd detail is worth questioning. If early modern listeners would find most plausible a story that was most conventional, can we simply reverse that process, finding most veracious those stories that are least conventional? The appearance of a vivid adjective or a slang term in a deposition might not necessarily signal authenticity. How are we to determine which are "real words" and which are "formulas" or impositions? Might not self-expression occur through rather than despite convention?

The Hole-in-the-Wall Convention or What Is a Legal Fiction?

Many of the collections of depositions I have discussed include at least one that addresses the conditions that made eyewitnessing possible.[110] Frances Lamb's deposition of September 1697, as presented in Frith's *Women and History* collection, explains her industrious efforts to secure a good view: "the wall which divided the bedchamber of Mrs. Weston from the room where [I] was then in, being an old decayed wall of plaster and an old ragged hanging before it, with [my] fingers [I] very easily made a hole, and through the old hanging and shattered wall [I] then saw Mrs. Weston in naked bed and her apprentice Frank Alchin lying upon her naked body in his clothes."[111] This deposition depicts Frances as a very determined peeper; it also helps explain precisely how she could have seen as much as the deposition describes. Martin Ingram has argued that the church court's own standards of proof promoted actions such as Frances's: "The various activities such as peering through a window or bringing witnesses to look too were specifically laid down in canon law as acceptable modes of proof. In short, these spying cases did not represent normal, spontaneous neighbourly behaviour but carefully planned, *legally purposeful* activity."[112]

While acknowledging that early modern households had abundant holes of one kind and another, many historians describe the frequent references to peepholes as conventional, that is, as a requirement of authoritative, credible speech as much as a description of a particular built environment or of the logistics of purposeful peeping.[113] For them, the peephole is a kind of legal fiction that enables the witnessing on which church courts depend: at the level of narrative, the bodies and acts described only exist from the observer's point of view and can only be entered into evidence and subjected to legal scrutiny from his or her perspective. Whether or not the holes actually existed, they argue, the convention of the hole in the wall authorized observers' knowledge while it also preserved their reputations by placing a barrier between them and those they viewed as transgressors, keeping the observer unseen. Depositions depict observers as imposed on but also drawn in by the sights and sounds that grab their attention, that compel them to watch and report. Catherine Richardson argues that the deponent's self is defined in relation to and in distinction from the persons he or she describes and those persons' actions; the peephole allows the deponent to have been present but not fully, an observer but not really a participant, in the know but uncorrupted by that knowledge. As Richardson explains, she is "not arguing that such a hole did not exist, rather about the reasons for *saying* one existed."[114] As George Haggerty argues of eighteenth-century accounts of witnessing sodomy, "For the obvious reason that proximity implies guilty association, then, such accounts are often framed as 'keyhole testimony,' in which an observer watches certain sexual activities from a distance and then reports them."[115] Shielding the witness from the imputation of sexual participation, these accounts also, Haggerty emphasizes, position the hearer or reader of the resulting story as the voyeur of a scene framed by the borders of the peephole that enables and restricts access to it. Richardson's and Haggerty's work suggests that witnesses must labor to insist that they are outsiders rather than insiders. That status is an achievement, not a given, and it is precarious. While the "hole-in-the-wall" convention works to protect and enable the third-person observer in church courts, the fact that the peephole then becomes a convention in erotic texts suggests that its effects were complicated. It might attach the viewer to the spectacle, enabling erotic response precisely by limiting participation and liability; it might secure a position for the voyeur by framing and focusing the spectacle; it might function as a reminder that stories, like spaces and erotic scenarios, are not contained. There is always a chink. There is always room for one more. That depositions insist that observers are not participants suggests all the ways in which, at some level, they were.

Lena Orlin takes issue with the emphasis on the peephole as a legal fiction in her valuable study of privacy in the early modern period. For her, the question is whether there really were so many chinks in the walls and also whether peeping was accidental—a function of truly permeable walls—or intentional. Orlin wants to emphasize that walls were flimsy, temporary, fissured by keyholes, windows, cracks, and knotholes, in short, by holes accidental and intentional: "Peepholes provided the grounds for narrative, dramatic, and probably also legal fictions without themselves being necessarily fictional." She concludes that "The mass of evidence suggests that there were indeed holes that were not what Laura Gowing calls 'conventional motifs' or 'legal fictions'."[116] But surely Gowing's point, which she shares with many social historians, is not that there were no holes. Her emphasis is that they figure so consistently in testimony that they function as a conventional form of self-authorization and self-protection. To work as a convention, as she says, the claim to have peeped through a hole needs to be plausible, needs to be made in a built environment in which it is easy to believe that a spy could find a hole through which to see or at which to listen. What is more, the peephole has the same effect on the narrative and on its object, the person spied on, whether it is real or fictive, whether it was found or created.

Orlin also argues that there was a moral imperative to peep into and report on others' conduct and that privacy was very hard to find or maintain because of the porosity of boundaries. People felt they had a right to know what their housemates and neighbors were up to. Under these conditions, peepholes were "instruments of resistance. They restored the old communal conventions of shared knowledge and mutual surveillance. Any newly erected boundary could be breached by a defiant chink or cranny." What is the difference between resistant peeping and what Ingram calls purposeful peeping? In both cases, we have witnesses who go out of their way to collect evidence against their neighbors. In both cases, the evidence they collect serves the project of policing the conduct of others. In both cases, this curiosity is an accepted and even expected community practice. Orlin sketches out sharply opposed options: "Either there was broad acceptance that there were holes in early modern walls, windows, floors, and doors, as is argued here, or, as Martin Ingram believes, there was collusion among all the parties involved, including litigants, defendants, and officers of the courts."[117] Are these really the options? Again, the convention of mentioning the hole through which one witnessed what was happening next door can only function to authorize speech if litigants, defendants, and officers of the court all know that such holes do indeed exist. This feature of the built environment underwrote and legitimized a reliable way to authorize one's testimony.

Defendants must have questioned the basis of testimony against them, pressing against this convention when it served their purposes. Capp describes a case in which a woman accused of sexual impropriety challenged what witnesses said they could see, "claiming that very little of the bed could be seen through the narrow gap over the chamber door" and that a parlor door "invariably swung shut of its own accord" so one could not see through it.[118] This example suggests that the legal fictions required to authorize eyewitness testimony were as open to challenge as the testimony itself. The fact that they were conventional did not mean that they were beyond discussion.

In this debate, the question becomes, from my point of view, what is gained and what is lost if we think of the hole in the wall as a "fiction," a fiction many deponents and clerks turn to in order to authorize narratives presented in evidence. If the speaking "I" is a fiction that readers today have to create for themselves, the hole in the wall is a fiction that the documents themselves provide to us. While identifying something as a legal fiction sometimes works to explain why we should stop talking about it, it might instead open a new conversation about what a fiction means, what it enables or constrains, and how "fictions" can outlast the original conditions of their production. For literary critics, surely identifying something as a fiction is an invitation to begin rather than an excuse to conclude.

When I have taught depositions, I have found that English majors ask questions that differ from those that guide supposedly textual or literary readings of depositions and that focus on the role of the witness as crucial to the story. I concede that students' questions result as much from the ways that they are untutored or undisciplined readers as from their training as literary critics. But attending to what they ask offers a useful experiment in the consequences of approaching a deposition as a story among other stories, since my students always read depositions as part of a mix that includes plays, poems, jests, and speeches. Let us take, for example, a 1598 deposition from the Bridewell Hospital Records, reproduced in Crawford and Gowing's *Women's Worlds*, in which Margaret Browne claims to have seen Clement Underhill and Michael Fludd engage in adultery:

Margaret Browne the wife of Henry Browne, citizen and stationer of London dwelling in Houndsditch in the parish of St Botolph without Bishopsgate in the ward of Bishopsgate London saith that upon the thirteenth day of this present month of May 1598 being Saturday Michael Fludd and Clement Underhill the wife of John Underhill were making merry together in the house of the said John Underhill being the next house unto this deponent's house in the parish and ward aforesaid he the said John being from home. And as they were eating their victualls Underhill's wife said unto Fludd these words eat no more cheese for that it will make your gear short and I mean to have a good turn of you soon, immediately after that went up into her chamber and lay upon her bed and there continued until six of the clock or thereabouts at what time she shut in her shop windows and went up unto him with a rapier in her hand and asked him whether he had spoken with all his friends or not whereupon the said Fludd took the rapier out of her hand laying it aside took her in his arms and brought her to the bed's foot and took up her clothes and she put her hand into his hose and he kissed her and pulled her upon him upon the bed's feet. And after that they went to the bed's side and he taking her in his arms did cast her upon the bed. He plucked up her clothes to her thighs, she plucked them up higher (whereby this deponent saw not only her hose being seawater green colour and also her bare thighs) then he went up to her upon the bed and putting down his hose had carnal copulation with her and having so done he wiped his yard on her smock and this deponent had in the meantime called up the said Henry Browne the husband of this deponent to see this deed, who came and saw Fludd come from the bed with his hose down whereupon this deponent's husband went away and would see no more. Then this deponent saw the said Fludd to go to a pail or a tub of water in the same chamber and washed his yard then Underhill's wife departed from him to fetch a pot of beer and out of the cupboard in the table took bread and butter which they did eat together and then she left up the pot and said to him, Here now I drink to thee.[119]

This deposition is crammed with arresting details: the detrimental effects of dairy consumption on gear performance, sea-water-green hose, yard hygiene, lunch preparation, and a postcoital toast.

While, as I have discussed, many scholars take vivid details as evidence of a deponent's voice, my students' concerns were slightly different. My students focused less on whether the remarkable details originated in Clement and Michael's conduct, or Margaret Browne's narrative or a clerk's shaping of it, and more on the relevance of these details to the charge. The very features that distinguish this deposition as evidence of social practices make it seem as if the court considering sex was interested in more than sex or as if its definition of adultery was more inclusive than theirs. How did these details help make the story seem true and the adultery domesticated? What is the importance of key objects, such as the rapier, in the progress of this story? Students in a course on the drama are trained to notice objects since they tend to be scarce and freighted with meaning, especially in Renaissance plays. If a weapon is mentioned, it will usually reappear at a climactic moment to effect the action. As a consequence, students in such a course expect the rapier's return.[120]

My students were also interested in the shape of the story: the gradual escalation from a meal, to the challenge with the rapier, to sex and then the denouement after Fludd "had carnal copulation with" Underhill. After all, sex is the most tersely and formulaically described exchange between the two. What is the relevance of the protracted negotiations before they have sex? After the couple has sex, why isn't the story over from the observer's point of view? Margaret's husband, whom she has called "to see this deed . . . went away and would see no more." Why does she stay glued to the peephole? Doesn't this suggest that her own curiosity is part of the story here and that this curiosity extends beyond the sex act? And why would a clerk continue to record details beyond those that describe the act in question? For my students, the literary question has to do with emplotment—where does the story begin and end?—and with audience or purpose—why would this story and all its apparently extraneous detail be considered evidence of adultery? For example, how is eating together—before and after sex—as important to the story of adultery as intercourse? Their response suggests that our attention to depositions as stories might need to include a different range of questions than those that have concerned most professional readers of these texts. As we have seen, while depositions are marshaled as evidence of many things, "close textual analysis" of them tends to focus on the deponent's interiority as manifested in voice and on word choice. What if we thought of the deposition not as giving us access to Margaret or to Clement and Michael or to the clerk but as what historians who work most extensively with these records would call it: a story? And what if we then evaluated it as such? As the object of analysis in itself?

What does this deposition tell us about the genre of the adultery story? What does it have in common with other stories of adultery? What distinguishes it? What does it tell us about the parameters of the adultery story: that is, when it begins and when it ends, what is included and what is not? What kinds of functions might we imagine such stories had and for whom? What does this story and others like it tell us about a community and a legal system invested in inviting, recording, and acting on such stories?

To sustain the widely repeated admission that church court records offer us only limited and problematic access to individuated subjects would be to undermine the interests and purposes that send many to the archives. Perhaps those literary critics committed to archival work are especially eager to find in archives what we do not have at home, what is not in the Norton anthology or on Early English Books Online. As Karen Newman points out, "the temptation to seek the marginal voice or lost women's speech, to read records as conveying the real the literary cannot, frequently overcomes better judgment."[121] But while Newman defends the value of literary modes of reading, as I do here, our emphases differ in that she ardently defends the literary as an object of analysis and disparages certain kinds of archival work. While I share her skepticism about what the archive can yield, I recognize that many historians share that very skepticism. Rather than turn away from the archive, we need to bring new questions and strategies to it. I argue for an interdisciplinary approach, one that aspires to create historical knowledge through literary analysis of a wide and various textual field. Like Valerie Traub, I attempt to "create knowledge of the past while keeping the past productively unknown."[122] Recognizing what we cannot know is an important part of creating historical knowledge, rather than a retreat from that project.

The importance of questions literary critics are trained to ask in the creation of historical knowledge is evident in the work of two historians who examine well-documented scandals among aristocrats, the Overbury scandal and trial of the earl of Castlehaven. Both cases shared terrain with church courts in their concern with sexual misconduct, although they did not appear in church courts because they focused on felonies: murder in one case and rape and sodomy in the other. They provoked a level of representation unimaginable regarding the local grievances and outrages that preoccupy the church courts. They were more visible, and their stakes were higher: Anne Turner, the earl of Castlehaven, and two of his servants were executed. Perhaps because everyone now knows what is and is not on the record regarding these much-studied cases and because many of the key players were aristocrats, the loudmouths of the historical record no one is straining to hear, historians have shifted their attention away from what really happened or the protagonists' interiority.

In his study of the processes by which the Overbury scandal became scandalous, Alistair Bellany contends that "the truth about the murder matters less than how the murder was represented and perceived," "talked about and given meaning" by contemporaries. Bellany's method turns a challenge into an opportunity. Although the superabundance of material related to the case presents a problem for anyone attempting to "investigate the mystery of Overbury's death, . . . studied as evidence of the vitality and diversity of scribal news culture, the plethora of reports becomes positively enlightening."[123] In her detailed study of the trial of the earl of Castlehaven, Cynthia Herrup recommends shifting focus from "which rendition of the trial is correct" to "which was persuasive to whom, when, and why"; we should ask, she suggests, "not *if* Castlehaven was guilty, but why knowing if he was seemed so important." She advises embracing "agnosticism on the verdict" since there will always be things we cannot know and trying "to find a balance on less solid ground, instead of trying to avoid it." This unsteady ground is the literary critic's boggy turf. Finally, she recommends that "textual remnants" of the law should be considered "within the demands of genre."[124] To concede that legal records have a genre is to demand tactics of literary analysis. The questions Bellany and Herrup pose are the kinds of questions with which literary critics have considerable experience. Acknowledging this might be a spur to engaging literary critics as experts on these very issues. The approach Herrup and Bellany take up suggests solutions to some of the methodological problems posed by court records and validates methods of reading that are sometimes disparaged in the hunt to pin down a speaking subject. Searching for a deposition's origin, we can lose track of its functions and effects; looking for the speaking subject, we can lose track of why capturing her seems so important.

The oft-repeated claim that depositions are stories might be taken not as a reminder of what they cannot prove but as an invitation to employ slow, wary reading practices, relating one text to others, defining kinds (such as the adultery story), grouping texts in these categories, and attending to how form, convention, audience, and venue shape textual content and consequence. Obviously, it is not reasonable to ask these kinds of questions when depositions are being used for quantification: patterns of slander charges, numbers of female plaintiffs, the types of courtship gifts given, etc. But when the pace slows, as it often does, so that the reader can consider particular depositions and deponents and the texture and shape of these stories, then it seems not only fair but helpful to point out the relevance of literary critics' expertise to the project of creating historical knowledge.

What this might mean is paying more attention to features those who rely on depositions already observe: the relations among the person telling the story, the characters he or she describes, and the clerk who teases out and takes down the deposition; the texts' status as stories with beginnings, middles, and ends and their debts to genre as well as event; settings and props; and language use. But it also means resisting the practice of surreptitiously investing these texts with exciting discoveries their readers also admit are not there: authors who know and can effect their intentions; voice as a reliable expression and therefore evidence of an accessible, self-aware, coherent subject; creativity unhampered by the venue, audience, or materials at hand; an "original" text accessible to an editor; or a clear boundary between the literary and the documentary, stories and evidence. A lot of effort has gone into casting doubt on these assumptions. Reactivating that doubt can be generative for readers in the archives, whatever their disciplinary affiliations. The reading practices I am suggesting contribute to the production of historical knowledge precisely by freighting and vexing it. Taking seriously the invitation to consider depositions as stories, an invitation, I want to reiterate, that historians themselves extend, can generate more interesting—and interdisciplinary—engagements with the textual traces of the early modern past. Mobilizing literary analysis will lead us to find both less and more in depositions. The result will be both new historical knowledge and an enhanced understanding of the operations, range, and effects of conventions we sometimes call literary. If there is fiction in the archives, literary criticism needs to be there as well.

Chapter 5

The Rule of Relation

Domestic Advice Literature and Its Readers

In the anonymous play *A Pleasant Conceited Comedie, Wherein is shewed how a man may chuse a good Wife from a bad* (1602), young Master Arthur physically and verbally abuses his wife, advising her that the best thing she can do for him is to "die sodainly." To hasten this outcome so that he can marry a prostitute, he gives her what he thinks is rat poison. It is, instead, a narcotic, made of poppy and mandrake, which only makes her appear dead. Arthur promptly marries his mistress but soon realizes his mistake: she spends freely, suits herself, defies him, and wishes for his death as devoutly as he wished for that of his first wife. In fact, she turns him in for murder, at which point his first wife reveals that she is still alive and thereby exonerates Arthur of a murder charge because, as she explains sagely, "Murther there cannot be where none is kild."[1] The play ends with Arthur pointing the moral that a good wife is long suffering and eager to please and will defend her husband's reputation and forgive his attempts to kill her, while a bad wife is a lustful, proud, willful prostitute who will gleefully try to get her husband charged with murder. This conclusion is rather obvious. As Jeremy Lopez speculates, "The audience's pleasure is bound up in watching what Arthur must go through to see what the audience already knows."[2] Arthur's process of learning by experience might not work out for everyone who poisons his first wife so as to enjoy a "second choice." It also demands a lot from the wife.

Reading was one alternative. A huge body of advice literature targeted at potential young Arthurs survives from the sixteenth and seventeenth centuries. But reading remained, as we will see, messy, risky, and interactive, rooted in and feeding back on experience rather than its alternative. Armchair

Arthurs could not count on staying out of the fray. Nor is domestic advice undramatic. Domestic advice included its own reprobates and heroes, its own scripts for performance, its own dramas of trial and error, suffering and regret, even if they are not quite as violent as young Arthur's. In this widely available literature of domestic advice, we might include guides to choosing a spouse, achieving a happy marriage, and running a household and family; printed collections of sermons; and volumes teaching cooking, husbandry, gardening, and medicine. Since magazines, newspapers, websites, television shows, and books bombard us today with suggestions on the same topics, these books document both the enduring market for domestic advice and the changing content of this advice. As described in advice literature, the early modern family and household sometimes appear very different not only from households today but from cherished assumptions about early modern households (as the birth place, for instance, of the "modern" marriage and family). In large part because of its abundance—there were many of these texts and some were printed many times—advice literature is a precious historical resource, offering page after page on topics such as marriage, household management, and child rearing. For readers now, it offers a treasure trove of information— domestic advice is heavily quoted—as well as a methodological challenge since it is also often disparaged as evidence.

Works of domestic advice sought to announce their relationship to other texts, to forge relationships to readers, and to direct those readers' relationships. Natalie Davis has argued that the printed book is "a carrier of relationships," helping establish "new relations" among people and cultural traditions. Building on this provocative comment, Natalie Glaisyer and Sara Pennell have argued that didactic texts in particular "establish and maintain relationships . . . between individuals and communities by being borrowed and lent" and by supplementing or substituting for an advisor to the reader: "The popularity of dialogue and question and answer formats in these books might be seen as a textual approximation of what the manual 'stood' for: a conversation between the 'expert' and the reader."[3] Thus these texts' form—their status as what might be called literature—is central to their project both of relating to readers and informing those readers' relationships. This is especially true of the advice on which I focus here, since these texts explicitly carry, establish, and maintain relationships by addressing how relationships should be conducted. They are, then, "relations" in two of the senses of that term I wish to activate: a verbal account and a relationship. While my earlier chapters have examined the contingency of truth claims on social relations, I here approach

true relations from another angle, examining how textual relations attempt
to shape social relations and stand as themselves vehicles of relation between
advisor and reader. But my emphasis remains on the interpretive demands
and opportunities that result for the reader pulled into relation and invited to
construct relations.

In this chapter, I compare how scholars from various disciplines describe
the value of these texts and then how they actually use them in support of their
arguments, building toward two case studies, of Miles Coverdale's translation
of Heinrich Bullinger's *The Christen State of Matrimonye* (in 1541) and William Gouge's *Of Domesticall Duties* (first published in 1622). Since the genre's
content has been much discussed, I focus instead on the books' engagement
with readers and their use of what might be called the literary, particularly
figures that posit relationships, such as simile, metaphor, and analogy, to foster
true domestic relations. In Gouge's exhaustive tome, I find a perhaps unlikely
modern analogue for how scholars might read.

As we will see, Bullinger and Gouge do not simply dictate how to conduct
one's relationships. Nor do they lay out analogies in the simplistic way that
is sometimes assumed: as the commonwealth is to the family, as Christ is to
his church so should the husband be to his wife. Instead, they instruct readers
in an interpretive practice that not only grasps relations between one kind of
relationship and another, between one biblical passage and another, between
ideals and daily life, but also crafts such relations in a skilled, flexible, and not
wholly predictable way. Domestic advice, in other words, instructs its readers
how to exceed its own intentions. It is not simply that readers resist advice.
In accepting invitations to posit relations of various kinds, they put advice to
their own uses and chart their own paths through mazes of relation.

Textual Relations of Domestic Relations

Some of these books explicitly address men like Arthur. For example, Roland
du Jardin's *A Discourse of the Married and Single Life* (1621) advises "the Masculine Reader" that "the benefit he shall get by reading of this, is, that though
perhaps hee cannot bee forewarned by wisdome to prevent [the incurable mis-
eries of marriage], yet he may be forewarned with patience to endure them;
which is the onely drift which herein is aymed at." The table of contents to
Alexander Niccholes's *A Discourse of Marriage and Wiving* (1615) concludes,
"If by this Jewell thou a good wife hit, / Thanke God that ere this Booke was

bought, or writ."[4] As these examples suggest, much of the literature of domestic advice was written largely by men and often addressed specifically to them, advising them both on their own conduct and on how to manage women.[5] Yet works in which mothers offer advice to their children, which have been much studied in the last few decades, demand inclusion in the capacious genre we call domestic advice literature precisely because they complicate how we define it. Maternal advice sometimes differed from what we might call paternal or pastoral advice in terms of its address to the reader, its claims to authority, and its purported goals.[6]

Just as all domestic advice was not written by or addressed to men, so it was not invariably Puritan or even Protestant. While the Reformation added urgency to the defense of marriage as an estate equal in honor to celibacy and made divorce a contentious topic in treatises on marriage, the writers of post-Reformation domestic advice occupied positions across the confessional spectrum; their advice sometimes borrowed from or restated pre-Reformation ideals or addressed the particular concerns of Catholic families and households in England after the Reformation. What was new, as Mary Beth Rose has argued, was "the emphasis, elaboration, and wide distribution" of domestic advice in the late sixteenth and seventeenth centuries.[7] In other words, the prescriptions for social relations were not necessarily new but the delivery system—the textual relation of domestic relations—was.

Some have argued that domestic advice was "bourgeois" or "middle class." For instance, in his still invaluable guide to *Middle-Class Culture in Elizabethan England*, Louis B. Wright argues that "most of these treatises were patently written from the middle-class point of view and express the ideals of the rising mercantile classes."[8] As our understanding of social and economic class in the early modern period has grown more nuanced, we have also achieved more precise knowledge of the range of positions from and ends to which such advice might be both proffered and consumed. Some critics have pointed out the ways in which the books themselves facilitate social mobility, enabling readers to adopt the manners and mores of their social betters or working to discipline readers by imposing on them values that were not necessarily their "own."[9] Householders might have purchased books and assigned others to do the edifying reading. Obviously, many household subordinates could not read these books even if they wanted to. But reading was not the only way to achieve access to their content. One might listen as a master or mistress, parent, or spouse read aloud. The fact that many printed conduct books were based on sermons should remind us that their advice was available aurally to large numbers of churchgoers.[10] People also had access to some of the content in the pithy form of printed broadside tables of domestic advice, which could be affixed to walls, where they might serve as an aid to memory.[11]

Even if it is hard to be sure how influential these treatises were, the huge numbers of them that were published and the many editions of certain titles can be taken as evidence that many households had, as Wright puts it, the "benefit of printed guidance."[12] In their work on printed playbooks, Alan Farmer and Zachary Lesser rely on reprints as evidence of publishers' informed speculations about what would sell.[13] Including printers and publishers in our consideration of domestic advice might enable us to see a particular title's relation not only to other printed works of advice but to other works by a given publisher. Farmer and Lesser suggest that plays did not sell as well as ballads because they were much longer and therefore more expensive; we might suspect that the market for the longest works of domestic advice would similarly have been limited by their expense and heft. Investing in a brief work, such as one of the broadside tables available from itinerant peddlers, would have entailed a different commitment than investing in a massive tome such as the 700-page *Of Domesticall Duties*, to which we will return below.[14] Who had the motivation and money to buy such volumes? Where one lived also determined access. These books would have been for sale in bookshops, most of which were located in London, so householders in the city were probably most likely to encounter and buy them.[15] Yet they also circulated widely through the Atlantic world; well into the eighteenth century, advice literature in English available in Massachusetts or Jamaica had been printed in England.[16]

Although reprints are one way of gauging popularity, and I include that information here, what constitutes the "popular" remains a question and a problem.[17] Some scholars doubt whether the numerous books published offering domestic advice, and the numerous editions of some of those books, have anything to do with whether people wanted to buy them or, having bought them, actually read them. Wright asserts that "the book of domestic advice became a work regarded as necessary in the household of every honest and thoughtful citizen," but, in saying so, he homogenizes domestic advice into "the book" and assumes he knows the citizen reader and how he or she used that book. In contrast, many wonder whether books of domestic advice were regarded as "necessary" and, if so, whether they were necessary as status objects or as fonts of vital information and instruction.[18] It has even been argued that survival might indicate underuse; according to Glaisyer and Pennell, for example, "It is indeed an irony of book history that the volumes of didactic material that survive today were those that were often little used or carefully preserved in libraries or closets."[19]

Domestic advice literature has long been assumed to be subliterary—background or context. Offering what remains the most comprehensive guide to the genre, Chilton Latham Powell insists that "the domestic book is utilitarian rather than literary, and whenever a passage of some artistic merit occurs . . . it is, like water in the desert, refreshing but seemingly out of place." Powell praises Robert Snawsel's expansion of an Erasmian dialogue, *A Looking Glasse for Maried Folkes* (1610), as "almost as good as a play," boasting "real literary qualities," but even this exception falls short of the literary mark because "its purpose seems to be utilitarian rather than artistic."[20] Powell's distinction between the utilitarian and the artistic is anachronistic. Artistic or "really literary" texts were assumed, even feared, to have the power to shape their readers. From the point of view of antitheatricalists, for example, the drama had the potential to change character and conduct in ways the preacher of a sermon or the author of domestic advice might envy as well as decry. Some theatergoers appear to have actively sought to be instructed and improved by the drama. Charles Whitney argues that early modern responses to drama suggest "an early modern, affirmative or pragmatic aesthetic aiming to find benefit or use," that is, an aesthetic that makes nonsense of Powell's distinction between the utilitarian and the artistic.[21] Furthermore, as we have seen, those early modern readers who documented their reading practice seem to have read purposefully, seeking for ways to put their reading to use. Didacticism, then, might lie not in an author's intention or a book's genre as much as a particular reader's use of a given work.[22]

Despite his reservations, Powell addresses the domestic book as a genre, identifying its four principal subjects (religious and secular perspectives on marriage; the legal process of contracting marriage; spousal relations; and government of the household and family) and discussing its typical stylistic features (including biblical and classical references and examples, as well as the use of dialogue "to add variety, which it usually failed to do, inasmuch as the writer, without changing his character or point of view, merely shouted through different masks"). He concludes that "as a rule . . . the style of the domestic book is pretty flat, pedantic, heavy. It reminds one of the atmosphere of a Puritan household."[23] In one sentence, Powell simultaneously disparages "Puritan" texual and domestic relations.

Powell concedes that his distinctions between the literary and nonliterary are "purely arbitrary." The arbitrary nature of such distinctions is one reason that so few of the scholars who quote from these texts tackle the question of whether they are "literature" and what that would mean. By treating the domestic conduct book as a genre and interrogating its formal and stylistic features, Powell opens up an approach whose potential few have exploited. Yet recent readings of some of these texts show that they reward sustained attention because they are more internally contradictory, nuanced, and expressive than they might at first appear. The fact that they announce their own purpose as instruction does not close the book on their intentions or effects. Like popular print accounts of Catholic treason or of witchcraft, domestic conduct books function inefficiently as delivery mechanisms for didacticism. The reader might be as puzzled as to what he has learned from them as from a Shakespeare play. The effect of that puzzlement is to be left to one's own devices to craft a lesson, to determine the relation between what the text offers and what one needs. For me, taking these texts as literature means reading cover to cover without a set of topics in mind, without mining them for evidence, in order to attend to how they convey their advice and how they relate to their readers. Doing so leads me back to their status as evidence, evidence particularly of interpretive practices—which turn out to be crucial to domestical duty.

Prescription Versus Practice

It has long been the convention to remind readers that the advice literature on which I am focusing here records "prescriptions" for how people should behave rather than descriptions of how they actually did. Printed advice, we are warned, is a poor guide to the social "practice" that is often contrasted to prescription. Advice literature's limitations as a form of evidence are often attributed to its status as "literary" as if literary and useful or descriptive are inevitably oppositions. For example, in an influential essay in 1981, Kathleen M. Davies explains that

> In recent years social historians have questioned the use of such
> sources as direct evidence of attitudes and behaviour, and have
> mounted a sustained attack on the theory that their contents can be
> taken at face value. Demographic studies show that literary sources
> have only a limited use in social history, since the patterns of
> behaviour which they describe may be highly unrepresentative. . . .

It would be very difficult now to maintain that the conduct books can be used on their own to show how men and women actually behaved.[24]

For Davies, "literary sources" seem to include all published writing or all discourse in wide circulation. Comparing this influential admonition to Powell's and Wright's dismissals of the literary claims of advice literature suggests that domestic advice literature is subliterary when the question is aesthetic value but suddenly becomes literary when emphasis is placed on its compromised evidentiary value. It is literary only to the extent that it is not reliable. The suggestion that it can be used only in relation to other forms of evidence rather than "on [its] own" gestures toward a relational reading practice that, I would argue, all sources require. But the caveats tend to focus on conduct books or advice literature rather than "demographic studies." The insistence that prescription should not be mistaken for description, that it is distinct from practice, is now commonplace. This distrust of advice literature as proof of behavior can be condensed into an admonition as terse as this one from Garthine Walker: "Do not be fooled by the prevalence of certain patriarchal discourses."[25]

Many scholars express particular unease about what advice literature can tell us about women's experiences and attitudes. Anthony Fletcher, for instance, advises that, because "[the didactic literature was written by men, some of it specifically to instruct women," it can "tell us how men wanted women to see the gender order, their place in it and themselves" but nothing at all "about what they thought."[26] Elaborating on a similar distinction between "what women were told, and possibly what they heard" on the one hand and "what women as a whole actually thought or how they went about their daily lives" on the other, Amy Erickson stresses the disparity between male writers' presumption that all women would marry and the demographic "fact" that "most adult women in the population at a given time were not married—they were either widowed or they had never married."[27] Similarly, many historians emphasize that conduct books have little or nothing to say about the many households that did not have a male head or depended on women's paid work; the ideal of a wife at home and a man going out to work simply did not pertain to many English households.[28] Recent studies of manhood, and of disparities and conflicts among men, have likewise revealed that some prescriptions we find in domestic conduct books were irrelevant to the lives and concerns of many men as well women.

But if we are frequently reminded that prescriptions did not always determine or describe practices, what is our evidence of practices, of what most women and men thought, and how they "went about their lives"? Legal records have often been considered the counterpoint to prescriptive texts, the real against the ideal. But as we have seen in the previous chapter, many scholars now describe court records as stories and value them as evidence of shared values rather than of particular actions or events. Depositions are most often described as evidence of "the underlying assumptions about how [social relationships] ought to work and how people ought to act," making them sound more like advice literature than unlike it.[29] When we look closely at court records, then, we find that they cannot hold down their job of representing the hard as against the soft, practice as opposed to prescription, the nonliterary against the literary.

Scholars turn to a range of other sources to bridge the gap between prescription and practice, including letters, diaries, wills, and account books. Each kind raises its own problems, of course.[30] According to Keith Wrightson, for example, "The picture [of marriage] which emerges" from diaries "indicates the *private* existence of a strong complementary and companionate ethos, side by side with, and often overshadowing, theoretical adherence to the doctrine of male authority and *public* female subordination."[31] Note that here prescription is literally performed or practiced; the ethos that exists in private is informed by prescriptions, which advise spousal companionship as well as female subordination, and so might also be viewed as "theoretical adherence" to an ideal, rather than a covert subversion or evasion of prescriptions. What is presented as a sharp opposition—private versus public, existence versus theoretical adherence—rapidly breaks down. These are clearly two sides of the same coin.

Many readers of *The Taming of the Shrew* have read the play's ending as instituting just such an arrangement by which Katharina will submit in public but remain excitingly untamed in private. Anthony Fletcher refers to this interpretation of the play when he adduces passages from conduct books celebrating marital sexuality, particularly one from William Gouge, to support the claim that "the normal rules of patriarchy . . . did not apply behind the chamber door." In other words, prescription dictates its own suspension in some areas of life. As a consequence, he ventures, "It is at least possible that many married couples, especially those who lived in households full of servants and children, did sustain a kind of public and private separation of the ordering of their married lives such as the fictional Petruchio appears to have had in mind for himself and Kate."[32] But in *Shrew*, Petruchio proposes only the opposite arrangement, supposedly so that he can co-opt Katharina's shrewishness as his own idea: "Tis bargained twixt us twain, being alone, / That she shall still be curst in company" (2.1.296–97).[33] Whether, after the play is over, a companionate ethos will prevail behind the scenes, while Katharina performs submission in public, is anybody's guess. We will discuss Shakespeare's status as evidence at greater length in the next chapter. At this point, I want to emphasize just how quickly the discussion of practice or lived experience returns to the literary, whether in terms of conduct literature, read to yield clues to how prescriptions might have scripted daily performances, or of court records, which turn out to be stories, or of a Shakespeare play, which provides the terms through which quotidian bargains can be construed. While we are frequently enjoined to stop trying to squeeze blood from the unyielding stones of advice literature and to delve into "the archives" instead, those archives, as I have tried to show in other chapters, offer more of the same rather than something completely different.

It is also possible to complicate the prescription/practice divide, and the way it is itself gendered, by thinking of these texts as literary and asking whose purposes they serve. Davies argues that advice literature catered to a bourgeois readership by presenting them to themselves as their own ideal: "It may be, therefore, that what we are seeing in the early seventeenth century is a collection of descriptive, rather than prescriptive texts, written by authors who were not advocating new ideals for marriage but were describing the best form of bourgeois marriage as they knew it" and "disseminating more widely a rather unchanging style of successful bourgeois family life, at a time when the thrifty and prudent habits of such a life may have appealed to some of their social superiors." This unchanging style of family life was the gendered division of labor, by which what the husband accumulated abroad the wife managed at home.[34] Challenging Davies's insistence on continuity and description, Lorna Hutson argues that she "devalues the genre, refusing to allow it any creative cultural force." In trying to refute the claim that the Reformation transformed attitudes toward marriage and thereby elevated women's status, Davies underestimates the "novelty and prescriptive force" of post-Reformation advice on marriage. Hutson counters that these texts "were not *descriptive* of existing practices, but advocative of practices currently ignored, undervalued or even actively disdained by their readers." As she points out, the spousal division of labor is "too symmetrical to be anything other than a fiction." Why bother to invent and repeat this fiction? Hutson argues that the "point" of this story "was not, primarily, to guarantee *in reality* the husband's governance of his wife, but to prove, through a persuasive fiction of the well-governed wife" the husband's credentials as a man among men.[35] For Hutson, then, prescriptions had practical uses—cultural or prescriptive force as she puts it—outside the home precisely as fictions, fictions that help promote relations among men and are thus evidence of historical realities outside the home.

I might expand Hutson's discussion of functional fictions to explore their effects within the home, where they operate in a range of ways as cover stories for female assertiveness, as justifications for men's dependence on women's work, or as idealizations of female consent.[36] This would counter the implication that the "secular and practical spheres of masculine activity" are somehow more real or more consequential than the domestic sphere. But Hutson's work here is a model of what it would mean for analysis to begin rather than end with the insight that a prescription is a fiction. Hutson is also a model for thinking the complex relationship between continuity and change. In her view, prescriptions for a gendered division of domestic labor advocate a discarded model of marital relations in the interests of a newly urgent need in homosocial relations. Whether the vision of marriage and domestic life presented in texts such as *Of Domesticall Duties* is new or old, descriptive or prescriptive or advocative, questions of content are inextricable from questions of address and effect. Do they attempt to describe or advocate existing practices? Do they promote change? If so, in what cultural arena? Do they tell stories about the domestic sphere to serve extradomestic purposes? Might the same text impose different kinds of prescriptive force on or invite different kinds of engagements from differently situated readers? It is very hard to manage the flickering distinctions between the fictional and the true here, let alone prescription and practice.

Because of the repetition in domestic advice, it is particularly challenging to pin down its relation to processes of change or its historical location. Early critics, such as Powell and Wright, emphasized continuity that amounts to stasis. According to Powell, "the similarity of all such treatises is so great that one wonders what moved the different writers to repeat over and over that which had been said so often before." Powell goes on to argue that, while later books elaborated on the foundation laid by books such as *The Christen State of Matrimonye*, "the household section of the domestic book remained the same in content and point of view from start to finish" so that "to read one is to read all."[37] Just as Powell focuses on the frustrated longing of the reader whose industrious attempt to read all yields nothing new, Wright focuses on a frustrated desire for development among the genre's scholarly readers: "The literary historian who likes to trace an evolutionary development in literature will find the manuals of domestic guidance peculiarly disappointing, for there is a strange sameness in point of view and treatment in the books read by the burgher of 1558 and by his grandson in 1640. . . . Except for differences of opinion regarding divorce and occasional differences about the subordination of woman, there is far more agreement than divergence in the treatises throughout the period."[38] Wright does not imagine that the burgher of 1558 and his grandson in 1640 might read even the same advice differently. He also imagines an indifference to women's subordination shared across time, among burgher, grandson, and literary historian.

While Powell's assertion that "to read one is to read all" might be taken as permission to stop at one, many readers have found greater variety—within and among texts and across time—than Powell and Wright claimed. The simple strategy of reading widely and deeply in the genre can yield new insights. While many scholars return again and again to the same few books and even the same passages from those books, often plucked from anthologies of excerpts, those who read often-cited books cover to cover and against lesser known works turn up eye-opening surprises; they are also able to challenge assumptions that still govern generalizations about this literature and the advice it offers. Many critics emphasize enormous diversity across the genre, the idiosyncrasies of individual authors and texts and internal contradictions. Just as those who dwell on textual continuity sometimes take it as evidence of cultural consensus, so those who emphasize textual variety often interpret it as evidence of "inconsistency in the culture at large."[39]

Still, there is considerable repetition in these books, and it sometimes poses a challenge for the reader. As Kathryn Schwarz puts it, "familiarity does not diminish the power" of an image or phrase.[40] It raises rather than resolves questions. Is repetition simply a product of the shared recourse to scripture— and a lack of controversy around scripture as Powell, rather implausibly, claims? Does it indicate consensus about "family values," which might include consensus about problem areas and anxieties, or at least particularly durable ways of talking about families?[41] Prescription might be read as negative evidence, as proof of what people were *not* doing but that some thought they should be. According to Bernard Capp, "It was indeed the gulf between patriarchal ideas and social practice that prompted the writing of conduct-books."[42] Perhaps discursive repetition had its pleasures, precisely because of an indirect relation to the real. Might not some readers find comfort or provocation in reading familiar formulations, enjoy revisiting the same debate or conversation from different perspectives, turn to discourse as an end in itself rather than a means of changing conduct? Or could authors plagiarize freely because no one was paying attention—in which case, as Powell asks, why keep churning out these books at all? And why keep reading them—not only then, but now? How and why did people read domestic advice? What are we to make of it now as a form of evidence?

Reading as Doing: The Active Reader

While we must often speculate as to reader responses, important new insights have been generated by thinking about implied readers. As soon as we focus on the reader, the distinction between prescription and practice erodes. Why? Because as soon as the reader is engaging a text and its prescriptions, he or she puts them into practice or refuses to do so or adapts them in unexpected ways. Readers are inevitably agents rather than or as well as objects of advice. Prescriptions are, of course, "directions for married persons," as one title puts it, and for anyone living in relation to others. As directions, they focus on how one should act and so depend on readers to enact them, to perform prescription, thus making it practice. Sometimes advice might take the place of practice, as when one watches cooking shows or reads food magazines rather than actually cooking. But whether or not it succeeded, domestic advice sought to propel its readers into action, to get them to "practice, practice, practice."[43]

The reader might be an agent, then, when he or she complied with prescription and not only when he or she resisted it, as many authors seem to assume readers will. The self is not defined only against or outside prescriptions (if such a thing is even possible) but through them.[44] Of course, this was as true for men as for women. In fact, householders might have been especially inspired to achieve the ideal of manhood they found in advice literature and to capitalize on the privileges it assigned them. They might have found in these books not a mirror of who they were but a model of who they could be.[45]

If, as some scholars argue, these books informed true relations among groups and countries as well as individuals, providing a template for ideal relatedness, then their application to the relationships among groups was as unpredictable as their application to the relationships among individuals because, in both cases, they depended on individuals to relate, for example, ideas about marriage to ideas about political unions, using gender hierarchy to justify and describe other forms of subordination.[46] Although domestic advice might provide a resource for assessing and managing extradomestic relations, the internal contradictions in the advice and its dependence on its readers to relate one register of relations to another made its effects unpredictable. For example, printed domestic advice could facilitate identification as well as subordination. As Jennifer Mylander has argued, for example, even when English books offered advice that was impracticable in the changed context of colonial America, the books could still perform valuable ideological work by sustaining a colonial reader's relationship to England and Englishness.[47]

Assuming domestic advice has political uses and implications without assuming what those might be can return us to the possibility of an active reader who finds in these texts affirmations and provocations more complex than discussions of prescription sometimes imagine. Let us take, for example, the political consequences of the emphasis in these books on "the Prince of the houshold, the domesticall King."[48] A number of scholars have linked the empowerment of the male householder addressed in many of these books to the English Civil War. In the system of analogies around which many constructions of domestic and political order were structured, the father was to his household as Christ was to his church, the king was to his people, and the minister was to his flock. While this system can seem deceptively fixed, changes in one set of relations sparked opportunities in another. According to Christopher Hill, the erosion of clerical power left the minister's position open, so that the householder could "step into" it. Householders "had been preparing" for the spiritual leadership they thereby assumed in part "by studying the large literature writing up their disciplinary duties."[49] The household head with an increased sense of his spiritual responsibilities could become a citizen empowered to resist and even oppose a ruler he perceived as ungodly.[50]

In this interpretation, the system of analogies remained in place, dictating interlocking hierarchies, and fathers simply stepped up to an enhanced version of their familiar role, which then led them to godly forms of resistance. It is also possible to see the revolutionary implications of domestic advice not as embedded in the system of analogies itself, and its changing relation to seventeenth-century circumstances, but as emerging from critical readings of those analogies and a willingness to think anew about the relations on which those analogies depended. In *Observations Upon Some of His Majesties Late Answers and Expresses* (1642), Henry Parker quotes Charles I's reminder that "*Princes are called Gods, Fathers, Husbands, Lords, Heads, etc. and this implies them to be of more worth and more unsubordinate in end, than their Subjects are, who by the same relation must stand as Creatures, Children, Wives, Servants, Members, etc.*" As Parker points out, the analogies to which the king refers serve his interests and insist on the fundamental *relation* of dominance and subordination between creators and creatures, heads and members, as well as a sliding scale of worth from top to bottom of a hierarchy. Parker argues that, although "these terms do illustrate some excellency in Princes by way of similitude" they "must not in all things be applied, and they are most truly applied to subjects, taken *divisim*, but not *conjunctim* [separately not collectively]."[51] For Parker, princes accrue excellency only "by way of similitude," rather than through an absolute equivalence, and such similitudes do not exist but rather have to be "applied." The sensible interpreter must consider when principles of similitude or relation truly apply and when they do not. Similarly, in *The Tenure of Kings and Magistrates* (1649), John Milton explains that the relation through which king and subject are both defined is consensual: "We know that king and subject are relatives, and relatives have no longer being than in the relation. The relation between king and subject can be no other than regal authority and subjection. Hence I infer past their defending that if the subject, who is one relative, take away the relation, of force he takes away also the other relative."[52] By fiat, then, the subject can "take away the relation" through which his king subjects him. Rather than "stepping into" an existing position, Milton's subject is an agential reader who challenges the whole system of analogies and redefines the relations through which king and subject are identified. The fiat Milton imagines here resembles divorce, reminding us of Milton's notorious reluctance to imagine that wives too might simply "take away" or reconfigure a relation that does not serve their interests.

If domestic advice had political effects, they would probably have extended beyond empowering the male householder/reader on whom Hill, Parker, and Milton focus. Extending her attention from the patriarch to the many other members of the household, Wendy Wall suggests that "English cookbooks, manuals, and plays in the hundred years prior [to the Civil War] offered indirect ammunition for the critique that social contract theorists would later wage against the traditional analogies of family and state."[53] It is possible to imagine female readers who dwelt on the political implications of their own roles as wives, mothers, and mistresses, or wives, servants, and younger sons who used the books to hold the male householder to a high standard of accountability or who seized on the liberty of conscience and spiritual equality the books invariably conceded to them. Readers who grasped that similitudes must be applied selectively and that relations can be taken away might begin to imagine radical possibilities, possibilities that emerge out of yet undo and exceed the texts that survive to us.

The active reader Parker and Milton imagine is a reader who, because his or her operations were not determined by the text, cannot be documented through it. The more we imagine an active reader, the more control we surrender over what these books meant to their readers and what we can use them to prove. Like the witness speaking in depositions, the agential reader is and is not there. We can approach him or her only through texts we know to be flawed. While domestic advice is often disparaged as too cut and dried, the challenge and opportunity it offers is that so much of what we learn there is uncertain. As we will now see, today's active scholarly readers of domestic advice may seek to wring historical knowledge from these tricky texts, but, at their best, they unsettle rather than fix our knowledge of these books and of early modern domesticity.

Scholars as Readers: New Evidence or New Reading Practices?

The injunction that prescription must not be confused with practice is so often repeated that it has become hard to think about what it means or where we should go from there. Yet we do proceed from there. Advice literature remains widely read and frequently cited because it is so copious. Advice literature is the workhorse of "context" in the classroom and in scholarly studies. But if it is used as evidence despite its much-vaunted shortcomings, what method overcomes its limitations? The reading practice advice literature requires is sometimes described as coercive or at least domineering. Sara Mendelson and Patricia Crawford advocate "reading male or popular sources 'against the grain'."[54] David Cressy advises that "through careful handling" such sources "can show the alteration of concerns over time and may also be made to illuminate the behaviour and opinions of the laity, the lesser folk, and of women."[55] These sources show only what they are made to. Such wary methods require showing dubious sources who is boss. Many scholars turn to these sources with the intention of prising new information from texts that sometimes appear to have been both overmined and overestimated. But they are not always as forthright as Cressy about the fact that they are not digging up new sources but rather returning to those sometimes dismissed as used up with new demands or seeking a new kind of relationship.

We often see a slight of hand by which those who emphasize the limitations of domestic advice literature and the importance of finding other kinds of sources return to them nonetheless, although with new questions. For example, Natasha Korda insists on the importance, "in attempting to comprehend the significance of women's changing historical relations to household stuff, to reach beyond such contextualizing texts as domestic manuals, conduct books, legal treatises, and so on, and consider as well sources of evidence that register the traces of material practice"; she suggests that we need to try harder to dig up "documents of practice."[56] She is a determined digger. Yet, in her first chapter, one of the most interesting things Korda does is to read what she calls "contextualizing texts" such as Gouge's *Of Domesticall Duties as* "documents of practice." Her fascinating book is distinguished not by wholly new evidence but by inventive ways of interpreting her evidence, looking for hints of practice within prescription itself.

Laura Gowing, who depends largely on ecclesiastical court records, as we have seen, moves rapidly beyond the caveat that prescription does not equal practice to a messier formulation of that relationship. Gowing reminds her readers that "the family itself was infinitely more complex than its literary model, and its relationships more awkward." Here "literature" is the category for all texts that do anything other than purport to describe what really happened: "Sermons and books made use of a common stock of ideas and images about marriage and the household to produce an ideal of social and familial order whose details were, for many households, largely irrelevant." If we grant that, then why should scholars or students care about this prescription that is divorced from practice? As Gowing suggests, "One starting-point might be to enquire how members of real households interpreted such ideology, and to what particular uses they put it: not how far household practice and gender order reflected ideology, but in what ways individuals sought to use such prescriptions."[57] While Gowing acknowledges "real households," she quickly shifts her attentions to some of those documents through which we have access to them—"records of marriage disputes" and of insults, records that register their indebtedness to popular literature. Furthermore, she stresses that what happened in real households, to the extent that we can imagine it, may well have been informed by, as it must also have fed into, prescriptive and imaginative texts. Yet again, not only does the real turn out to be accessible through "stories" but it is also inseparable from "literary" and "contextual" forms of evidence, which shape its terms. Alexandra Shepard describes advice literature as "a product of reality, rather than somehow separate from and comparable with it."[58] One might also add that advice literature is *productive of* reality. Just as Valerie Traub argues that "male-authored discourses were an intrinsic, indeed, constitutive part of women's lived experience," so discourses of domestic advice were intrinsic indeed constitutive parts of men's lived experiences.[59] When we look closely at thoughtful discussions of "hard" evidence or of practice regarding how people lived their lives in their real households, the literary often reasserts itself, not as the banished alternative but as the unavoidably integral.

With the help of the *ODNB*, among other resources, we are gaining new perspectives on advice literature by paying more attention to its authors and the differences among them. But what we are learning is that the point of origin for these texts is hard to pin down, fractured and shifting. Authors wrote from a wide range of social and doctrinal positions. A few were unmarried; many were married. Most were ministers, but some were not.[60] Those who were ministers were often embroiled in doctrinal controversy, sometimes as a result of their writings. For example, the first printing of *A Bride-Bush. Or, a Direction for Married Persons* in 1617 does not name an author. In the epistle dedicatory to a much-expanded 1619 edition, which describes the work as "compiled and published" by William Whately, a popular Puritan preacher known as "the Roaring Boy of Banbury," Whately explains to his father-in-law that a wedding sermon he preached ten or eleven years earlier was published "without my privity" by a friend to whom he had given a copy. His hand forced, Whately consulted his notes on the subject of marriage and published this fuller treatment of the subject. Once named, Whately was then accountable for the content of his text. He was called before the Court of High Commission for his claim that willful desertion or adultery should be grounds for divorce and that remarriage should be possible after such a divorce. He recanted this view in 1621 and the 1623 edition of *A Bride-Bush* includes his two-page retraction as well as the offending passages, which he claims the printer forgot to delete.[61]

The signature of the retraction (Ff3r–v) indicates that the page was printed last and then inserted after the dedicatory epistle, the epistle to the Christian reader, and the table of contents. In the 1623 edition, then, Whately both reproduces and retracts his controversial views on divorce.[62] For our purposes here, I want to stress, first, that Whately has views so particular that he was compelled to recant them; second, that he depicts himself as unable to control the printing of his texts yet as accountable for their contents; and third, that *A Bride-Bush*, like many of the more popular, frequently reprinted conduct books, is not one text but several. Did Whately really change his mind, or did he recant for expediency's sake? Which text is *the* text? Learning more about Whately and his text effectively unsettles rather than stabilizes our knowledge.

Although we look to authors to anchor these text's meanings, in one way or another, they are not there. Just as the first edition of *A Bride-Bush* identifies its author only as "W. W." of Banburie, writing August 20, 1608, so it is often difficult to identify an author beyond dispute. For example, the title page of the 1615 printing of *A Godly Forme of Houshold Government*, which was printed at least eight times between 1598 and 1630, presents John Dod and Robert Cleaver as the amenders and augmenters of a text first "gathered" by "R. C." Most scholars refer to the authors as "Dod and Cleaver." In *Family Reformation Promoted* (1656), his redaction of this book and Gouge's *Of Domesticall Duties*, Daniel Cawdrey claims that his father, Robert Cawdrey, first wrote and published *A Godly Forme of Houshold Government*. He insists that he does not object to Dod and Cleaver repackaging the material, but only to the fact that they put "to their Booke their own Names, concealing (or at least obscuring) the Name of the first Father of it; onely putting the two first letters of his names, R.C. which signifies nothing to a *strange Reader*."[63] If, looking for an author, we turn to the *ODNB*, we find an entry for Cawdrey, listing him as the "probable" author of this work, but not for Cleaver. In the *ODNB*, Cleaver is a shadowy presence, remembered only in association with Dod, just as Cawdrey is a kind of ghost writer on the title pages of *A Godly Forme*. Estranged by centuries, we find ourselves the "strange readers" about whom Daniel Cawdrey worries, unable to figure out the author's identity.

Another productive strategy for prising new information out of domestic advice literature is to apply the venerable technique of textual analysis to books that have often been dismissed as subliterary. As we have seen, Chilton Latham Powell and Louis B. Wright treated what Powell called "the domestic conduct book" as a genre, even as they disparaged its literary pretensions. Some of the most revealing analyses of domestic advice books have taken the time to examine a few works in depth, attending to conventions, structure, and the reappearance of particular metaphors and plots. Lorna Hutson offers a detailed analysis of Xenophon's *Oeconomicus* "and its seventeenth-century 'marriage guidance' derivatives"; Wendy Wall has a wonderful chapter on "Familiarity and Pleasure in the English Household Guide, 1500–1700"; Natasha Korda offers sustained readings of texts including Gervase Markham's *The English Huswife* and Gouge's *Of Domesticall Duties*.[64] By placing particular works in the foreground rather than the background, Hutson, Wall, and Korda help us think about these texts as texts, with authors and publication histories and influence, rather than as troughs of free-floating quotations. By examining a few texts closely, even as they position them in genres, these critics attend to internal contradictions within individual texts and to change over time.

Following in the footsteps of these and other critics, I would like to conclude this chapter with case studies of Miles Coverdale's translation of Bullinger's *The Christen State of Matrimonye* and William Gouge's *Of Domesticall Duties*.[65] Rather than offer comprehensive readings of the texts or exhaustive histories of publication and reception, although such a project would be valuable, I focus on the ways in which these books address the issue of how their readers will put prescription into practice. As the work I have surveyed in this section suggests, new reading practices can make old texts yield new knowledge, knowledge that unsettles rather than shoring up what we think we know about the early modern period. I return to these oft-cited texts to find evidence not about early modern domestic life but about methods for reading prescriptions then and now. How do these texts teach their readers to use them? How is that instruction related to how scholars use them now?

The Christen State of Matrimonye

Heinrich Bullinger was a Reformed theologian from Switzerland closely connected to reformers in England through a correspondence network; more than 12,000 of his letters survive. Like Luther, he was a former priest who married a former nun (in 1529). When Miles Coverdale, another former cleric, undertook his translation of Bullinger's work, he had himself recently married. Coverdale lived in Strasbourg for several years starting in 1540, and he probably completed the translation then.[66] Coverdale's translation was first published in Antwerp in 1541. According to Carrie Euler, who offers the most thorough account of the book's publication history, it went through eight editions, seven of them between 1541 and 1552.[67] Editions in 1542 and 1543, entitled *The Golden Boke of Christen Matrimonye*, included a preface by Thomas Becon writing under the pseudonym Theodore Basille. Becon later explained that the work was "for the more redy sale set forth in my name by the hungry printer with my preface."[68] The title pages of these two editions name Coverdale and Becon, but not Bullinger. Indeed, according to Euler, "Bullinger's name does not appear on or in any of the English editions."[69] Coverdale's translation did not include all of Bullinger's text, truncating Bullinger's discussion of household management.[70] The adaptation of Bullinger's text did not end with Coverdale's expurgation and translation of it. Only the first Antwerp edition contains all of Coverdale's translation. Subsequent editions exclude chapters on clerical marriage, divorce, and other controversial topics—that is, the very parts of the book Coverdale seems to have privileged.[71] This seminal text was, then, several texts, leaving in doubt what it was that made it influential: its discussion of domestic life, which Coverdale condensed, or its discussion of doctrinal controversy, which most editions suppressed.

Scholars continue to debate the importance of *The Christen State of Matrimonye* to the history of printed domestic advice in England. Does it mark a beginning or an end? It is often praised as a first— "The first important Protestant formulation on marriage to be published in English"—and as foundational—"the basis on which the genre of Protestant marriage books would develop."[72] Yet Powell describes the book as nothing new in itself and as marking the end of "the formative period of our type" because in the books that follow, "we find no new elements of any importance"; Bullinger's successors can only elaborate on what they find in him. At the same time, Powell also praises Coverdale's translation of Bullinger as "one of the most broad-minded, unbiased, and modern in principle of any before Perkins' *Christian Oeconomie*" in 1609.[73] Like Powell, Karen Newman depicts the book as the end of an era, but she emphasizes that its content is retrograde rather than "modern," pointing out that, in Coverdale's translation, Bullinger spends a great deal of time explaining what one should not do, that is, commit whoredom before or adultery after marriage. He is so absorbed in defending marriage against abuses—redeeming the idea of marriage from its debasement in practice— that he has little time for the details of daily life.[74]

Euler argues that the influence of *The Christen State of Matrimonye* stems from the fact that it was both new and old: "Bullinger's unique blend of pre-Reformation, Protestant, and specifically Reformed ideas is what made the book so popular among the English." Furthermore, according to Euler, the part of the book that most influenced subsequent works of domestic advice was the part that Coverdale trimmed and altered.[75] In time, the discussion of domestic conduct proved influential, especially after some of Bullinger's more controversial Reformist views, such as his defense of divorce in the case of adultery, failed to take hold in England and so were cut out. While the discussion of controversial topics such as clerical marriage was especially addressed to other reformers and ministers, the discussion of domestic conduct appealed to lay readers as well.

I am less interested in the content of this volume than in its method—how it addresses its own status as advice literature and how it goes about explaining to readers how they might use it to manage matrimony. In part because he enters the field so early, Bullinger reflects on why he has chosen to print his advice rather than or in addition to preaching it. Whereas "the worde of preaching prospereth not on every side," he writes, "that which is written / endureth longer and goeth further than it that is spoken / therfore have I gathered this boke concernyng holy wedloke / and sent it out in wrytyng" (C3r). This statement can stand as a justification for all advice literature. Bullinger values reading not only as the means by which his words reach their destination but as an important part of training up Christians in the home. He suggests that the householder impose a reading program on his subordinates, including the active exercise of the pen (in taking notes) and the tongue (in discussion): "Let them excersye their penne & their tongues in readyng diverse printed bokes pertayninge to the holy scriptures / and come to heare the trewe prechers of goddis worde & in anewise let them not heare the papistike prechers." For Bullinger, to learn aurally one must be able to produce a true relation of what one has heard: "when they come home from any good sermone aske them what they have borne awaye / & exhorte them to marke diligently a nother tyme and to reherse it when they come home" (I7v).

Bullinger frequently draws in the reader using a tactic that reappears in later works: anticipating and articulating possible objections. For example, he interrupts a critique of how marriage is celebrated with a question he assigns to the reader: "Thou wilt say: What? hath god then forbydden honest folkes to make mery together or to daunce honestly in all good maner?" (G6v). He imagines male and female queries. For instance, from a wife who is enjoined not to be overly familiar with her servants he imagines: "Thou wilt saye: I can not be so boysterous nor shew my selfe so terryble" (I1v). The wife's eruption into first-person speech is arresting here, but, as so often, this is a first-person statement the author assigns to her so that he can counter it. When he raises possible objections, Bullinger reminds the reader that this text is not only about how they should conduct their relationships but is itself also a conduit of relations between writer and reader, relations in which the author presumes to supply the words thou wilt say.

Some of Bullinger's most interesting appeals are to the reader's existing knowledge. For example, Bullinger advises the newly married couple to get off to a good start "by this ensample folowyng: yf two boordes at the first be not well coupled and joyned the one to the tother / they never are fastened right afterward. But yf the first couplyng & joyning together be good/then can ther afterward no violence dryve the boordes a sunder / yee the whole boord doth sooner breake / then the glewing of them together" (G7r–G7v).[76] This "ensample" will make most sense to those who already have some experience of poor joins that fail to hold. But more generally, it emphasizes that a strong coupling, of spouses or of boards, does not just happen. It has to be crafted. This crafting is Bullinger's emphasis throughout.

In another example, he compares a poor marital start to an injury that is not properly treated. "For yf at the begynnyng of mariage there chaunce such rudenesse and uncomely discorde / then will it allwaye be breakyng out / even as it is with greate woundes & broken legges / which seldome are so thorowly healed / but somtyme they have payne at the chaunge of the wether." If a couple allow discord to begin, it will never quite heal but will reopen or ache: "Then come such unsemely wordes as these be: Thus dyddest thou serve me also afore. It were my parte to lerne to geve litle credence unto the / etc. And after thys maner doth that to earlye discorde / make ye whole life & the whole state of mariage / bytter and sower" (G7v). The festering impostume of marital discord issues in the unseemly yet, he claims, predictable words spouses accustomed to arguing will find coming out of their mouths. He is, briefly, a prophet and a playwright, anticipating and scripting the dialogue he hopes to help Christian spouses avoid.

If the spouses who get their marriage off to a good start are skillful carpenters or physicians, then Bullinger's domestic advice is both analogous to practical advice about managing the material world and dependent on those books and the knowledge they convey to provide the model of the kind of skilled, careful work he requires of married persons. One of his most detailed similes expands on his reference to the bitter taste of ill-made matrimony, comparing those who do not follow his advice to an impatient vintner who, upon buying the vineyard, tests the grapes before their time and, if he finds them "yet hard and sower / that is unseasonable and not rype," decides to "plucke up the vynes / and destroye the whole yarde." In "first commynge together," as in winemaking, one must recognize that good results take time. Given Bullinger's investment in defending monogamy, wine proves a useful analogy to marriage as a long-term investment: in both cases, "the longer the better and the more pleasaunt." But this very detailed simile assumes that the reader already knows that wine is first juice and then grape must and then sour wine before it becomes drinkable wine, that one must nurture vines rather than tearing them up in a fit of pique, and that the person who does not invest the time required will "lacke wyne at his nede." At one level, the wife might be viewed as the vine or the sour wine. But in all these examples it seems to be the marriage that is the join knit by a carpenter, the mended leg that does or does not throb when it rains, the well-tended vineyard and the sweet wine it produces. The vineyard example ends with the advisory that "yf thou whilt suffre no infirmyte nor blemishe / thou must take none to be thy spouse" (G8v). The rather abstract marital virtue of patience here becomes concrete through a simile that appeals to the reader's knowledge of vintry and ability to relate it to marriage. Assuming that a relationship can, through skill, be forged, Bullinger's printed advice guides the reader in creating this bond.

The similes in Coverdale's translation of Bullinger are so specific that they at first seem idiosyncratic. But the book's content, including some of these similes, was widely reproduced.[77] Thomas Gataker uses "glewed" as a synonym for cleaving unto one's spouse: he elaborates on Genesis 2.24 by explaining that a man shall leave his father and mother and "be glewed unto, or cleave fast to his wife."[78] William Gouge, to whom we will turn next, elaborates on Bullinger's discussion of the couple as joined or glued together. Of Ephesians 5.31, he explains,

> To set forth the firmnesse of the marriage bond he [Paul] addeth this Emphacicall phrase, *shall be joined,* (or as the word properly, according to the naturall notation thereof signifieth, *shall be glued) to his wife.* Things well glued together are as fast, firme, and close as if they were one intire peece. Yea we observe by experience that a table will oft times cleave in the whole wood, before it will part asunder where it is glued: so as an husband ought to be as firme to his wife as to himself: and she to him. (H8r–v)

Later, Gouge again advises that when, at first, "there be a good liking mutually and thorowly setled in both their hearts of one another, love is like to continue in them for ever, as things wich are well glued, and setled before they be shaken up and downe, will never be severed asunder: but if they be joyned together without glue, or shaken while the glue is moist, they cannot remaine firme. Mutuall love and good liking of ech other is as glue" (O3r).[79] If love is a glue that seals a join, it can be applied by choice. While the Book of Common Prayer marriage ceremony describes husband and wife as those whom "God hath joined together," this imagery suggests that, at one level, husband and wife must join themselves. But Gouge admits the possibility of circumstances beyond the control of spousal craft. The glue must be applied in a timely fashion; it cannot be counted on to emerge from the join, and it is needed immediately rather than in the fullness of time. Finally, one must hope that the join is not "shaken while the glue is moist," surely a situation over which one would have only limited control.

The material practices of textual production in the early modern period often involved joining, drawing together the efforts of multiple workers and multiple textual parts into a whole. As we have seen in the introduction, readers too were "joiners," piecing together notes from or memories of texts they had read into commonplace books, adding marginalia or interleaving blank pages into books to include their own commentary, pasting slips of paper over printed texts, disassembling printed and manuscript texts and reassembling them into new forms.[80] Making meaning was, like making a marriage or family, a matter of skilled joinery and the judicious application of glue. Even as Bullinger anticipates and tries to control readers' responses, he simultaneously enjoins readers to a form of craft that is not simply a matter of following his directions or submitting to his authority. He thereby compromises his own authority to prescribe and activates readers whose responses might vary—even as the advice stays the same.

The more we learn about the huge and heterogeneous body of domestic advice literature, the clearer it becomes that we cannot formulate one all-purpose formulation of the evidence value of these texts, although the admonition that we should not mistake them for descriptions of practice attempts to do so. In its diversity and richness, advice literature raises the same question we have entertained with regard to witchcraft pamphlets and depositions: Does consistency across samples—convention—make a statement valuable as evidence or is it the excessive, remarkable, and idiosyncratic that most compels attention if not belief? The answer is that scholars tend to respond to both, depending on what they are trying to prove: to patterns and eccentricities, conventions and bizarre outbursts. When we focus, as I am doing here, on the advisor's engagements with and representations of the reader and the employment of figuration to explain domestic relations, we find both plagiarism and innovation, convention and experimentation, continuity and idiosyncrasy, directives and invitations to improvise. The texts make claims on our attention and can prove valuable as evidence both when they repeat what we have already read countless times and when a particularly vivid passage leaps out from the page as remarkable. Because the texts themselves encourage readers to interpret, use, and do, they point us toward what they cannot document: readers' applications and practices.

Of Domesticall Duties

At 700 pages, William Gouge's *Of Domesticall Duties* is one of the longest printed books of domestic advice; it has sometimes been called the best or at least the best seller.[81] The table of contents alone is twelve closely printed pages. Gouge reassures his reader at the outset: "Though for such a matter as is handled in these Treatises, the worke may seeme at first sight to be too copious, yet I hope the observant Reader will not finde it too tedious. It is the variety of many, not the prolixity of few points, which hath made this booke to swell to that bignesse which it hath" (¶2v–3r). It is so big that it is most often represented through extracts.[82] While William and Malleville Haller praise it as "encyclopedic," they also call it "authoritative, exhaustive, compendious, systematic, and dull."[83] As I will show, Gouge's aggressively copious text undermines many of the dichotomies through which it is most often understood. Gouge builds assumptions about practice into his prescriptions, thus destabilizing an opposition between the two; he demands and instructs active readers, opening up the possibility that they will apply his lessons in ways he does not predict; and, in what has become the most discussed, but I think least understood, feature of his book, he builds resistant female readers into his text, establishing them as alternate sites of authority. At the center of the oppositions and tensions in *Of Domesticall Duties*, we often find the figure of the wife, whom Gouge has installed there, I will argue, as a kind of countertheorist of domestic life.

In an epistle dedicating the book to his parishioners, Gouge addresses an active reader, whom he urges to amend printers' errors "with a pen" (sig. A1r) and for whom he facilitates a selective reading process, offering that detailed table of contents as well as his parallel listing of duties at a glance so that "you may the more readily finde out such particular points as you desire most especially to read" (¶4v). In discussing his own method, Gouge refuses the prescription/practice divide by claiming that he modeled his recommendations on behavior he observed. He then moves from observation to what he calls "disposition," which the *OED* defines as "The action of setting in order, or condition of being set in order; arrangement, order; relative position of the parts or elements of a whole." If Gouge installed his observations of lived relations in his textual relation, through disposition he relied on his own apprehension of relatedness, of how one thing follows from another and implies the next, as a principle of organization and a spur to inclusion: "My method and

manner of proceeding brought many things to my minde, which otherwise
might have slipped by. For by method sundry and severall points appertaining
to one matter are drawne forth, as in a chaine one linke draweth up another."[84]
For Gouge, chains or threads of association should guide the memory as well
as the composition of a text: "As method is an helpe to Invention, so also to
retention. It is as a thread or wier whereon pearles are put, which keepeth
them from scattering. And if a man by abundance of matter be cast into a
labyrinth, by the helpe of method he may easily and readily finde out the way
againe" (¶4v–5r). Acknowledging that the reader requires guidance through
his labyrinthine text, Gouge also suggests that one can best remember the
details by embracing the "disposition" by which parts are parallel to other
parts and related to the whole. On the one hand, Gouge's tables and cross
references provide the method, unspooling the thread to guide the reader out.
On the other hand, Gouge's allusion suggests that the reader must find his or
her own way out, playing both Theseus and Ariadne at once. In *Areopagitica*,
Milton privileges individual agency over submission: "For those actions which
enter into a man, rather than issue out of him, and therefore defile not, God
uses not to captivate under a perpetual childhood of prescription, but trusts
him with the gift of reason to be his own chooser."[85] Although Gouge is in the
business of prescriptions that might be called infantilizing, he empowers his
readers as their own choosers.

Gouge has sometimes been praised for grounding his advice in experience. Powell, for instance, claims that Gouge's book offers "practical instructions for family life along the best human lines." Alison Wall describes Gouge
as writing "a more balanced guide" and being "more realistic" about family life
than the unmarried "Protestant zealots" who, according to her, wrote other
books.[86] But what, if anything, might make Gouge's advice more practical
than, say, Bullinger's?

What little access we have to Gouge's practical experience comes through
two hagiographic biographies written shortly after his death, one by his son
Thomas and one by William Jenkyn, his successor as pastor of Blackfriars
church. These sources demonstrate the terms in which interested contemporaries idealized Gouge as a preacher and family man, but not necessarily how
he carried out his own domestical duties. These biographies explain that, while
he was at Cambridge, "He was so strict and observant in the course of his life,
as they then counted him, an *Arch-Puritan*, which was the terme then given
in scorne to those who were conscionable of their waies."[87] He was pastor of
Blackfriars for forty-five years, never holding another position, although, his

biographers are eager to point out, he had offers of preferment. He had detractors, including those who claimed he was too wealthy and even practiced usury, but his preaching was so popular that his Blackfriars church had to be expanded. Devoted to preaching, he refused to retire; at the end of his life, suffering with kidney stones and asthma, he had to be carried to the pulpit but insisted on preaching anyway.

His biographers root Gouge's preaching in a robust life as a reader and a writer. He was always in his study by five in the morning. According to his son, he had "white paper bound betwixt the leaves of the Bible" so that he could write any observations and interpretations that would not fit under the heads in his commonplace book. He was as resistant a reader as he was assiduous, refusing to read the Book of Sports aloud in his church. He spent summers in the country with his family, which enabled him to write and publish his treatises.[88] Gouge at home, then, was Gouge at work, studying scripture, writing sermons and books.[89]

One might presume that Gouge's household was also the laboratory for his ideas about domestical duties. His biographers offer tantalizing glimpses of a complicated distribution of power in the Gouge household. His son claims that "his mind was so addicted to the University" that he only left it under duress, because his father had "prepared" a marriage for him "much against his mind." From Thomas's point of view, this marriage helped lead William into the ministry and was thus providential. Thomas writes of Elizabeth Caulton Gouge, his mother, that "To her care he [William] committed the providing for of his family, himself only minding his studies, and weighty affaires of his heavenly calling."[90] As Brett Usher's entry on Gouge in the *ODNB* points out, this was "a strange thing to do to a girl of seventeen."[91] In *Of Domesticall Duties*, Gouge reproves those "masters of families who commit all the care of their house either to their wives, or to some servant, and misspend their whole time in idlenesse, riotousnesse, and voluptuousnesse" (sig. C2r) and warns "those who have publike offices in Church or common-wealth" that "they may not thereupon thinke themselves exempted from all family-duties. These private duties are necessarie duties" (C2v). Although "many a husband because the wives office is especially to abide at home, will put off all government to the wife" (S2v), Gouge advises against this. Whether his own practice, as described by his early biographers, ran counter to his advice depends on what we think he left to Elizabeth's care.

Thomas Gouge suggests that, if William left Elizabeth to "provide for" the family, he took a strong role in "governing" it:

> The government of his Family was exemplary, another *Bethel*, for he
> did not only make conscience of morning and evening prayer and
> reading the word in his family, but also of Catechising his Children
> and Servants: wherein God gave him a singular gift, for he did
> not teach them by any set form, but so as he brought them that
> were instructed to express the Principle taught them in their own
> words . . . never any Servant came to his house, but gained a great
> deal of knowledge.

William Jenkyn concurs that if one "looks upon" Gouge at home, one will
find him "daily dropping upon" his children and servants "with holy instructions."[92] Throughout *Of Domesticall Duties*, Gouge stresses the household
head's obligation to catechize—and the obligation of all subordinates to listen
and learn.[93] If Jenkyn's description of Gouge "dropping upon" his children
and servants sounds menacing, his own favorite figure for instruction is even
more so. Defending his reliance on repetition, Gouge reminds the reader that
"The Apostle thought that this naile of love had need be fast beaten into the
heads and hearts of husbands, and therefore addeth blow to blow to knock
it up deepe, even to the head" (F8r). Later, he reminds us that "That which
at first is little heeded, by much urging and pressing will for ever be held, as
a naile that at one blow scarse entreth, with many blowes is knockt up to the
head" (L7v). He repeats this figure in his discussion of parents teaching their
children (Nn3r). Like Bullinger's metaphors, Gouge's favorite image for instruction draws on a knowledge of manual skills, in this case carpentry.

Even if Elizabeth provided for the house, freeing William to hammer
away within and outside it, she appears in both biographies largely as an occasion of his patience. According to Thomas Gouge, his father William "was of
a most sweet and meek disposition; yea such was his meeknesse of Spirit, that
it seemeth unparallel, for though he had lived with his Wife above 20. years
together, yet neither Child nor Servant could ever say, that they observed an
angry countenance, or heard an angry word proceed from him towards her,
all her life."[94] Thomas says nothing of his mother's disposition; nor does he
include her death as an event in his father's life. The emphasis on William's
meekness suggests that it was somehow remarkable, that many another in his
circumstances would have given way to anger. But his wife's provocations,
hovering as the occasion of his laudable restraint, remain just outside these
biographies.

Driven by the project of praising the dead, the biographies of William cannot be taken as evidence of the Gouges' domestic experience. Although that experience is largely inaccessible, it figures in some discussions of Gouge's domestic advice. Alison Wall argues that "he knew a great deal more than most of the male writers about the realities of childbirth and family life," since he and his wife had thirteen children, and that this manifests itself in various ways, including his suggestions on how to treat a pregnant wife.[95] Yet many others argue that Gouge's theoretical commitment to domestic hierarchy resisted the pressure of his household experience. According to Kathleen Davies, for example, "Gouge expressed the theory of male dominance in its strongest form, and it is the most important theme of his *Of Domesticall Duties*."[96] For Davies and others, then, Gouge's advice is more about "theory" than about "the realities of childbirth and family life." Whether Gouge is praised as rooted in realities or as committed to the theory of male dominance, the assumption is that the realities of childbirth and family life are somehow contrary to the theory of male dominance, as if one could not be equally invested in both.

The question of theory versus reality, of prescription versus practice if you will, often centers as above on the wife's status and duties. This is not because Gouge's prescriptions for the wife are any more harsh or contradictory than anyone else's but because he draws our attention to his female parishioners' resistance to them. In his dedicatory epistle, Gouge recalls that "when these Domesticall Duties were first uttered out of the pulpit, much exception was taken against the application of a wives subjection to the restraining of her from disposing the common goods of the family without, or against her husbands consent. But surely they that made those exceptions did not well thinke of the Cautions and Limitations which were then delivered, and are now againe expressly noted" regarding that property the wife might control (¶3v). He urges readers to keep these cautions in mind. As Gouge makes clear, what was at issue was how one would apply the scriptural precept of wifely subjection to the daily management of property; some parishioners objected to how he applied an abstraction to the conduct of daily life and how they thought that applied to them.

Gouge introduces his female parishioners as characters in his story by positioning them as examples of readers who bristle at any obligation imposed on them: "Let everyone, as their conscience (an impartiall Judge) shall bear them witnesse, make a right application of everything to themselves. Thus shall we Ministers be freed from many evill surmizes" (¶3r–v). Each reader, then, is responsible for the "right application of everything to themselves." Even at his most defensive, then, Gouge enjoins readers to do their part.

Gouge blames his organization—and auditors' and readers' inability to comprehend it—for provoking resistance. Following "the Apostle" (Paul), he treated the wife's duties first, and women objected to his depiction of "the uttermost extent of that subjection under which God hath put her" (the wife) because they had not yet seen his discussion of a husband's duties (¶3v). Read against the "Apologie I have beene forced to make, that I might not ever be judged (as some have censured me) an hater of women" (¶4), Gouge's explanations in the book itself seem more inflammatory than conciliatory. As he later explains more bluntly, the Apostle begins with the husband and wife because they were the first couple in the world and "even to this day . . . the first couple is ordinarily an husband and a wife" who erect and bring together a family (C3r). Of the two spouses, he begins with the wife because of her inferiority to her husband (sig.C3r–v). His organization, then, paradoxically acknowledges the wife's importance in the family—that she stands "in the first rank" with her husband—and her subordination to him. Her duties must be "more fully expressed, and placed in the first ranke" because "for the most part inferiours are most unwilling to undergoe the duties of their place" (C3v). Wives' objections just confirm his claim that "inferiours that are under subjection thinke their burden the heaviest, and are lothest to beare it, and most willing to cast it away"; "Not without cause therefore doth the Apostle first declare the duties of inferiours" (C4r). Perhaps Gouge includes his parishioners' objections in part because they confirm this point.

According to Gouge, his organization, grounded in Ephesians, prevented wives from seeing that he imposes limits on husbands' authority as well:

> But when I came to deliver husbands duties, I shewed, that he ought not to exact whatsoever his wife was bound unto (in case it were exacted by him) but that he ought to make her a joynt Governour of the family with himselfe, and referre the ordering of many things to her discretion. . . . In a word, I so set downe an husbands duties, as if he be wise and conscionable in observing them, his wife can have no just cause to complaine of her subjection. That which maketh a wives yoake heavy and hard, is an husbands abuse of his authority. (¶4)

So Gouge chastises female readers for being overhasty—caviling with his depiction of the wife's duties before they get to his depiction of the husband's. But he also suggests that, while he must explain what a wife is "bound unto," he depends on husbands to ameliorate the effects of wives' subjection. In other words, he builds assumptions about practice into his prescriptions.

Gouge's design materializes a particular vision of marital reciprocity by which husband and wife both have duties and responsibilities:

> Now that in all those places where a wives yoke may seeme most to pinch, I might give some ease, I have to every head of wives duties made a reference, in the margin over against it, to the duties of husbands answerable thereunto, and noted the reference with this marke *, that it might the more readily be turned unto. Yea I have further parallel'd, and laid even one against another in one view, the heads of husbands and wives duties, as they answer each other. (¶4r)

By "one view" Gouge means that he has presented across four columns and two pages—one opening of the volume—the "particular" duties of husbands and wives side by side on one page and, on the facing page, two parallel columns of the wives' and husbands' "aberrations" from these particular duties (sigs. A1v–A2r). Just as the asterisks are cues to consider relations, so this layout invites readers to grasp parallels between their own and others' duties. As a consequence of the equilibrium so beautifully displayed across these four columns, "if both of them be conscionable and carefull to performe their owne duty, the matrimoniall yoke will so equally lie on both their necks, as the wife will be no more pinched therewith then the husband" (¶4r). The matrimonial yoke will pinch, but it will pinch both equally. Whether the duties Gouge assigns to spouses are so absolutely parallel has been much discussed. I am most concerned here not with the content of his advice but with his relation to his readers, who must grasp how their own duties fit into a larger schema and who must be "conscionable and carefull to performe" the advice he offers, starting with those female parishioners to whom he draws our attention.

Although Gouge's early biographers do not mention his conflict with his female parishioners, it has become the one thing about *Of Domesticall Duties* that most discussions of domestic advice mention.[97] Many of those who comment on Gouge's contentious female parishioners present him as defending a theory that was untenable in practice and wives in his parish as experts on that practice. According to Wright, "in actuality women of the commercial classes in the later sixteenth and seventeenth centuries had a remarkable amount of independence."[98] Anthony Fletcher describes Gouge's expectations as "unrealistic." Alison Wall too emphasizes the "discrepancy between theory

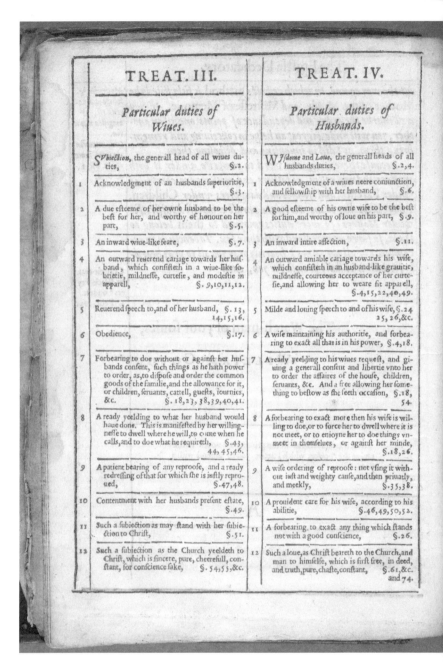

TREAT. III.	TREAT. IV.
Particular duties of Wiues.	**Particular duties of Husbands.**
S Vbiection, the generall head of all wiues duties, §.2.	W Isdome and Loue, the generall heads of all husbands duties, §.2,4.
1 Acknowledgment of an husbands superioritie, §.3.	1 Acknowledgment of a wiues neere coniunction, and fellowship with her husband, §.6.
2 A due esteeme of her owne husband to be the best for her, and worthy of honour on her part, §.5.	2 A good esteeme of his owne wife to be the best for him, and worthy of loue on his part, §.9.
3 An inward wiue-like feare, §.7.	3 An inward intire affection, §.11.
4 An outward reuerend cariage towards her husband, which consisteth in a wiue-like sobrietie, mildnesse, curtesie, and modestie in apparell, §.9,10,11,12.	4 An outward amiable cariage towards his wife, which consisteth in an husband-like grauitie, mildnesse, courteous acceptance of her curtesie, and allowing her to weare fit apparell, §.4,15,22,40,49.
5 Reuerend speech to, and of her husband, §.13,14,15,16.	5 Milde and louing speech to and of his wife, §.24,25,26,&c.
6 Obedience, §.17.	6 A wise maintaining his authoritie, and forbearing to exact all that is in his power, §.4,18.
7 Forbearing to doe without or against her husbands consent, such things as he hath power to order, as, to dispose and order the common goods of the familie, and the allowance for it, or children, seruants, cattell, guests, iournies, &c. §.18,23,38,39,40,41.	7 A ready yeelding to his wiues request, and giuing a generall consent and libertie vnto her to order the affaires of the house, children, seruants, &c. And a free allowing her something to bestow as she seeth occasion, §.18,54.
8 A ready yeelding to what her husband would haue done. This is manifested by her willingnesse to dwell where he will, to come when he calls, and to doe what he requireth, §.43,44,45,46.	8 A forbearing to exact more then his wife is willing to doe, or to force her to dwell where it is not meet, or to enioyne her to doe things vnmeet in themselues, or against her minde, §.18,26.
9 A patient bearing of any reproofe, and a ready redressing of that for which she is iustly reproued, §.47,48.	9 A wise ordering of reproofe: not vsing it without iust and weighty cause, and then priuatly, and meekly, §.35,38.
10 Contentment with her husbands present estate, §.49.	10 A prouident care for his wife, according to his abilitie, §.46,49,50,52.
11 Such a subiection as may stand with her subiection to Christ, §.51.	11 A forbearing to exact any thing which stands not with a good conscience, §.26.
12 Such a subiection as the Church yeeldeth to Christ, which is sincere, pure, cheerefull, constant, for conscience sake, §.54,55,&c.	12 Such a loue, as Christ beareth to the Church, and man to himselfe, which is first free, in deed, and truth, pure, chaste, constant, §.61,&c. and 74.

Figure 10. William Gouge's "parallel'd" duties from his *Of Domesticall Duties* (1622). Reproduced by permission of The Huntington Library, San Marino, California.

TREAT. III.

Aberrations of Wiues from their particular duties.

AMbition, the generall ground of the aberrations of wiues, §.2.

1. A conceit that wiues are their husbands equals, §.4.

2. A conceit that she could better subiect her selfe to any other man then to her owne husband, §.6.

3. An inward despising of her husband, §.8.

4. Vnreuerend behauiour towards her husband, manifested by lightnesse, sullennesse, scornfulnes, and vanitie in her attire, §.9,10,11,12.

5. Vnreuerend speech to and of her husband, §.13, 14,15,16.

6. A stout standing on her owne will, §.17.

7. A peremptorie vndertaking to doe things as she list without and against her husbands consent. This is manifested by priuie purloyning his goods, taking allowance, ordering children, seruants, and cattell, feasting strangers, making iourneyes, and vowes, as her selfe listeth, §.42.

8. An obstinate standing vpon her owne will, making her husband dwell where she will, and refusing to goe when he calls, or to doe any thing vpon his command, §.44,45,46,67.

9. Disdaine at reproofe; giuing word for word; and waxing worse for being reproued, §.47,48.

10. Discontent at her husbands estate, §.50.

11. Such a pleasing of her husband as offendeth Christ, §.53.

12. Such a subiection as is most vnlike to the Churches, viz. fained, forced, fickle, &c. §.56,&c.

TREAT. IV.

Aberrations of Husbands from their particular duties.

WAnt of wisdome and loue, the generall ground of the aberrations of husbands, §.3,5.

1. Too meane account of wiues, §.8.

2. A preposterous conceit of his owne wife to be the worst of all: and that he could loue any but her, §.10.

3. A Stoicall disposition, without all heat of affection, §.12.

4. An vnbeseeming cariage towards his wife, manifested by his basenesse, tyrannicall vsage of her, loftinesse, harshnesse, and niggardlinesse, §.5,15,17,41,44,53.

5. Harsh, proud, and bitter speeches, to and of his wife, §.24,25,30,32,36,39.

6. Losing of his authoritie, §.5.

7. Too much strictnesse ouer his wife. This is manifested by restraining her from doing any thing without particular and expresse consent, taking too strict account of her, and allowing her no more then is needfull for her owne priuate vse, §.19,55.

8. Too lordly a standing vpon the highest step of his authoritie: being too frequent, insolent, and peremptorie in commanding things friuolous, vnmeet, and against his wiues minde and conscience, §.30,32.

9. Rashnesse and bitternesse in reprouing: and that too frequently, on sleight occasions, and disgracefully before children, seruants, and strangers, §.36,38,39.

10. A carelesse neglect of his wife, and niggardly dealing with her, and that in her weaknesse, §.46,51,53.

11. A commanding of vnlawfull things, §.26, 30,32.

12. Such a disposition as is most vnlike to Christs, and to that which a man beareth to himselfe, viz. complementall, impure, for by-respects, vnconstant, &c. §.62,&c. and 74.

and practice" in *Of Domesticall Duties*: "Despite its large size and convenient index, his treatise does not seem to have offered much practical help to any Blackfriars parishioner who found herself faced with" conflicting advice regarding her subordination and obedience.[99] In all these assessments of the inadequacies of *Of Domesticall Duties*, the London wife stands for "actuality," the realistic, workable, and practical for which prescription cannot account.

Yet as the statement from Alison Wall suggests, the question is not just one of a discrepancy between theory and practice but of discrepancies within theory. However neatly and symmetrically organized, Gouge's advice is riddled with internal contradictions. Precisely because he alerts us to female parishioners' objections to some of his discussions of the wife's role, particular attention has been paid to contradictions within Gouge's descriptions of the wife's status. Gouge constantly insists that the wife is both a subordinate and almost a companion or partner: "Her *place* is indeed a place of inferiority, and subjection, yet the nearest to equality that may be: a place of common equity in many respects, wherein man and wife are after a sort even fellowes, and partners" (Aa2v). Anticipating the objection that fellowship and inferiority do not go together, he announces rather crossly, "They are of very meane capacity that cannot see how these may stand together" (Aa3r). As Susan Amussen crisply summarizes, the contradiction underlying Gouge's depiction of the wife was that he, like other Puritan ministers who wrote such books, was "trying to define an unequal partnership between spiritual equals."[100]

The contradictions that riddle Gouge's constructions of duty could prove opportunities because they placed the burden of choice on the reader, who had to decide how to perform duties that, however carefully organized in tables, remained ambiguous and contradictory. Since subordinates must limit their obedience to God's will, they must constantly make judgments: "*Gods will is that which must direct and settle every one in the things which they doe:* for Gods will is the rule of that which is right. Every thing is very right which he willeth: and nothing is right that swerveth from his will" (M4r). Clear enough. But Gouge devotes considerable space to the gray areas this opens up. All human relationships should be understood "*comparatively* in relation to God" (M5r). The burden falls, then, on fallen humans, who must compare or relate their relations to other humans to those with God: "Now let masters take notice hereof: and know that God the great Lord of all hath made this relation betwixt master and servant" (M6v). But "in relation to God," "*Master and servants are in the same subjection*" (M8r)—which must remind the master not to tyrannize: "For when masters command and forbid any thing against God, they goe beyond their commission, and therein their authoritie ceaseth" (Ss7v). Similarly, a wife may act without her husband's consent if he will not agree for her to do what God "expressly commands." But to act without his consent, she must "be sure that God hath commanded her that which she doth without or against her husbands consent" (Y3v). Any doubts should cause her to hesitate before acting. This caveat about the limits on the householder's authority is constantly repeated. It alerts us to the fact that performing domestic duty requires subordinates to engage in ongoing acts of interpretation and analysis.

Focusing on the point of contention Gouge himself identifies—the wife's relation to marital or household property—Natasha Korda argues that *Of Domesticall Duties* does not just reveal "discrepancies between legal theory and material practice" but attempts to rework prescriptions in the face of changing household practices. She focuses particular attention on a practice she argues is new: the housewife's role as "keeper" exercising "increasing managerial control over the things that entered and (more disturbingly) exited the home." In her view, "Gouge's many mitigating exceptions to the law of coverture capitulate to the daily exigencies of household management, which necessitated flexibility and autonomy in the decision-making process." His prescriptions, then, are in dialogue with changing practices and sometimes in conflict with themselves. At one point, for instance, as Korda stresses, Gouge "astonishingly condones, under certain circumstances, a wife's keeping or concealing goods from her husband."[101] That is, even at the level of prescription or theory, Gouge works to acknowledge all the ways in which wives, to fulfill their obligations to their husbands and their households, had to exercise their own judgments, making decisions that could not be anticipated. This is not, then, a prescription out of touch with practice but a prescription that is itself a dynamic conversation. Since Gouge says in the dedicatory epistle that he "remembers" his female parishioners' objections when he first preached on this topic, one might imagine that he has taken their objections into account in this detailed discussion, filled with objections and responses, so that they assume a place not as the resistant reminder of what is done in practice and how it contraverts theory but as countertheorists with whom he must negotiate.

An auditor's notes on Gouge's sermon on Ephesians, when compared to *Of Domesticall Duties*, suggest that Gouge may have qualified and softened his pronouncements as well as elaborated on them. As an "Advertisement to the Reader" appended to the 1631 edition of *An Exposition of the Whole Fifth Chapter of S. Johns Gospell* explains, "These notes were about eighteene yeares agoe taken by *Mr. William Pemble*, from the mouth of *Mr. William Gouge*, as hee publickly preached them in *Black-fryers* Church, and they were found in the studie of the said *Mr. William Pemble* after his death. Take them therefore as here they be, and be pleased to passe by all imperfections."[102] It is impossible to know how accurate Pemble's notes are. Gouge himself fulminated against publications based on notes, perhaps as a consequence of this text. In the advertisement to the reader of Gouge's *A Recovery from Apostacy* (1639), he expresses concern that short-hand techniques tempt listeners "to publish their owne notes," wronging both readers and the author because of "omissions, additions, mis-placings, mistakings." He assures his reader that "If severall Workes of one and the same Author (but some published by himselfe, and others by an *Exceptor*) be compared together, they will easily be found in matter and manner as different, as Works of different Authors."[103]

Despite Gouge's reservations, Pemble's published notes strikingly resemble parts of *Of Domesticall Duties*; many passages are the same word for word, either because Gouge's book followed his sermons closely and Pemble took very accurate notes or because Pemble consulted the published volume. But there are also telling differences between Pemble's published notes and *Of Domesticall Duties*. Pemble's notes on Ephesians are a fraction of the size of Gouge's final product. This version lacks the detailed justification of Gouge's organization and emphases, as well as his exegetical detail and subtlety. The published book expands on and complicates everything in this compressed version. But Pemble's notes also include much that does not appear in *Of Domesticall Duties*. These differences may indicate either that Pemble simplified Gouge's pronouncements on wifely duty or that Gouge changed them.

Pemble's recollection of the sermon begins with "the negative part of obedience," that is, all the wife cannot do (Dd3v). It includes more inflammatory comments about women, including gratitude for "the great favour of God in giving us such a King as we now have, of the strongest sex" (Bb3v) and a reminder that, between husband and wife, "there is a most neere relation: yea [wives share] a common equity in many things with their husbands: and so in some things there is an equality; but yet for all this, to conclude as women do, that there is an equality in all, is but a womans reason, &c." (Bb4r). Pemble's account of the sermon's discussion of wifely subordination is also less nuanced than *Of Domesticall Duties*, reminding the audience that "of whatsoever state or degree shee was before her marriage, yet must she, though a Queen, &c. but married to a meane subject, after her marriage acknowledge her selfe inferiour to him, though for her Regiment and the like she may be his superiour" (Cc2r).

Regarding the wife's relation to marital property, Pemble's sermon notes dictate bluntly "That the wife abstaine to doe any thing of her owne head, and after her owne minde, eyther without or against the consent of her husband" (Pemble Cc4v). In *Of Domesticall Duties*, this becomes "A wife must doe nothing which appertaineth to her husbands authoritie simply without, or directly against his consent" (Gouge V1v), and Gouge explains that he includes the qualifying phrase "which appertaineth to her husbands authoritie" since he does not wish to restrain the wife's liberty in "sundry things proper and peculiar to a wife" (Gouge V1v). According to Pemble, the sermon includes its own qualifications regarding the wife's control over property: she may operate with her husband's implied or intuited consent; she may make decisions within the purview of being deputized to run the household; she may act in exceptional cases in which her husband is an imbecile or irresponsible; she is free to dispose of those "proper goods" of which she herself "hath a property and right, not only in the use, but in the possession of them." But the sermon's conclusion in Pemble's version is unequivocal: "For goods that are common, which come eyther by the wife or by the husband; the property, right, and possession belongs onely to the husband, the wife hath onely the use of them and no more" (Pemble Dd1v). "And the Law of our Land sheweth it, saying, that the woman is under covert baron, and therefore she may not give, sell, buy, or borrow without her husband consent to it, for otherwise her husband may revoke all againe" (Pemble Dd1v). In *Of Domesticall Duties*, Gouge also refers to coverture, but he takes the time to argue for its relevance (Gouge V4v). In Pemble's sermon notes, in contrast, Gouge offers the bewildered wife a final clarification:

> Heere there is a generall direction for wives in this matter, that what a sonne, who is under the government of his parents, may doe in this case, in disposing of the goods of his father, the same may the wife doe in the disposing of her husbands goods, and no more. Neither let the wife plead that shee brought maintenance with her, and therefore shee may doe what shee list; but she must consider the subjection that God hath laid upon her, and that now her goods are not her owne, but her husbands: And though they be yoke-fellowes, yet it is in familiarity, not in authority. (Pemble Dd2v)

The views offered at such length in *Of Domesticall Duties* are not all that different. But there we see Gouge working hard to persuade, phrasing things carefully. In *Of Domesticall Duties*, the last word is also that husband and wife are "yoak-fellowes in mutuall familiaritie, not in equall authoritie; and in relation to others as children and servants, not in opposition each to other. In this respect she is subject, not equall. If therefore he will one thing, and she another, she may not thinke to have an equall right and power, she must give place and yeeld" (Gouge V8r). But Gouge does not make the inflammatory claim that the wife has no more authority than her own son. What is most striking in comparing Pemble's sermon notes to *Of Domesticall Duties* is that, in the latter, Gouge presents this issue as a debate rather than a given: "It is a question controverted whether the wife hath power to dispose [the goods of the family] without or against the husbands consent" (Gouge V2r). An assertion in the sermon becomes a point of debate in the expanded book of domestic advice. It seems reasonable to conjecture that the female parishioners might have had something to do with that.

Are wives, then, the "keepers" of the actual and the daily, as many commentators on Gouge's resistant female parishioners suggest? Or might we view Gouge's female parishioners as rival prescribers, as theorists as well as actors? Since Gouge grounds everything in scriptural exegesis, might not they challenge him at the level of interpretation? It is important to remember that the wives in Gouge's London congregation appear in Gouge's text—and in our discussion of that text's reception—because he put them there. Perhaps one of the reasons that Gouge's conflict with his female parishioners has attracted so much attention is that, in his account of it, he uncovers what Kathryn Schwarz calls "negotiations that masquerade as prescriptions."[104] The wives he depicts not only negotiate with their husbands, and with the prescriptions imposed in *Of Domesticall Duties*, but with Gouge himself, compelling him to acknowledge, in print, that negotiation underpins, undermines, and masquerades as prescription.

Just as women cannot simply represent practice, standing for the real interrupting constructions of the ideal, so men do not align neatly with theory. For one thing, theory landed differently on some men than on others, creating conflicts between patriarchs and potential patriarchs, their sons and servants. Alexandra Shepard points out that "there were as many internal contradictions *within* prescriptive accounts of male authority as between prescription and practice."[105] Shepard places these contradictions at the "prescriptive source" of "the patriarchal model of manhood associated with marriage," but the fissures within texts like *Of Domesticall Duties* suggest that prescription is as much an effect as it is a cause, that it is a destination as well as a source, and that its contradictions emerge from the fact that it is already a debate and a relation between scripturally inspired rules and the demands of daily life, demands for which Gouge attempts to account at every turn.

We can see the complexities of gendered response in two cases of readers who left some record of their appropriation of Gouge's *Of Domesticall Duties*. These are the two most-discussed readers of advice literature—in part because we have so little evidence of how readers actually responded to these texts. Nehemiah Wallington, a wood-turner living in London, married in 1621 (when he was about twenty-three) and shortly after purchased a copy of the newly published *Of Domesticall Duties*, "so everyone of us may learn and know our duties and honor God every one in his place where God has set them," as he recorded in one of the fifty notebooks he kept. His claim that he made the purchase not for "me" or for "them" but for "us" suggests that he imagines the book's contents can be made available to everyone in the household and might help him weld the household's members into a collective, focused not on him as its head but on a shared submission to God.[106] He confirmed this when—years later— he drew up a list of 31 articles to which he required the adults in his family, including an apprentice and servants, to subscribe.[107] For Anthony Fletcher, what makes Wallington's references to *Of Domesticall Duties* remarkable is that "Here, unusually, we can trace action following from prescription."[108] Yet Wallington's action was the creation of more prescription— redacting advice into a document he required everyone to sign. The articles he drafted focus on shared duties to pray, fast, study the Bible, and avoid cursing and lying. Erica Longfellow analyzes the articles Wallington drew up, pointing out that they seem only loosely connected to Gouge's elaborate charts of reciprocal family duties, and concludes that "Nehemiah Wallington conceived of the Christian reform of his 'private family life' not in terms of intimate relations among family members but in terms of duty to God and upright life within the community."[109] The relation that matters, then, is the relation all family members have with God.

The other record-keeping reader of Gouge's *Of Domesticall Duties* is Lady Sarah Cowper. Although Lady Sarah and her husband, Sir William, travelled in a rather different social circle than the Wallingtons and lived in a later era, she shared with Wallington a passion for self-documentation. In the period 1670–1700, she compiled and indexed eleven commonplace books (3,500 pages). In 1700, she began keeping a detailed diary instead. Anne Kugler shows the complex ways in which Lady Sarah appropriates domestic advice in her extensive daily entries. She often invokes advice writers including Gouge in order to take her husband to task for failing to fulfill his obligations and for encroaching on or disrupting her ability to fulfill hers. According to Kugler, "Lady Sarah, then, did not so much feel repressed by patriarchy as she was outraged that its prescriptions, as she understood them, were not being fulfilled."[110] In short, Lady Sarah Cowper borrows method as well as content from Gouge in that she engages, as he does, in a reading practice in which she recruits evidence in support of her views and agenda. She also writes in her diary as a way to theorize about, supplement, comment on, and redirect her relationship with her husband. She manages her marital relations in part by relating her experience of marriage to the model she finds in books and in part by composing a textual relation that compensates her for her grievances by defending her own dutifulness and indicting her husband's irresponsibility and interference.

In these two exceptional and therefore much cited cases, we have a tradesman and a gentlewoman, a master and a mistress, living and writing almost a century apart. But each turns to the same book, Gouge's *Of Domesticall Duties*, as a resource in managing domestic relationships or at least in writing about them. Their very different positions seem to shape the forms their written responses take: Wallington's set of articles to which others must subscribe versus Cowper's diaries, apparently written to solace herself or, at best, to shame and instruct her husband if he should read them after her death. But for both, reading and writing are crucial to the process of gaining some kind of mastery over their relations, in part by turning domestic relations into textual ones.

In appropriating *Of Domesticall Duties* to their own ends, Wallington and Cowper were simply practicing the robust reading practice Gouge models throughout his text. The disgruntled female parishioners he remembers in the preface are not alone; throughout he conjures objectors. This practice seems to install on the page his favored pedagogical practice. His son Thomas writes that Gouge would restage his sermons at home for his household and neighbors "(wanting helpes in their own families)," but "he would do so after such a familiar manner" that many "have professed they were much more benefited by them in that repetition, then in the first hearing, for he did not use word by word to read out of notes what was preached, but would by Questions and Answers draw from those that were under his charge, such points as were delivered." Just as Bullinger urges the householder to get his subordinates to "rehearse" what they have learned, so Gouge tests his auditors' comprehension and memory of his sermons, inviting his neighbors to relate back to him what he has related to them as part of his project of bringing those he instructed to "expresse the Principle taught them in their own words."[111] In *Of Domesticall Duties*, Gouge reproduces this dialogic method by introducing the questions he will then answer, the objections he will counter.

Gouge also places his advice in dialogue by means of negative prescriptions, to which he devotes hundreds of pages. As he explains in his preface, "because contraries laid together doe much set forth in their lively colours, I have to every duty annexed the contrary fault, and aberration from it" (¶3). His table of parallel duties includes parallel "aberrations" from duty as well. He notes that many readers and listeners do not fully grasp what is at issue in a prescription for dutiful conduct until they are invited to imagine "contrary vices." In Gouge's negative prescriptions, the badly behaved come to life in ways that the well behaved seldom do. Contrary to the mildness required of wives, we learn, "is a frowning brow, a lowring eie, a sullen looke, a powting lip, a swelling face, a deriding mouth, a scornefull cast of the armes and hands, a disdainfull turning of this side and that side of the body, and a fretfull flinging out of her husbands presence" (T3v–T4r). This amounts to a set of directions for how to perform defiance. If one attempts to enact Gouge's description here, one not only achieves the appearance of ill-temper but can begin to experience it emotionally as well. The book does not describe mildness in equally graphic terms, nor does it offer a set of steps one can mime in order to embody it.

When he is not describing gestures, facial expressions, and postures one should *not* take up, Gouge describes negative examples in terms of evocative similes. Contrary to husbands who yield to their wives' humble suits are those "who yeeld to their wives request as an hard-milch-cow letteth downe her millke, not without much adoe" (Aa7r). Gouge laments a parallel grudgingness in his description of the "heavinesse of spirit, and discontentednesse of minde, when servants doe their service lowringly, grudgingly, by compulsion (as Beares are brought to a stake) and of necessitie, as slaves in a galley" (Rr6r). Throughout, Gouge renders his negative examples with arresting specificity. Contrary to good step-parents are those who "envy at the prosperity of their husbands and wives children: and secretly endevour to hinder it in what they can: and cunningly seeke to alienate the naturall parents affection from them: whence fearefull tragedies have beene made, and lamentable mischiefes have followed" (Pp3r). Contrary to truly generous masters are those who care for their sick servants, as Gouge advises, but "so mutter at their servants, and fling out such discontented speeches (namely, that they tooke them for their worke, and not to keepe them in their bed: to get some thing by them, not to be at such cost with them: or that they make themselves more sicke then needs: they may rise, if they will, (with many other like discontented speeches) that the poore sicke servants are more grieved and troubled with their masters discontent, then with their sicknesse" (Xx3r).

Why go to such trouble to imagine these discontented speeches? Gouge explains that "Notice is to be taken of these inhumane cariages, that the detestations of them may make other masters more tender hearted towards their servants" (Xx3v). But if negative prescription is supposed to inspire readers and listeners to do better, it can also act as a kind of script for the contrary but unimaginative. Furthermore, bad husbands, fathers, and masters emerge as characters in a drama more than the positive ones do because Gouge has put so much effort into imagining them and engaging the reader's imagination as well. Just like young Arthur, the protagonist in a play that might be called *How Not to Treat Your Wife*, so the bad apples in *Of Domesticall Duties* help the reader see how not to behave but also perhaps how one actually does or might want to.

If Gouge offers scripts for what one might be thinking, for questions one might wish to ask or objections one might want to offer, and for the kinds of things one should not say, his text also gives considerable attention to what one does, to performance or practice, as a kind of evidence. At one point, he advises a wife to testify to her husband's superiority by "some outward obeisance" such as bowing to him because such a courtesy "cannot but much worke on the heart of a good and kinde husband, and make him the more to respect his wife, when he beholdeth this evidence of her respect to him" which is also a model for children and servants to follow (T4r). Fletcher has singled this out as a particularly unrealistic expectation,[112] and Gouge himself recommends it rather cautiously, hastening to say that he does not expect the wife "to bow at every word that she speaketh to her husband." While children and servants should show more submissive obeysance more frequently than a wife, a wife should "testifie her reverend respect of her husband" only sometimes, as when he arrives home or departs or when she sues to him or he offers her a great favor (T4r). Gouge anticipates that "scornfull dames" may "deride these outward evidence[s] of their subjection" (T4v) but insists that even equals are sometimes willing "to performe this kinde of courtesie." A wife's conduct should "give evidence of the reverence which she beareth to her husband" (T5r). What interests me in this particular recommendation is that Gouge so self-consciously describes obeisance as a performance that then constitutes a form of evidence of an inward state.

Gouge presents all members of the family as needing to give evidence and to receive it. Husbands who interfere in how wives run their households "afford no opportunity to their wives of giving proofe of that understanding, wit, wisdome, care, and other gifts which God hath endowed them withall" (Aa8v); in contrast, the husband who commends his wife for a job well done affords her "an undoubted evidence of his good acceptance of her duty" (Bb1r). Gouge advises that children's carriage is a "surer evidence" of their reverence to their parents than speech, "for actions are better signes of the disposition of the heart then words" (Ff2v). Just as performance is a way of "giving proof," so practice is the best form of prescription: "Example is a reall instruction, and addeth a sharpe edge to admonition. Much more shall a religious parent doe by practise then by precept. . . . Practise is an evident proofe of the necessitie of the precept delivered" (Mm7v). Gouge's asseveration that practice proves precept closes the gap that is supposed to define this genre. The husband, too, is bound to the "practise and performance of the forenamed duties"; he must not just assert love but put it to "the truest triall, the *deed*" (Dd7v). Throughout his prescriptions, Gouge insists on the importance of putting them into practice so as to prove inward states that would otherwise remain inscrutable or to create inward states through acting the part.

The emphasis on conduct as evidence of interiority, of course, opens up the possibility that it might be tampered with so that it conceals rather than reveals: "Men are deceitfull, and may deale doubly, pretending one thing with their mouthes, and intending another with their heart, and never meane to performe what they promise" (Ii8r). While the ideal is the sincerely dutiful—"Sincerity is that grace that maketh one to be *within* even in *truth*, what *without* he appeareth to be *in shew*" (Y6v)—Gouge, as always, invites the reader to consider its opposite: "Contrary to sinceritie is dissimulation, and meere outward, complementall subjection: when a wife doth even despise her husband in her heart" (Y7v). In such a case, the performance of duty is not sufficient: "the subjection of a wife respecteth not her practise only, but her judgement and opinion also: which if she can bring to the lawfulnesse and meetnesse of that which her husband requireth, she will much more cheerefully performe it" (Z1r–v). Gouge here suggests that it is not only easier for everyone if the wife "cheerfully performs" her duty but that the whole elaborate system of reciprocal duties crumbles if her "judgement and opinion" do not subtend her "practise" and performance. Her husband must secure her consent to "the lawfulnesse and meetnesse" of his requirements, thus revealing not only the complexity of those requirements but the extent of his dependency on her.[113] Still, when necessary, superiors may at least compel conduct if not conscience. Of servants Gouge writes, "Though the conscience be free to a man, and out of anothers power, yet their outward actions are not free. . . . Though they cannot be forced to have a religious and righteous heart, yet they may be forced to doe religious and righteous duties" (sig. Tt8v). This is Gouge's bluntest statement of the necessity of forcing practice, which he depicts as the master's prerogative and as the limit of his power.

For the most part, Gouge focuses not on force but on persuasion, enjoining subordinates and superiors alike to understand *why* they must perform the duties he sets out for them, so that they can put their hearts in their practice. The key to understanding domestical duty, he suggests, is learning to grasp the concept of relatedness at its heart. Fascinated by the relation between syntactical and rhetorical structures on the one hand and human relationships on the other, Gouge offers his treatise on Ephesians as an extended meditation on relatedness. Gouge particularly dwells on Ephesians 5.24: "Therefore as the Church is subject to Christ, so let wives be to their owne husbands in every thing." As he explains to his readers, "The proposition is grounded on that resemblance which is betwixt the Church in relation to Christ, and a wife in relation to her husband" (C8r). Just as the mystery of Jesus's relation to his church can only be understood by analogy, so the importance of human relations can only be explained through comparisons. Gouge calls "so" "the particle of relation" (F6r). It "sheweth that that which hath before beene delivered" is "to be referred and applied to" the second term (F6r–v). This helps explain why simile is one of the crucial figures in all accounts of domestic relations, including Gouge's *Of Domesticall Duties*. The simile, like metaphor and analogy, trains readers in thinking relationally. But the system of analogies around which much domestic advice is structured treats as a given what Gouge presents as requiring thoughtful analysis and selective application. Rather than explaining relations to which the reader must simply assent, these figures demand that the reader imagine the extent and limits of similarity, rightly applying the figurations.

Gouge assumes figuration to be the language of scriptural truth, but he also presents himself as a guide to deciphering it. Discussing Proverbs 5.18.19, "*Rejoice with the wife of thy youth: Let her be as the loving Hind, and pleasant Roe, and be thou ravisht alwaies with her love,*" he advises the reader, "Here note both the *metaphors*, and also the *hyperbole* which are used to set forth an husbands *delight* in his wife. In the *metaphors* againe note both the *creatures* whereunto the wife is resembled, and also the attributes given to them. . . .

These metaphors hath *Salomon* used to set forth that unfained and earnest, intire and ardent affection which an husband ought to beare unto his wife." They are "fit" and "pertinent" but only if "rightly applied"; "if we stretch them beyond modesty, we wrong the pen-man of them, or rather the Holy Ghost that directed him, and propound a pernicious patterne unto husbands" (Aa4v–Aa5r). Sometimes Gouge finds the language in the Song of Songs a bit too "metaphoricall, and hyperbolicall" (Bb2v). He says of the proverb that the good housewife never puts out her candle, "That is a *tropicall* speech: and some-what *hyperbolicall*" (Xx1v).[114] So the reader must always be an interpreter, knowing how to "apply" metaphors "rightly" and not to "stretch" them too far. For Gouge, then, as for Bullinger to a lesser extent, figuration is not the icing on the cake but rather a way of practicing the cognitive skill that is crucial to understanding the Bible and performing one's domestical duties. The reader must be able to gauge the relation between scriptural metaphor and right application, between mystical relations and their human equivalents, between vehicle and tenor. Gouge frequently explains how one figure "hath relation to" another, one verse to another. He refers readers to the "rule of relation," by which, for example, what the Apostle says of one spouse applies to the other. Of Ephesians 5.31, "For this cause shall a man leave his father and mother, and shall be joined unto his wife: and they two shall be one flesh," he writes, "Yet is not the man only tied hereby, but the wife also: the nature and rule of relation requireth as much: if a man must inseparably cleave to his wife, the wife must answerably cleave to her husband" (H8r).[115] The reader must supply what is only implied by the rule of relation.

This skill of understanding how to apply rules of relation is one Gouge cultivates in and requires of all the members of the household who must grasp structural parallels, the relatedness of wives to children and servants and to a lesser extent of mistresses, masters, and parents to husbands. Each member of the household must constantly compare one vector of relation to others. By the last of eight treatises, he is saying of the duties of masters, for example, "A like dutie to this was enjoyned to an husband in relation to a wife, Treat.4.s.4. Some of the reasons, directions, & other points there handled, may be here applied. Read it therefore" (sig. Tt5v; see also Vv3r). He invites children to think about the relation between mother and father as spouses as well as the relation they share as parents to the child: "Though there be a difference betwixt father and mother in relation of one to another, yet in relation to their children they are both as one, and have a like authority over them. Now children are not to looke to that difference that is betwixt their parents in that mutual relation that is betwixt husband and wife, but to that authority which both parents have other their children: and so to carry an equall respect to both" (Ii3r). Gouge here imagines children who can recognize but then ignore the status difference between their parents in order to focus on their parents' shared authority. This is a fairly tricky maneuver.

For Gouge, domestic relations are analogous to the relation of Christ to his church, all roles and identities are defined relationally, and being in relation to God and to others entails a constant interrogation of interrelatedness. The rule of relation is, thus, a habit of thought, an exegetical guide, and a principle of social organization. As a consequence, we cannot separate content from form, prescription from practice, erudition from practical knowledge, interpretation from application in *Of Domesticall Duties*. Even as Gouge lays down the law about domestical duties—directing the reader through his chart of parallel duties and aberrations therefrom, asterisks, marginalia, and cross references—he also includes as a duty an obligation to apply, interpret, imagine, and relate that activates rather than subjects his reader. Slowing down to reread *Of Domesticall Duties* reveals that, in addition to being an encyclopedic compendium of advice on domestic relatedness, it is also a treatise on interpretive practices, on how to comprehend the world relationally. As soon as we attempt to abide by the rule of relation, as Gouge enjoins us as readers to do, the divisions between prescription and practice, theory and action, interpretation and conduct, literature and evidence begin to break down.

I began with a play. This might be considered putting the cart before the horse. Some critics argue that, if advice literature is sub- or extraliterary, it is also preliterary. That is, it contributes to the development of literary genres, which emerge to address its concerns more effectively than it can. Many scholars have linked advice literature to the drama, for instance, arguing that plays explore the contradictions that advice literature registers but often ignores or leaves unresolved.[116] Others argue that the problems advice literature addressed were engines of literary invention, spurring writers to appropriate or create genres better suited to grappling with social change and struggle.[117] In contrast, I have argued that advice literature is neither more primitive nor less resourceful than other genres and that, as a consequence, we might view it *as* literature rather than as a developmental stage on the road to it. But that is not to say it is not evidence. The question, as so often, is what it is evidence of.

While advice literature has been roundly dismissed as a record of what actually occurred in particular households, or how individuals felt about it, it can be recuperated as a source by rethinking some of our assumptions about it. Literary critics and historians are exploring how advice literature supplied terms and scripts through which people could understand their experience, afforded fictions that disguised and thereby helped to resist or manage change, and exposed and explored areas of debate and contradiction. I have particularly focused on how advice literature invited its readers into an active interpretive practice that, once underway, could not be predicted or controlled. This interpretive practice was as indebted to craft as to exegesis; it employed the rule of relation to make connections from the abstract to the concrete, from one kind of relationship to another, from the ideal to the actual situations in which one would have to attempt to achieve it. A writer such as William Gouge both lectured from the pulpit and took questions from the floor, attempted to persuade and provoked, recorded, and entertained objections, observed how people actually behaved, anticipated how they might, and advocated how they should. As I have suggested, the texts of advice literature themselves offer valuable clues toward a protocol for reading this genre as both literature and evidence. This protocol requires us to attend to "rules of relation" and to proceed actively as readers who constantly compare, connect, apply, supply, or take away relations.

In the preceding chapter and this one, we have seen how church court depositions and advice literature, genres that have not usually been claimed as literature, are sometimes disparaged or qualified as evidence because of the ways they are fictions of one kind or another, "stories" or "prescriptions." If we take a dismissal as an invitation, I have argued, we might find more literary ways of reading these texts that can make them yield new kinds of meaning, new forms of evidence. These reading strategies require a slower pace, an openness to the unexpected, an attention to both the specifics of a given text and its relations to other texts, and an awareness of our own investments in and active contributions to the relations we posit. Far from standing as a context for or background to literature, advice literature offers a model for how we might read literature—particularly the drama, to which we will now turn—as evidence.

Chapter 6

Relational Truths

Dramatic Evidence, *All Is True*, and *Double Falsehood*

I have shown that the official account of Fr. Henry Garnet's trial, Thomas Potts's account of the trials of the Lancashire witches, and the "true and faithful account" of the parliamentary inquiry into the London Fire obscure the processes by which they were composed and the complex interests they served. I have argued that depositions are collaborative compositions and that even advice literature was far less univocal than it might at first appear. Crises of evidence and the texts they generated called on readers to be relators, grasping and creating relationships between one situation and another, one social relation and another, one text and another, texts and their own experience. Plays too can be seen as "pieced together out of a collection of odds and ends"; some of their readers then disassembled and reassembled them to suit themselves, as they did with many of the texts they read.[1] Plays thus, like costumes and the identities they helped constitute, were stitched together out of fragments that bore their own histories, might circulate independently, and could be reassembled into different compositions. Such plays were, then, "joins" of disparate pieces, like joint stools, doublets, persons, or marriages.[2] Nor were plays fixed once they were ready to be performed. As Margaret Jane Kidnie puts it, "a play, for all that it carried the rhetorical and ideological force of an enduring stability, is not an object at all, but rather a dynamic *process* that evolves over time in response to the needs and sensibilities of its users."[3] Its meaning is, then, in its targets as much as its sources.

Our efforts to grasp both plays and the theater as an institution require that interpreters themselves pitch in to the work of unearthing and assembling fragments. As Natasha Korda shows, the largely invisible labor that under-pinned performances must be pinned and laced together like the very costumes it produced. Locating the "scattered traces" of women's work in the public theaters "often requires laboriously collecting many shards or fragments of evidence that would remain, when viewed in isolation, indecipherable" but that "take on significance or value only *relationally*, when strung or stitched together to form a pattern."[4] Plays and performances were, then, built from shreds and patches; as scholars of the drama, our work is similarly a process of collecting what pieces remain of those jigsaws and puzzling over how to reassemble them. Here too we must act as relators, positing relations among the fragments that constitute the drama and between plays and other kinds of evidence.

Because of the evidence we do not have about the early modern theater—for example, the box office receipts and reviews we would love to have but do not—the theater as an institution has inspired inventive evidence collection;[5] the surviving plays have inspired extraordinary methodological innovation. Critics have shown that grouping plays by company or by publisher helps us see them differently than grouping them by playwright(s).[6] They have also shown that we can uncover new evidence not by "finding" hitherto unknown sources but by reading familiar texts in strikingly new ways. Simon Palfrey and Tiffany Stern, for instance, manufacture new evidence from much-studied Shakespeare plays by dividing them into actors' parts, which they call "imagi-natively reconstructed part-scripts."[7] In short, recent work on the drama reveals it to be a pile, a process, a conjecture, rather than a stable object of analysis and reveals our own work to be not only digging up remains but imaginatively reconstructing their relations and speculating about what is missing. We join in the fabrications the drama has always required. Yet plays continue to be valued as evidence and relied on as illustration, even as they are revealed as unstable and disparaged as unreliable. Here again, as throughout this book, the question is what they are evidence of.

Apologies for the use of plays as evidence often refer back to Peter Laslett's cautionary "note" on the use of "literary evidence" in the writing of social history. Recognizing that many kinds of texts might be considered "literary," Laslett restricts his remarks to "universally famous" and "conspicuous" literary texts. He compares those who want to insist on the historical truth of literature to those who take scripture literally, not without some justice. But he counters such literal reading with his own uncritical faith in the superior truth value of demographic statistics: "all issues about typical or untypical, more or less, short time or long time, in fact all properly effective discussion of social descriptions, are finally numerical."[8] It is on the basis of demography that he famously asserts that Shakespeare's depiction of young women such as Juliet marrying in their early teens is "not true." To make this claim, he must elide the distinction between "women in Shakespeare's plays" and "Englishwomen of Shakespeare's day."[9]

Laslett warns that using literature as historical evidence is a troublesomely "theory-laden activity," by which he means that the investigator "has to have a theory, and an inclusive one, about how fantasy is related to real life, now and in the past" as well as "a theory of the relationships between 'truths' of disparate kinds, poetic truths and historic truths especially."[10] Although Laslett draws a firm line between "fantasy," which he aligns with literature, on the one hand and evidence on the other, "fantasy" is as likely to reside in a deposition, a true relation of witchcraft or the cause of a fire, or a book of domestic advice as it is in a play, as I have shown. But in this chapter, I will argue that using literature, particularly the drama, as evidence does, indeed, require one to have a theory of relationships among kinds of evidence and kinds of truths. While Laslett discusses literature in general, and not just the drama, I will focus on the drama because, when historians use literature as evidence, they tend to rely particularly heavily on plays, because critics and historians have been particularly self-conscious about their use of the drama as evidence and because plays showcase the challenge of true relations: of trusting another's report and making knowledge for ourselves out of inevitably partial and interested relations. Often, on the stage, this problem is part of the play's content and of the process in which the drama engages its audience.

In this chapter, I examine how both historians and literary critics recruit Renaissance plays, especially those by Shakespeare, as evidence, building to a discussion of critical response to Shakespeare and John Fletcher's *Henry VIII* or *All Is True* (1613). Critical debates about the play, I argue, suggest that the apprehension of historical truth requires the ability to comprehend new information by means of what one already knows, relating a particular individual to a well-known type, a text or event to a familiar genre, one historical figure to another, one era to another. Such a process requires the interpreter to bring as much as she takes away. In short, the play is not the thing in that historical meaning is not invested in the play itself as much as it is in the relations it invites the interpreter to spin out from it. The play is simultaneously indebted to particulars of the historical conflicts it depicts—which I bring to bear through a text Henry circulated presenting his own case for a divorce, *The Glasse of the Truthe*—and available to engagements with multiple periods, including our own. In this very availability, I argue, it is historical evidence, but evidence not of what happened in Henry's reign or in the time of Shakespeare but of an interpretive practice that has early modern affiliations and present-day applications. The same year that Shakespeare and Fletcher wrote *All Is True*, they also might have written *Cardenio*, a supposedly lost play that has recently been "discovered" embedded in Lewis Theobald's adaptation *Double Falsehood* (1728). Whereas *Henry VIII* or *All Is True* provokes the reader to move across time and to reach outside it, *The Double Falsehood* stakes its claim to both literary value and historical evidence entirely in terms of what stands behind or is buried within it. But, as we have seen so often in this book, the original that is supposed to resolve uncertainty is just not there. In its absence, we are left with our own desire and ability to posit relations.

Drama as Evidence

Although literary critics are as likely to disparage the evidentiary value of literature as are historians, historians are especially inclined to admonish their readers that "however tempting, we must never see literature as a mirror of reality." Such caveats are often correctives to an earlier historiography that succumbed to temptation. Lawrence Stone, for example, was heavily criticized for the ways in which he used literature in *The Family, Sex, and Marriage in England*, eliding the distinction between characters and historical persons, between literature and other forms of evidence. My favorite example is his wonderfully scrambled assurance that "There were plenty of cheerful and affectionate Wives of Bath in real life as well as in the works of Shakespeare."[11] Although Stone may confuse wives of Bath with merry wives of Windsor, his description of the Wife of Bath as "cheerful and affectionate" is more jarring than her attribution to Shakespeare. Stone's breezy reference to real life suggests that he did, indeed, take literature as a mirror of reality. But his misreading here is as likely to disappoint literary critics as it is social historians.

In part because of critiques of Stone's practice, historians have become more cautious and more defensive. In fact, caveats are usually the prelude to an apology for the use of literary evidence. For example, Elizabeth Foyster, who issues the warning above, proceeds to explain the value of plays and ballads as "a route into the otherwise hidden depths of the male psyche," revealing "the fears and anxieties" underlying norms and ideals for masculine conduct.[12] Anthony Fletcher sheepishly excuses his reliance on ballads and drama, "neither of which is the usual stock in trade of the early modern social historian." While Fletcher seems to feel a little guilty, he is obviously not doing anything all that unusual in taking "literary texts of all kinds seriously as historical source material"; many social historians employ literature as a "source" as well as ornament and illustration.[13] David Cressy similarly insists that, while "It is still something of a novelty for social historians to engage with creative literature," they must overcome their reluctance because "the printed output of English Renaissance drama provides a huge trove of text, almost entirely neglected by historians, that calls for cautious investigation." Investigate it he does, reading a bracing range of plays for evidence of the varied meanings of cross-dressing. Although Cressy criticizes others' assertions that "creative or polemical literature was grounded in social practice"—that is, that drama is evidence of widely held attitudes or everyday actions—he also draws on plays as one form of valuable but neglected evidence.[14] In his *Antichrist's Lewd Hat*, Peter Lake claims that he takes "supplementary evidence from the plays," which he links to "contemporary social reality." Lake's description of plays as supplements is borne out in moves such as "To clinch the argument, let us turn back for a moment to *A Warning for Fair Women*."[15] But Lake sometimes makes plays his main focus, devoting considerable time to reading them, as does Cressy.

Plays, especially those by Shakespeare, most often appear not as the main object of analysis or even the means of clinching the argument but as illustrative. They serve as "dramatic" evidence, then, by offering a memorable example. Discussing church court litigation in Sileby in the 1630s, for example, Bernard Capp brings in *The Winter's Tale* to clarify his discussion of jealousy:

> The uncertain boundaries of propriety [specifically whether it was appropriate for married persons to kiss someone other than their spouses] created problems that reached beyond Sileby, of course, for this was a society obsessed with female chastity. The issue drives the plot in Shakespeare's *A Winter's Tale*, where Hermione's innocent warmth towards a guest triggers a murderous jealousy in her husband, the king. Kissing might signify far more, as Leontes believes, and the word frequently appears in defamation cases as a euphemism for sexual intercourse.[16]

Capp here uses *The Winter's Tale* as evidence of an obsession with female chastity and the problems caused by unclear codes of conduct for married persons. But then his gesture back from the play to defamation cases seems to confirm

Leontes's jealousy, presented as unfounded just a sentence before: "Kissing might signify far more, as Leontes believes." When Capp next identifies kissing as a euphemism for sexual intercourse, he elides the distinction between the "innocent" action of kissing and the use of the term "kiss" to describe "far more." Doing slides into saying and back to doing, not only in Leontes's muddled logic but in Capp's analysis of the social meanings of extramarital kissing. His reference to defamation cases confuses whether Leontes misunderstands Hermione's "innocent warmth" or rightly grasps that the word kiss can stand in for intercourse. Rather than establishing the fact that the boundaries of social propriety were uncertain, this discussion stirs up confusion as to the value of either Shakespeare's play or defamation cases as evidence of that problem.

We see a similar slippage in Paul Griffiths's use of plays in his magisterial *Lost Londons*. Griffiths begins a chapter on policing by insisting, in a way that resembles Laslett, that we now can see that Shakespeare's constables are caricatures:

> we ought by now to have got rid of the stereotypes of the dithering clown constables Dogberry and Elbow who traipse through *Much Ado About Nothing* and *Measure for Measure*. This was dry caricature, but believable. Comic constables were stock literary characters at the time, but there were enough bumbling officers across the land for them to be instantly recognizable.

Still, Griffiths reminds us, "Dogberry did a good job." Griffiths cannot turn away from Shakespeare's comic constables, in part because they allow him to personalize early modern constables, who otherwise remain abstract and anonymous figures in his discussion. He goes on to complicate the evidentiary status of these caricatures even farther:

> The pair are nowhere near representative of constables, whose performances ranged anywhere from careful to careless, and they should remain as paper caricatures if we always pick out their funny sides, forgetting perhaps that Elbow served in his post for seven-and-a-half years, although steps were being taken to replace him as the play draws to a close.
>
> Yet much previous work sees early modern constables as second-rate amateurs for the most part, neighbours who served by turn for one year only and were not paid for their troubles.[17]

Should these characters be dismissed as stereotypes? Or are they, in fact, evidence that enables us to revise some of those stereotypes? In this confusing discussion, Griffiths depicts them as both. What were the functions and effects of such stereotypes? What purposes were served by the "paper caricature" of the bumbling constable and what interplay between paper (or performance) and reality made such caricatures "believable"? Did the caricature shape constables' ability to do their jobs? These are questions to which we will return in our discussion of *Henry VIII* or *All Is True*. It is not clear what *Much Ado* has to say about constables or *The Winter's Tale* has to say about jealousy or marriage. Critics zestfully disagree about these plays all the time. As a consequence, the plays historians draw on as accessible, clarifying examples are very likely to slip out of control, veering away from or contradicting the assertion they are supposed to support.

Plays' status as evidence becomes more rather than less vexed when we turn our attention to the methods of literary critics. Literary critics sometimes employ plays as corroboration, supplements, illustrations, or caricatures to be corrected. But they also invest them with heightened significance as vessels of cultural meaning or as so deeply embedded that they cannot be understood out of context and bear with them clots of the turf in which they were once rooted. Eric Mallin, for instance, values Shakespeare's drama, "as a historical repository, with a direct, participatory relation to its time."[18] The nature of that relation is inseparable from the nature of the plays' claims as repositories of evidence concerning the period in which they were first produced. To read Shakespeare historically or to "historicize" Shakespeare, as so many propose to do, requires some model of the relationship between the play and history. Some critics draw a sharp line between fictions and realities with a two-fold purpose: (1) to shore up the status of the real as a counterpoint to the representational, as the truth fictions attempt to manage or deny, and (2) to emphasize the operations of fiction in prompting, ignoring, or resisting processes of social change.

For example, in an essay on *The Taming of the Shrew*, Lynda Boose argues that it marginalizes or suppresses histories that nonetheless "leak back in" to it or "travel" from one register to another. In Boose's view, "historicizing the play" is "to insist upon invading privileged literary fictions with the realities that defined the lives of sixteenth-century 'shrews'" and to hold the play "accountable for the history to which its title alludes." Boose is a diligent researcher, turning up a range of sources and drawing attention to their provenance, that is, the role of nineteenth-century antiquarians in selecting, expurgating, and glossing the documents they preserve and transmit. Certain elements of her practice remain widely used: reading a play against other kinds of evidence, interpreting that other evidence warily, and questioning the drama's cultural functions rather than assuming them to be benign. But her argument in this essay assumes a distinction between "privileged literary fictions" and past "realities" that has since eroded; it also expresses confidence in our access to the stories of "real village Kates."[19] While Boose rolled up her sleeves and found unfamiliar evidence to shore up her reading of *Shrew*, she also relied heavily on David Underdown's argument that there was a "gender crisis" in early modern England, so her conclusions were vulnerable to attacks on that hypothesis.[20] Many other historicist critics were criticized for relying too heavily on grand narratives of only one or two historians or failing to grasp that historiography is a series of debates rather than conclusions.

In the wake of these critiques, literary critics of a historical bent are no less eager to seek history, even as they recognize that it offers shaky ground rather than solid. As we have seen in previous chapters, the bedrock tends to erode or fracture just as we are about to reach it. As literary critics have come to think of themselves as engaged in the creation of historical knowledge, rather than applying someone else's historical hypotheses to literary texts to confirm their interpretations, they have struggled to find ways to describe the relation of literature to history and, correspondingly, the value of literature, in this case specifically drama, as evidence.

As Fredric Jameson puts it, "The literary or aesthetic act . . . always entertains some active relationship with the Real," but the question, as we have seen in preceding chapters as well, is what that relationship is and how to explain it.[21] Historical readings of the drama have often been taxed with asserting what Walter Cohen diagnosed as "arbitrary connectedness": "The strategy is governed methodologically by the assumption that any one aspect of a society is related to any other. No organizing principle determines these relationships: any social practice has at least a potential connection to any theatrical practice."[22] I will not propose here a "true relation" between drama and culture, representation and reality, as opposed to an arbitrary connection. But I want to focus on the ongoing struggles to articulate what that true relation might be, what Julian Yates identifies as "the kinds of wrangles literary critics typically find themselves in when they try to parse out the relation between something called a literary representation and the so-called real world that made it."[23] I also propose to make a virtue of arbitrariness in that it focuses our attention on the role of the critic as relator—insisting on relations that are not there but rather made. Such a practice is both anachronistic and related to the interpretive practices we find under discussion in the seventeenth century. It does not originate there, nor do we inherit it. But attending to descriptions of collecting and gluing then might prompt us to acknowledge our own actions and agency now.

To venture any claim about the relation between one text and another requires one to choose a verb and venture a method. Numerous assumptions underpin that choice of verb; numerous consequences unspool from it. This methodological challenge arises when we discuss the relationship between any two texts, as we saw in attempts to discuss the relationship between depositions and other discourses, or between any kind of text and the real. Here, I want to focus on formulations of how the drama relates to social processes, often themselves described as "relations." The widely used tactic of describing some phenomenon or other "on the Renaissance stage" works to avoid making any overt claim about how the depiction of this phenomenon on the stage relates to anything else. But it is hard to avoid making some kind of claim about that. Most critics employ several different terms, even in a given essay. I have done this myself. It shows how hard we struggle to describe this vexed relation.

The challenge of describing this relationship intensifies as we move away from or beyond the model of reflecting social reality and as we attempt to name and explore messier relationships, relationships in which the real is neither distinct nor stable and the text's relationship to it is more active than reflection or representation suggests.[24] I should note here that the many claims that drama registers or exposes certain conflicts or social processes closely resemble the claim that it reflects reality, although these terms acknowledge that what is registered might be partial or distorted and sometimes credit (or blame) the stage for selecting some concerns and excluding others. For Michael Neill, "literary texts," especially plays, are "among the richest historical repositories that we possess—not because they often have much to tell us about the 'facts' of history but because they are unfailingly sensitive registers of social attitudes and assumptions, fears and desires." The "information" plays are "dense with," according to Neill, "often found its way more or less unconsciously into the work because it was integral to the world the writers inhabited, inscribed in the very language by which they knew it."[25] In this description, plays operate as containers that record and preserve evidence that somehow finds its way into them.

The first step in the movement away from verbs such as "reflect" or "register" is to describe plays as parallel or analogous or similar to other discourses.

Most critics acknowledge that they are not talking about drama's relation to the unmediated real, but rather to other genres, other discursive strains, often legal documents—or stories as we have so often seen them called. For example, Lena Orlin discusses a "telling analogy" between a Canterbury Consistory Court case and *Arden of Faversham*, describes the servant Nick in Thomas Heywood's *A Woman Killed with Kindness* as having a "cognate" in a figure in another court case, and argues that the structure of *Arden* resembles that of a case: "Like a church-court case, with its variety of perspectives aired in sequential depositions, *Arden* shows each character viewing the world through his or her own fears and desires."[26] Perhaps analogy is a particularly useful way to excavate plays' "possible relations to historical origins and contexts," because, as Mallin argues, many of Shakespeare's plays are themselves "occupied with tropes of similarity" which serve as "rhetorical models for the dramas' intercourse with the culture they recreate."[27] Another advantage of describing analogies or parallels between the theater and other cultural institutions, the drama and other discourses, is that it does not require one to explain whether one realm is prior to another or whether one has an effect on the other and if so what effect and by what means.[28]

But this strategy can also obscure a relator's own agency. For example, Subha Mukherji examines a legal case that "provides remarkable analogies with, and suggestive insights into, the process that Heywood dramatises" in *A Woman Killed with Kindness*. Of another case, she argues that it "provides a suggestive real-life comparison" to a play. In her discussions of plays, Mukherji often says that they "recall" or "remind us of" legal cases or that we are "made to think of" particular cases. But how can plays recall legal cases most spectators or readers know nothing about?[29] The telling and remarkable connections critics apprehend, while not arbitrary, depend on the critic whose reading across evidentiary genres supplies them.

Many scholars want to insist on the drama's cultural agency without explaining the nature or effects of that agency very precisely. To this end, many describe the drama as *participating* in social processes; participating has been one of my own favorite verbs since it attributes agency to the drama without assigning it intention, crediting it as a cause, or committing to a particular model of how that agency operates or even to what effect. Another advantage of "participating" is that it describes relations that are messier, less predictable, and more mobile than models of reflecting or paralleling would allow. It concedes that the drama and real life are not neatly separable.

Increasingly, the theater as a place is depicted as one site among many; the drama as a form is depicted as one genre among many; both are considered as nodes in larger networks. Considering the stage as a site, if a supercharged one, leads critics to track tropes or concerns across discursive registers and "conceptual ecologies," or to track a particular word through a promiscuous and errant reading practice that wanders across genres "without a map," or to track the circulation of particular objects through plays and beyond them.[30] Arguments that focus on circulation, exchanges, conversations, or networks also tend to land some place other than new readings of old plays. That is, they tend to employ plays as part of a larger arsenal of evidence in the service of arguments about attitudes toward, say, politics, sexuality, or crime, rather than in the service of an interpretation of a particular play or plays. Such arguments often focus our attention on disparities among different representations of a particular problem, issue, or event. But, at the same time, they often accord the drama an important role as a site or document of, or a catalyst to or consequence of, the subject under discussion.

In an influential early formulation, Stephen Greenblatt describes the drama as one of many sites through which social energy circulates. Mapping the flow of social energy, "we can ask how collective beliefs and experiences were shaped, moved from one medium to another, concentrated in manageable aesthetic form, offered for consumption. We can examine how the boundaries were marked between cultural practices understood to be art forms and other, contiguous, forms of expression."[31] Greenblatt's use of passive constructions here is typical of a critical practice that wants to discuss energy, agency, and movement, but without assigning too much demonstrable agency to authors or to texts. If there is a generator or pump in this model, it remains unnamed. As other critics have picked up on the notion of "circulation," the question has arisen as to whether the drama is a site or vessel through which energies circulate or is itself in motion. Many specify that the drama participates in conversations, exchanges, or networks with other cultural forms.[32] Recently, critics using actor network theory have built on this existing convention to describe plays as "mobile commodities participating within larger networks of social change and exchange," networks that extend across time and place.[33] Refusing teleology, network models can also avoid explaining cause and effect, even as they emphasize the agency of various actors, including texts. This work answers Richard Levin's provocative if cranky critique that new historicist critics shifted agency from authors to texts by embracing it.[34] Texts do, indeed, "make moves," even if they are neither intentional nor the origin or end point of the energies circulating through them.

Any attempt to understand drama's movement through these networks, what it brings to and takes from an exchange or conversation, requires us to think about its form in new ways. What is it about drama's form that distinguishes it from the other players in networks, exchanges, or conversations and demands our attention? One strategy for privileging the drama makes a virtue of its collaborative authorship, a feature that often counts against the evidentiary value of depositions, as I have argued in chapter four, and is, therefore, downplayed. In contrast, plays are sometimes valued as evidence precisely because they were produced collaboratively, even at some level communally, rather than by an individual. For instance, Anthony Fletcher argues that, since plays "derive as much from a 'social milieu' as from an authorial point of view," they "can thus properly be used as historical evidence, not of realities but of the imaginative and ideological constructions of the period, of its mentality."[35] Thus, for Fletcher, a movement away from "the author," with a presumably idiosyncratic, if locatable, point of view, elevates the value of plays and ballads as evidence. While Fletcher keeps "reality" distinct from "the imaginative and ideological," he also, in his very method, concedes that he cannot quite reach "reality" except through "constructions." Wendy Wall argues that plays "are particularly well suited for airing incompatible social discourses," both because of their dialectical form—"they imagine a wide range of positions put in conversation with each other"—and their conditions of production and consumption: "theater reached a wide array of people in and outside London and was collaboratively produced by people of different social backgrounds."[36] In both its institutional matrix and its dialogic form, drama commands attention as a participant in and register of social community, as designed to appeal to and activate response in heterogeneous spectators. In other words, it is valuable as evidence because it was inherently *relational* in its production and its form. Its content too is often described as dictated by or responding to new or changing "relations" among classes, genders, and nations, between country and city, old and new.

According to many scholars, the dialogism that defines drama and elevates its value as evidence renders it less successfully didactic than some other sources, because it exploits and explores conflict rather than resolving it. To give just a few examples among many, Mary Beth Rose argues that the exploitation of the ideological conflicts that bedevil advice literature "became the task not of sermons, but of the drama, in which a greater attachment to the concrete, an obligation to action, and a dependence on conflict brought paradox into the light of representation, giving visibility and significance to contradiction and seeking to resolve it through the operations of form."[37] Many critics point out that the drama was better at exploring conflict than at resolving it. As a consequence, the conflicts at a play's heart might override even an overtly moralizing conclusion; the hard work and cranking machinery required to achieve closure or coherence might cast doubt on that achievement. Carla Mazzio, for instance, suggests that the drama "often thrived precisely by exposing fictions of coherence (and the fictions of incoherence that helped to define them)."[38] This generic resourcefulness might allow drama to anticipate and promote processes of change, rather than simply registering or responding to them.

Drama's failure or refusal to be simply didactic was a matter not only of its relationship to its content but its relationship to its audience. Katharine Eisaman Maus argues that the theater's "radically synechdochic" method, "endlessly referring the spectators to events, objects, situations, landscapes that cannot be shown them" fostered "theatre goers' capacity to use partial and limited presentations as a basis for conjecture about what is undisplayed or undisplayable. Its spectacles are understood to depend upon and indicate the shapes of things unseen."[39] By this account, the theater's didacticism is not a matter of content but of venue and process. The theater does not teach a lesson as much as it teaches spectators a critical mode of evaluating evidence and the truth claims it supports. What distinguishes the drama, then, is not just what it is but what it calls on the spectator to do and to supply.

When we shift our focus from the drama to the theater, from the play script to the stage as a space, then we are presented with the question of what that space makes possible and what can happen thereupon. Speaking of the connection between city drama and London, Jean Howard, whose formulations have been particularly influential, argues that "the theater helped to make sense of city life" by weaving new developments "into stories that interpreted, hierarchized, and distinguished the incompetent from the boorish, the insider from the pariah, in the process figuring new social relations for an expanding metropolis and new solutions to pressing urban problems."[40] Howard, who tackles the "evidence of fiction" head on, concedes that the plays on which she focuses are not particularly valuable as evidence of, for example, women's lived relationship to property but that "these plays provide us with *other* kinds of historical knowledge: less of 'facts' than of the often contestatory *terms* through which historical experience was rendered emotionally and ideologically intelligible."[41] Joining Howard in viewing the theater as both a site of and an engine for figuring new social relations, Amanda Bailey characterizes "the early modern theatre as a site of contradiction, one that was simultaneously oriented towards the desires of its audience and against authorities." In this description of the theater as site, it is the visitors who are cultural agents. The theater simply offers them the opportunity, the venue, the strategies, and the materials through which to rework "dominant codes."[42] Drama generates, at best, or at least collects, preserves, and displays, the resources through which contemporaries can narrate and thus make meaning of their experience.

The theater might also provide terms and narratives that stymie change, that perpetuate continuities. Even as the stage accustomed spectators to seeing the new—Turks and Africans, Jews and Dutchmen, for example—it might also limit understanding of what these strangers might look like, how they might act, and who they could be.[43] While the stage included many kinds of persons, it also relied on exclusions in terms of who made theater, who consumed it, and who could be represented.[44] Furthermore, the ways drama helped its consumers manage change might also limit its ability to do so. Old bottles can make it hard to taste what is different about the new wine. It is precisely as bearers of history that plays might perform this limiting function; but it is also as they appear to resist or ignore change that plays might help audiences manage it.[45] Sometimes, then, the drama provides compensatory fantasies, which might muffle recognition or impede change.

Many critics who challenge the assumption that the theater was necessarily oppositional—a site of struggle in Howard's terms or oriented against authorities in Bailey's—still depict it as both the arena in which cultural battles took place and the warehouse from which combatants might draw the materials they could use in those struggles. Anthony Dawson and Paul Yachnin call the theater "a kind of waystation, a place where different cultural avenues cross"; Peter Lake describes it as "a sort of playpen in which participants could adopt and lay aside, ventriloquise and caricature, try on for size, test and discard a whole variety of subject positions, claims to cultural authority, arguments and counter-arguments about legitimacy and power."[46] As Henry S. Turner argues, "The crucial question that awaits further scholarly work on early-modern drama . . . is not *whether* the theatre operated as a site for refracting social and ideological contradictions of its moment but *how* specifically it did so, and how this process is itself determinative of English 'dramatic form' in fundamental ways."[47] Many critics and historians who rely on the drama as evidence and who assert the theater's significance as a cultural site evade both the question of how it functioned and of how the theater as a space is connected to the drama as a form. While Turner, among others, has proposed that the connection in part emerges from spatial mastery—in which theatrical construction, performance, spectatorship, and plots conjoin—the force of Turner's challenge remains unmet.[48]

If critics agree on anything, it is only that drama can do things that other genres cannot and that the stage opens up possibilities foreclosed in other cultural venues. This notion of the theater's and the drama's particular tasks and capabilities leads us back, in all these formulations, to the resources specific to dramatic form, to what it is about the drama that enables it to play a very particular role, a role many agree is important, even if they cannot agree on what it is, and a role that is connected to its status as evidence because the nature of drama's "relation" to early modern England is inseparable from its qualifications as a "true relation" of that time and place.

The stances of the historian and the literary critic are less distinct than my discussion thus far may have suggested. I have described historians and critics in the third person, as they rather than we. Yet I identify with some practitioners in both groups and have engaged in practices I assign to both sides of the aisle, so to speak. I also query practices associated with both disciplines, including my own, and emphasize the debates within disciplines as much as those between them. Here as throughout this book I attempt to include the reader in an interdisciplinary we—one that attends to both the historical and the literary simultaneously—so as to muddy rather than redraw disciplinary distinctions and to explore shared evidence, common methodological problems, and the possibilities of collaboration. In this chapter as in others, historians and literary critics will find themselves sharing the same practices, plays, and paragraphs.

Although, as we have seen, some historians and critics argue that the drama's value as evidence depends on its origins in an institution or collective rather than an individual, others privilege drama as the expression of a particular author. And not just any author. Whatever their disciplinary base, those who approach the plays historically or adduce them as evidence tend to return to Shakespeare more than any other playwright. In part, this is because when plays are used as illustrative examples it helps when the passages and plots cited are familiar to most readers. Thus, Shakespeare has a special claim as evidence simply because of his cultural dominance. Historians such as Cressy, Griffiths, and Lake read just as widely as specialists in the drama, even if they also read differently or to different ends. Yet Shakespeare retains pride of place among examples. We quote Shakespeare because everyone knows him; everyone knows him in part because we quote him so much. But many who turn to Shakespeare as evidence also claim that he deserves a special status. This is sometimes based, predictably, on a claim that Shakespeare's plays are better as literature. Greenblatt, for instance, argues that Shakespeare deserves particular attention because his works are "easily the most powerful, successful, and enduring artistic expressions in the English language." [49] But how does Shakespeare's stature shape the status of his plays as historical evidence? Although Lake complains that most historicizing "exercises" conducted by literary critics "end up discussing the most canonical of canonical texts," he too builds toward Shakespeare and Ben Jonson but only because "they happen to contain some of the most sophisticated and developed contemporary discussions of many of the themes and concerns around which the book is organized." Lake concedes that his work on *Measure for Measure* and *Bartholomew Fair* "perhaps paradoxically serves to reinscribe the canon in contemporary terms, albeit through historical means and procedures," but this is only because "in those texts Jonson and Shakespeare identify with uncanny precision many of the issues, tensions and conflicts that lie . . . at the heart of the culture and politics of post-reformation England." [50] From Lake's perspective, then, certain plays may have become canonical in part because they are more closely or truly related to culture and politics and so more useful as objects of analysis and more valuable as evidence. As David Schalkwyk claims, Shakespeare's representation of the voices of female servants "is considerably greater and more varied" than we can find in other sources, such as advice literature, "although not by any means comprehensive." [51] While not perfect, then, Shakespeare is better, not just aesthetically but as evidence.

If some claims that Shakespeare's plays have special value as evidence assert that they offer more sophisticated, developed, precise, and varied articulations of what lies at the heart of early modern England, others paradoxically defend the plays' value as a function of their indirect relation to history. They are also often referred to as evidence of timelessness, of aspects of the human condition that are outside history. [52] Critics who focus on performance emphasize the ways in which the plays are unstuck in time, perpetually works in progress, bearing the marks of various times and places and creating new meanings in new mountings. [53] The widely made claim that Shakespeare is less topical than other playwrights yields different answers to the question of how this shapes his plays' status as evidence. Leah Marcus ascribes to Shakespeare a "puzzling immunity" or imperviousness to "history at the level of specific factual data, the day-to-day chronicling of events"—what I might call an imperviousness to being recruited as evidence. [54] But other critics argue that Shakespeare's untimeliness makes his plays a particularly useful object of study. According to Bruce Smith, Shakespeare plays on the ambiguous meanings of proof as both "demonstration by evidence or argument" in a law court or a scientific laboratory "and knowing through firsthand experience," exploring "the subjective aspect of what purports to be objective truth."[55] In his argument for historical phenomenology, that is, subjective experience as a route to historical knowledge, Smith reminds us that Shakespeare's relation to proof remains an open question rather than a given. Kathryn Schwarz argues that "Shakespearean belatedness . . . creates an oblique refraction of reified norms."[56] Acknowledging that Shakespeare "represents things of his own time and place only implicitly if at all," Valerie Forman explains that focusing "on a playwright with a tendency toward abstraction, who reduces thematic content to forms" allows her to demonstrate how "debates about economic practices . . . could be rendered as tragicomedy."[57] Immune, subjective, belated, alienated, and abstract, this Shakespeare commands attention because of his oblique relation to his time and place.

Apologies for using the drama, especially Shakespeare, as evidence tend to focus not just on what is in the play but how we can get at it. This often entails taking up an oblique relation to the texts themselves. David Glimp suggests that, in liminal parts of play scripts such as inductions and epilogues, "Shakespeare reflects upon the relation of the stage to its audience and to society at large."[58] Many critics have isolated the scene not only as a crucial building block of the drama but as a resonant unit of meaning in other genres as well; in the drama, some scenes seem to demand more attention and to pack a stouter evidentiary punch than others.[59] Focusing on parts of plays is a consequence both of interpretive fatigue—we need to look anew in order to see some plays at all—and of approaching "the drama" as an archive. When the object of analysis is not a play or a playwright but a particular object, word, pun, or crisis in the culture as a whole or as depicted on the stage, then one must read across the field of drama and read drama in relation to other kinds of evidence. But this raises its own problems. Wall, for instance, puts pressure on the habit of choosing a single passage or scene as evidence in support of a narrative of historical development; her case in point is the relation of the Duchess of Malfi's prescription of syrup for her daughter's cough to the history of domesticity: "How can a passage from a literary work be read as 'evidence' for a particular historical social formation? How does a passage's place within a play's specific discursive thematic, or its reference to synchronic material practices, complicate its usefulness for telling this well-known historical narrative?"[60] These are important questions.

In her analysis, Wall focuses on what Laslett suggests is the only viable use for literary evidence—the meaning of something as concrete as sugar syrup. And yet, by considering the place of that syrup in the play as a whole as well as tracking the meanings of syrup across a range of texts, Wall demonstrates that syrup might not mean what many readers assume it means and that its meaning requires painstaking reconstruction if we are to grasp "the sheer uncanniness of the early modern everyday." Although Wall emphasizes "how literary texts can be drained of their figurality and historicity when conscripted to serve as evidence for macrohistorical narratives," she uses the play, and the syrup, to tell us a different story of discontinuity or rupture between the early modern everyday and our own.[61] Wall makes *The Duchess of Malfi* yield evidence by dwelling on its figurality and its historicity and by delineating the early modern meanings of sugar syrup, which, as she demonstrates, were both figural and historical.

As Wall's practice shows, evaluating the evidentiary value of plays requires close attention to how we read. Jean Howard advises that it is possible to create historical knowledge through reading practices that attend to "the content and forms of cultural texts themselves. They must be *read*, not just *read through*, as if they were transparent windows to something else." Such reading resists the assumption that a play must be about either one thing or another, to argue instead that the persons, objects, actions, and relations depicted on stage "are capable of bearing several significations at once, or, to put it another way, are simultaneously part of more than one discursive struggle."[62] A literary reading practice, then, while committed to discovering "literature's productive role in history," values literature and, in this case plays in particular, because of their indeterminacy or multiplicity of meaning, their availability to varying interpretations, their relevance to different kinds of arguments or narratives and their embeddedness in multiple webs of relation. As we have seen, even texts that are not usually counted as literature, including printed true relations, depositions, and advice literature, reward such a reading practice as well.

The kind of reading practice Howard recommends takes us back to the formalism of critics such as Northrop Frye but with a twist. Attention not to parts of the play but to the plot as a whole, to what happens in what order and with what consequences, can include attention not only to the history of forms but, as Howard suggests, to the role of form in history, to literature's productivity or generativity. As Kathryn Schwarz puts this, "Reading against the grain becomes reading for the plot."[63] This is an approach Margreta de Grazia takes to *Hamlet*, arguing that, for two centuries, critics have fundamentally misrecognized the play's premise because they have ignored its plot—a plot about dispossession—and *Hamlet's* embeddedness therein.[64] In rereading for the plot we may be reclaiming a skill that was relatively new to sixteenth- and seventeenth-century audiences and that the drama helped them learn. Lorna Hutson argues that sixteenth-century readers were learning to read for the plot in a very particular way because "the shaping epistemology of plot is . . . derived from the common ground which English dramatists perceived to exist between the forensically based plots of Latin intrigue comedy and the popular practices of detection and evidence evaluation that defined their own culture of trial by jury." Hutson also links the development of Renaissance dramatic plots to the ability to convey "a more complex sense of layers of fictional time," which requires the reader to conjecture possible futures as a consequence of the actions they see unfold on stage or that are narrated as having occurred earlier or elsewhere. By reading for the plot, we learn, as contemporaries once did, "ways of thinking about proof and evidence" as well as ways of thinking about motives, actions, and their effects. We also learn to relate what is represented to what we can remember or anticipate or what we can imagine as happening meanwhile but offstage.[65] To read for the plot, then, is to read historically as well as creatively.

What I want to add to these injunctions to read is a more self-conscious mode of reading for relations modeled on that William Gouge advocates in *Of Domesticall Duties*. This is, I realize, a counterintuitive, perhaps even a deliberately perverse, choice. As we saw in the preceding chapter, Gouge describes a finite system of relations into which one should place one's self and a limited set of parallels one might draw. But in focusing on figures of relation such as simile, metaphor, and analogy and what he calls the "rule of relation" by which what is true in one hierarchical relation can be applied to another, he gestures toward an interpretive process that is interactive rather than predetermined. As Gouge argues, relations must be *apprehended* through a practice that constantly attends to rules and figures of relation: how is this like or connected to this and to what effect? But relations must also be crafted or joined by the reader and so, in Milton's terms, they can be "taken away" by the reader. The practice Gouge proposes opens a door we might force a bit further to expand the range of relations we trace and how far we trace them, just as time has simultaneously expanded and contracted what we can bring to our practice as relators, sparking new associations and occluding others. The constant repetition of the words "relate" and "relation" in attempts to discuss the drama as a form of historical evidence suggest that Gouge's reading method might be especially useful with regard to plays.

At first, the drama appears to be visibly, loquaciously there—on the page, as the surviving witness to a performance that is now lost to us. But, like the deposition, it is a text that stands in the place of presence and that draws our attention to what is not there. In doing so, it advises us of elusive points of reference, of the difficulty of distinguishing one version of a story from another, or of privileging one version over another, and of our own imaginative opportunities and interpretive obligations. It thus requires a reading practice that not only reads in rather than through, against the grain and for the plot, but also attends to what a text does not include and requires the reader to supply: that is, its true relations to the networks of association we must join if we are to make meaning of it.

In Shakespeare and Fletcher's *Henry VIII* or *All Is True*, we encounter a superabundance of referential gestures, to other versions of this history, to what is not shown, to what is about to happen after the play's story ends and what has happened by the time the audience watches, to rumors that become truths and are then dismissed as rumors again. As a consequence, to the extent that the play can serve as historical evidence, what it documents is an interpretive process that extends outside it and depends on readers or spectators' active engagement. In drawing our attention to how we go about making historical knowledge, the play also leads us back to the reign it depicts and the ways in which Henry VIII intervened to shape what constituted knowledge of his wife's sexual history. The relator's interpretive practice is both historically rooted—in Henry's reign, in attitudes toward gossip, in a wide-ranging practice of thinking about evil favorites—and available for our appropriation and repurposing.

Henry VIII or *All Is True*

In some ways, we know more about *Henry VIII*, the original title of which appears to have been *All Is True*, than we do about many other plays. According to Gordon McMullan, the editor of the superlative Arden edition, it has the "firmest dating evidence" as well as "one of the longest and most stable theatrical histories" of "any play in the Shakespeare canon."[66] A 1628 performance "bespoken" by the duke of Buckingham at the Globe has been called "one of the best recorded performances in early modern stage history."[67] The play is infamous as the occasion of the burning of the first Globe theater, when the shooting off of ordinance set the thatch on fire at the first performance of the play on June 29, 1613. According to Sir Henry Wotton, the fire "kindled inwardly," since the spectators were "more attentive to the show" than to the danger. Several contemporaries commented on this disaster in letters and almanac entries.[68] For Ellen MacKay, the fire, in which the feigned proved all too dangerously real, "signaled the theatre's dangerous relation to the 'real' world" and "the unsecured relation" theatrical desire "orchestrates between the palpably real and the manifestly illusory."[69] The play's own history, then, is secured on the record by its instantiation of that unsecured relation at the core of theatricality and by kinds of evidence extraneous to it.

Whereas the play's performance history is more fully documented than that of many another play, it has long been dismissed as embarrassingly simplistic, even jingoistic. In recent decades, however, a critical consensus has emerged that the play's relation to its sources, to available genres (history play, late play, masque), to its titular protagonist, and to historical truth is vexed; that the title "all is true" is ironic; and that this uncertainty is not the play's failure or bad faith but one of its central concerns. In a turning point in criticism of the play, Lee Bliss insisted on "an essential ambiguity in the play's 'truths'" because, in the play, "establishing the 'truth' in any given situation is exceedingly complicated; prior certainty repeatedly dissolves in the face of later revelations," until we are suddenly and abruptly shifted to a more idealizing plane in Archbishop Cranmer's prophecy, which presents the monarch with a hortatory ideal, a flattering glass of what should be true.[70] Judith Anderson argues that the prologue, repeating the word "truth" three times, signals that the play will subject "the very notion of objective truth" to scrutiny. For her, the play revolves around "the changing relation between fiction and truth, poetic feigning and history."[71] As we have seen in previous chapters, the project of determining what might make a relation true depends on the shifting relations between Protestants and Catholics, men and women, court and commons. As McMullan summarizes, in the play, "What we are not given is a sense of testimony as the recounting of the truth: as with the numerous pamphlets entitled 'A True Report' or 'A True Account' that were printed in the period, there is no need to assume that all is true." Or perhaps the point is that there are multiple relations with equal, and equally vexed, claims to be true. If so, then the burden is on the reader or viewer, who learns to negotiate among competing truth claims in part by encountering their rivalry.[72]

Despite its meticulously detailed historical pageants, which would seem to lull the viewer with spectacle, the play makes stout demands of viewers and readers, requiring us to compare what we already know about this story to what we see staged. The play does not give us scenes we might expect: intimate scenes between Anne and Henry, or Katherine and Henry, or a trial for Anne Boleyn. Blackfriars, the venue for the divorce hearing at the heart of the play, was also the home of the king's company and perhaps even the location of the first performances of the play.[73] References to the setting might, then, invite the audience to consider the relation between the hearing and the play, then and now. By leaping at the end from Henry's reign to James's, the play, as Barbara Kreps points out, erases "decades of traumatic change and uncertainty in English history" while yet reminding viewers that they know what happens next.[74] Depicting a relatively recent, notorious, and widely known sequence of events, the play toys with what audiences already know and what they expect, requiring one to bear in mind not only what did happen but what would. According to many of its critics, then, *All Is True* is a play that requires one to understand various relations, most of which exist outside it and that the spectator or reader must help supply.

As a consequence, *All Is True* requires the same set of skills William Gouge inculcates as essential to Christian family life: apprehending relations, in this case between past and present, one king and another, one era and another. As Chris Kyle puts it, "What is at stake here is the precise relationship between two historical moments, not just one"[75] and the relationship, consequently, between two monarchs, Henry and James, not just because Cranmer's prophecy at Elizabeth's christening anticipates James as "another heir" to Henry (5.4.41), but because, as various critics have noted, Henry and his court resemble James and his in a range of ways.[76] Several critics have pointed out the resemblance between Henry's wife Katherine and James's wife Anne.[77] Nor are these relations as simple as one-to-one correspondences between Henry and James, Katherine of Aragon and Anne of Bohemia. According to Denis Kezar, in the play "the identity of Henry's 'queen' blurs into a palimpsest of his many wives" and "a future queen is indistinguishable from two kings (Henry and James)."[78]

More broadly, as Frye points out, "the play's piecemeal, loosely organized structure asks readers and audiences to relate characters and political contexts to one another, to interpret historical events in the light of specifically Jacobean anxieties."[79] McMullan describes the play's structure not as piecemeal but as cyclical: "we see each subsequent event in its past and future relations with others." For McMullan, this interpretive focus on relatedness extends to the typological, as it would for Gouge, by which the audience sees a connection not only between kings Henry and James but between these earthly kings and the biblical David.[80] Holger Schott Syme argues that all of Shakespeare's late plays call on the viewer or reader to, in the words of the prologue to *Henry V*, "piece out our imperfections with your thoughts," which, he elaborates, is "the action of supplying precisely what is not there, visibly or otherwise." While I agree, I would emphasize that precision is a challenge in this operation. Once one begins to piece out, there is no telling what one might supply or what joins one might solder. Turning to the prologue of *All Is True* and its request that the viewer "think ye see / The very persons of our noble story / As they were living," Syme argues that "The audience is asked to make a deliberate decision to treat the actors on stage as identical to the historical characters they impersonate, and only if they make that decision will they be able to 'see' anything else."[81] Yet as readings of the layered identifications of the key players in *All Is True* suggest, we are not required to identify an actor with only one historical character but rather invited to grasp the associations among the various contenders who move in and out of the positions of king, queen, favorite, or phoenix.

Even as the play requires the viewer or reader to apprehend the social relations at its heart and the contingent truth claims they generate, these relations also challenge the notion of succession on which the play otherwise depends. One queen replaces another, and one king replaces another, and yet the reader or viewer seems to move backward as well as forward. Succession is a political challenge not only because of the reproductive failures that bedeviled the Tudors but because it was so tricky to finesse the movement forward that was supposed to ensure both continuity and change. For example, several years after his accession but before *All Is True*, James rearranged corpses in Westminster so as to sideline Elizabeth I and relate himself to the male Tudors, as the ending of *All Is True* attempts to do. In 1606, he had Elizabeth's remains removed from her grandfather's central tomb and placed in a new tomb built for her and Mary Tudor. Coupling the two childless Tudor queens as a marginal, fruitless pair, James built a larger, more expensive tomb for his mother, visually and symbolically associating her and himself with their blood connection to Henry VII, founder of the Tudor dynasty, and with the founding of a new, fertile Stuart dynasty.[82] I rehearse that particular history, so vividly reconstructed by Julia Walker, to point out both how concrete narratives of lineal relatedness could be, literally moving corpses into new spatial arrangements, and how available to revision.

The play's usefulness for exploring the relations between reigns and monarchs is not limited to Henry and James. *All Is True* was available for application to a third monarch, James's son Charles I. Thomas Cogswell and Peter Lake argue that, in the 1628 performance commissioned by another duke of Buckingham, George Villiers, "the audience witnessed a full-blown exercise in propaganda in which a major political figure used the revival of an old Shakespeare play to send certain messages about his career and his fate not merely to the Globe's audience, but also, via newsletter and gossip networks, to the wider political nation." Cogswell and Lake make relatedness their method and their argument about this particular performance: "To make this case, we will relate the political dynamics of the play both to Buckingham's complicated relations with the politics of performance and popularity and to his immediate political circumstances in the summer of 1628." They also consider "Buckingham's relation to the politics of 'theatrical' performance, in both its literal and metaphoric senses." In their view, Buckingham depended on viewers to be able to place the reading "of what he was and had been" that they could derive from the performance in dialogue with other available (and more negative) readings, just as the play itself depended on viewers to link what it depicted to other versions they knew of these personalities and events.[83]

Cogswell and Lake's depiction of Buckingham's scheme in 1628 depends on an assessment of Buckingham's dilemma and proposed solution that is deeply literary as well as scrupulously historical. For Cogswell and Lake, Buckingham's problem and his attempted solution both emerged from another kind of relational interpretive process, that is, the compulsion or necessity of relating a particular individual to a familiar type, a particular event to a genre. Buckingham could connect himself to Cardinal Wolsey in the play because of "the dominant stereotypes of the evil councillor and favorite that critics of a royal regime had long used to describe the workings of court and conciliar politics."[84] This way of understanding the particular by relating it to the stereotypical was widely practiced by contemporaries, as we have seen. Cogswell and Lake argue that, when *All Is True* was first performed, some spectators connected Wolsey to Robert Cecil, secretary of state to both Elizabeth I and James I. A decade and a half later, it was the relationship between king and councilor that audiences recognized, and they could recast the players to suit the political moment: "given the stability of the stereotype and the political structures upon which it commented, the same body of maxims, archetypes, exemplary narratives, and morally satisfying endings were available to describe—and excoriate—the next great English favorite, George Villiers."

For Cogswell and Lake, Buckingham had become the victim of a political culture in which there were too few plots and too few roles: "when trying to understand political conflict, contemporaries only had available scripts with a limited number of starring roles and satisfactory outcomes."[85] This is a narrative dearth to which the character Buckingham in *Henry VIII* refers when he describes himself as "one in fortunes" with his "wretched father": "both / Fell by our servants, by those men we loved most— / A most unnatural and faithless service" (2.1.120–23). According to Cogswell and Lake, a man like Buckingham could be a loyal servant (a Buckingham) or an evil councilor (a Wolsey). He used the performance to expose his place in a fatally limited system of relations: "For his entire career, Buckingham was cast between those two poles—caught, as it were, within the plot of the play," so that all he could do was try to recast himself, "to manipulate the relative paucity of the master narratives of virtuous rule and evil counsel through which seventeenth-century English subjects interpreted their political system, not to the duke's detriment, but rather to his advantange." Addressing Buckingham's dilemma in terms of "narrative paucity," "vicious bipolar oppositions," and inescapable plots, Cogswell and Lake suggest that, for Buckingham, who was ultimately assassinated, a cultural failure of imagination proved fatal.[86] All the performance could do was remind the audience of the dire consequences of holding either position in this vicious opposition. Buckingham and Wolsey both fall out with the king and die in the course of the play. The play seems to predict that things cannot end well for Buckingham.

These two historians assign drama the powerful role of shaping conceptual, affective, and political possibilities with life-and-death stakes. At the same time, of course, this analysis is deeply historical in that the images, tropes, roles, and plots to which they refer were historically specific, even as they shaped possibilities for continuity and change. We can see in this analysis of a command performance of *All Is True*, then, what might be called robust interdisciplinarity of goals and tactics.

Although Mario DiGangi does not discuss this play or this performance, his identification of the "sexual type" offers an illuminating complement to Cogswell and Lake's analysis. DiGangi includes the "monstrous favorite" as one of his sexual types, arguing both that attacking Charles I's favorites offered a safe way to focus and displace resentments about the dangers of the king's personal rule and that the demonization of favorites had broader implications for homoerotic relations outside the particular situation of Charles and his court. For DiGangi, as for Cogswell and Lake, the stage provides an opportunity to subject the available types to scrutiny, suggesting their "partiality or inadequacy as a standard for classifying and evaluating the social practices of an individual."[87] DiGangi emphasizes "social and sexual ideologies," whereas Cogswell and Lake anatomize Caroline court politics in detail. DiGangi dwells on the agency of dramatic characters and sometimes, by implication, the agency they might facilitate for some individuals; Cogswell and Lake detail the strategies and contemplate the motives of a notorious historical person. But both interpretations—one from a literary critic and one from two historians—view types as socially consequential and the drama in performance as a vehicle for exposing and contesting the tyranny of type.

If we take the drama only as evidence of the common-sense understanding of a familiar type—the monstrous favorite, the friend, the lusty widow, the witch, the pirate, or the cursed shrew—we can miss its role in complicating as well as exploiting such stereotypes. We can also miss the varied ways in which those stereotypes might have defined possibilities off the stage, becoming conditions of unforeseen possibility on the one hand or limiting imagination on the other. Through what Ian Hacking calls "the looping effect of human kinds," by which people alter their conduct in order to "fit or get away from the very classification that may be applied to them," taxonomies prescribe as much as they describe, offering scripts for how one might choose to act or not to act.[88] Reading the drama in relation to other kinds of evidence, and opening to question the functions of stereotypes, enables us to compare manifestations of robust types in different kinds of texts with consequences as various as laughter or assassination and to compare the usefulness of stereotypes for Buckingham and his detractors, for example. Finally, focusing on the specifics of a particular performance can help us think about how the meanings of a play can be put to highly context-specific uses. Discussing the "typological inclination" in histories of sexuality, Valerie Traub shifts her own focus from the contents of typologies to "the cultural conditions that render such types culturally salient at particular moments."[89] This shift in emphasis suggests a perhaps surprising convergence between work such as hers and Cogswell and Lake's into why the type of the favorite was salient in particular ways in 1628 and how and why Buckingham used a performance of a play to critique that salience and its consequences for him. In this performance, court politics, the history of sexuality, and the narrative paucity of political polemic coalesce in an interpretive process by which particular salience is assigned to durable type.

Why should *All Is True* be the play that requires relational imagination from its audiences, that Buckingham should choose, that should inspire such careful attention to how verbal relations shape social relations, how political (and sexual) life requires an ability to apprehend and assess relations between individual and type, event and plot? One answer lies in the reign the play depicts, which can be read as an early evidentiary crisis emerging in the aftermath of the Reformation, on a par with those I examined in my first three chapters. In these crises, the contingency of truth claims was both undeniable and unsettling. Inquiries as various as Henry Garnet's trial for treason, witchcraft prosecutions, and the parliamentary investigation into the causes of the London Fire, depended on rumor and gossip. "Official" accounts of these inquiries register this dependence even as they scrutinize, suspect, or dismiss some evidence as implausible or malicious. In Henry VIII's efforts to secure a divorce, gossip similarly proved a crucial form of evidence, alternately relied on and disparaged.

We can see the emphasis Henry and his advisors placed on managing information and controlling public opinion in *A Glasse of the Truthe* (1532?), which was probably written by the king's advisors, perhaps with his input.[90] J. Christopher Warner argues that Henry's agents spread the claim that Henry had written it himself. The text's authorship, according to Warner, is beside the point: the "salient fact" is that readers understood that they should take the text as the king's and as rehearsing and justifying the perspective on the divorce that he wanted them to take.[91] The treatise warns readers not to hearken to malicious gossip against the king and not to give too ready credence to arguments contrary to those it presents. They should instead "manfully" refuse "to suffre any suche reportes" (C4r–v). But then it defends the evidentiary value of the reports it disseminates itself.

The treatise consists of a dialogue between a lawyer and a divine, a dialogue whose effect manages to be univocal, thus reminding us that it is possible to be both dialogic and didactic, despite claims that it is dialogue that makes drama particularly useful for exploring conflict if not for resolving it. Whereas, as we have seen, the drama is sometimes valued as giving us access to a kind of collective consciousness, this pamphlet reminds us of the process by which such a consciousness might be manufactured and controlled. The two interlocutors in *A Glasse of the Truthe* repeatedly return to the question of whether truth resides in "That whiche appereth in dede only: or that by report? And if by reporte, whether that whiche some men say & depose, is true: or onely that all men say and holy agree unto, is true?" (E3r).

As we have seen, "that whiche some men say & depose" was often taken as truth because truths "all men say and holy agree unto" were hard to find in a contentious culture. Nor was it always possible to distinguish what appeared indeed from what one knew by report. The lawyer concludes that one must begin with evident appearances but, when they are in question, one must recur to precedents, that is venerable reports (E3r–E3v): the law requires that we be persuaded by "sufficient wrytinges and sayenges," and what the lawyer seems to accept as "sufficient" is what appears plain to most other people.

The lawyer takes paternity as his crucial example. One can only prove "the truthe of his owne lynadge or parentage . . . by auctoritie of the lawe." The law, in the absence of any way of proving paternity, accepted that a woman's husband was always the legal father of her child, "whether it be so in dede or no," even in cases when he manifestly could not be because, for instance, he had been at sea (E3v–E4r).[92] Paternity was only an issue in church courts when the mother was not married. Paternity, that bedrock, was, then, widely known to be a legal fiction. For the lawyer, it serves as an example of how the law steps into the breach of the unprovable.

The lawyer moves from this—both a given and a sobering challenge to everything that is given about patrilineage—to the question of how one can secure "ocular proof" of copulation, given that commonly no witnesses "depose of the very acte." As we have seen, this is a crucial concern in church courts, in which witnesses assert the plausibility of their testimony by explaining the lengths to which they have gone in order to see others engaged in prohibited sex acts. Here, the lawyer, warming up for the question of Katherine and Arthur's marriage, argues that, in the absence of eyewitnesses, one must accept what would later be called "circumstantial evidence" and what he describes here as "the nere circumstances precedynge or folowynge the acte," which include age and opportunity, and "conversation in bedde" as reported by others, the very bases of the claim that Arthur and Katherine must have consummated their marriage.

The divine concludes that it will "lytel avayle the quene to alledge, that she was nat knowen by prince Arthur" because he has heard that there are noble witnesses

> that knew prince Arthure & the quene at the tyme of their mariage, and knewe them bothe to be of competent age, feete [as in feated, suited or equipped?] apte & prone to that naturall acte: bedded to gyther at sondrye tymes, lyvinge at libertie, in one house beynge: no lette or impediment in lawe why they shulde nat, but many

provocations of nature why they shulde accomplysshe their natural
desire in that be halfe. (E4r–v)

Common knowledge of what constitute natural desires and acts here conjoins
with the authority of noble men and a very specific description of circumstances such as being "bedded together" on various occasions and having the
run of a shared house. Just as paternity is taken to be likely, so the likelihood
that Katherine and Arthur consummated their marriage is taken as proof
enough. But while the legal fiction of a husband's paternity takes a woman
at her word, here the circumstantial operates to silence Katherine's account of
her sexual experience.

Having already adduced as proof what he has "heard said," the divine
then turns from common knowledge of what is likely to have happened to the
hearsay account of what Arthur said did: "some men of great house say and (as
I am enfourmed) depose upon theyr othe: that prince Arthur dyd report hym
selfe unto them, that he hadde carnally knowen her" (E4v). Here again, it is
striking how closely this testimony resembles that offered in church courts,
in which sexual relations exist as verbal ones, available by the "attestacion of
credible folkes" (E4v–E5r). This evidence is at three removes from the act: the
divine has been informed of depositions of Arthur's report. The discussion
builds toward the much repeated joke that Arthur supposedly made, asking for a drink the morning after his wedding night because he was parched
from having been in Spain. The version repeated here is "Mary if thou had-
deste bene as often in Spayne this nyghte as I have bene: I thynke verely
thou woldest have ben moche dryar" (E5r).[93] Both the divine and the lawyer
recognize that a joke or a boast is being taken as proof. But they insist on it
nonetheless. The lawyer claims that in the face of this evidence the queen can
hardly claim that her marriage was not consummated: "I thynke the quene
wyll never erenestly alledge that matter: which hath nat only no probabilite
of truth, but also that beyng proved whiche you speke of: that is to say, the
mariage, livinge, beddinge, and conversation together of her and prince Ar-
thure, a plaine conclusion to the contrarie" (E4v). There is only doubt about
it because the queen insists that she was not carnally known "and she sayth
that she knoweth it better than all the worlde beside" (E6v). And yet, "this her
ostentacion & affirmation is nothinge true" (E5v). More to the point, it does
not matter whether it is true or not. It is no longer possible to prove it, "seynge
that she hath bene knowen syns" (E7r). So the issue is not what happened but
whose allegation carries the most weight. In this case, a jest taken in earnest

trumps the queen's "earnest" allegations of a nonconsummation assumed to be laughably unlikely.

Offering an example of what would happen if both his parents denied that he was their son, the lawyer concludes that "the question is not what they know: but what is to be bileved. And truly no man is to be bileved in his owne matter" (E8r). That is, the queen is both the best witness—"It cannot be denied, but she knoweth it best of folke nowe living" (E6v) since Arthur, presented as a superior witness because male, is now dead—and the worst in that she has a vested interest and so is incredible. The lawyer ignores the fact that, just as his parentage is as much his own matter as it is his parents', so Katherine and Henry's marriage is as much the king's "owne matter" as it is hers. The conclusion of this rather one-sided dialogue is that the proximity of Arthur and Katherine in bed "so clerely setteth for the truthe of carnall knowledge" that the queen's "asseveration to the contrary" should not be able to counter it.

In *A Glasse of the Truthe*, then, while "untrue reports" should not be heeded, what counts as truth is still a matter of reports, reports from noble men and women as to the natural course that relations between young kings and queens in bed will most probably take. Because that is the case, Henry has sought out and then published rumors and stories about Katherine. In *A Glasse of the Truthe*, we see how Henry might turn the inability to know or prove—the inability that makes gossip so dangerous because it stirs up uncertainties that cannot be resolved—to his advantage. Only Katherine can be sure whether Katherine and Arthur's marriage was consummated. As we have so often seen in this book, just as we glimpse a definitive form of evidence—Arthur's testimony, or Katherine's body, if it could have been examined after her wedding night—that incontrovertible proof recedes out of reach. Arthur is dead, and Katherine has been known since. Her report on her "owne matter," the matter of her own body, cannot counter Henry's investment in his great matter. In such a vacuum, plausibility ("what is to be bileved") and power ("the playne truthe of our mooste noble and lovinge princis cause" [A2v]) suffice as proof. *A Glasse of the Truthe* suggests that it is not arbitrary that *All Is True* should be about Henry VIII or that Buckingham should choose this particular play because what is at issue in it is the role of verbal relations in negotiating social relations.

The press was not Henry's only mechanism for managing gossip. He used the law as well. Kreps draws particular attention to the laws Henry enacted "to accommodate his changes in heart and mind and turn his will into law."[94] Eric Ives's biography of Anne Boleyn explains some of these acts in helpful terms:

The Succession Act [25 Henry VIII, c. 22] required every person to
take an oath to support the Boleyn marriage, and a massive attempt
was made to swear all adult males in the country. The Act also made
it a treasonable offence to write or act against the marriage with
Anne, with lesser penalties for gossip or for refusing to take the oath
specified. . . . Another Act [26 Henry VIII, c. 13], passed later in the
year, extended the definition of treason to cover anything spoken,
written or done which deprived the king of his title or seriously
defamed him.[95]

These acts thus made gossip treason; Anne Boleyn's treason trial, then, depended on rumor and was defended by spreading rumors that justified the
verdict. An act after Anne's death retroactively clarified that a queen's adultery
was treason; an act following the execution of Catherine Howard made it treason for a woman the king intended to marry, assuming her to be a virgin, to
keep it a secret that she was not; it also made it treason for any subject to fail
to report to the king or Privy Council knowledge of the queen's "lightness of
body"—thus licensing gossip and making a refusal to relate it into treason.[96]
For Henry, executing his marital relations in the interests of the succession
(among other things) required the skillful regulation of verbal relations, suppressing some and promoting others as suited his shifting needs for different
truths. In *Henry VIII*, Wolsey praises Henry for the precedents he sets: "Your
grace has given a precedent of wisdom / Above all princes in committing
freely / Your scruple to the voice of Christendom" (2.2.94). Resolving multiple
voices into one, the play presents popular opinion as how "the voice is now"
(3.2.405); how "the voice goes" (4.2.11); how "it stands agreed, I take it, by all
voices" (5.3.121–22); and what "the common voice" says (5.3.209). *A Glasse of
the Truthe* and Henry's statutes suggest that his precedent was not committing
his scruple to the common voice but dictating what that voice should be.

Whereas *A Glasse of the Truthe* intervenes when Henry's great matter remains undecided, attempting to sway his subjects to his version of the truth,
All Is True weighs in long after the fact, when Cranmer's prognostications
have come true. And from that perspective, it offers a very cynical spin on *A
Glasse of the Truthe's* treatment of what exactly the truth is. To the insistence
that the plausible is the true, Shakespeare and Fletcher add the suggestion
that "what is to be believed" is often what is expedient and that, while this
version may triumph over others, it cannot eliminate them entirely. What we
see in the play is a depiction of Henry relying on gossip to justify eliminating

a favorite and a wife of whom he has grown tired. If the historical Henry criminalized gossip later, he did so because he understood its power, or so the play would suggest.

Although critics routinely use the words "relate" and "relation" in their discussions of this play, the play itself never uses the word "relation"—a word that appears relatively rarely in Shakespeare's works. Perhaps unsurprisingly, it occurs most often (three times) in *The Winter's Tale*, which is so interested in dubious verbal relations of fraught emotional relations.[97] Regardless, critics emphasize the importance of both narrative and social relations in *All Is True*. It thus participates in what Syme describes as "the late plays' perverse interest in exploiting spectacle as well as narrative while casting doubt on the autonomous validity of both."[98] The play begins with what Bliss describes as "Norfolk's relation to Buckingham of the events of the Field of the Cloth of Gold," a relation that functions to put us on guard: "caught once in easy acceptance of what we thought was a conventional report speech"—that is, a true relation—"we are now less ready to accept either the grand appearance of the moment or any single person's assertion."[99] *All Is True*, then, opens with conflicting relations, dramatizing the conflict among competing truth claims from a notably cool distance, both temporal and political. Long after Henry VIII's death, the play stages the sovereign's role in promoting and relying on rumor as interested proof.

The word "relate" appears twice in the play, both times with reference to a witness against Buckingham. Henry first demands:

> Let be called before us
> That gentleman of Buckingham's: in person
> I'll hear him his confessions justify,
> And point by point the treasons of his master
> He shall again relate. (1.2.4–8)

When this gentleman appears, Wolsey says, "Stand forth, and with bold spirit relate what you, / Most like a careful subject, have collected / Out of the Duke of Buckingham" (1.2.129–31). The only evidence against Buckingham is words, evidence "collected out of" Buckingham and then related to others and against him. In this, the treason trial shares ground with the relatively low-stakes disputes between neighbors heard in church courts. Both depend on witnesses' uncorroboratable testimony, what might be called gossip. Buckingham's surveyor exists first as an "examination" (1.1.116) or a deposition, a text that, as we have seen, stands in the place of a witness, until Buckingham demands a face-to-face confrontation with him, a confrontation related rather than shown to us. As the First Gentleman reports to the Second,

> The great Duke
> Came to the bar, where to his accusations
> He pleaded still not guilty and alleged
> Many sharp reasons to defeat the law.
> The King's attorney, on the contrary,
> Urged on the examinations, proofs, confessions
> Of diverse witnesses, which the Duke desired
> To have brought *viva voce* to his face;
> At which appeared against him his surveyor,
> Sir Gilbert Park his chancellor, and John Court,
> Confessor to him, with that devil monk,
> Hopkins, that made this mischief. (2.1.11–22)

Although these "diverse witnesses" outface him, refusing to back down, the duke never accedes to their relation of his relation to the king. Like Henry Garnet and the Popish Plot traitors we considered in chapter one, Buckingham withholds the confession the state seeks and requires, instead reasserting his loyalty and pardoning those who have brokered his execution. In the play, this refusal to confess generates a discursive competition in which the state, promoting and depending on rumor, cannot distinguish its official story from the other versions. Rumors turn out to be accurate and official versions little more than self-serving gossip. The play suggests but never confirms that the evidence against both Buckingham and Katherine might be trumped up.

A discussion between two gentlemen in 2.1 leads from Buckingham's conviction to an even worse "ensuing evil" related to a secret "so weighty, 'twill require / A strong faith to conceal it"—that is, the estrangement between Katherine and Henry (2.1.140, 143–44). The second gentleman asks if the first has heard "A buzzing of a separation / Between the King and Katherine" (147–48). The first says that, while he heard this buzzing, he did not "hold it" since the king, when he heard it, angrily "sent command to the Lord Mayor straight / To stop the rumour, and allay those tongues / That durst disperse it" (150–52). But, as the second gentleman explains, the status of that buzzing or rumor has changed with the times:

> But that slander, sir,
> Is found a truth now, for it grows again
> Fresher than e'er it was, and held for certain
> The King will venture at it. Either the Cardinal,
> Or some about him near have, out of malice
> To the good Queen, possessed him with a scruple
> That will undo her. (2.1.152–58)

In the next scene, the lord chamberlain remarks that "These news are every-where—every tongue speaks 'em, / And every true heart weeps for't" (2.2.37–38). Slander becomes truth when the king says so, when he no longer acts to stop it but rather freshens it with his credence.

The play does not stage the debate regarding whether Katherine ever consummated her first marriage to Henry's brother Arthur, that is, whether she was a virgin when she married Henry. As we have seen in *A Glasse of the Truthe*, this issue was at the center of legal, theological, and popular inquiries into the status of Henry and Katherine's marriage; Henry claimed that his doubts on this score occasioned his belated scruple regarding the marriage. *Henry VIII* does not offer a clear answer to the question of the origin of Henry's prick of conscience, although it does depict him meeting Anne before we are told that there is a rift between king and queen. Does Anne spur him to get rid of Katherine, whom he claims he would keep if he could be reassured, or does he manufacture a scruple to serve his own ends, or does Wolsey possess him with it or instill it in him? Wherever it came from, Henry's scruple spurred him to promote the rumors he had previously suppressed. This is no different from the process by which "evidence" is gathered or manufactured against Bucking-ham. In the proceedings against Katherine, as depicted in *All Is True*, we see Henry promoting slander about Katherine, even if the content of that slander is not rehearsed in detail.[100]

The Henrician statutes defending the historical Henry's marriage to Anne, and *The Glasse of the Truthe*, suggest that the legitimacy of a marriage depends on the sorts of talk about it that are allowed. This is particularly true of a royal marriage, of course, where the legitimacy of the heir to the throne is at stake. But the Act of Supremacy, no matter how exceptional its circumstances and aims, shares with advice literature the view that refusing to countenance ru-mors is an important tactic in defending marriages. Perhaps it is not surprising to see connections between Henry's statutes and advice literature. Although the statutes carry considerably more "prescriptive force," both presume to direct speech and action, especially "relations." Chilton Latham Powell argues that Heinrich Bullinger's *Christen State of Matrimonye*, which, as we have seen in chapter five, is often considered a prototype for English domestic advice, "gives considerable evidence of a connection with the divorce of Henry VIII," including tables of consanguinity and affinity, the grounds on which Henry repudiated Katherine, and an exasperated statement about tyrants who defend their "own fond fleshly" whims by coining new and ungodly laws:

> what is the cause of all this dissension cruell persecucion tyrannye
> evell lawes making unjust actes/false religion/wyked ordinances
> & ungodly decrees & institucions but onely the blynd ignorance
> of unlerned rulers? which mesure all thing aftyr theyr owne fonde
> fleshly aspects and reason besydes all scriptures: & wold have their
> owne carnall willes to stonde in the stede/yea rather tto be above
> god & his lawes.[101]

In this passage, which goes a long way toward explaining why Bullinger's book was censored, he emphasizes Henry's knack for turning his "carnal will" into law, the knack that makes him the perfect protagonist for a play like *All Is True*, with its emphasis on interested versions of the truth.

Wright extends Powell's point about Bullinger to argue that the proliferation of domestic advice literature after the Reformation responded in part to Henry's divorce: "Out of the effort to clarify and codify marriage relations, an effort which was stimulated to a considerable degree by the popular interest in the discord in the royal household, a whole literature developed."[102] This relation between Henry's marriages and divorces and the emergence of advice literature may or may not be true. But the proposal that a royal divorce and the controversy surrounding it spurred the development of this genre might provoke us to think again about "rules of relation" by which an impulse to "clarify and codify marriage relations" emerges in relation to the king's marriages and the changes they threaten to a whole system of orderly, scripturally informed relatedness.

In *Of Domesticall Duties*, printed almost a century after Henry's divorce, William Gouge warns that giving credence to and promoting gossip is the way to undo a marriage. Gouge was the pastor of Blackfriars, where the play was performed by the King's Men and where the divorce hearing at its heart took place. Gouge argues that it is a crucial duty of relatedness not to disseminate or even receive defamatory relations about one's family members. He discusses this at greatest length with regard to spouses, but he recurs to it as a crucial duty in the relationships of parents and children, masters and servants as well. In a section on "husbands and wives preventing each others discredit," Gouge advises that to "prevent an ill name," the spouses must attend to "What one relateth of another, and how." First and foremost, "husbands and wives may in no case delight to discover unto others, and spread abroad the infirmities, and imperfections of one another, or any thing that may tend to the discredit of either of them: but rather cover and conceale them as much as they may with good conscience." It is also important that spouses be careful "What eare they give to things related by others": "husbands and wives must not have their eares wide opened to heare every tale and report that shall be brought to one against the other, but rather shew themselves displeased and offended with them that are ready to relate things of evill report." Spouses who show an interest in "tales and reports of one another" will find "flattering tale-bearers" all too eager to tell them "untrue, or slight reports." Finally, spouses must be careful not to turn evil report into censure: "If one heare reported any notorious crime of the other, they may not be over-headie or hastie to judge and condemne, no though they thinke they see some evidence thereof, but rather suspend their judgement"; "they must not rashly beleeve any evill report of one another, but rather suppresse all light suspitions as much as they can."[103] In this advice, Gouge emphasizes how much relations in the sense of reports or accounts matter to the maintenance of intimate relationships by arguing that one enacts loyalty by neither spreading nor listening to relations about one's spouse—even if true but especially if not.

Focusing my discussion of the relational interpretation of drama on Shakespeare and Fletcher's *All Is True*, I have considered relation in its meaning of relationships—to spouses and favorites—and in its meaning of a verbal relation, particularly a rumor of dubious veracity but powerful effect. As I have shown, controversies surrounding Henry's divorces, at the time and in retrospect, insisted on the relationship between the two, particularly the role rumors played in constituting the truth of marital and political relations. I have, thus, considered the play as itself evidence of a seventeenth-century awareness of this connection. I have looked backward from *All Is True* to *A Glasse of the Truthe* and forward from it to Gouge's articulation of the proper protocol for handling reports about one's family members. These relations cannot be charted in any linear way. They keep twisting back and around. Rather than assuming that *A Glasse of the Truthe* or *Of Domesticall Duties* are "contexts" for *All Is True*, I have insisted that the relationship I posit among these texts is not a given; I have woven a particular web of textual relations in order to draw attention to how the play both stages the process of relational interpretation and requires it of its own interpreters. The interpretive practice of grasping relations is simultaneously historically specific and a possible model for our own practice.

Double Falsehood

The interpretation of *Henry VIII* or *All Is True*, as many critics have argued, requires its viewers or readers to join what is in the play with what is not, what they find with what they bring to bear. The controversy I now turn to, over the status of another supposed Fletcher-Shakespeare collaboration, exposes critics' investment in something that is not there and the ingenuity with which we launch ourselves into the void and create the truth we require. If we view Lewis Theobald's *The Double Falsehood* as having some relation to the lost *Cardenio*, then it emerges, in some way, from the brief Fletcher/Shakespeare collaboration that also issued in *Henry VIII* or *All Is True*. While R. A. Foakes's Arden edition of *Henry VIII* argued for Shakespeare as sole author, McMullan's edition presents the play as a collaboration. With regard to *All Is True*, Fletcher's involvement has often been acknowledged and then ignored, the methodological sleight of hand we have seen elsewhere in this book.[104] Even more dramatically, *The Double Falsehood* presents us with the challenge of imagining its origin not in a person but in a relationship—among texts as well as authors and across time.[105] Publication of *The Double Falsehood* in the New Arden Shakespeare and a recent spate of productions, including one in London sponsored by Arden, offer a new opportunity to address what it means to think about authorship, like truth, as relational, by which I mean here both transactional and referential.

The most interesting thing about *Double Falsehood*, in my view, is not the play itself but how critics talk about it, especially how they address the relations among its textual forms and its authors. Was Theobald working with a Renaissance play, what Tiffany Stern calls a "Shakespeare-related manuscript"? Just as, in previous chapters, we have seen how the archival manuscripts that are supposed to subtend print frequently elude us, so Stern casts doubt on the very notion of a lost Fletcher/Shakespeare *Cardenio*, let alone Theobald's ownership of it or its survival in some form within *Double Falsehood*.[106]

Theobald's self-justifications follow a pattern that should, by now, be familiar. His authorization rests on a manuscript, but a manuscript that we cannot see. In the dedicatory epistle to what he calls "this Orphan Play," "this Remnant of [Shakespeare's] Pen," Theobald hopes that his patron's support will silence "the Censures of those *Unbelievers*, who think it impossible a Manuscript of *Shakespeare* could so long have lain dormant." Theobald claims that the text he offers us is based on not one but three manuscripts that he has in his possession. Of the oldest and therefore most closely connected to Shakespeare, he acknowledges that

> It has been alledg'd as incredible, that such a Curiosity should
> be stifled and lost to the World for above a Century. To This my
> Answer is short; that tho' it never till now made its Appearance on
> the Stage, yet one of the Manuscript Copies, which I have, is of
> above Sixty Years Standing, in the Handwriting of Mr. *Downes*, the
> famous Old Prompter; and, as I am credibly inform'd, was early in
> the Possession of the celebrated Mr. *Betterton*, and by Him design'd
> to have been usher'd into the World. What Accident prevented This
> Purpose of his, I do not pretend to know: Or thro' what hands it
> had successively pass'd before that Period of Time.[107]

In evidence, Theobald offers what he presents as knowable and certain—Mr. Downes's handwriting—what he has on credible information—the early ownership of the manuscript—and what is unknown—its subsequent provenance. He adds in a "tradition" that Shakespeare gave the manuscript "as a Present of Value" to his "Natural Daughter," for whom he had written it. This claim posits a series of relations, assigning Shakespeare a natural daughter and making her both the inspiration of the play and a key link in the chain connecting back to Shakespeare. Theobald also mentions two other manuscripts of varying ages and degrees of perfection. But none of these survives now, so his account is the only evidence we have that they ever existed. In his self-justification, we find a dizzying chain of relations, among persons and texts and across time, relations we must accept on faith.

Although *The Double Falsehood* was long dismissed as a forgery, it has received renewed attention because of the decision to include it in the New Arden series of editions of Shakespeare's plays and because of press coverage of it as the discovery of a "lost" play by Shakespeare.[108] The editor of the new Arden edition, Brean Hammond, acknowledges that "all students of the play have recognized that Theobald must himself be responsible for at least some

aspects of the final product" and uses his introduction to argue that there
is "some relationship between the lost play performed in 1613 and the play
printed in 1728."[109] The question, of course, is just what that relationship is.
And what was Theobald's role in transacting it? Was he, as John Freehafer puts
it, "a liar who fabricated a Shakespeare play or a vandal who destroyed one"?[110]
Hammond warns that "it would be rash to make too many judgements about
Cardenio on the evidence of *Double Falsehood*, given the adaptation the script
certainly underwent at Theobald's hands." He argues, in fact, that the play
"had probably already suffered [adaptation] before Theobald ever saw it," by
which he means that Theobald was working from a Restoration abridgement
or adaptation (43, 50–54, 96). Hammond ultimately concludes that it is impossible to determine with any certainty: "Sooner or later, all scholars putting
their minds to the *Cardenio / Double Falsehood* question will be forced upon
speculation" (57). But he offers his edition as the fruit of "a growing conviction that Theobald's adaptation is indeed what remains to us of an otherwise
lost Shakespeare-Fletcher collaboration once called *Cardenio* or *The History
of Cardenio*" (5). Its claim on our attention and its place in the Arden Shakespeare both depend on the play's purported relation to Shakespeare, however
tenuous. *The Double Falsehood* is, in turn, a conduit of relation, as our search
for this missing play emerges from, as Philip Lorenz puts it, "the desire not
only to authenticate and to know, but also to *have* a certain *relation* to Shakespeare—to 'touch' him in one way."[111]

Theobald called the play "this *dear Relick*," but whether he meant that as a
relic of the original play or a relic of Saint Shakespeare is hard to determine.[112]
Others have called *The Double Falsehood* a ghost of that earlier play or its
"mangled" remains or a container for the "bones of a Shakespearean play";[113]
a new collection of essays devoted to the question promises that "new research
provides stronger evidence than ever before that a lost Fletcher/Shakespeare
Cardenio can be discerned within *Double Falsehood*."[114] Rather than rehearse
the debate or come to a conclusion here, I want to focus on how several influential analyses address the issue of relations between what survives to us and
what we wish to find. Hammond describes the relationship between *Double
Falsehood* and *Cardenio* in a variety of ways: "what we now have is a palimpsest or pentimento—at all events, nothing that is *straightforwardly* Shakespeare-Fletcher. Nevertheless . . . Shakespeare's hand, and even more plainly
Fletcher's, can be detected in the eighteenth-century redaction" (6); "the lost
play has a continuing presence in its eighteenth-century great-grandchild" (8).
Double Falsehood is "what remains of an otherwise lost Shakespeare-Fletcher

collaboration once called *Cardenio*" (94) and "harbours an authentic Jacobean layer" (95). Other critics agree that the play has some things in common with other plays on which Fletcher and Shakespeare collaborated in these years.[115] But Stern counters that such claims imagine a more individuated sense of style than pertains to a master of pastiche like Theobald, who "wrote comfortably in at least two voices: his own and Shakespeare's," and who spoke fluent Cervantes and Fletcher as well.[116]

According to Barbara Fuchs, "the dubious text continues to live or die by its relationship to Shakespeare; its only claim to fame its evanescent link to the Bard. No one is interested in discredited apocrypha, also-rans in the contest for canonicity, however fascinating these may prove in their own right."[117] So, however we figure the relation between *Double Falsehood* and *Cardenio*, it is that relation that matters, that grants the play its value, that constitutes its claim on our attention. Throughout this book, I have focused on the fervent but thwarted compulsion to dig behind printed remains to manuscripts. Again and again, we have found that those manuscripts simply do not exist. In the case of the missing *Cardenio*, we find the apotheosis of this obsession: we value a printed text as a kind of reliquary, whose value resides in what it holds or once held. We also find that the manuscript that constitutes its worth does not now exist and may never have.

The evidence that Theobald was working with manuscripts of a lost play and not forging from whole cloth mostly consists of assumptions about what Theobald is unlikely to have done or known as much as qualities in the play itself that can be taken as Shakespearean or Fletcherian. Evidence that casts doubt on Theobald, suggesting a forgery rather than a discovery and adaptation, includes the fact that Theobald was charged with plagiarism in another case and declined to include *Double Falsehood* in his own 1733 edition of Shakespeare's works—a stunning omission that advocates for the play's status as "Shakespeare-related" must address. Hammond tackles this by suggesting that "Theobald did have a literary property that he at first considered to be a play composed solely by Shakespeare, but that he lost faith in it very soon after it was published, because he came to be convinced that it was, after all, more likely to be a Shakespeare-Fletcher collaboration than pure Shakespeare" (75–76) and for him that mitigated its value (91). But even if we accept the argument that Theobald was working with the manuscript of a Renaissance play or a Restoration adaptation of a Renaissance play and even that this play was a collaboration between Fletcher and Shakespeare, perhaps the lost *Cardenio*, it remains in question what the relation of that earlier play is to Theobald's adaptation, how we would know, and why we would care.

The Double Falsehood itself, whatever it is, contains references to how textual relations shape lived ones, always articulated by female characters who apprehend their situations as familiar stories with predictably unhappy endings. Their own experience is "like an old tale still" as *The Winter's Tale* puts it. Violante says to her rapist, Henriquez,

> I have read stories,
> (I fear too true ones), how young lords like you
> Have thus besung mean windows, rhym'd their suff'rings
> Ev'n to th'abuse of things divine, set up
> Plain girls, like me, the idols of their worship,
> Then left them to bewail their easy faith,
> And stand the world's contempt. (1.3.40–46)

Henriquez's falsehood is "double" because he both rapes and abandons Violante and schemes to marry Leonora, his friend Julio's beloved. When Leonora resists her father's (Don Bernard's) insistence that she marry Henriquez, protesting that she loves Julio instead, she reminds him of the fact that her mother chose for love, disobeying her father to marry him. He responds, "No doubt you have old stories enough to undo you. What, you can't throw yourself away but by precedent, ha?" (2.3.121–23). For Violante, an old story sets the precedent for her ruin; for Leonora, the story sets a precedent for love and defiance; for her father, "old stories" are "precedents" for young women's self-destruction. In each case, it is impossible to think the options without recourse to the stories already available, stories that, this play suggests, tend to limit rather than expand the options.

When Violante disguises herself as a shepherd boy, she narrowly escapes being assaulted by her master. Violante bargains that, if he quenches his "foul Affections," she will "be a woman and begin / So sad a story" that it will move him to pity, but he insists "No stories now" (4.1.180–84). She manages to escape despite her attempt to counter what she has already recognized as a familiar story with yet more stories, as if these stories could be a defense against the violence that is their content and defines her identity. Henriquez marries and redeems Violante with his father's consent. If the two heroines achieve conventionally happy endings, by which they are married rather than undone, they are still following precedents set by old stories.

The texture of *The Double Falsehood* often feels thin; it does not at first glance seem to offer the critic much to work with. If we try to read it as historical evidence, which era might we take it as evidence of—the Renaissance, the Restoration, or the eighteenth century? Yet whether mangled remains or forgery, *The Double Falsehood* reflects on the horrible paucity yet exacting tyranny of old stories, the reason that Buckingham might have chosen to manage his image problems by staging a play. In the face of the desperate finitude of plots and roles, and their tyrannical effects on one's prospects, all one can do is cultivate awareness of those stories and their precedents, insisting on telling them in moments of crisis, as Violente and Leonora do. This finitude is, of course, also part of the reason that someone in the eighteenth century would adapt or forge an old play rather than writing a new one.

Two interesting readings of this play connect it to yet other stories, not only the story of Shakespeare's career and oeuvre, and his relation to Fletcher, but to two other stories of relatedness: the story of Catholics versus Protestants (and Shakespeare's embeddedness therein) and the story of what Barbara Fuchs calls "Anglo-Spanish relations." Richard Wilson's inventive and provocative reading of the remains of *Cardenio* he finds entombed in *The Double Falsehood* returns us to the antihero of my first chapter, whom Wilson calls "the serpentine Henry Howard, earl of Northampton," the author of *A True and Perfect Relation*, whose code name was El Cid, who received a pension from Madrid, and who dominated the Privy Council at the time *Cardenio* seems to have been performed. Wilson argues that "the pro-Spanish and crypto-Catholic culture of the Howard faction" might "explain why the new work performed for their first Christmas in power was the sole Shakespearean drama set in Spain, and one of the few Jacobean plays with sympathetic Spanish characters." Wilson also connects the play to the Howard family's politics: "it would have been very difficult for the Whitehall audience of *Cardenio* not to recognise in this torrid melodrama the case of Frances Howard" and her marriage to the earl of Essex, which was annulled in 1613, so that she could marry Robert Carr.[118] It is hard to demonstrate conclusively what an audience would have found it difficult or impossible not to recognize, especially since even at court different members of the audience would bear varying degrees of knowledge about and opinions regarding a scandal in the process of unfolding.

Wilson does a wonderful job of contextualizing *Cardenio*. But his evidence that the Howard faction was behind the play lies in the play itself, a play that is widely held to be "lost":

So, it is the incipient violence of *Cardenio*, in the hindsight of the
Overbury affair, which suggests that the prime movers of the 1612
celebrations were . . . the Lord Chamberlain and the Howards.
Thus, the picture emerges of Shakespeare at the end of his career
in the orbit of England's last great Catholic family, and writing his
romances as a legitimation of the Howard programme of religious
reconciliation. Some time in late summer, we might therefore speculate, the first three acts of this tragicomedy were sent from Shakespeare to be completed by Fletcher, for their urgency is signalled
with a drumming providentialism that is typical of the late plays.

Wilson here speculates not only about the motives and involvement of the
Howards but about Shakespeare's motives and the menace and providentialism of the play itself, as well as what we can "therefore" assume about the
division of labor between the two collaborators, who pass the story from one
to the other as if it were a baton. In general, he downplays the ways in which
Theobald's text at best mediates our access to *Cardenio*. For him, for the most
part, the surviving play *is* the play. He recalls its odd status now and again:
"if *Cardenio* did open with a ruler spying on his son . . . its scenario could
hardly come closer to English politics in 1612 . . ."; "if Frances Howard's father
did sponsor *Cardenio* . . ." then it "would seem to reflect" the family's guilt
at marrying her off so young; "if Theobald's text is faithful to *Cardenio*, then
its emotions do seem to register the ambivalence of those who organised the
funeral towards this 'flower of his country and admiration of the world'," that
is, the recently deceased Prince Henry. Much virtue in if, perhaps, but those
are big ifs. Wilson assumes that "an astonishing scene [5.2] that has no literary source . . . cannot, surely, be by Theobald," taking his own evaluation of a
scene's success as evidence in itself that it is "Shakespeare-related."[119]

Fuchs limits her analysis of "the *Cardenio/Double Falshood* dyad" to the
play's paratexts, its prologue and epilogue, and the ways in which they "enact
Shakespearean greatness at the expense of his sources," erasing the story's debt
to Cervantes and illogically praising a Bard who could "charm the heroes of
that glorious reign, / Which humbled to the dust the pride of Spain" (Epilogue
35–36). Fuchs adds to the tissue of relations I have been discussing in *Henry
VIII* or *All Is True* the relations between nations, between language traditions,
and between drama and other genres. If we look at these relations, she argues,
we will begin to see the possibility of "a *pirated* national corpus," and the
ways appropriation is "itself coded in relation to the national project" so that

Cardenio's disappearance has played a role "in how we read Anglo-Spanish re-lations in early modern drama" by allowing us to miss "what otherwise should have been no surprise: the widespread reliance by English dramatists of the early modern era on contemporary Spanish prose, and particularly on Cer-vantes."[120] As Fuchs turns our attention to the Spanish texts that, she argues, both *Cardenio* and *Double Falsehood* depend on and efface, these English texts that are both missing and obstructive disappear from view in favor of a new object of analysis, an object that is, yet again, a network of relations.

All Is True requires audiences to relate what they see to what they do not and to relate its version of the truth to what they already know. It also reveals Henry's manipulation of relations in terms of stories, intimacies, and cor-respondences. *Double Falsehood* claims our attention only in its relation to something else that is not there, that we cannot quite reach or apprehend, that in despair we might just invent, as Gary Taylor and Stephen Greenblatt have written their own versions of *Cardenio*, as historians sometimes invent the "I" who speaks in depositions. Whatever we are looking for, it is not all there. But both *All Is True* and *Double Falsehood* suggest that, while "it" is not there, we are, that the apprehension of relatedness is our work; ranging across genres, disciplines, and time, it is always work in progress.

Notes

INTRODUCTION

1. William Shakespeare, *The Norton Shakespeare*, ed. Stephen Greenblatt, Walter Cohen, Jean E. Howard, and Katharine Eisaman Maus (New York: Norton, 1997).

2. Barbara J. Shapiro, *A Culture of Fact: England, 1550–1720* (Ithaca, N.Y.: Cornell University Press, 2000), 91.

3. *A True Relation of the Unjust, Cruell, and Barbarous Proceedings against the English at Amboyna In the East-Indies* (London, 1624), sigs. A2v, A2v–A3r.

4. Richard Sutton, *A True Relation of the Cruelties and Barbarities of the French upon the English Prisoners of War* (London, 1690), sig. H1r.

5. *True Relation of the Travailes and most miserable Captivitie of William Davies, Barber-Surgion of London* (London, 1614), sig. A4r.

6. In *A True Narrative of a Wonderful Accident, Which occur'd upon the Execution of a Christian Slave at Aleppo in Turky* (London, 1676), the relator directs us to a coffeehouse where we can find witnesses to his story. Many other texts advise the reader on where he or she can view a body or include lists of witnesses. See David Cressy, *Agnes Bowker's Cat: Travesties and Transgressions in Tudor and Stuart England* (Oxford: Oxford University Press, 2000), on how texts tried to document their credibility by including lists of witnesses (34–35). Shapiro points out that "News reports of apparitions and mermaids were as filled with proofs for these matters of fact as were the accounts of the Royal Society" (*Culture of Fact*, 102). See also Lorraine Daston and Katharine Park, *Wonders and the Order of Nature, 1150–1750* (New York: Zone, 2001), 246–53.

7. J. Q., *Hell Open'd, Or, The Infernal Sin of Murther Punished. Being A True Relation of the Poysoning of a whole Family in Plymouth* (London, 1676), sig. B1v; *A True Relation of the Wonderful Cure of Mary Maillard, (Lame almost ever since she was Born)* (London, 1694), advertisement before the title page.

8. For the claim that Fr. Henry Garnet's severed head did not decay, see *The Condition of Catholics Under James I: Father Gerard's Narrative of the Gunpowder Plot*, ed. John Morris (London: Longmans, 1872), 305. On a coroner's discovery, see *Murther, Murther. Or, A bloody Relation how Anne Hamton . . . by poyson murthered her deare husband* (London, 1641), sig. A4r. For an accusing ghost, see *A Full and True Relation of the Examination and Confession of W. Barwick and E. Mangall, of Two Horrid Murders* (London, 1690), 1.

9. Paul Griffiths, *Lost Londons: Change, Crime and Control in the Capital City, 1550–1660* (Cambridge: Cambridge University Press, 2008), 255.

10. Roy Porter, "The Rise of Physical Examination," in *Medicine and the Five Senses*, ed. W. F. Bynum and Roy Porter (Cambridge: Cambridge University Press, 1993), 179–97, esp. 181. See also Eve Keller, *Generating Bodies and Gendered Selves: The Rhetoric of Reproduction in Early Modern England* (Seattle: University of Washington Press, 2007), 166; and Julia Rudolph, "Gender and the Development of Forensic Science: A Case Study," *English Historical Review* 123, 503 (August 2008): 1–23, esp. 15. Law courts and physicians relied on physical examination as well. But even when they did, physical examination often entered into evidence as a true relation. See Sara D. Luttfring, "Bodily Narratives and the Politics of Virginity in *The Changeling* and the Essex Divorce," *Renaissance Drama* 39 (2010): 97–128; Holger Schott Syme, *Theatre and Testimony in Shakespeare's England: A Culture of Mediation* (Cambridge: Cambridge University Press, 2012), 209–13.

11. On the increasing role of primary sources in early modern historiography, see Jennifer Summit, *Memory's Library: Medieval Books in Early Modern England* (Chicago: University of Chicago Press, 2008). On the value placed on documents in legal courts, see Syme, *Theatre and Testimony*.

12. Alexandra Walsham, *Providence in Early Modern England* (Oxford: Oxford University Press, 1999), 218.

13. Daston and Park, *Wonders*; Deborah Harkness, *The Jewel House: Elizabethan London and the Scientific Revolution* (New Haven, Conn.: Yale University Press, 2007); John H. Langbein, *The Origins of the Adversary Criminal Trial* (Oxford: Oxford University Press, 2003); Katharine Park, *Secrets of Women: Gender, Generation, and the Origins of Human Dissection* (Brooklyn, N.Y.: Zone, 2006); Mary Poovey, *A History of the Modern Fact* (Chicago: University of Chicago Press, 1998); Jonathan Sawday, *The Body Emblazoned: Dissection and the Human Body in Renaissance Culture* (London: Routledge, 1995); Steven Shapin and Simon Schaffer, *Leviathan and the Air-Pump: Hobbes, Boyle, and the Experimental Life* (Princeton, N.J.: Princeton University Press, 1985); Keith Thomas, *Religion and the Decline of Magic* (New York: Scribner's, 1971).

14. Stephen Greenblatt, *Marvelous Possessions: The Wonder of the New World* (Chicago: University of Chicago Press, 1991), 122; Andrea Frisch, *Invention of the Eyewitness: Witnessing and Testimony in Early Modern France*, North Carolina Studies in the Romance Languages and Literatures 279 (Chapel Hill: UNC Department of Romance Languages, 2004), 13.

15. Mary C. Fuller, *Voyages in Print: English Travel to America, 1576–1624* (Cambridge: Cambridge University Press, 1995), 2.

16. Philip H. Round, *By Nature and By Custom Cursed: Transatlantic Civil Discourse and New England Cultural Production, 1620–1660* (Hanover, N.H.: University Press of New England/Tufts University Press, 1999), 25–26, 29, 33–36; Alix Cooper, *Inventing the Indigenous: Local Knowledge and Natural History in Early Modern Europe* (Cambridge: Cambridge University Press, 2007), 10; Mary Baines Campbell, *The Witness and the Other World: Exotic European Travel Writing, 400–1600* (Ithaca, N.Y.: Cornell University Press, 1988).

17. Lennard J. Davis, *Factual Fictions: The Origins of the English Novel* (New York: Columbia University Press, 1983; reprint Philadelphia: University of Pennsylvania Press, 1997), 67.

18. Shapiro, *Culture of Fact*, 60; see also 211.

19. Malcolm Gaskill, *Crime and Mentalities in Early Modern England* (Cambridge: Cambridge University Press, 2000), 279.

20. On truth as a narrative effect, see Michael Witmore, *Culture of Accidents: Unexpected Knowledges in Early Modern England* (Stanford, Calif.: Stanford University Press, 2001), 11; Karen Cunningham, *Imaginary Betrayals: Subjectivity and the Discourses of Treason in Early Modern England* (Philadelphia: University of Pennsylvania Press, 2002), 15; and Lorna Hutson, *The Invention of Suspicion: Law and Mimesis in Shakespeare and Renaissance Drama* (Oxford: Oxford University Press, 2008), 126.

21. Elizabeth Eisenstein, *The Printing Press as an Agent of Change* (Cambridge: Cambridge University Press, 1979), 74. Elizabeth Spiller also emphasizes this aspect of Eisenstein's argument, in *Science, Reading, and Renaissance Literature: The Art of Making Knowledge, 1580–1670* (Cambridge: Cambridge University Press, 2004), 12–14.

22. Ann Blair, "Reading Strategies for Coping with Information Overload ca. 1550–1700," *Journal of the History of Ideas* 64, 1 (2003): 11–28.

23. On the overlap of written and oral culture, see Roger Chartier, "Leisure and Sociability: Reading Aloud in Early Modern Europe," trans. Carol Mossman, in *Urban Life in the Renaissance*, ed. Susan Zimmerman and Ronald F. E. Weissman (Newark: University of Delaware Press, 1989), 103–20; Richard Cust, "News and Politics in Early Seventeenth-Century England," *Past & Present* 112 (1986): 60–90; and Adam Fox, *Oral and Literate Culture in England, 1500–1700* (Oxford: Clarendon, 2000), 172. On the overlap of print and manuscript cultures, see Harold Love, *Scribal Publication in Seventeenth-Century England* (Oxford: Clarendon Press, 1993); and Harkness, *Jewel House*, 181–210, 258, and passim.

24. Adrian Johns, *The Nature of the Book: Print and Knowledge in the Making* (Chicago: University of Chicago Press, 1998).

25. Shapin and Schaffer, *Leviathan and the Air-Pump*, 60–72, 327, 336.

26. Ibid., 60; Harkness, *Jewel House*, passim and esp. 181–210; Spiller, *Science, Reading, and Renaissance Literature*, 137–77; Richard Cunningham, "Virtual Witnessing and the Role of the Reader in a New Natural Philosophy," *Philosophy and Rhetoric* 34, 3 (2001): 207–24.

27. *Anna Trapnel's Report and Plea, or, A Narrative of her Journey from London into Cornwal* (London, 1654), sig. F1v.

28. *A True and Perfect Relation of that execrable and horrid fact, committed in White-Lyon-yard* (London, 1674), 3.

29. *The Cry of a Stone: Or a Relation of Something Spoken in Whitehall by Anna Trapnel, being in the Visions of God. Relating to the Governors, Army, Churches, Ministry, Universities: And the Whole Nation* (London, 1654), sigs. A1v, a2v, A1v, C2r (see also H4v), I1v.

30. Steven Shapin, *A Social History of Truth: Civility and Science in Seventeenth-Century England* (Chicago: University of Chicago Press, 1994), 238.

31. Daston and Gallison challenge "one of the most deeply entrenched narratives about the Scientific Revolution and its impact," which describes "how knower and knowledge came to be pried apart," by arguing that "as long as knowledge posits a knower, and the knower is seen as a potential help or hindrance to the acquisition of knowledge, the self of the knower will be at epistemological issue" (Lorraine J. Daston and Peter Galison, *Objectivity* [Brooklyn: Zone, 2007], 39, 40).

32. Several important studies demonstrate that there was broad "lay" participation in the contested processes of determining fact and evaluating evidence in the early modern period. See especially Harkness, *The Jewel House*; Hutson, *The Invention of Suspicion*; and Shapiro, *Culture of Fact*, 119–20 and passim. In the proliferation of printed true relations in the seventeenth century, the purported eyewitness emerged as the condition under which a text could be presented as true at the very moment that doubt was cast on the reliability of vision. New technologies, especially the telescope and the microscope, revealed that even the most reliable witness could not necessarily trust his eyes. In *Vanities of the Eye: Vision in Early Modern European Culture* (Oxford: Oxford University Press, 2007), Stuart Clark attends to "sceptical tropes" about vision that suggested that visual experience was "something relative, not absolute" (4).

33. Peter Dear, "Totius in Verba: Rhetoric and Authority in the Early Royal Society," *Isis* 76, 2 (1985): 145–61, 159.

34. *True Narrative of a Wonderful Accident*, sig. A2r.

35. *A True Relation of the Wonderful Cure of Mary Maillard*, sigs. A4v–B1r.

36. Peter Burke, *Eyewitnessing: The Uses of Images as Historical Evidence* (Ithaca, N.Y.: Cornell University Press, 2001), 19.

37. Johns, *Nature of the Book*, 31.

38. R. W. Serjeantson, "Testimony and Proof in Early-Modern England," *Studies in History and Philosophy of Science* 30, 2 (1999): 195–236; Ian Atherton, " 'The Itch grown a Disease': Manuscript Transmission of News in the Seventeenth Century," *News, Newspapers, and Society in Early Modern Britain*, ed. Joad Raymond (London: Frank Cass, 1999), 39–65, esp. 53.

39. Sharon Achinstein, *Milton and the Revolutionary Reader* (Princeton, N.J.: Princeton University Press, 1994), 27–70; Mark Knights, *Representation and Misrepresentation in Later Stuart Britain: Partisanship and Political Culture* (Oxford: Oxford University Press, 2005), 209, 273; Todd Wayne Butler, "The Haunting of Isabell Binnington: Ghosts of Murder, Texts, and Law in Restoration England," *Journal of British Studies* 50 (April 2011): 1–29, esp. 4.

40. Lisa Jardine and Anthony Grafton, " 'Studied for Action': How Gabriel Harvey Read His Livy," *Past and Present* 129 (November 1990): 30–78, esp. 30, 31, 32.

41. On the reading practices of women and of men outside elite scholarly circles, see Margaret W. Ferguson, *Dido's Daughters: Literacy, Gender, and Empire in Early Modern England and France* (Chicago: University of Chicago Press, 2003); Heidi Brayman Hackel, *Reading Material in Early Modern England: Print, Gender, and Literacy* (Cambridge: Cambridge University Press, 2005); Julie Crawford, "Reconsidering Early Modern Women's

Reading, or, How Margaret Hoby Read Her de Mornay," *Huntington Library Quarterly* 73,2 (2010): 193–223; and Lara Dodds, "Reading and Writing in *Sociable Letters*: Or, How Margaret Cavendish Read Her Plutarch," *English Literary Renaissance* 41, 1 (2011): 189–218.

42. William H. Sherman, *John Dee: The Politics of Reading and Writing in the English Renaissance* (Amherst: University of Massachusetts Press, 1995), 65, 66, 71.

43. Roger Chartier, "Culture as Appropriation: Popular Cultural Uses in Early Modern France," in *Understanding Popular Culture: Europe from the Middle Ages to the Nineteenth Century*, ed. Steven L. Kaplan (Berlin: Mouton, 1984), 229–53; and "Communities of Readers," *The Order of Books: Readers, Authors, and Libraries in Europe Between the Fourteenth and Eighteenth Centuries*, trans. Lydia G. Cochrane (Stanford, Calif.: Stanford University Press, 1994), 23. On appropriation, see also Scott Cutler Shershow, *Puppets and "Popular" Culture* (Ithaca, N.Y.: Cornell University Press, 1995), 109–82.

44. William H. Sherman, *Used Books: Marking Readers in Renaissance England* (Philadelphia: University of Pennsylvania Press, 2008), xiii. See also Love, *Scribal Publication*, on "user publication"— the role of readers in creating new texts and in creating "scribal communities," "interlocking networks" of family members, friends, and neighbors who shared scribal copies of texts (81). D. R. Woolf contrasts the intensive scholarly reading assessed by Grafton and Jardine, among others, to a "much more leisurely form of 'extensive' reading that follows little pattern beyond the individual reader's tastes, personal concerns, and daily whims," *Reading History in Early Modern England* (Cambridge: Cambridge University Press, 2000), 9.

45. Kevin Sharpe, *Reading Revolutions: The Politics of Reading in Early Modern England* (New Haven, Conn.: Yale University Press, 2000), 278. See also Sasha Roberts, *Reading Shakespeare's Poems in Early Modern England* (Houndsmills.: Palgrave Macmillan, 2003), 8; and Fred Schurink, "Manuscript Commonplace Books, Literature, and Reading in Early Modern England," *Huntington Library Quarterly* 73, 3 (2010): 453–69.

46. Adam Smyth, " 'Rend and teare in peeces': Textual Fragmentation in Seventeenth-Century England," *Seventeenth Century* 19 (2004): 36–52; Jeffrey Todd Knight, "Making Shakespeare's Books: Assembly and Intertextuality in the Archives," *Shakespeare Quarterly* 60, 3 (2009): 304–40. See also Summit, on how Sir Robert Cotton, among others, "unbound his own manuscripts in order to reorganize and rebind them into volumes of his own making" (*Memory's Library*, 146); and Patricia Fumerton, "Remembering by Dismembering: Databases, Archiving, and the Recollection of Seventeenth-Century Broadside Ballads," in *Ballads and Broadsides in Britain, 1500–1800*, ed. Patricia Fumerton and Anita Guerrini (Farnham: Ashgate, 2010), 13–34, on the practices of collectors such as Samuel Pepys in cutting, pasting, and reassembling printed texts.

47. Harkness, *Jewel House*, 196, 197.

48. Juliet Fleming, *Graffiti and the Writing Arts of Early Modern England* (Philadelphia: University of Pennsylvania Press, 2001), 10; Tessa Watt, *Cheap Print and Popular Piety, 1550–1640* (Cambridge: Cambridge University Press, 1991), 199; Tiffany Stern, *Documents of Performance in Early Modern England* (Cambridge: Cambridge University Press, 2009), 62.

49. John Milton, *Norton Critical Edition of Milton's Poetry and Prose*, ed. Jason P. Rosenblatt (New York: Norton, 2010), 369.

50. "To All Lovers of Ingenuous and Artificial Conclusions" from John White, *A Rich Cabinet, with Variety of Inventions* (London, 1668), sigs. A4r–v.

51. John Barton, *The Art of Rhetorick Concisely and Completely Handled* (London, 1634), sigs. B1r, B6v, B7v.

52. Annabel Patterson, *Censorship and Interpretation: The Conditions of Writing and Reading in Early Modern England* (Madison: University of Wisconsin Press, 1991), 81, 63, 31; Stephen B. Dobranski, *Readers and Authorship in Early Modern England* (Cambridge: Cambridge University Press, 2005), 41, 62, 17.

53. Roger Chartier, "Texts, Printing, Readings," in *The New Cultural History*, ed. Lynn Hunt (Berkeley: University of California Press, 1989), 154–75, esp. 156.

54. Michel de Certeau, *The Practice of Everyday Life*, trans. Steven Rendall (Berkeley: University of California Press, 1984), 169. Barthes, too, emphasizes that a text's meaning resides in its destination rather than its origin, in Roland Barthes, "The Death of the Author," *Image, Music, Text: Essays Selected and Translated by Stephen Heath* (New York: Hill and Wang, 1977), 142–48, esp. 148.

55. Margaret W. Ferguson, "Sidney's *A Defence of Poetry: A Retrial*," *boundary 2* 7, 2 (1979): 61–96, esp. 62, discussing Sidney's letter to his brother Robert. I am grateful to Ferguson for directing me to this phrase in Sidney.

56. Francis Bacon, *Advancement of Learning* (Rockville, Md.: Serenity Publishers, 2008), 36.

57. Daston and Park, *Wonders*, 232.

58. Sharpe, *Reading Revolutions*, 264.

59. Fumerton, "Remembering by Dismembering," 34. See also Knight, "Making Shakespeare's Books," 340. Alan B. Farmer and Zachary Lesser, "Early Modern Digital Scholarship and DEEP: Database of Early English Playbooks," *Literature Compass* 5/6 (2008): 1139–53, esp. 1149. On combining old and new reading methods, slow reading and database searches, see Robin Valenza, "How Literature Becomes Knowledge: A Case Study," *English Literary History* 76, 1 (2009): 215–45.

60. Fredric Jameson, *The Political Unconscious: Narrative as a Socially Symbolic Act* (Ithaca, N.Y.: Cornell University Press, 1981), 82.

61. Louis Montrose, "Renaissance Literary Studies and the Subject of History," *English Literary Renaissance* 16, 1 (1986): 5–12, esp. 6, 8.

62. Patrick Collinson, "Truth, Lies, and Fiction in Sixteenth-Century Protestant Historiography," in *The Historical Imagination in Early Modern Britain*, ed. Donald R. Kelley and David H. Sacks (Cambridge: Cambridge University Press, 1997), 37–68, esp. 58, 61.

63. Catherine Gallagher and Stephen Greenblatt, *Practicing New Historicism* (Chicago: University of Chicago Press, 2000), 30, 31.

64. Quentin Skinner, *The Machiavellian Moment: Florentine Political Thought and the Atlantic Republican Tradition* (Princeton, N.J.: Princeton University Press, 1975); and *Virtue, Commerce, and History* (Cambridge: Cambridge University Press, 1985); Kathleen

Canning, "Feminist History After the 'Linguistic Turn:' Historicizing 'Discourse' and 'Experience,' " *Signs* 19, 2 (Winter 1994): 368–404.

65. Carlo Ginzburg, "Checking the Evidence: The Judge and the Historian," *Critical Inquiry* 18,1 (1991): 79–92, esp. 83.

66. Stuart Clark, "Introduction," in *Languages of Witchcraft: Narrative, Ideology, and Meaning in Early Modern Culture*, ed. Stuart Clark (Houndmills: Macmillan, 2001), 8, 10.

67. Mary Fissell, *Vernacular Bodies: The Politics of Reproduction in Early Modern England* (Oxford: Oxford University Press, 2004), 161.

68. Peter Lake and Steven Pincus, "Rethinking the Public Sphere," in *The Politics of the Public Sphere in Early Modern England*, ed. Peter Lake and Steven Pincus (Manchester: Manchester University Press, 2007), 1–30, esp. 18.

69. Sharpe, *Reading Revolutions*, 26.

70. Gallagher and Greenblatt, *Practicing the New Historicism*, 28. While Mark Knights describes later Stuart Britain as a "culture of fiction and epistemological uncertainty" (278), for him fiction consistently means the false: the "misleading and fictional" (292); "dangerous representations and fictions" (291). "Imagined fictions pervaded the political culture, imagined both in the sense of fancied and as something 'uncertain, imperfect . . . opposite in some measure to real' " (*Representation and Misrepresentation*, 305). For contemporaries, I argue, the distinctions between fiction and the real were less clear.

71. Jean E. Howard, "The New Historicism in Renaissance Studies," *English Literary Renaissance* 16, 1 (1986): 13–43, esp. 25, 29.

72. Greenblatt, *Marvelous Possessions*, 6, 12–13, emphasis mine.

73. In her work on solving problems of social justice, Janet Halley articulates her desire "for a pragmatic posture, a sense of being *in relation to* problem seeing and problem solving," *Split Decisions: How and Why to Take a Break from Feminism* (Princeton, N.J.: Princeton University Press, 2006), 7. I too desire a pragmatic posture of being "in relation to." Catherine Belsey argues that "To the degree that the present informs our account of the past, we make history *out of a relation, which is always a relation of difference between the present and the past. . . . we make* a relation, in both senses of that term, out of *our* reading practices and *their* documents," *Shakespeare and the Loss of Eden: The Construction of Family Values in Early Modern Culture* (New Brunswick, N.J.: Rutgers University Press, 1999), 12. I do not think that the relation between past and present is always and only a relation of difference or that "their documents" are neatly separable from "our reading practices." But I agree that we *make* the relations that constitute history. As Wendy Brown puts it, "The complex *political* problem of the relation between past and present, and of both to the future, is resolved by neither facts nor truth" (*Politics Out of History* [Princeton, N.J.: Princeton University Press, 2001], 141)—because it is not a given but is a choice and a work. My emphasis on a method of tracing associations, collecting and assembling fragments, and keeping open a productive uncertainty is also indebted to actor-network theory. See Bruno Latour, *Reassembling the Social: An Introduction to Actor-Network Theory* (Oxford: Oxford University Press, 2005).

74. Hayden White, " 'Figuring the Nature of the Times Deceased': Literary Theory

and Historical Writing," in *The Future of Literary Theory*, ed. Ralph Cohen (New York: Routledge, 1989), 19–43, esp. 31. See also *The Content of the Form: Narrative Discourse and Historical Representation* (Baltimore: Johns Hopkins University Press, 1987); and "The Historical Text as Literary Artifact," in *Tropics of Discourse: Essays in Cultural Criticism* (Baltimore: Johns Hopkins University Press, 1978). Building on White, LaCapra argues that "The stress on 'grubbing in the archives' reinforces the idea that only the reporting and analysis of (preferably new) facts satisfy the conditions of strictly historical knowledge," Dominick LaCapra, *History & Criticism* (Ithaca, N.Y.: Cornell University Press, 1985), 92.

75. Jacques Derrida, *Archive Fever: A Freudian Impression* (Chicago: University of Chicago Press, 1998), 17.

76. See Karen Newman, *Cultural Capitals: Early Modern London and Paris* (Princeton, N.J.: Princeton University Press, 2007), esp. 133–51; and Summit, *Memory's Library*, 10, 8. See also the special issue of *Studies in the Literary Imagination* 32, 1 (Spring 1999) devoted to "The Poetics of the Archive"; and Pierre Nora, "Between Memory and History: *Les Lieux de Mémoire*," trans. Marc Roudebush, *Representations* 26 (1989): 7–25.

77. Shapiro identifies as discourses of fact chorography, political and scientific description, travel reporting, news media, and accounts of scientific experiments (*Culture of Fact*, 161).

78. J. Q., *Hell Open'd*, sig. G3r.

79. Shapiro, *Culture of Fact*, 19.

80. According to Victoria Kahn, *Wayward Contracts: The Crisis of Political Obligation in England, 1640–1674* (Princeton, N.J.: Princeton University Press, 2004), "early modern writers and readers recognized genre as a kind of social contract, a set of shared assumptions to which each party consented" (17). Focusing on the relation of texts to readers and among texts in some ways resembles the "distant reading" Franco Moretti recommends, placing particular texts as members of classes, considering the relationships among these classes, and assessing the patterns that then emerge, Franco Moretti, *Graphs, Maps, Trees: Abstract Models for a Literary Theory* (London: Verso, 2005). But it also resembles Valenza's "slow reading" ("How Literature Becomes Knowledge," 226) in its close attention to individual texts and might best be called proximate or relational reading in its attention to relations among texts within and across classes.

81. Henry S. Turner, "Lessons from Literature for the Historian of Science (and Vice Versa): Reflections on 'Form'," *Isis* 101 (2010): 578–89, esp. 582.

82. Natalie Davis, *Fiction in the Archives: Pardon Tales and Their Tellers in Sixteenth-Century France* (Stanford, Calif.: Stanford University Press, 1987).

83. William and Malleville Haller, "The Puritan Art of Love," *Huntington Library Quarterly* 5 (1942): 235–72, esp. 241–42.

CHAPTER I. TRUE AND PERFECT RELATIONS: HENRY GARNET,
CONFESSIONAL IDENTITY, AND FIGURATION

1. *The Condition of Catholics Under James I: Father Gerard's Narrative of the Gunpowder Plot*, ed. John Morris (London: Longmans, 1871), 290. I will cite this as Gerard's *Narrative*. Gerard laments that, because he had limited access to prisoners, "we could not have such means as we desire to meet and talk with those that were eye-witnesses of many notable accidents, which we hope to do hereafter" (*Narrative*, 159). His narrative was written around 1607 when he was in exile, and circulated in manuscript, but was not itself printed until the nineteenth century. Gerard's text offers a reminder that oral and written reports, manuscript and print circulation, coexisted and that even the most authoritative narratives were contested from the very start.

2. Peter Lake, with Michael Questier, *The Antichrist's Lewd Hat: Protestants, Papists, and Players in Post-Reformation England* (New Haven, Conn.: Yale University Press, 2002), 307. The miraculous straw inscribed with Garnet's face is hand drawn on the inside cover of the British Library copy of *A True Relation* (STC 11619). On this copy, it performs an aptly ambiguous function: for skeptics, it is a contemptuous joke, confirming that the whole text is a refutation of the very idea that Garnet could be a saint or martyr; for devout Catholics, it could frame the text as itself the relic of a process by which Garnet achieved transcendence. On the straw and this drawing of it, see Julian Yates, *Error, Misuse, Failure: Object Lessons from the English Renaissance* (Minneapolis: University of Minnesota Press, 2003), 28–62. Hagiography and horror, Catholic relics and state propaganda, torture and martyrdom came together in a copy of *A True and Perfect Relation* that went on the auction block in 2007 for the "hammer price of 5,400 pounds" as "a rare and macabre" anthropodermic book—that is, a book supposedly bound in human skin. News coverage of the auction claimed both that the skin was Garnet's and that his "spooky" face could be seen on its cover, http://news.bbc.co.uk/2/hi/uk_news/england/south_yorkshire/7115174.stm.

3. I quote from the British Library copy of this text. I will cite signature numbers parenthetically. The first issue of this text appears to have left "whole" out of the title; subsequent reissues, also in 1606, introduced it. Arthur Marotti offers a helpful introduction to *A True and Perfect Relation* (133–43), and attributes material consequences to it, especially in its international distribution: "It was, in effect, a work that led directly to the international controversy over the subsequent Oath of Allegiance in which some of the same issues were at stake." Arthur F. Marotti, *Religious Ideology and Cultural Fantasy: Catholic and Anti-Catholic Discourses in Early Modern England* (South Bend, Ind.: University of Notre Dame Press, 2005), 142.

4. See Margaret W. Ferguson's reading of Elizabeth Cary's *The Tragedy of Mariam* in *Dido's Daughters: Literacy, Gender, and Empire in Early Modern England and France* (Chicago: University of Chicago Press, 2003); and, on *Macbeth*, Stephen Greenblatt, "Toil and Trouble," *New Republic* (November 14, 1994): 32–37; Rebecca Lemon, who reads Garnet's scaffold speech as an example of how "even the formulaic speech produced interpretive chaos rather than upholding state power" and argues more generally that the scaffold

speech was "a secular form of" the now prohibited and distrusted Catholic confession, in *Treason by Words: Literature, Law, and Rebellion in Shakespeare's England* (Ithaca, N.Y.: Cornell University Press, 2006), 79–159, esp. 89, 88; and Steven Mullaney, "Lying like Truth," in *The Place of the Stage: License, Play, and Power in Renaissance England* (Chicago: University of Chicago Press, 1988), 116–34.

5. Mark Nicholls, "Investigating Gunpowder Plot," *Recusant History* 19, 2 (1988): 124–45, esp. 131, 138.

6. Lewis Owen, *The Unmasking of All Popish Monks, Friers, and Jesuits* (London, 1628), sigs. S4r–S4v. In Garnet's trial, it was actually John Gerard who was accused of administering communion to the conspirators. In Jesuit Oswald Tesimond's account, he calls this a "slanderous fable" invented by Coke and "a sample of a thousand other falsehoods and stories of the kind" that should warn the reader not "to believe such stories without first seeing very clear proof." See *The Gunpowder Plot: The Narrative of Oswald Tesimond alias Greenway*, trans. from the Italian and ed. Francis Edwards, S.J. (London: Folio Society, 1973), 208.

7. What constitutes a "true and perfect" confession remains open to question. See Peter Brooks, *Troubling Confessions: Speaking Guilt in Law and Literature* (Chicago: University of Chicago Press, 2000). Throughout his study, Brooks points to the ways in which confessions are "equivocal." He cites Edward Coke on the development of a notion of "a reserved domain, concerning matters of personal conscience and belief, on which persons cannot be required to speak in proceedings that could lead to their condemnation for this belief" (16)—but obviously Coke did not allow such mental reservation to Garnet.

8. In response to the Popish Plot, much of the material in *A True and Perfect Relation* was reprinted as *The Gunpowder-treason: with a Discourse of the Manner of its Discovery; and a Perfect Relation of the Proceedings against those Horrid Conspirators* (London, 1679). This provides an extensive epistle to the reader (about 50 pages) and then cobbles together a number of texts about the plot but, as Marotti points out, leaves out the earl's longest speech: "After this, the Earl of *Northampton* made a Learned Speech, which in it self was very copious; and the intention being to contract this Volume as much as might be, and to keep onely to matter of Fact, it was thought convenient to omit the same" (L4r). See Marotti, *Religious Ideology*, 192–93. Some of the material is also repackaged in *The Tryal and Execution of Father Henry Garnet, Superior Provincial of the Jesuits in England* (London, 1679), which follows *A True and Perfect Relation* pretty closely, except for the addition of the claim that Garnet was morally superior to the popish plotters because he blushed when caught in a lie.

9. See Michael C. Questier, *Conversion, Politics and Religion in England, 1580–1625* (Cambridge: Cambridge University Press, 1996), on Garnet's own comments about the demand at assize courts that conformists repeat their recantations (112). On the common practice of reading depositions aloud in criminal trials, see Holger Schott Syme, *Theatre and Testimony in Shakespeare's England: A Culture of Mediation* (Cambridge: Cambridge University Press, 2012), 26–71. While I take his point that recording practices focused on capturing the gist of a statement rather than its details, I focus on how texts register an anxiety about the disparity between what had been said and what could be "taken."

10. Similarly, *His Majesties Speach in This Last Session of Parliament* (London, 1605), known as the King's Book, presents James's words "as neere to the life of his owne wordes, as they could bee gathered" (sig. A3; cf. A4).

11. Gerard, *Narrative*, 227, 228. Indeed, Crooke's speech as Gerard presents it condenses the same points as the version presented in *A True and Perfect Relation* and includes some of the same key phrases. Interestingly, the Latin phrases are the same in both. Compare *True and Perfect Relation*, sigs. N4v–O2r, and Gerard, *Narrative*, 227–28.

12. In contrast, Gerard dispatches with this speech in a paragraph (*Narrative*, 263).

13. Linda Levy Peck, *Northampton: Patronage and Policy at the Court of James I* (London: George Allen & Unwin, 1982), 81–83, 111–13.

14. Kevin Sharpe, *Sir Robert Cotton, 1586–1631: History and Politics in Early Modern England* (Oxford: Oxford University Press, 1979), 126, 41. See also Jennifer Summit, *Memory's Library: Medieval Books in Early Modern England* (Chicago: University of Chicago Press, 2008), 136–96.

15. Northampton practiced just the kind of occasional and strategic conformity against which Garnet had argued. See Michael C. Questier, *Conversion, Politics and Religion*, 179–80.

16. Peck, *Northampton*, 112. On Northampton, see also Pauline Croft's *ODNB* entry.

17. Peck, *Northampton*, 82–3; Alastair Bellany, *The Politics of Court Scandal in Early Modern England: News Culture and the Overbury Affair* (Cambridge: Cambridge University Press, 2002), 205.

18. Gerard, *Narrative*, 310–11, 162; see also Tesimond, *Gunpowder Plot*, 178. Gerard comes close to authorizing "that first relation and discourse of all this treason" (the King's Book) since it did not include the "absurd fiction" that Garnet (in fact, Coke claimed it was Gerard himself) heard the conspirators' confessions and ministered communion to them because the author was "said to be of no less authority than the King himself" and as a consequence "was so careful of his authority and the credit of his narration, that he would not blemish the same with reporting any known untruth" (199; Tesimond follows this closely on his p. 210).

19. Philip Caraman, *Henry Garnet, 1555–1606, and the Gunpowder Plot* (New York: Farrar, Straus, 1964), 394n1, n2.

20. David Jardine, *Criminal Trials II: The Gunpowder Plot* (London: Charles Knight, 1835), 235.

21. Ibid., 236, 237.

22. Nicholls, "Investigating Gunpowder Plot," 129–30.

23. Nicholls dismisses the possibility that documents were forged, distorted, or destroyed by explaining that "the loss of some original documents," while regrettable, is also unsurprising given their heavy use and poor storage. The only surprise is that so many have survived. He concludes confidently that "vanished testimony can be reconstructed from accounts of those most public of public trials which none of the accused saw fit to contradict" (Nicholls, *Investigating Gunpowder Plot* [Manchester: Manchester University Press, 1991], 217). Syme's description of Coke's procedure as "harvesting," or winnowing, excerpting,

and shaping testimonies and documents into a compelling narrative, supports Nicholls's contention by showing how little value Coke placed on preserving the raw materials with which he worked (*Theatre and Testimony*, 73).

24. *A Treatise of Equivocation*, ed. David Jardine (London: Longman, 1851), 31, 103. This text was only circulated in manuscript in the period. See the *ODNB* entry on Francis Tresham. On the widespread reliance of religious minorities, clergy and laity, on some form of equivocation to survive, see Alexandra Walsham, *Charitable Hatred: Tolerance and Intolerance in England, 1500–1700* (Manchester: Manchester University Press, 2006), 194–206.

25. On fear of equivocation and distrust of Catholic speech as the legacy of the Gunpowder Plot, see Marotti, *Religious Ideology*, 137. See also Lowell Gallagher, *Medusa's Gaze: Casuitstry and Conscience in the Renaissance* (Stanford, Calif.: Stanford University Press, 1991); Katharine Eisaman Maus, *Inwardness and Theater in the English Renaissance* (Chicago: University of Chicago Press, 1995), 19–24; Olga L. Valbuena, *Subjects to the King's Divorce: Equivocation, Infidelity, and Resistance in Early Modern England* (Bloomington: Indiana University Press, 2003).

26. Gerard, *Narrative*, 261. On interruptions of Garnet, see also 262, 264, 299.

27. Nicholls, "Investigating Gunpowder Plot," 125, 137. Nicholls argues that James and his council refrained from torture, for the most part, because they recognized that it "does not necessarily produce the truth" and they "desperately wanted to know the truth" (Nicholls, *Investigating Gunpowder Plot*, 57–8). If the torture of Fawkes—like the threat of treason—is exceptional, then English law can both boast that it does not countenance torture and rely on it. See Scott Michaelsen and Scott C. Shershow, "Does Torture Have a Future?" *boundary2* 33, 3 (2006): 163–99.

28. *His Majesties Speach*, sig. Hv; *The Araignment and Execution of the Late Traytors* (London, 1606), sig. C3v.

29. Philip Caraman's biography concurs (*Henry Garnet*, 375). In his 1991 book, Nicholls is a bit more equivocal than he appears in his *ODNB* entries. He concedes that Garnet wrote his declaration on March 9 "after either being tortured or at least being threatened with torture" (*Investigating Gunpowder Plot*, 65).

30. Gerard and Caraman both make this claim. Note that Catesby was dead by this point.

31. Alice Hogge, *God's Secret Agents: Queen Elizabeth's Forbidden Priests and the Hatching of the Gunpowder Plot* (New York: HarperCollins, 2005), 363. Both *A True and Perfect Relation* and Gerard's *Narrative* depict Garnet as questioning how accurately the witnesses heard what he and Oldcorne said. There were two witnesses, who claimed they took notes, omitting from their testimony anything about which they could not agree (Gerard, *Narrative*, 255). Nicholls praises "their conscientious and truthful efforts" (*Investigating Gunpowder Plot*, 64).

32. Lena Cowen Orlin, *Locating Privacy in Tudor London* (Oxford: Oxford University Press, 2007), esp. 226–61. According to Orlin, it was incriminating simply to seek "conversational privacy" (229).

33. Gerard, *Narrative*, 169; Caraman, *Henry Garnet*, 360; Tesimond, *Gunpowder Plot*, 187.

34. Ferguson, *Dido's Daughters*, 268, 277, 280. See also Catherine Belsey, *Shakespeare and the Loss of Eden: The Construction of Family Values in Early Modern Culture* (New Brunswick, N.J.: Rutgers University Press, 1999), 83.

35. Similarly, Maus describes a "shared arsenal" from which both Catholics and Protestants drew their "rhetorical weapons" (*Inwardness*, 43); Elizabeth Hanson describes "rhetorical cooperation" between Jesuits and legal personnel and the ways in which "the narrative of Jesuitical secret labors and the narrative of torture not only imitate each other but become, on occasion, the same story," *Discovering the Subject in Renaissance England* (Cambridge: Cambridge University Press, 1998), 48, 52. As Barbara Shapiro argues more generally, "In spite of much talk of impartiality and 'naked truth,' it was not clear to contemporaries how one could construct a meaningful persuasive narrative without rhetoric," *A Culture of Fact: England, 1550–1720* (Ithaca, N.Y.: Cornell University Press, 2000), 62,

36. This was an anonymous letter given to William Parker, Baron Monteagle, which he passed on to James. The author has never been conclusively identified but is widely suspected to have been Francis Tresham, whose sister, a recusant, was Monteagle's wife (although Fr. Francis Edwards suggests Robert Cecil, the earl of Salisbury). In his *ODNB* entry on Tresham, Mark Nicholls claims that he "almost certainly" wrote the letter. The letter was given to Monteagle's servant in the street; he then interrupted a dinner party to present it to his master, who handed it to someone else to read aloud, "an extraordinary action if he was not already aware of its contents," S. M. Toyne, "Guy Fawkes and the Powder Plot," *History Today* 1 (1951): 16–24, esp. 21. Questions have also arisen regarding the nine days that intervened between the receipt of the letter and the capture of Fawkes.

37. Ibid., sig. F3v.

38. Ibid., sig. F3r.

39. Ibid., sig. B4r.

40. Gerard, *Narrative*, 100.

41. Alison Shell, *Catholicism, Controversy and the English Literary Imagination, 1558–1660* (Cambridge: Cambridge University Press, 1999), 115; Marotti, *Religious Ideology*, 141.

42. Gerard, *Narrative*, 241n.1 (this has been erased in the manuscript); Tesimond, *Gunpowder Plot*, 181, 182.

43. This was a strategy used to disparage Garnet's friendship with and dependence on Anne Vaux, as Arthur Marotti has discussed (Marotti, *Religious Ideology*, 54–55).

44. According to Gerard, "this was their misconstruing, not his equivocating" (259) because Tresham meant he had not seen him 14 years before the Spanish treason rather than for the last 14 years. *True and Perfect Relation* describes the period in question as 16 years.

45. These include *Confession and Execution of Leticia Wigington of Ratclif* (London, 1681) and *The True Relation of the Tryals At the Sessions of Oyer and Terminer* (London, 1681), both available in facsimile in Randall Martin, *Women and Murder in Early Modern News Pamphlets and Broadside Ballads, 1573–1697* (Burlington, Vt.: Ashgate, 2005). Philip D. Collington offers a helpful introduction to an excerpt from *Confession and Execution of Leticia*

Wigington in *Reading Early Modern Women: An Anthology of Texts in Manuscript and Print, 1550–1700*, ed. Helen Ostovich and Elizabeth Sauer (New York: Routledge, 2004), 50–52. As he points out, Wigington's lodger, John Sadler, rumored to be her lover, was executed as her accomplice in the murder; Martin also emphasizes Sadler's contested role in this brutal crime. On Sadler, see *The Last Dying Speeches and Confessions of the Three Notorious Malefactors. . . . John Sadler, For Whipping a Girl to Death in Ratcliff* (London, 1680/1) and *The Tryal and Condemnation of Several notorious Malefactors . . . And most remarkably of John Sadler* (London, 1681).

46. For a detailed and useful overview of this case and the various print accounts of it, see Randall Martin, *Women, Murder, and Equity in Early Modern England* (New York: Routledge, 2008), 33–35.

47. Ibid., 32–33.

48. Catholics sometimes used this phrase. For instance, Fr. John Gerard averred that "the Attorney brought against Father Garnett all other former matter that had been forged against the martyrs in Queen Elizabeth's time, with which (if they had been true) yet they could no more have charged Father Garnett with them in justice, than the child that was then unborn" (Gerard, *Narrative*, 225). Even more important, variations on this phrase were not always associated with Catholics. In *A True Relation of the Unjust, Cruell, and Barbarous Proceedings against the English at Amboyna In the East-Indies* (London, 1624), one Colson subscribes his confession but says "you make mee to accuse my selfe and others of that which is as false, as GOD is true: for, God is my witnes, I am as innocent as the childe new borne" (sig. D1r). In *A True Relation of the Unjust Accusation of Certain French Gentle-men, (Charged with a Robbery, of which they were most Innocent)* (London, 1671), Denzell Lord Holles asserts that these gentlemen "were as free as the Child new born" (sig. Br) of the charges.

49. See also *The True Narrative of the Confession and Execution of the Prisoners at King-stone-upon-Thames* (London, 1681), 3. *The True Protestant Mercury* (February 23–26, 1681) claims that "Eliz. Wigenton" had been condemned but "Reprieved for Her Belly."

50. For example, a woman convicted of poisoning her master's family claims, "My Lord, I am Innocent, I am with Child, do not kill two Innocents. If I must die, let my Child live!" (J. Q., *Hell Open'd, Or, The Infernal Sin of Murther Punished* [London, 1676], C4r). She persists in this claim on the scaffold, despite being searched several times by midwives (F6r). She also identifies herself with the newly born, insisting "I am as free from this Crime, as the Child that is now Born" (C7r).

51. *An Account of the Behaviour of the Fourteen Late Popish Malefactors* (London, 1679), sigs. D1v, E1v. On Smith, and the ordinaries more generally, see Andrea McKenzie, *Tyburn's Martyrs: Execution in England, 1675–1775* (London: Hambledon Continuum, 2007), esp. 121–55, 267–68. Just a few years later, Smith could present a prisoner's use of this trope as neither inculpatory nor associated with Catholicism. *A True Relation of the Execution of John Smith* (London, 1684), subscribed by Samuel Smith as ordinary, emphasizes the piety of Edward Jackson, hanged for coin clipping, and reports that he avowed on the scaffold that "he was as clear as that Child, (*pointing to a little Child*)" (2), and left a written statement

contesting the evidence against him and concluding "that as to any actual or personal Clipping, or diminishing the King's Coin, I am as Innocent as the Child in the Mothers Womb."

52. Benjamin Harris, *Domestick Intelligence or News Both from City and Country*, 1 (Wednesday, July 9, 1679). See also Benjamin Keach's poem *Sion in Distress, or the Groans of the Protestant Church* (London, 1681; Boston, 1683), in which Justice attributes this phrase to the Whore, telling Jehovah, "Thy *Judgment Seat* she seems to slight and scorn, / Says she's *as guiltless as the Child unborn*" (88). I am grateful to Laura Stevens for directing my attention to this text.

53. *A Letter from the Lady Creswell to Madam C. the Midwife* (London 1680), 2. On this text, and the complexity of its politics, see Melissa M. Mowry, *The Bawdy Politic in Stuart England, 1660–1714: Political Pornography and Prostitution* (Aldershot: Ashgate, 2004), 44–46.

54. Sir Matthew Hale, *Historia Placitorum Coronae: The History of the Pleas of the Crown* (London, 1736), 635. I am thus arguing that early modern confessional antagonisms produced a "hermeneutics of suspicion" long before what Paul Ricoeur calls the "school of suspicion," Marx, Nietzsche, Freud, and Paul Ricoeur, *Freud and Philosophy: An Essay on Interpretation*, trans. Denis Savage (New Haven, Conn.: Yale University Press, 1970), 32 and passim. While Ricoeur opposes faith to suspicion, in seventeenth-century England, faith bred suspicion.

CHAPTER 2: SHAM STORIES AND CREDIBLE RELATIONS: WITCHCRAFT AND NARRATIVE CONVENTIONS

1. A nineteenth-century editor of seventeenth-century depositions from the Castle of York, James Raine, routinely dismisses testimony regarding witchcraft as delusional. Of Jane Milburne's testimony against Dorothy Stranger in Newcastle in 1663, he remarks that "It is strange that any magistrate should write down such ridiculous evidence"; of another deposition by one Mary Moor in 1674, he marvels "one would scarcely believe it possible that any magistrate could sit down to write such nonsense from the lips of any one." *Depositions from the Castle of York, Relating to Offences Committed in the Northern Counties in the Seventeenth Century* (Publications of the Surtees Society 40, 1861), 112, 208.

2. Carlo Ginzburg, *Ecstasies: Deciphering the Witches' Sabbath*, trans. Raymond Rosenthal (New York: Pantheon, 1991), 10; Sarah Ferber, "The Abuse of History? Identity Politics, Disordered Identity and the 'Really Real' in French Cases of Demonic Possession," in *Women, Identities and Communities in Early Modern Europe*, ed. Stephanie Tarbin and Susan Broomhall (Aldershot: Ashgate 2007), 29–41, esp. 37. Marion Gibson asks, "Suppose accounts agree on something we now find incredible?" Marion Gibson, "Thomas Potts' 'dusty memory': Reconstructing Justice in *The Wonderfull Discoverie of Witches*," in *The Late Lancashire Witches: Histories and Stories*, ed. Robert Poole (Manchester: Manchester University Press, 2002), 42–57, 43.

3. Christina Larner, *Witchcraft and Religion: The Politics of Popular Belief*, ed. Alan

Macfarlane (Oxford: Blackwell, 1984), 21; Keith Thomas, *Religion and the Decline of Magic* (New York: Scribner's, 1971), 460.

4. James Sharpe, *The Bewitching of Anne Gunter: A Horrible and True Story of Deception, Witchcraft, Murder, and the King of England* (New York: Routledge, 2000), 80.

5. Thomas Cooper, *The Mystery of Witchcraft* (London, 1617), sig. Bb6v. According to John Cotta, however, witches' confessions "tend more to the satisfaction of curiositie then of use, and therefore are not without some danger published," *The Triall of Witch-craft, Shewing the True and Right Methode of the Discovery* (London, 1616), sig. L4r.

6. For how popular and elite cultures collaborated and overlapped in facilitating witchcraft prosecutions, see Stuart Clark, "Inversion, Misrule and the Meaning of Witchcraft," *Past and Present* 87 (1980): 98–127; and *Thinking with Demons: The Idea of Witchcraft in Early Modern Europe* (Oxford: Oxford University Press, 1997); Annabel Gregory, "Witchcraft, Politics, and 'Good Neighbourhood' in Early Seventeenth-Century Rye," *Past and Present* 133 (November 1991): 31–66; Clive Holmes, "Popular Culture? Witches, Magistrates, and Divines in Early Modern England," in *Understanding Popular Culture: Europe from the Middle Ages to the Nineteenth Century*, ed. Steven L. Kaplan (Berlin: Mouton, 1984), 85–111, esp. 87; and "Women: Witnesses and Witches," *Past and Present* 140 (August 1993): 45–78, esp. 50–51; and E. P. Thompson, "Anthropology and the Discipline of Historical Context," *Midland History* 1, 3 (1972): 41–55.

7. Henry Goodcole, *The Wonderfull Discoverie of Elizabeth Sawyer a Witch, late of Edmonton* (London, 1621), sigs. A3r–A3v.

8. Randall Martin, *Women, Murder, and Equity in Early Modern England* (New York: Routledge, 2008), 98–101.

9. On this passage in Goodcole, see Anna Bayman, " 'Large hands, wide eares, and piercing sights': The 'Discoveries' of the Elizabethan and Jacobean Witch Pamplets," *Literature & History* 16, 1 (2007): 26–45, esp. 27; Jonathan Gil Harris, *Foreign Bodies and the Body Politic: Discourses of Social Pathology in Early Modern England* (Cambridge: Cambridge University Press, 1998), 128–38; Dennis Kezar, "*The Witch of Edmonton* and the Guilt of Possession," in *Solon and Thespis: Law and Theater in the English Renaissance*, ed. Dennis Kezar (Notre Dame, Ind.: University of Notre Dame Press, 2007), 124–60, esp. 131–34; Diane Purkiss, *The Witch in History: Early Modern and Twentieth-Century Representations* (London: Routledge, 1996), 237.

10. Marion Gibson, *Women and Witchcraft in Popular Literature, c. 1560–1715*, vol. 7 in The Early Modern Englishwoman: A Facsimile Library Series 3 Pt. 2 (Aldershot: Ashgate, 2007), x.

11. Alan Macfarlane, *Witchcraft in Tudor and Stuart England: A Regional and Comparative Study* (London: Routledge, 1970), 86. As Macfarlane's practice shows, we can often compare assize indictments to pamphlets. There are also rare cases in which we can compare a manuscript account to a pamphlet. For one such, see Marion Gibson, *Reading Witchcraft: Stories of Early English Witches* (London: Routledge, 1999), 66–72. What we do not have are full transcriptions of trials.

12. According to Gibson, who has written at length on how to read these pamphlets,

"Perhaps the best way of reading these accounts is as records of a kind of oral history—the magistrate and his clerk acting as partial and selective recorders of conflicting and unfixed stories circulating in the community, which come to be retold and reused as evidence of crime" ("Thomas Potts' 'dusty memory'," 51). The benefit of this approach is that it shifts attention from tellers to tales—since the true relation between the two is one we cannot determine now. See also Gibson's *Reading Witchcraft*, in which she argues that pamphlets "will not necessarily tell us what happened but what those involved believed happened, or wanted us to believe" (75). See also Stuart Clark, "Introduction," in *Languages of Witchcraft: Narrative, Ideology, and Meaning in Early Modern Culture*, ed. Stuart Clark (Houndmills: Macmillan, 2001), 1–18, esp. 10.

13. See, among others, Bayman, "'Large Hands'"; Frances E. Dolan, *Dangerous Familiars: Representations of Domestic Crime in England, 1550–1700* (Ithaca, N.Y.: Cornell University Press, 1994); Malcolm Gaskill, *Crime and Mentalities in Early Modern England* (Cambridge: Cambridge University Press, 2000); Gibson, *Reading Witchcraft*; Karen Newman, *Fashioning Femininity and English Renaissance Drama* (Chicago: University of Chicago Press, 1991); Purkiss, *Witch in History*; and Deborah Willis, *Malevolent Nurture: Witch-Hunting and Maternal Power in Early Modern England* (Ithaca, N.Y.: Cornell University Press, 1995).

14. Richard Bovet, *Pandaemonium, or the Devil's Cloyster* (London, 1684), sigs. D7v, E12v. *A Tryal of Witches, at the Assizes Held at Bury St. Edmond . . . 1664* (London 1682), presented as "Taken by a Person then Attending the Court," explains its mission in its preface "To the Reader": "I thought that so exact a Relation of this Tryal would probably give more satisfaction to a great many persons, by reason that it is pure Matter of Fact, and that evidently Demonstrated; than the Arguments and Reasons of other very Learned Men, that probably may not be so Intelligible to all Readers."

15. Peter Elmer, "Toward a Politics of Witchcraft in Early Modern England," in *Languages of Witchcraft*, ed. Clark, 101–18, esp. 103. See also Clark, *Thinking with Demons*, 549–682.

16. *The Lawes Against Witches, and Conjuration. And Some Brief Notes and Observations for the Discovery of Witches* (London, 1645), sig. A3r.

17. On searching witches, see John Stearne, *A Confirmation and Discovery of Witchcraft* (London, 1648), sigs. G1r–G4v. For a skeptical view of corporeal evidence, see Thomas Ady, *A Candle in the Dark* (London, 1656). On witches' marks, see Dolan, *Dangerous Familiars*, 191–94; Holmes, "Women: Witnesses and Witches," 65–75; Gail Paster, *The Body Embarrassed: Drama and the Disciplines of Shame in Early Modern England* (Ithaca, N.Y.: Cornell University Press, 1993), 246–60; Purkiss, *Witch in History*, 238–41; James Sharpe, "Women, Witchcraft and the Legal Process," in *New Perspectives on Witchcraft, Magic and Demonology*, vol. 3, *Witchcraft in the British Isles and New England*, ed. Brian P. Levack (New York: Routledge, 2001), 58–75; and Willis, *Malevolent Nurture*, 51–81. Sharpe points out that, while witches' marks were variously located in the sixteenth century, "by the mid-seventeenth century familiars sucked from a teat on the pudenda or near the anus of the female witch," thus suggesting a more eroticized vision of the relation between witch and

familiar. James Sharpe, "The Witch's Familiar in Elizabethan England," in *Authority and Consent in Tudor England: Essays Presented to C. S. L. Davies*, ed. G. W. Bernard and S. J. Gunn (Aldershot: Ashgate, 2002), 219–32, esp. 226.

18. On suspicion of Hopkins's standards of evidence, see Malcolm Gaskill, "Witchcraft and Evidence in Early Modern England," *Past and Present* 198 (2008): 33–70.

19. On early modern debates regarding standards of evidence and the heavy reliance on evidentiary narratives, see, in addition to Gaskill, Macfarlane, *Witchcraft*, 16–20, 170, 197; Katharine Eisaman Maus, *Inwardness and Theater in the English Renaissance* (Chicago: University of Chicago Press, 1995), 104–27; and Barbara Shapiro, *Probability and Certainty in Seventeenth-Century England: A Study of the Relationships Between Natural Science, Religion, History, Law, and Literature* (Princeton, N.J.: Princeton University Press, 1983).

20. On acceptable witnesses and standards of evidence, see Reginald Scot, *The Discoverie of Witchcraft* (London, 1584), sig. D2r, and Book II, passim; Macfarlane, *Witchcraft*, 17–20, 57, 170; and Wallace Notestein, *A History of Witchcraft in England from 1558 to 1718* (New York: Russell and Russell, 1965), 44–45, 108–14. On women's increasingly significant role as witnesses after 1590, see Holmes, "Women: Witnesses and Witches." Holmes argues that women witnesses "were being mobilized by men, who were the driving force behind the decision to bring local suspicions and fears to the attention of the courts" (56). On child witnesses, see Michael Witmore, *Pretty Creatures: Children and Fiction in the English Renaissance* (Ithaca, N.Y.: Cornell University Press, 2007), 171–211; and Elizabeth A. Foyster, "Silent Witnesses? Children and the Breakdown of Domestic and Social Order in Early Modern England," in *Childhood in Question: Children, Parents and the State*, ed. Anthony Fletcher and Stephen Hussey (Manchester: Manchester University Press, 1999), 57–73. On child witnesses regarding witchcraft, see James Crossley's introduction to his edition of Potts, *Discovery of Witches in the County of Lancaster* (Manchester: Chetham Society, 1845), in which he refers to the Throgmorton children in the Warboys's case as "these little incarnate fiends" (iv) and says of nine-year-old Jennet Device in the 1612 Lancashire case that "A more dangerous tool in the hands of an unscrupulous evidence-compeller, being at once intelligent, cunning and pliant, than the child proved herself, it would not have been easy to have discovered" (li).

21. William Perkins, *A Discourse of the Damned Art of Witchcraft* (London, 1608), sig. O5r.

22. Cotta, *Triall of Witch-craft*, sig. Dv.

23. John Gaule, *Select Cases of Conscience Touching Witches and Witchcrafts* (London, 1646), sig. I5r. On caution in prosecuting witches, see also Richard Bernard, *A Guide to Grand-Jury Men* (London, 1627); Robert Filmer, *An Advertisement to the Jury-men of England, Touching Witches* (London, 1653); and George Gifford, *A Dialogue Concerning Witches and Witchcraftes* (London, 1593), sigs. H2v–H3r.

24. James Sharpe has calculated that in the Home Circuit counties (Essex, Hertfordshire, Kent, Surrey, and Sussex) only 32 percent of cases ended in the conviction and punishment of the accused, 22 percent in execution and 10 percent in the lesser penalty of a year's imprisonment and four stints in the pillory (*Instruments of Darkness: Witchcraft in*

Early Modern England [Philadelphia: University of Pennsylvania Press, 1997], 111). Sharpe uses numbers from C. L'Estrange Ewen, *Witch Hunting and Witch Trials: The Indictments for Witchcraft from the Records of 1373 Assizes Held for the Home Circuit, 1559–1736* (London: K. Paul, 1929), 99, 117–89; Macfarlane's analysis of Essex assize court records (*Witchcraft*, 57); and J. S. Cockburn's calendar of Home Circuit assize court indictments. Working with Ewen's figures, Malcolm Gaskill calculates that "of 258 persons indicted at the Home Circuit assizes, 1560–1600, just fifty-nine (23 per cent) were found guilty" ("Witchcraft and Evidence," 40). Brian Levack claims that "in the early seventeenth century, more than fifty percent of all English witchcraft trials ended in acquittals." In Levack's view, the relative absence of torture and inquisitorial procedure contributed to the high acquittal rate in England, as did the fact that judges from the central courts supervised local justices. Brian Levack, "Possession, Witchcraft, and the Law in Jacobean England," *Washington and Lee Law Review* 52, 5 (1996): 1613–40, esp. 1624.

25. See, for example, *An Account of the Tryal and Examination of Joan Buts* (London, 1682).

26. Scot, *Discoverie*, sig. C4r.

27. Gaule, *Select Cases*, sigs. B2v–B3r.

28. Gaule, *Select Cases*, sigs. E5r–E5v.

29. George Gifford, *A Discourse of the Subtill Practises of Devills by Witches and Sorcerers* (London, 1587), sigs. G4r–G4v.

30. Bernard, *Guide to Grand-Jury Men*, sigs. K8r, K12v, L1v.

31. References to *Macbeth* and later to *Othello* are from *The Norton Shakespeare*, ed. Stephen Greenblatt, Walter Cohen, Jean E. Howard, and Katharine Eisaman Maus (New York: Norton, 1997).

32. The thesis that witchcraft began with a refusal of charity and then guilty feelings can be found in Thomas, *Religion and the Decline of Magic*; and Macfarlane, *Witchcraft*.

33. A particularly good example of this is the Gunter case, discussed below.

34. Gaskill, *Crime and Mentalities*, 35, 48.

35. For example, Marion Gibson argues that this plot predominates only in texts published before 1590 and written by legal personnel, because victims, over time, ceased to feel any guilt about their conflict with those they accused. After 1590, "victims get more blameless, witches get wickeder" as stories are more likely to be told from the victim's perspective and in his/her interests. "Understanding Witchcraft? Accusers' Stories in Print in Early Modern England," in *Languages of Witchcraft: Narrative*, ed. Clark, 41–54.

36. As Hayden White argues, "the value attached to narrativity in the representation of real events arises out of a desire to have real events display the coherence, integrity, fullness, and closure of an image of life that is and can only be imaginary." *The Content of the Form: Narrative Discourse and Historical Representation* (Baltimore: Johns Hopkins University Press, 1987), 24.

37. Bovet, *Pandaemonium*, sig. E2r.

38. *A Relation of the Devill Balams Departure Out of the Body of the Mother-Prioresse of the Ursuline Nuns of Loudun* (London, 1636), sig. C4r.

39. Gibson identifies a passage that "presents the witch [in this case Agnes Samuel] sympathetically, and thus it may be true" (Gibson, *Reading Witchcraft*, 66); Purkiss argues that "traces of the agency of the witch rather than the questioner" can be found in "material unassimilable by the categories of the learned" (Purkiss, *Witch in History*, 167).

40. Peter Brooks, *Troubling Confessions: Speaking Guilt in Law and Literature* (Chicago: University of Chicago Press, 2000), 4, 55.

41. Gaule, *Select Cases*, sig. I12v.

42. Matthew Hopkins, *The Discovery of Witches* (London, 1647), sig. B2r.

43. Scot, *Discoverie*, sigs. D3v–D5r; John Wagstaffe, *The Question of Witchcraft Debated; or a Discourse against Their Opinion that Affirm Witches* (London, 1669), F1r.

44. Thomas Potts, *The Wonderfull Discoverie of Witches in the Countie of Lancaster* (London, 1613), sig. E2r. See also Perkins, *Discourse*, O2r–O2v.

45. Goodcole, *Wonderfull Discoverie*, sigs. B4r, D2r. For the role of interrogators in shaping confessions, see [W. W.], *A True and Just Recorde, of the Information, Examination and Confession of all the Witches, taken at S. Oses in the Countie of Essex* (London, 1582); Hopkins, who claims to discount confessions "drawn from" the accused by violence or flattery, or "interrogated to her, and words put into her mouth" (*The Discovery of Witches*, sig. B2r); and Edmond Bower, *Doctor Lamb Revived, or, Witchcraft condemn'd in Anne Bodenham, A Servant of his* (London, 1653), who insists that he has "obliged" himself in this account "to use the same words and expressions" his subjects did and that he has "not made them speak my words in this relation" (sig. G2r).

46. Ginzburg, *Ecstasies*, 10.

47. Newman, *Fashioning Femininity*, 67–70. See also Catherine Belsey, *Subject of Tragedy: Identity and Difference in Renaissance Drama* (London: Methuen, 1985), 178–91.

48. Purkiss, *Witch in History*, 145, 170. Purkiss goes so far as to claim that accused witch Anne Bodenham "got some pleasure and satisfaction from her self-fashioning as witch even if it also killed her" (153). On the agency of the confessor, see also Louise Jackson, "Witches, Wives and Mothers: Witchcraft Persecution and Women's Confessions in Seventeenth-Century England," *Women's History Review* 4, 1 (1995): 63–83; Michael Witmore, *Pretty Creatures*, 183; and Kirilka Stavreva, "Fighting Words: Witch-Speak in Late Elizabethan Docu-fiction," *Journal of Medieval and Early Modern Studies* 30, 2 (2000): 309–38.

49. *A Series of Precedents and Proceedings in Criminal Causes, Extending from the Year 1475 to 1640 Extracted from the Ecclesiastical Courts in the Diocese of London*, ed. William Hale (London, 1847), 147. "Dive" may simply mean "die" here, or it might suggest both the literal plunge of hanging and a more metaphorical fall.

50. Levack, "Possession, Witchcraft, and the Law," 1636.

51. Ibid., 1631; Sharpe, *Bewitching*, 191. Levack emphasizes that, although the Gunter case was heard in a prerogative court that followed something like inquisitorial procedure, it was a turning point in the history of judicial skepticism that would lead to declining conviction rates and ultimately the end of witchcraft prosecutions.

52. According to Levack, it is likely that Brian was convicted and fined, while Anne was given "a royal pardon and a dowry" ("Possession, Witchcraft, and the Law," 1635). On

the outcome of the case and on the pardon and dowry for Anne, see Sharpe, *Bewitching*, 194–97, 204–6.

53. Sharpe, *Bewitching*, xii.

54. Ibid., 62, 135.

55. Levack "Possession, Witchcraft, and the Law," 1621–23; see also Sharpe on the script for demonic possession (*Bewitching*, 156–57). For an interesting take on the role of performance in the Gunter case, see Todd Wayne Butler, "Bedeviling Spectacle: Law, Literature, and Early Modern Witchcraft," *Yale Journal of Law & the Humanities* 20, 2 (2008): 111–29.

56. Sharpe, *Bewitching*, 8.

57. Gaskill, *Crime and Mentalities*, 40. See also Holmes, "Women: Witnesses and Witches," 62.

58. On the influence of learned witchcraft treatises on one another, see Gaskill, *Crime and Mentalities*, 37–48, and Clark, *Thinking with Demons*, passim.

59. Sharpe, *Bewitching*, 141.

60. Peter Rushton, "Texts of Authority: Witchcraft Accusations and the Demonstration of Truth in Early Modern England," in *Languages of Witchcraft: Narrative, Ideology and Meaning in Early Modern Culture*, ed. Stuart Clark (Houndmills: Macmillan, 2001), 21–39, esp. 27.

61. Witmore, *Pretty Creatures*, 181.

62. See Dolan, *Dangerous Familiars*, on the role of "subject-extensions" in witchcraft (180–94).

63. Witmore, *Pretty Creatures*, 181.

64. Ibid., 181, 175. See also, Marion Gibson, *Reading Witchcraft*, 1–10.

65. Lena Orlin, "Rewriting Stone's Renaissance," *Huntington Library Quarterly* 64, 1–2 (2001): 189–230, esp. 219, 221.

66. Witmore points out that the notion that child witnesses were suborned is structurally parallel to the idea of the bewitched or possessed victim as a passive instrument or vehicle, a sponge, a mimic, a puppet (*Pretty Creatures*, 173–74, 177).

67. Sharpe, *Bewitching*, 195.

68. Ibid., 204.

69. Levack "Possession, Witchcraft, and the Law," 1628.

70. Sharpe, *Bewitching*, 169. The uncertain future for a woman who had been accused might lead her to prefer death. Sir George Mackenzie reported that "a silly creature" confided in him that she had confessed to witchcraft because she was poor and dependent on charity and that having been "defam'd for a Witch, she knew she would starve, for no person thereafter would either give her meat or lodging, and that all men would beat her, and hound Dogs at her, and that therefore she desired to be out of the World." *Laws and Customes of Scotland in Matters Criminal* (Edinburgh, 1678), sig. M4R.

71. Potts, *Wonderfull Discoverie of Witches*, sig. B1v. Subsequent citations to this text will appear in parentheses. Since the nineteenth-century, the town of Lancaster has been distinguished from the county of Lancashire that surrounds it, but Potts does not make that

distinction. In modern usage, Samlesbury and Lancaster are both towns in the county of Lancashire; I follow that usage here.

72. Stephen Pumfrey, "Potts, Plots, and Politics: James I's *Daemonologie* and *The Wonderfull Discoverie of Witches*," in *The Lancashire Witches* ed. Poole, 22–41, esp. 30, 31; Gibson, "Thomas Potts' 'dusty memory'," 53. The Gunpowder Plot haunts this text. Potts's account suggests that some of the accused testified that, during a meeting at one of their homes, Malkin Tower, they had cooked up a scheme to blow up Lancaster Castle, where several accused witches were already imprisoned. Given the connection between the Lancashire witches' plot and the other Gunpowder Plot, it then becomes especially interesting that Potts dedicates his text to Thomas Knyvett, who, as James I's keeper of Whitehall Palace, had searched the undercrofts of the House of Lords on the evening of November 4, 1605, and, allegedly, found Guy Fawkes and his barrels of powder. By dedicating his text to Knyvett, Potts draws our attention to the connection between discovering the Gunpowder Plotters and discovering witches.

73. James Crossley, "Introduction" to his 1845 edition of *Potts' Discovery of Witches in the County of Lancaster*, lii–liii (my emphasis).

74. Gibson, "Thomas Potts' 'dusty memory'," 51, 49, 50.

75. Michael Dalton, *The Countrey Justice* (London, 1630), sigs. Aa6v–Aa7r.

76. James Sharpe, "Introduction," in *The Lancashire Witches*, ed. Poole, 1–18, 3.

77. Pumfrey, "Potts, Plots, and Politics," 35.

78. Edgar Peel and Pat Southern, *The Trials of the Lancashire Witches: A Study of Seventeenth-Century Witchcraft* (New York: Taplinger, 1969), 83; Robin Briggs, *Witches and Neighbors: The Social and Cultural Context of European Witchcraft* (New York: Penguin, 1996), 332. See also Jonathan Lumby, *The Lancashire Witch-Craze: Jennet Preston and the Lancashire Witches, 1612* (Preston: Carnegie Publishing, 1995), 136–42.

79. Richard Bernard uses the "notable example of one *Grace*, or rather gracelesse, *Sowerbutts*" to demonstrate the problem caused for prosecutions by witnesses who "feigne their accusations, yea and confirme them by oath to be true" (*Guide to Grand-Jury Men*, sigs. K1v–K2r).

80. On the differences between English and Continental witch lore, see, for instance, Clark, *Thinking with Demons*; Larner, *Witchcraft and Religion*, 69–78; Macfarlane, *Witchcraft*, 3–22; and Thomas, *Religion and the Decline of Magic*, 435–68. On sex with demons, see Walter Stephens, *Demon Lovers: Witchcraft, Sex, and the Crisis of Belief* (Chicago: University of Chicago Press, 2002).

81. Pumfrey, "Potts, Plots, and Politics," 22. The introduction of the sabbath was probably caused in part by the fact that the Jacobean witchcraft statute of 1604 (1 Jac. I, c. 12) had specified that it was a felony to "consult covenant with entertaine employ feede or rewarde any evill and wicked Spirit to or for any intent or purpose." See Pumfrey, 28; C. R. Unsworth, "Witchcraft Belief and Criminal Procedure in Early Modern England," in *Legal Record and Historical Reality*, ed. Thomas G. Watkin (London: Hambledon Press, 1989), 71–98, esp. 77. Barbara Rosen identifies *News from Scotland* (1591) as "the first pamphlet account [in English] of the Witches' Sabbath as it was said to occur on the Continent" but

also points out that this idea did not really catch on in England, Barbara Rosen, *Witchcraft in England, 1558–1618* (Amherst: University of Massachusetts Press, 1991), 190. According to John Demos, in Salem eighty years later, "there were a few reports of dancing and 'sport,' but very little of the wild excitements associated with witch revels in continental Europe. Most striking of all is the absence of allusions to sex; there is no nakedness, no promiscuity, no obscene contact with the Devil." As in Lancashire, the focus was on a compact between witch and the devil, but not one celebrated to continental excess. John Demos, "Underlying Themes in the Witchcraft of Seventeenth-Century New England," *American Historical Review* 75, 5 (1970): 1311–26, esp. 1321.

82. Ania Loomba, *Gender, Race, and Renaissance Drama* (Manchester: Manchester University Press, 1989), 42.

83. *Othello* 1.2.71–74; 1.3.61–64, 106. Critics have connected the play to inquiries into evidence: see Joel Altman, *The Improbability of Othello: Rhetorical Anthropology and Shakespearean Selfhood* (Chicago: University of Chicago Press, 2010); Maus, *Inwardness and Theatre*, 104–27; and Patricia Parker, *Shakespeare from the Margins* (Chicago: University of Chicago Press, 1996), 229–72.

84. When Thomas Rymer dismisses *Othello* as "fraught . . . with improbabilities," miscegenation ranks high on his list of "improbable lyes" (*The Critical Works of Thomas Rymer*, ed. Curt A. Zimansky [New Haven: Yale University Press, 1956], 134).

85. *The Witches of Huntingdon, Their Examinations and Confessions* (London, 1646), sig. A3v.

86. *CSPD* 1634–35 (CCLXIX) 78; C. L'Estrange Ewen, *Witchcraft and Demonianism: A Concise Account Derived from Sworn Depositions and Confessions Obtained in the Courts of England and Wales* (London: Heath Cranton, 1933), 248–49.

87. H. F., *A True and Exact Relation of the Severall Informations, Examinations, and Confessions of the Late Witches, Arraigned and Executed in the County of Essex* (London, 1645), sig. A1v.

88. Stearne, *Confirmation and Discovery*, sig. C3r.

89. Ibid., sig. C2r.

90. Pumfrey, "Potts, Plots, and Politics," 34; Thomas, *Religion and the Decline of Magic*, 445–46. See also Sharpe, "Witch's Familiar"; and James A. Serpell, "Guardian Spirits or Demonic Pets: The Concept of the Witch's Familiar in Early Modern England, 1530–1712," in *The Animal/Human Boundary: Historical Perspectives*, ed. Angela N. H. Creager and William Chester Jordan (Rochester, N.Y.: University of Rochester Press, 2002), 157–89, esp. 167, 179. Appearing frequently after 1566, the familiar was explicitly identified in the 1604 witchcraft statute and proved an important form of evidence for the witch finder Hopkins.

91. Francis Bacon, *Advancement of Learning* (Rockville, Md.: Serenity Publishers, 2008), 36.

92. Lawrence M. Friedman, "Law, Lawyers, and Popular Culture," *Yale Law Journal* 98, 8 (1989): 1579–1606, 1595.

93. John Gee, *Foot Out of the Snare* (London, 1624), sig. H3r.

94. On the connection between witchcraft and Catholicism, see, among others, Stephen Greenblatt, *Shakespearean Negotiations: The Circulation of Social Energy in Renaissance England* (Berkeley: University of California Press, 1988), 94–128; Harris, *Foreign*, 118–40; Norman Jones, "Defining Superstitions: Treasonous Catholics and the Act Against Witchcraft of 1563," in *State, Sovereign and Society in Early Modern England: Essays in Honour of A. J. Slavin*, ed. Charles Carlton et al. (Phoenix Mill: Sutton, 1998), 187–203; Purkiss, *Witch in History*, 154–56.

95. James Sharpe, *Instruments of Darkness*, 77, 238, see also Sharpe, "Introduction," *Lancashire Witches*, 4; Lumby, *Lancashire Witch-craze*, 141; and Alison Findlay, "Sexual and Spiritual Politics in the Events of 1633–34 and *The Late Lancashire Witches*," in *The Lancashire Witches*, ed. Poole, 146–65, esp. 159.

96. Witmore, *Pretty Creatures*, 186.

97. *CSPD* (1634–35), 79.

98. *CSPD* (1634–35), 98, 129–30. See also Ewen, *Witchcraft and Demonianism*, 250.

99. John Webster, *The Displaying of Supposed Witchcraft* (London: 1677), sigs. Nn3r–Nn3v. Webster discusses both the Samlesbury and Lancaster cases in a chapter on impostures (sigs. Mm3v–Nn4r). Webster's exposure of the boy's counterfeiting prompts him to assert his own credibility: "And that this is most certain truth, there are many persons yet living, of sufficient reputation and integrity, that can avouch and testifie the same; and besides, what I write is the most of it true, upon my own knowledge, and the whole I have had from his own mouth more than once" (Nn3v). "His own mouth" is presumably the boy's, Edward Robinson's, since Webster claims to have confronted him long before he was brought up to London. But it is interesting that Webster should aver that what he writes is "the most of it true." He may mean that most of it is true "upon my own knowledge" and all of it is "certain truth," but he opens up a little room for doubt.

100. On Robinson's demand for money, see *CSPD* (1634–35), 78–79.

101. For the boy's recantation, see *CSPD* (1634–35), 141, 152–53. A version of the boy's first examination is presented by John Webster at the end of his text, sigs. Yy2r–Yy3r.

102. *CSPD* (1634–5), 78–79.

103. Webster, *Displaying*, sig. Yy1v.

104. Witmore, *Pretty Creatures*, 172. Purkiss claims Robinson's testimony was "an object lesson in how to construct a plausible narrative using cultural materials" (*Witch in History*, 233, 247n3, 4).

105. *Newsletters from the Caroline Court, 1631–1638: Catholicism and the Politics of Personal Rule*, ed. Michael C. Questier, Camden Fifth Series 26 (Cambridge: Cambridge University Press, 2005), 226. A few days later he writes that "The witches, which in a former I did mention, will not be believed to be witches, notwithstanding that one doth confesse her selfe a witch, and therefore shall returne into Lancheshire agayne" (227–28).

106. Andrew Gurr, *The Shakespeare Company, 1594–1642* (Cambridge: Cambridge University Press, 2004), 12. While the title page of the 1634 edition calls the play *Late Lancashire Witches*, the running title is *The Witches of Lancashire*; that is what Nathaniel Tomkyns calls it, as does the Globe Quartos edition: Richard Brome and Thomas Heywood,

The Witches of Lancashire, ed. Gabriel Egan (London: Nick Hern, 2002). The title page also identifies the play as "a well received Comedy."

107. These inversions are a vivid example of those that Stuart Clark argues structured witchcraft belief (*Thinking with Demons*).

108. Herbert Berry quotes Tomkyns's letter in full in "The Globe Bewitched and *El Hombre Fiel*," in *Shakespeare's Playhouses* (New York: AMS, 1987), 121–48, esp. 123. So does Gurr, *Shakespeare Company*, 265–66, among others. Berry is responsible for making this letter central to recent interpretations of the play.

109. Berry, "Globe Bewitched," 131. See also Gurr, *Shakespeare Company*, 155–56.

110. Purkiss, *Witch in History*, 245.

111. Findlay, "Sexual and Spiritual Politics," 149.

112. Thomas Heywood and Richard Brome, *The Late Lancashire Witches* (London, 1634), sig. L4v. An excellent digital edition by Helen Ostovich is available at Richard Brome Online, http://www.hrionline.ac.uk/brome/home.jsp.

113. Heather Anne Hirschfeld, *Joint Enterprises: Collaborative Drama and the Institutionalization of the English Renaissance Theater* (Amherst: University of Massachusetts Press, 2004), 118–144, esp. 119.

114. Findlay "Sexual and Spiritual Politics," 160; Hirschfeld, *Joint Enterprises,* 140, 143; Purkiss, *Witch in History*, 183. On the connection between playwrights and witches, see also Stephen Greenblatt, "Shakespeare Bewitched," in *New Historical Literary Study: Essays on Reproducing Texts, Representing History*, ed. Jeffrey N. Cox and Larry J. Reynolds (Princeton, N.J.: Princeton University Press, 1993), 108–35, especially his claim that Shakespeare's theatrical conjuration "places him in the position of the witch" (127).

115. Hirschfeld, *Joint Enterprises*, 143, 174n78.

116. *Remains Historical & Literary Connected with the Palatine Counties of Lancaster and Chester, Published by the Chetham Society*, vol. xxxix (Chetham Society, 1856), 27. Ffarington's list also includes some who were convicted in Lancaster but were not sent up to London, such as Jennet Device. In the end, all count as "witches."

117. *A Narration of the Life of Henry Burton* (London, 1643), sigs. C4v–D1r. Berry explains that "the women in London were sent back to Lancashire in December, 1634, still 'condemned,' and nine of the convicted people were still in prison there in 1637, including three who had been in London" ("Globe Bewitched," 145n17; see also 137). See also Findlay "Sexual and Spiritual Politics," 151, 162; Purkiss, *Witch in History*, 244; Thomas Heywood and Richard Brome, *The Late Lancashire Witches*, ed. Laird H. Barber (New York: Garland, 1979), 60–61.

118. On the basis of Ffarington's list, C. L'Estrange Ewen concludes, judiciously, that "Of the survivors of the condemned women it seems not improbable that they lingered in Lancaster Castle until death released them" (*Witchcraft and Demonianism*, 251). More recent conclusions are bolder. According to Sharpe, "a number of the reprieved witches died in gaol" (*Instruments of Darkness*, 127). Hirschfeld and Witmore both make this claim (Hirschfeld, *Joint Enterprises*, 172n47; Witmore, *Pretty Creatures*, 185).

119. Dolan, *Dangerous Familiars*, 223; Dennis Kezar, "*The Witch of Edmonton* and the

Guilt of Possession"; Kathleen McLuskie, *Renaissance Dramatists* (Atlantic Highlands, N.J.: Humanities Press International, 1989), 76; Purkiss, *Witch in History*, 183; David Underdown, *Revel, Riot and Rebellion: Popular Politics and Culture in England 1603–1660* (Oxford: Oxford University Press, 1985), 38.

120. Ian Bostridge, *Witchcraft and Its Transformations, c. 1650–1750* (Oxford: Oxford University Press, 1997), 91; Sharpe, "Introduction," *Lancashire Witches*, 13–14.

121. Emphasizing the powerlessness of Elizabethan and early Stuart theater to influence its audience, Paul Yachnin argues that plays' indeterminacy meant that their meanings could easily be "appropriated to opposing political points of view" (17); "the powerlessness of the theater should be understood as the price the players paid for their liberty to address topical issues and so to appeal to a public audience." *Stage-Wrights: Shakespeare, Jonson, Middleton, and the Making of Theatrical Value* (Philadelphia: University of Pennsylvania Press, 1997), 11.

122. Shapiro, *Probability*, 208; cf. 211–12; Barbara J. Shapiro, *A Culture of Fact: England, 1550–1720* (Ithaca, N.Y.: Cornell University Press, 2000), 19. On the disaggregation of elite from popular culture, see Holmes, "Popular Culture?" and "Women: Witnesses and Witches"; Shapiro, *Probability*, 212–21; Thompson, "Anthropology and the Discipline of Historical Context"; and D. R. Woolf, "The 'Common Voice': History, Folklore and Oral Tradition in Early Modern England," *Past and Present* 120 (August 1988): 26–52.

123. Ady, *Candle in the Dark*, sig. B3r.

124. Webster, *Displaying*, sig. a2v.

125. Joseph Glanvil, *Saducismus Triumphatus: OR, Full and Plain Evidence Concerning Witches and Apparitions* (London, 1681), sig. F4r; see also sigs. Aa2v–Aa3r.

126. Phyllis J. Guskin, "The Context of Witchcraft: The Case of Jane Wenham (1712)" *Eighteenth-Century Studies* 15, 1 (1981): 48–71, esp. 50, 59, 70.

127. Bostridge, *Witchcraft and Its Transformations*, 135.

128. Gaskill, *Crime and Mentalities*, 113–16. On changes in this period, see Bostridge, *Witchcraft and Its Transformations*.

129. Wagstaffe, *Question of Witchcraft Debated*, sig. D5r. Roper makes a similar argument about baroque Germany: "No longer a death-dealing harpy, the old woman was finally cut down to size, reduced to a bogey for frightening children" and as a consequence "shriveled into a caricature of herself, an old, toothless, fairytale hag to scare children." Lyndal Roper, *Witch Craze: Terror and Fantasy in Baroque Germany* (New Haven, Conn.: Yale University Press, 2004), 256, 12.

130. Gaule, *Select Cases*, sigs. D5r, D9r.

131. Unsworth, "Witchcraft Beliefs and Criminal Procedure," 73; see also Gaskill, "Witchcraft and Evidence."

132. Gaskill, *Crime and Mentalities*, 110.

CHAPTER 3. A TRUE AND FAITHFUL ACCOUNT?
THE LONDON FIRE, BLAME, AND PARTISAN PROOF

1. Nigel Smith reminds us that the city of London was regularly consumed by fire: "'Making Fire': Conflagration and Religious Controversy in Seventeenth-Century London," in *Imagining Early Modern London: Perceptions and Portrayals of the City from Stow to Strype, 1598–1720*, ed. J. F. Merritt (Cambridge: Cambridge University Press, 2001), 273–93, esp. 278.

2. I quote here the numbers inscribed on the monument, discussed below. These tallies seem to have been based on assessments by the city surveyors. See also Walter George Bell, *The Great Fire of London in 1666* (London: John Lane, 1920); John Bedford, *London's Burning* (London: Schuman, 1966); John E. N. Hearsey, *London and the Great Fire* (London: William Clowes, 1965).

3. Neil Hanson, who offers a vivid account of the fire's damage, contests this oft-repeated claim, arguing that "the true death toll of the Great Fire of London is not four or six or eight, it is several hundred and quite possibly several thousand times that number," especially if we take into account the starvation, disease, and exposure that followed in its wake. Neil Hanson, *The Great Fire of London in That Apocalyptic Year, 1666* (Hoboken, N.J.: John Wiley, 2001), 250.

4. Cynthia Wall, *The Literary and Cultural Spaces of Restoration London* (Cambridge: Cambridge University Press, 1998).

5. Regarding the discursive contests around the fire, in addition to Wall, I am indebted to Michael McKeon's *Politics and Poetry in Restoration England: The Case of Dryden's "Annus Mirabilis"* (Cambridge, Mass.: Harvard University Press, 1975); and Laura Lunger Knoppers, *Historicizing Milton: Spectacle, Power, and Poetry in Restoration England* (Athens: University of Georgia Press, 1994). Joseph Monteyne argues that "the aesthetic pleasure and distance offered by visual representation" offered a way of managing "the intimate and frightening prospect of the city's loss of order and autonomy." *The Printed Image in Early Modern London: Urban Space, Visual Representation, and Social Exchange* (Aldershot: Ashgate, 2007), 122.

6. *Burnet's History of My Own Time, Part I, the Reign of Charles the Second*, 2 vols., ed. Osmund Airy (Oxford: Clarendon, 1897), 1:410.

7. Samuel Pepys, *The Diary of Samuel Pepys*, ed. Henry B. Wheatley, 9 vols. (London: George Bell, 1900), 5:392–411, esp. 405.

8. Evelyn and Pepys both take this view. See also Thomas Brooks, *Londons Lamentations* (London, 1670); T[homas] D[oolittle], *Rebukes for Sin by God's Burning Anger* (London, 1667); William Sandcroft, *Lex Ignea: Or The School of Righteousness. A Sermon Preach'd before the King, Octob. 10. 1666. At the Solemn Fast appointed for the late Fire in London* (London, (1666); O.S., *Counsel to the Afflicted: Or, Instruction and Consolation for such as have suffered Loss by Fire* (London, 1667); Rege Sincera, *Observations Both Historical and Moral Upon the Burning of London* (London, 1667); Edward Stillingfleet, *A Sermon Preached before the Honourable House of Commons* (London, 1666); Thomas Vincent, *Gods Terrible Voice in*

the City (London, 1667); Samuel Wiseman, *A Short and Serious Narrative of London's Fatal Fire* (London, 1667); and William Wray, *The Rebellious City Destroyed. Being an Anniversary Sermon in Memory of the Dreadful Fire of London* (London, 1682).

9. Edward Waterhouse, *A Short Narrative of the Late Dreadful Fire in London* (London, 1667), sig. B5r.

10. Bernard Capp, "Arson, Threats of Arson, and Incivility in Early Modern England," in *Civil Histories: Essays Presented to Sir Keith Thomas*, ed. Peter Burke, Brian Harrison, and Paul Slack (Oxford: Oxford University Press, 2000), 208. Capp talks about scapegoating Catholics at times of political tension and refers to Robert Hubert as "the deluded French Catholic" (208). But others refer to Hubert as a Huguenot. On Hubert, see Hanson, *Great Fire of London*, 97–106, 201–25.

11. Pepys, *The Diary of Samuel Pepys*, 5:402; *The life of Edward, Earl of Clarendon* (Oxford: Clarendon Press, 1827), 3:93.

12. This scapegoating process was not unique to England. See Penny Roberts, "Arson, Conspiracy, and Rumour in Early Modern Europe," *Continuity and Change* 12, 1 (1997): 9–29.

13. Peter Stallybrass and Allon White, *The Politics and Poetics of Transgression* (Ithaca, N.Y.: Cornell University Press, 1986), 53.

14. For differing interpretations of the peculiar status of Catholics in post-Reformation England, see, in a growing body of scholarship, Frances E. Dolan, *Whores of Babylon: Catholicism, Gender, and Seventeenth-Century Print Culture* (Ithaca, N.Y.: Cornell University Press, 1999); Arthur F. Marotti, *Religious Ideology and Cultural Fantasy: Catholic and Anti-Catholic Discourses in Early Modern England* (South Bend, Ind.: University of Notre Dame Press, 2005); Michael Questier, *Catholicism and Community: Politics, Aristocratic Patronage and Religion, c. 1550–1640* (Cambridge: Cambridge University Press, 2006); and Ethan Shagan, ed., *Catholics and the "Protestant Nation": Religious Politics and Identity in Early Modern England* (Manchester: Manchester University Press, 2005).

15. *A Sad Relation of a Dreadful Fire at Cottenham* (London, 1676), 3. See also Robert Elborough, *London's Calamity by Fire Bewailed and Improved* (London, 1666), sig. B4v. For other true relations linking Catholics, fire, and servants, see *The Jesuites Firing-Plot Revived . . . Being the Full and true Relation how Elizabeth Owen . . . set fire to the House of one Mr. Cooper* (London, 1680) and *Trap ad Crucem; Or, The Papists Watch-word . . . Also a Relation of The several Fires That of late have hapened in and about the said CITY* (London, 1670), a collection of "true and impartial relations" of papist perfidy (sig. C1r).

16. E. C., *A Final Proof of the Plot from the Revelations* (London, 1680), sig. A2v.

17. Samuel Rolle, *Shlohavot Or, The Burning of London in the Year 1666* (London, 1667), Part II, sig. I7v. According to Nigel Smith, "That seventeenth-century people seemed to move so effortlessly from the literal to the figurative and back again in their talk about fire suggests that they made little distinction between the two categories" (Smith, "Making Fire," 292).

18. *A Full and True Account of the Sad and Dreadful Fire which happened in the Borough of Southwark* (London, 1689), reverse side.

19. J. P. Kenyon, *The Popish Plot* (London: Heinemann, 1972), 3.

20. Vincent, *Gods Terrible Voice in the City*, sig. D3r.

21. William Bedloe, *A Narrative and Impartial Discovery of the Horrid Popish PLOT Carried on for the Burning and Destroying the CITIES of London and Westminster* (London, 1679), sig. B1r.

22. *The Burning of London by the Papists* (London, 1714), sig. B3v.

23. Rolle, *Shlohavot Or, The Burning of London in the Year 1666*, Part III, sig. A2v.

24. *A True and Perfect Relation of the Whole Proceedings against the late most barbarous Traitors* (London, 1606), sigs. Hh1v–Hh2r.

25. *The Act of Parliament of the 27th of Queen Elizabeth* (London, 1679), 5; *The Burning of London by the Papists*, sigs. A2v–A3r.

26. Thomas Scott, *Exod. 8.19. Digitus Dei* (Holland, 1623), sig. A4v.

27. *Pyrotechnica Loyolana, Ignatian Fire-works. Or, the Fiery Jesuits Temper and Behaviour* (London, 1667), sig. R2v. See also E. C., *A Final Proof of the Plot from the Revelations*, sig. A2r.

28. Bedloe, *Narrative and Impartial Discovery*, sig. B1v; *Warning for Servants, and a Caution to Protestants, or The Case of Margret Clark* (London, 1680), sigs. B2v–B3r. See also J. J., *Heaven Upon Earth. Or the Best Friend in the Worst Times* (London, 1667), sig.A8v; and *The English Pope* (London, 1643), sigs. F2v–F3r.

29. See Keith Thomas, *Religion and the Decline of Magic* (New York: Scribner's, 1971); and Michael Witmore, *Culture of Accidents: Unexpected Knowledges in Early Modern England* (Stanford, Calif.: Stanford University Press, 2001), 12, 138, 146.

30. *The Diary of John Milward, Esq. Member of Parliament for Derbyshire*, ed. Caroline Robbins (Cambridge: Cambridge University Press, 1938), 7, 31–32; Bell, *Great Fire of London*, 196. On the investigation, see Hanson, *Great Fire of London*, 179–99.

31. Bell, *Great Fire of London*, 201. See also Hearsey, *London and the Great Fire*, 172–73.

32. Edward Hyde, Earl of Clarendon, *The History of the Rebellion and Civil Wars in England* (Oxford: Oxford University Press, 1843), 1187.

33. Wall, *Literary and Cultural Spaces of Restoration London*, 15.

34. *Journal of the House of Commons* 8 (1660–67), 627, 681.

35. Milward, *Diary of John Milward*, 68–69.

36. Burnet, *Burnet's History of My Own Time*, 1:415.

37. *CSPD* (1666–1667), 175.

38. The City of London's detailed and helpful website for the monument offers, as its description of the fire itself, the account from the London Gazette.

39. *An Account of the Burning of the City of London* (London, 1721), sigs. D4r–D4v.

40. *A True and Faithful Account of the Several Informations Exhibited to the Honourable Committee appointed by the Parliament to Inquire into the late Dreadful Burning of the City of London* (London, 1667), sigs. B1v, D1v. Given how many copies of this text were confiscated and destroyed, it is striking how many survive. Some members of Parliament may have chosen to leak this report. According to Adrian Johns, Parliament often struggled to control the publication of its proceedings with limited success. *The Nature*

of the Book: Print and Knowledge in the Making (Chicago: University of Chicago Press, 1998), 173, 172.

41. Bell, *Great Fire of London*, 203. See also Bedford, *London's Burning*, 173.

42. *CSPD* (1667), 290, 393. On other attempts to control print representations of the fire, especially those incendiary texts that blame Catholics, see *CSPD* (1666–67), 214–15, 430.

43. *Diary of Samuel Pepys* 8:108 (September 16, 1667).

44. These include *London's Flames Discovered by Informations Taken before the Committee Appointed to Enquire after the Burning of the City of London* (London, 1667); *London's Flames: Being an Exact and Impartial Account of Divers Informations Given in to the Committee of Parliament* (London, 1679); Bedloe, *A Narrative and Impartial Discovery of the Horrid Popish PLOT*; *The Burning of London by the Papists*; and *Pyrotechnica Loyolana*.

45. *State Trials*, ed. Thomas B. Howell, 33 vols. (London: R. Bagshaw, 1809–26), 4.807–64.

46. Charles II seems to have converted to Catholicism only on his deathbed, so this author's certainty regarding the point requires the benefit of hindsight. For an account of Charles's death and his reconciliation with Rome, see the broadside *A True Relation of the late King's death* (London, 1685).

47. *True Protestant Account of the Burning of London, Or, An Antidote, Against the Poyson and Malignity of a Late Lying Legend, Entituled, An Account of the Burning of London, &c.* (London, 1720). Citations appear in the text.

48. Mark Knights, *Representation and Misrepresentation in Later Stuart Britain: Partisanship and Political Culture* (Oxford: Oxford University Press, 2005), 5, 60, 6, 7.

49. Ernest Renan, "What Is a Nation?" in *Nation and Narration*, ed. Homi K. Bhabha (London: Routledge, 1990), 8–22.

50. John E. Moore, "The Monument, or, Christopher Wren's Roman Accent," *Art Bulletin* 80, 3 (September 1998): 498–533, esp. 520, 522. On the options Wren considered for topping the pillar, see also Christine Stevenson, "Robert Hooke, Monuments, and Memory," *Art History* 28, 1 (February 2005): 43–73, esp. 55–60.

51. Moore, "The Monument, or, Christopher Wren's Roman Accent," 506. According to Moore, "The extensive writing on the Monument constitutes an overlooked example of epigraphy in London, a city where monumental Latin inscriptions . . . were rarely found on the exteriors of public buildings" (498). This epigraphy worked to connect the London Fire to the fire in Rome during Nero's reign. On the classical antecedents and resonances of these inscriptions, Moore is invaluable; he transcribes all of the inscriptions in his appendix (525).

52. *Journals of the House of Commons* 9 (1667–87), 703. See Kenyon, *Popish Plot*, 13.

53. On October 26, 1678, Tonge addressed the Commons on the firing of the city. See *Journals of the House of Commons* 9 (1667–87), 522.

54. Moore, "The Monument," 516.

55. *The Burning of London by the Papists*, sig. A4v. Some versions of the inscription refer to London as an ancient rather than a Protestant city. See, for instance, Samuel Arnott, *The*

Column Called the Monument, Described, Erected to Perpetuate the Dreadful Fire of London in the Year 1666 (London, 1805), 15.

56. This sentence appears both in Robert Seymour, *An Accurate Survey of the Cities of London and Westminster* (London: 1736), 612; and Arnott, *The Column Called the Monument*, 15.

57. This translation is the one provided on a plaque at the monument (see Figure 6). Stevenson questions whether this Latin line was ever actually inscribed since it "has left no physical trace" ("Robert Hooke, Monuments, and Memory," 66); she has found "no seventeenth- or eighteenth-century print references to the Latin additions." Henry Thomas does refer to the Latin inscription in 1828 (see below). At the site today, the Latin inscription is more present than the English one.

58. On the fluctuating fortunes of this English inscription, see *True Protestant Account of the Burning of London*, sigs. A4v–B1r, C4v. See also *The Diary of John Evelyn*, ed. William Bray, 2 vols. (London: Dent, 1966, 2: 229); and Bell, *Great Fire of London*, 208–9.

59. *Burning of London by the Papists*, sig. A4r.

60. *True Protestant Account*, sigs. C4v–D1r. For this other inscription, see also Bedford, *London's Burning*, 176. Moore reproduces this stone plaque, which is now in the Museum of London (516). Hanson explains that it was removed in 1830, at the time the inscriptions were removed from the monument, and "thought lost, but in 1877 it was found in the cellars of 23 Pudding Lane" (*Great Fire of London*, 233). On these inscriptions, see also Charles Welch, *History of the Monument* (London, 1893), 25–41.

61. David Cressy, "National Memory in Early Modern England," in *Commemorations: The Politics of National Identity*, ed. John R. Gillis (Princeton, N.J.: Princeton University Press, 1994), 61–73, esp. 70–71. On memory and Protestant nationalism, see also David Cressy, *Bonfires and Bells: National Memory and the Protestant Calendar in Elizabethan and Stuart England* (Berkeley: University of California Press, 1989); and Ronald Hutton, *The Rise and Fall of Merry England: The Ritual Year, 1400–1700* (Oxford: Oxford University Press, 1994). On monuments, see Sanford Levinson, *Written in Stone: Public Monuments in Changing Societies* (Durham, N.C.: Duke University Press, 1998). While Christine Stevenson describes the 1681 inscriptions as a "spectacularly public failure of memory," they might also be called a spectacularly public *triumph* of memory in that they work to produce a memory of the fire that conforms to the presumption of Catholic treachery that resists evidence to the contrary ("Robert Hooke, Monuments, and Memory," 43).

62. John Noorthouck, *A New History of London, including Westminster and Southwark* (London, 1773), 252.

63. *A Critical Review of the Publick Buildings, Statues, and Ornaments in and about London* (London, 1734), sig. C1r.

64. *The Ambulator; or, A Pocket Companion for the Tour of London and its Environs* (London: Scatcherd and Letterman, 1811), 17. In contrast, the 1744 edition of this guide does not mention the inscriptions and expresses only admiration for the monument.

65. *The Picture of London for 1807; Being a Correct Guide*, 8th ed. (London: Longman, 1807), 131. This is repeated in many subsequent editions of this guide.

66. Henry Thomas, *The Wards of London; Comprising a Historical and Topographical Description of Every Object of Importance Within the Boundaries of the City* (London: J. Gifford, 1828), 2 vols., 1:211, 216.

67. James S. Ogilvy, *Relics and Memorials of London City* (London: Routledge, 1910), 31.

68. A. K. Bruce, *Memories and Monuments in the Streets of the City of London* (London: Methuen, 1931), 109.

69. *A Description of the Monument, Erected in Commemoration of the Dreadful Fire of London in the Year 1666* (London: John Bleaden, 1834), 16. This is an updated version of Arnott's *The Column Called the Monument*, similarly aimed at tourists.

70. http://www.themonument.info/history/.

71. http://www.museumoflondon.org.uk/Explore-online/Past/LondonsBurning/objects/record.htm?type=object&id=119401. Under the heading Catholics, as a subset of "heroes and villains" among those "people" relevant to London's Burning, this website also includes images of *Pyrotechnica Loyolana* as an "anti-Jesuit book," and of *A True and Faithfull Account* as a "report on the cause of the fire," which it describes as "causing great anti-Catholic feeling" and as, in its flimsy evidence, expressing "the prevailing prejudices of the time." Among proceedings from a 2007 study day on "myths and realities" regarding the fire, the website offers a pdf of a lecture by Colin Haydon, answering the question "Why was it claimed that the fire was started by a Catholic conspiracy?"

72. http://www.museumoflondon.org.uk/Explore-online/Past/LondonsBurning/Themes/1417/.

CHAPTER 4. FIRST-PERSON RELATIONS: READING DEPOSITIONS

1. The courts carried over from before the Reformation "elaborate procedures whereby claims were made, witnesses called, depositions taken in private, and sentences rendered on the basis of the written depositions," Richard M. Wunderli, *London Church Courts and Society on the Eve of the Reformation* (Cambridge: Medieval Academy of America, 1981), 41. On procedures, see also Martin Ingram, *Church Courts, Sex and Marriage in England, 1570–1640* (Cambridge: Cambridge University Press, 1987), 47–49; and Eric Josef Carlson, *Marriage and the English Reformation* (Oxford: Blackwell, 1994), 142–80. Important studies include Susan Amussen, *An Ordered Society: Gender and Class in Early Modern England* (New York: Blackwell, 1988); Ian Archer, *The Pursuit of Stability: Social Relations in Elizabethan London* (Cambridge: Cambridge University Press, 1991); Laura Gowing, *Domestic Dangers: Women, Words, and Sex in Early Modern London* (Oxford: Clarendon, 1996); and Ingram, *Church Courts*, 38, 32, 36, 48, 250–51. On the subsequent history of the courts, see David Lemmings, "Women's Property, Popular Cultures, and the Consistory Court of London in the Eighteenth Century," in *Women, Property, and the Letters of the Law in Early Modern England*, ed. Nancy E. Wright, Margaret W. Ferguson, and A. R. Buck (Toronto: University of Toronto Press, 2004), 66–94.

2. Of the statements taken at Bridewell Court, Paul Griffiths writes, "Examinations and confessions were read back to prisoners to let them check that words had not been put in their mouths, and to give them a chance to go through their stories once more," *Lost Londons: Change, Crime, and Control in the Capital City, 1550–1660* (Cambridge: Cambridge University Press, 2008), 248. On how the process of giving a deposition, having it read back, emending it, and signing it worked in the Court of Chancery, see Christine Churches, " 'The Most Unconvincing Testimony': The Genesis and Historical Usefulness of the Country Depositions in Chancery," *Seventeenth Century* 11, 2 (Autumn 1996): 209–27. As Churches points out, depositions were not "the last word" in that they were contested and the credibility of deponents called into question. Churches also emphasizes how much the questions shaped the answers. Furthermore, even if the clerk recorded exactly what a deponent said, it was not necessarily true. Joanne Bailey argues that "the factual basis of the records is itself debatable, considering that the cases were adversarial," Joanne Bailey, *Unquiet Lives: Marriage and Marriage Breakdown in England, 1660–1800* (Cambridge: Cambridge University Press, 2003), 23. While I particularly focus on interpretations of church court records, I sometimes draw on the comments made by scholars working with depositions from other English courts so as to demonstrate areas of methodological consensus and conflict among those working on depositions as a genre.

3. Peter Rushton, "Texts of Authority: Witchcraft Accusations and the Demonstration of Truth in Early Modern England," in *Languages of Witchcraft: Narrative, Ideology and Meaning in Early Modern Culture*, ed. Stuart Clark (Houndmills: Macmillan, 2001), 21–39, esp. 25; see also John G. Bellamy, *Criminal Law and Society in Late Medieval and Tudor England* (New York: St. Martin's, 1984), 48–49.

4. This remains an operative assumption in courts. In her instructions to the jury in Yolo County, Judge Janet Gaard reminds jurors that "you are to take the court reporter's record as accurate" with regard to testimony heard in court. A juror cannot challenge that record on the basis of his or her own notes or memory.

5. Unlike the records Arnold examines, the church court deposition was not a confession, nor was it produced through an inquisitorial process. See John H. Arnold, "The Historian as Inquisitor: The Ethics of Interrogating Subaltern Voices," *Rethinking History* 2, 3 (1998): 379–86, esp. 383.

6. Bernard Capp, "Life, Love and Litigation: Sileby in the 1630s," *Past and Present* 182 (February 2004): 55–83, esp. 75.

7. Focusing on criminal trials, particularly state trials, "in the age of Shakespeare," Holger Schott Syme argues that the mediation of court records constituted rather than mitigated their value for contemporaries. I agree with Syme that mediation was integral to depositions, that contemporaries were acutely aware of this fact, and that scholars should interrogate what that means rather than ignoring it. My broader chronological and generic scope leads me to emphasize contemporary unease about this mediation rather than acceptance, even dependence on it, as he does. Furthermore, I focus on what this mediation means to scholars today and how it undermines some of the uses to which these texts are

now put. See Holger Schott Syme, *Theatre and Testimony in Shakespeare's England: A Culture of Mediation* (Cambridge: Cambridge University Press, 2012).

8. Natalie Zemon Davis, *Fiction in the Archives: Pardon Tales and Their Tellers in Sixteenth Century France* (Stanford, Calif.: Stanford University Press, 1987), 2. See also James Oldham, "Truth-Telling in the Eighteenth-Century English Courtroom," *Law and History Review* 12, 1 (1994): 95–121.

9. David Cressy, "Gender Trouble and Cross-Dressing in Early Modern England," *Journal of British Studies* 35, 4 (October 1996): 438–65, esp. 445–6. See also Amanda Flather, *Gender and Space in Early Modern England* (Woodbridge: Royal Historical Society/Boydell, 2007), 12; Malcolm Gaskill, "Reporting Murder: Fiction in the Archives in Early Modern England," *Social History* 23, 1 (1998): 1–30; and Cressy, *Birth, Marriage, and Death: Ritual, Religion, and the Life-Cycle in Tudor and Stuart England* (Oxford: Oxford University Press, 1997), 7.

10. Lena Cowen Orlin, *Locating Privacy in Tudor London* (Oxford: Oxford University Press, 2007), 153; Alexandra Shepard, *Meanings of Manhood in Early Modern England* (Cambridge: Cambridge University Press, 2003), 131.

11. Amussen, *An Ordered Society*, 6; Capp, "Life, Love and Litigation," 63; Bernard Capp, *When Gossips Meet: Women, Family, and Neighbourhood in Early Modern England* (Oxford: Oxford University Press, 2003), 186; David Cressy, *Agnes Bowker's Cat: Travesties and Transgressions in Tudor and Stuart England* (Oxford: Oxford University Press, 2000), 7; Cressy, "Gender Trouble," 446; Orlin, *Locating Privacy*, 153.

12. Gowing, *Domestic Dangers*, 45. See also Griffiths, *Lost Londons*, 137. Griffiths argues that, in the Bridewell Court books, one of the principles of selection was making the court and its procedures look good. The records that survive "speak first and foremost for the Bridewell court. The clerk chose words carefully when he was taking notes, and sat down afterwards picking out what to put in the courtbook and what to leave out, framing entries to create sound images of procedure" (233).

13. Gowing, *Domestic Dangers*, 45.

14. Lawrence Stone, *Road to Divorce: England 1530–1987* (Oxford: Oxford University Press, 1990), 31. By "character," Stone seems to mean here "credit" or reputation, what we might call a "character reference." But his choice of term also reminds us that, if depositions are stories, then those discussed in them might be considered characters as much as persons.

15. Amy Louise Erickson, *Women and Property in Early Modern England* (London and New York: Routledge, 1995), 19, 223. See also Adam Fox, *Oral and Literate Culture in England, 1500–1700* (Oxford: Clarendon, 2000), 173; and Lynda Boose, "The Priest, the Slanderer, the Historian and the Feminist," *English Literary Renaissance* 25, 3 (1995): 320–40. In his earlier work, Paul Griffiths tentatively suggested that in depositions "we are perhaps closer to the authentic voice of the bawd and prostitute than in print depictions," "The Structure of Prostitution in Elizabethan London," *Continuity and Change* 8, 1 (1993): 39–63, esp. 41; see also his reference to depositions as women's "own narratives" (49).

16. Timothy Stretton, *Women Waging Law in Elizabethan England* (Cambridge: Cambridge University Press, 1998), 13.

17. Sara Mendelson and Patricia Crawford, *Women in Early Modern England, 1550–1720* (Oxford: Clarendon Press, 1998), 11.

18. Diane Purkiss, "Losing Babies, Losing Stories: Attending to Women's Confessions in Scottish Witch-Trials," in *Culture and Change: Attending to Early Modern Women*, ed. Margaret Mikesell and Adele Seeff (Newark: University of Delaware Press, 2003), 143–58, esp. 145. To hear these voices, we must "weed and prune" (145). This approach also requires considerable confidence that we can figure out what a witness was actually trying to say. Although Louise Jackson refers to witches' confessions as "layered" and as "palimpsests," she also claims, "I have tried to listen for their voices, however faint." "Witches, Wives and Mothers: Witchcraft Persecution and Women's Confessions in Seventeenth-Century England," *Women's History Review* 4, 1 (1995): 63–83, 64, 69, 79.

19. For challenges to the equation of voice with subjectivity, see Gina Bloom, *Voice in Motion: Staging Gender, Shaping Sound in Early Modern England* (Philadelphia: University of Pennsylvania Press, 2007); and Carla Mazzio, *The Inarticulate Renaissance: Language Trouble in the Age of Eloquence* (Philadelphia: University of Pennsylvania Press, 2008). Patricia Fumerton stakes out a middle ground, looking at "multividual" subjects—"serial 'selves'—variously defined occupationally, relationally, or spatially—that could be taken up, adjusted, and cast off as occasion demanded" and the voices they adopt and discard. Conceding that the subject we discover is often "largely conjectural, an imaginative creation of a virtual 'I,'" she enjoins researchers to "seek out the individuals behind the statistics and . . . listen for their different voices": "although we cannot hear directly from most of these dispossessed dead, we are not reduced to silence. We can at least catch momentary voicings." *Unsettled: The Culture of Mobility and the Working Poor in Early Modern England* (Chicago: University of Chicago Press, 2006), 51, 47, xx, 49.

20. According to Griffiths, writing of the Bridewell courts, "Stuttering or silence could both be taken as evidence that suspects were unsure of themselves and their stories, or that they were trying to hide something significant" (*Lost Londons*, 247). Fumerton argues that vagrants were defined in part by their inability to give a proper "reckoning" of themselves (*Unsettled*, 49). On pressing, see Andrea Mckenzie, "'This Death Some Strong and Stout Hearted Man Doth Choose': The Practice of Peine Forte et Dure in Seventeenth- and Eighteenth-Century England," *Law and History Review* 23, 2 (2005): 279–313.

21. Lawrence Stone, *The Past and the Present Revisited*, rev. ed. (London: Routledge and Kegan Paul, 1987), 241. See also Diana O'Hara, *Courtship and Constraint: Rethinking the Making of Marriage in Tudor England* (Manchester: Manchester University Press, 2000), 2; Orlin, *Locating Privacy*, 153; and Anne Laurence, "Real and Imagined Communities in the Lives of Women in Seventeenth-Century Ireland: Identity and Gender," in *Women, Identities and Communities in Early Modern Europe*, ed. Stephanie Tarbin and Susan Broomhall (Aldershot: Ashgate, 2008), 13–27, esp. 26.

22. Fox, *Oral and Literate Culture*, 83, 84.

23. Shepard, *Meanings of Manhood*, 12, emphasis mine.

24. For example, see David M. Turner, *Fashioning Adultery: Gender, Sex and Civility in England, 1660–1740* (Cambridge: Cambridge University Press, 2002): "An analysis of

church court records brings us into a world of conjugal infidelity more firmly grounded in material actuality and lived experience than the printed materials examined in previous chapters. However, the words of participants in the legal process were no less subject to mediation and cultural construction than other genres of fashioning adultery. . . . *Nevertheless*, the rich social detail of testimonies enables us to ask questions about adultery and marital relations the answers to which cannot be derived, or at least are not readily accessible, from other sources" (143–44, emphasis mine). See also a "none the less" on 168. Loreen L. Giese offers another version of this common move of acknowledging and then subordinating mediation. *Courtships, Marriage Customs, and Shakespeare's Comedies* (Houndmills: Palgrave Macmillan, 2006), 6–7.

25. Valerie Frith, ed., *Women and History: Voices of Early Modern England* (Toronto: Coach House, 1995); John N. King, ed. *Voices of the English Reformation: A Sourcebook* (Philadelphia: University of Pennsylvania Press, 2004). See also Jonathan Bastable, *Voices from the World of Samuel Pepys* (Cincinnati, Oh.: David and Charles, 2007). In *A City Full of People: Men and Women of London, 1650–1750* (London: Methuen, 1994), Peter Earle presents a cacophony of unplaced voices, in a section he calls "Voices of Londoners." Imtiaz Habib's *Black Lives in the English Archives: 1500–1677: Imprints of the Invisible* (Aldershot: Ashgate, 2008) is both skeptical about and committed to "the project of reconstructing the irrecoverable history of early modern English black people speaking from silence" (17).

26. Diane Purkiss, *The Witch in History: Early Modern and Twentieth-Century Representations* (London: Routledge, 1996), 93. See also Purkiss's astute critique of feminist critics' investments in identifiably female voice and agency in Diane Purkiss, "Material Girls: The Seventeenth-Century Woman Debate," in *Women, Texts, & Histories, 1575–1760*, ed. Clare Brant and Diane Purkiss (London: Routledge, 1992); and Loreen Giese's introduction to her helpful guide, *London Consistory Court Depositions, 1586–1611: List and Indexes*, ed. Loreen L. Giese (London: Record Society, 1995), ix.

27. A signature proclaims ownership of and accountability for a letter. And yet, as Jonathan Goldberg asks, "what does a signature authenticate when a person can produce multiple versions of the signature in different hands and spellings?" Jonathan Goldberg, *Writing Matter: From the Hands of the English Renaissance* (Stanford, Calif.: Stanford University Press, 1990), 242.

28. James Daybell, "Female Literacy and the Social Conventions of Women's Letter-Writing in England, 1540–1603," in *Early Modern Women's Letter Writing, 1450–1700*, ed. James Daybell (Houndmills: Palgrave, 2001), 59–76; *Letterwriting in Renaissance England*, ed. Alan Stewart and Heather Wolfe (Washington, D.C.: Folger Shakespeare Library, 2004), 55, 181–83; and Alison Thorne, "Women's Petitionary Letters and Early Seventeenth-Century Treason Trials," *Women's Writing* 13, 1 (March 2006): 23–43. In the particular context of the law, women were especially dependent on men to represent their words and their interests. See Stretton, *Women Waging Law*, 123; Geoffrey L. Hudson, "Negotiating for Blood Money: War Widows and the Courts in Seventeenth-Century England,"in *Women, Crime and the Courts in Early Modern England*, ed. Jenny Kermode and Garthine Walker (Chapel Hill & London: University of North Carolina Press, 1994), 146–69; Carolyn Sale,

"The 'Roman Hand': Women, Writing and the Law in the *Att.-Gen. v. Chatterton* and the Letters of Lady Arbella Stuart," *English Literary History* 70 (2003): 929–61.

29. As Karen Cunningham asks, "What is the relationship between the one who wields the pen and the one who authors the letter?" *Imaginary Betrayals: Subjectivity and the Discourses of Treason in Early Modern England* (Philadelphia: University of Pennsylvania Press, 2002), 110–40, esp. 118.

30. See Goldberg, *Writing Matter*, 233–78, on the collaborative formation of the self through writing; and Karen Newman, "Sundry Letters, Worldly Goods: The Lisle Letters and Renaissance Studies," *Journal of Medieval and Early Modern Studies* 26, 1 (Winter 1996): 139–52, esp. 144, 149. For a fascinating example, see Lucy Hutchinson, *Memoirs of the Life of Colonel Hutchinson* (London: Longman, 1808), who famously alternates between third and first person references to herself in this biography. Strategizing to save her husband from execution as a regicide, Hutchinson claims *she* wrote a letter to the Speaker of the House in an effort to test the waters. She says she was going to show it to her husband, but, on her way to do so, a friend told her that the House was kindly disposed toward her husband that day. So she signed the letter and sent it: "being used sometimes to write the letters he dictated, and her character not much differing from his" (407). When she is later questioned about this letter, she says she "could not absolutely say that was her writing, though it had some resemblance" (451). The authorship of the letter is still in dispute.

31. James Daybell, *Women Letter-Writers in Tudor England* (Oxford: Oxford University Press, 2006), 76; see also 80. For an earlier version of this statement, see Daybell's "Women's Letters and Letter-Writing in England, 1540–1603: An Introduction to Issues of Authorship and Construction," *Shakespeare Studies* 27 (1999): 161–86. Daybell distinguishes between reading letters as "historical documents" and "as texts," emphasizing the value of reading them as something more than "straightforward depositories of historical fact" (Daybell, *Women Letter-Writers* 12, 116, 46). See also Sara Jayne Steen, "Behind the Arras: Editing Renaissance Women's Letters," *New Ways of Looking at Old Texts: Papers of the Renaissance English Text Society, 1985–1991*, ed. W. Speed Hill (Binghamton, N.Y.: MRTS/RETS, 1993), 229–38, esp. 237.

32. Orlin emphasizes that we must also consider what deponents did not think of, or did not think mattered, or that no one bothered to ask them (*Locating Privacy*, 264).

33. Lynne Magnusson, "A Rhetoric of Requests: Genre and Linguistic Scripts in Elizabethan Women's Suitors' Letters," *Women and Politics in Early Modern England, 1450–1700*, ed. James Daybell (Aldershot: Ashgate, 2004), 50–66, esp. 52. On how letters challenge assumptions about authorship and intellectual property, see also *Women, Property, and the Letters of the Law in Early Modern England*, ed. Nancy E. Wright, Margaret W. Ferguson, and A. R. Buck (Toronto: University of Toronto Press, 2004).

34. Jeffrey Masten, *Textual Intercourse: Collaboration, Authorship, and Sexualities in Renaissance Drama* (Cambridge: Cambridge University Press, 1997); and Jeffrey Masten, "Material Cavendish: Paper, Performance, 'Sociable Virginity'," *Modern Language Quarterly* 65, 1 (March 2004): 49–68; on productive cross-sex collaborations, see also Catharine Gray, *Women Writers and Public Debate in Seventeenth-Century Britain* (New York:

Palgrave, 2007), 29–31; and Maureen Quilligan, *Incest and Agency in Elizabeth's England* (Philadelphia: University of Pennsylvania Press, 2005).

35. Leah Marcus, "Confessions of a Reformed Uneditor," *PMLA* 115, 5 (2000): 1072–75, esp. 1073.

36. *Elizabeth I: Collected Works*, ed. Leah S. Marcus, Janel M. Mueller, and Mary Beth Rose (Chicago: University of Chicago Press, 2000), xii. For a speech delivered by someone else, but in Elizabeth's presence, see 79–80.

37. Ibid., xiii.

38. John Guy, review of *Elizabeth I: Collected Works*, in *Albion* 33, 4 (2001): 638–42, esp. 639.

39. *Elizabeth I: Collected Works*, xv, xxi. See also Leah Marcus, "From Oral Delivery to Print in the Speeches of Elizabeth I," *Print, Manuscript, and Performance: The Changing Relations of the Media in Early Modern England*, ed. Arthur F. Marotti and Michael D. Bristol (Columbus: Ohio State University Press, 2000), 33–48, 37.

40. In contrast, Guy complains that the edition, by omitting some of Elizabeth's revisions to manuscript texts, has "emasculated" "nuances." Guy too is driven by a desire for presence, a presence he fascinatingly genders masculine and attaches to Elizabeth's "own hand." Yet this presence consistently eludes the reader in part because so many hands went into producing Elizabeth's authenticity (Guy, review of *Elizabeth I: Collected Works*, 640). See also Steven W. May, who looks to new editions to restore the queen's "genuine discourse" and "own voice," " 'Tongue-Tied Our Queen?': Queen Elizabeth's Voice in the Seventeenth Century," in *Resurrecting Elizabeth I in Seventeenth-Century England*, ed. Elizabeth H. Hageman and Katherine Conway (Madison, N.J.: Fairleigh Dickinson University Press, 2007), 48–67, esp. 63.

41. Stone, *Road to Divorce*, 31, 32; Lawrence Stone, *Broken Lives: Separation and Divorce in England, 1660–1857* (Oxford: Oxford University Press, 1993), 4; and Stone, *Uncertain Unions: Marriage in England, 1660–1753* (Oxford: Oxford University Press, 1992), 7. Adam Fox makes a similar claim that depositions allow us to "eavesdrop on the domestic chatter, market-place gossip, and ale-house discussion of men and women as they went about their daily business" (Fox, *Oral and Literate Culture*, 136).

42. Garthine Walker, "Rereading Rape and Sexual Violence in Early Modern England," *Gender & History* 10, 1 (1998): 1–25, esp. 8.

43. Gowing, *Domestic Dangers*, 46.

44. Miranda Chaytor, "Husband(ry): Narratives of Rape in the Seventeenth Century," *Gender & History* 7, 3 (1995): 378–407, esp. 381.

45. Gowing, *Domestic Dangers*, 239, 46; and Laura Gowing, "Bodies and Stories," in *Culture and Change: Attending to Early Modern Women*, ed. Margaret Mikesell and Adele Seeff (Newark: University of Delaware Press, 2003), 317–32, esp. 321; Fox, *Oral and Literate Culture*, 172; Joanne Bailey, "Voices in Court: Lawyers' or Litigants'?" *Historical Research* 74, 186 (November 2001): 392–408, esp. 408.

46. Peter Brooks, *Troubling Confessions: Speaking Guilt in Law and Literature* (Chicago: University of Chicago Press, 2000), 40, 13. On the imbalance of power between

inquisitor and witness, see Edward Muir and Guido Ruggiero, "Introduction: The Crime of History," in *History from Crime: Selections from Quaderni Storici*, ed. Edward Muir and Guido Ruggiero (Baltimore: Johns Hopkins University Press, 1994), vii–xviii, ix; and Arnold, "The Historian as Inquisitor," 383–84. On the less adversarial process by which church court depositions were shaped, which Malcolm Gaskill goes so far as to describe as a "consensual dialogue," see Malcolm Gaskill, *Crime and Mentalities in Early Modern England* (Cambridge: Cambridge University Press, 2000), 308; see also Gowing, *Domestic Dangers*, 42; Garthine Walker, "Just Stories: Telling Tales of Infant Death in Early Modern England," in *Culture and Change: Attending to Early Modern Women*, ed. Margaret Mikesell and Adele Seeff (Newark: University of Delaware Press, 2003), 98–115, esp. 105.

47. Lorna Hutson, *The Invention of Suspicion: Law and Mimesis in Shakespeare and Renaissance Drama* (Oxford: Oxford University Press, 2008), 254. See also Cornelia Hughes Dayton, "Rethinking Agency, Recovering Voices," *American Historical Review* 109, 3 (2004): 827–43, esp. 842.

48. Cynthia Herrup, *The Common Peace: Participation and the Criminal Law in Seventeenth-Century England* (Cambridge: Cambridge University Press, 1987); Barbara J. Shapiro, *"Beyond Reasonable Doubt" and "Probable Cause": Historical Perspectives on the Anglo-American Law of Evidence* (Berkeley: University of California Press, 1991); John Brewer and John Styles, "Introduction," in *An Ungovernable People: The English and Their Law in the Seventeenth and Eighteenth Centuries*, ed. John Brewer and John Styles (New Brunswick, N.J.: Rutgers University Press, 1980), 14–15; J. A. Sharpe, "The People and the Law," in *Popular Culture in Seventeenth-Century England*, ed. Barry Reay (New York: St. Martin's, 1985), 249–56.

49. Gowing, *Domestic Dangers*, 52–53.

50. See, for instance, Laura Gowing, *Common Bodies: Women, Touch and Power in Seventeenth-Century England* (New Haven, Conn.: Yale University Press, 2003): "Legal forms have been removed from this quotation for clarity" (210n1; see also 223n20, 225nn64, 81). This means that, among other changes, Gowing replaces "this examinant" with "he" or "she."

51. In her work on letters, Lynne Magnusson advises that relations of deference extend beyond formulaic salutations: "power relations in civil exchanges come to extend more deeply into the grain of the language—into the discourse that enacts the heart of the business rather than the flourishes that accompany it." Lynne Magnusson, *Shakespeare and Social Dialogue: Dramatic Language and Elizabethan Letters* (Cambridge: Cambridge University Press, 1999), 37, 55.

52. Gaskill, *Crime and Mentalities*, 21. In *The Trials of Frances Howard: Fact and Fiction at the Court of King James* (New York: Routledge, 1993), David Lindley also identifies "archeological layers" of evidence, with "pre-trial examinations" as the "bottom layer, and that which might be assumed to be nearest the 'facts'." But when he reaches the top, representations of the "characters" of particular defendants, Lindley points out that "the analogy of archeological layers breaks down—for this topmost 'layer' must, logically, already have shaped" the lord chief justice's "approach to the examinations which constituted the first

level. There is a circular negotiation between event and cultural assumptions as they are encoded in surviving texts" (151–56).

53. Martha Howell and Walter Prevenier, *From Reliable Sources: An Introduction to Historical Methods* (Ithaca, N.Y.: Cornell University Press, 2001), 22.

54. Carolyn Sale, "Slanderous Aesthetics and the Woman Writer: The Case of *Hole v. White*," in *From Script to Stage in Early Modern England*, ed. Peter Holland and Stephen Orgel (New York: Palgrave, 2004), 181–94, esp. 194. Sale quotes White's examination on her p. 193. I quote it here as reproduced in *Records of Early English Drama, Somerset Including Bath*, ed. James Stokes (Toronto: University of Toronto Press, 1996), 1: 282–83. The italics indicate the editor's expansions of abbreviations in the record.

55. *Depositions and Other Ecclesiastical Proceedings from the Courts of Durham, Extending from 1311 to the reign of Elizabeth*, ed. James J. Raine (London: J.B. Nichols, 1845), 310–12, 282. See also 243.

56. *Depositions*, ed. Raine, 312.

57. Barbara Shapiro, *Culture of Fact: England, 550–1720* (Ithaca, N.Y.: Cornell University Press, 2000), 113, 161, and passim. Andrea Frisch argues that, in France, the witness was transformed from a second person to a first person in the sixteenth century. Before that, "as a participant in a dialogic exchange, the witness functioned as a *second* person whose ethical relations with his juridical interlocutors determined the credibility of his testimony"; "in the pre-modern context, the individual, autobiographical 'I' is not the subject of testimony: the *intersubjective* I is." As we have seen, the shift Frisch describes had not yet occurred in English seventeenth-century church court depositions, which continued to "suppress the dialogic encounter out of which [they] had emerged." Andrea Frisch, *Invention of the Eyewitness: Witnessing and Testimony in Early Modern France*, North Carolina Studies in the Romance Languages and Literatures 279 (Chapel Hill: University of North Carolina Press, 2004), 13, 40, 117.

58. Amussen, *Ordered Society*; Ingram, *Church Courts*.

59. Stone, *Broken Lives*, 7. Stone gives virtually the same methodological statement in the companion volume, *Uncertain Unions*, 5.

60. Chaytor, "Husband(ry)," 40in1; Walker, "Rereading Rape," 20n4. In her book, Walker says, "Examinations, depositions and petitions are rendered in the first rather than the clerical third person." Garthine Walker, *Crime, Gender and Social Order in Early Modern England* (Cambridge: Cambridge University Press, 2003), xv.

61. Walker, "Rereading Rape," 19.

62. Frith, ed., *Women and History*, xxiv.

63. John Beattie, "'Hard-pressed to make ends meet': Women and Crime in Augustan London," in *Women and History*, ed. Frith, 103–15.

64. Helen Ostovich and Elizabeth Sauer, "Legal Documents/Women's Testimony," in *Reading Early Modern Women: An Anthology of Texts in Manuscript and Print, 1550–1700*, ed. Ostovich and Sauer (New York: Routledge, 2003), 15–19, esp. 16, emphasis mine.

65. G. R. Elton, *Star Chamber Stories* (London: Methuen, 1958). See also F. G. Emmison, *Elizabethan Life: Disorder (Mainly from Essex Sessions and Assize Records)*

(Chelmsford: Essex County Council, 1970), which purports to offer "a big corpus of new evidence" (vii) by synthesizing the material into a narrative, since offering extracts would produce too much "wasted space" (xii).

66. Discussing the work of E. P. Thompson, Catherine Gallagher and Stephen Greenblatt argue that leaving the unfamiliar aspects of a text in place can actually engage readers more actively with it: "Deprived of certain orthographic conventions, the reader must subvocalize, supplying stops and producing a meaning in an extraordinarily active manner, so that the language seems intimately 'inside' the reader and unusually palpable in strict proportion to its foreignness, its violations of the reader's linguistic and social conventions." Catherine Gallagher and Stephen Greenblatt, *Practicing New Historicism* (Chicago: University of Chicago Press, 2000), 56.

67. See Gary Taylor and Michael Warren, eds., *The Division of the Kingdoms: Shakespeare's Two Versions of King Lear* (New York: Oxford University Press, 1983).

68. Gowing, *Common Bodies*, 69–70 (Lichfield Record Office, B/C/5 1685). For her explanation of putting it in the first person, see 221n70. On 120, she offers us a deposition that "was noted by the coroner's clerk in the first person."

69. Lichfield Record Office, B/C/5/1685/262. I depended on Gowing's research to locate and understand this deposition.

70. Gowing, *Common Bodies*, 70.

71. Patricia Fumerton argues that the ballad is the perfect form for the multividual "imagining and voicing diverse serial personae and subject positions through an anonymous, mutating, generic form" (*Unsettled*, 58). On ballads, see the essays in *Ballads and Broadsides in Britain, 1500–1800*, ed. Patricia Fumerton and Anita Guerrini (Burlington, Vt.: Ashgate, 2010).

72. All these ballads are available in the English Broadside Ballad Archive, http://emc. english.ucsb.edu/ballad_project/. George Herbert's "The Sacrifice" is written in Christ's voice, but, in one stanza, it switches to third person—"They buffet him, and box him as they list, / Who grasps the earth and heaven with his fist, / And never yet, whom he would punish, missed"—only to move back to the first in the refrain "Was ever grief like mine?" and the next stanza "Behold, they spit on me." Most editors change the third-person stanza to first person for continuity, but John P. Rumrich and Gregory Chaplin, editors of *Seventeenth-Century British Poetry, 1603–1660* (New York: Norton, 2006), leave it for its "irony" (230n9).

73. Bruce R. Smith, "I, You, He, She, and We: On the Sexual Politics of Shakespeare's Sonnets," in *Shakespeare's Sonnets: Critical Essays*, ed. James Schiffer (New York: Garland, 1999), 411–29, esp. 424, 416, 427, 424.

74. Margreta de Grazia, *Shakespeare Verbatim: The Reproduction of Authenticity and the 1790 Apparatus* (Oxford: Clarendon, 1991), 132–76. De Grazia shows that Malone's was an editorial project of positing relations: between Shakespeare and the "I" of the sonnets, between the sonnets and Shakespeare's plays, and between Shakespeare and his readers. On the conjectural nature of the relations editors and readers discover in the sonnets, see William Nelles, "Sexing Shakespeare's Sonnets: Reading Beyond Sonnet 20," *English Literary*

Renaissance 39, 1 (2009): 128–40. On editorial interventions to regender or degender pronouns in the sonnets, see also Margreta de Grazia and Peter Stallybrass, "The Materiality of the Shakespearean Text," *Shakespeare Quarterly* 44, 3 (1993): 255–83, esp. 270–72.

75. Smith, "I, You, He, She, and We," 427.

76. Chaytor, "Husband(ry)," 399; Boose, "The Priest, the Slanderer," 328; Bailey, "Voices in Court," 392–93.

77. Henry Goodcole, *The Wonderfull Discoverie of Elizabeth Sawyer a Witch, late of Edmonton* (London, 1621), sigs. C1r–v.

78. Jonathan Gil Harris, *Foreign Bodies and the Body Politic: Discourses of Social Pathology in Early Modern England* (Cambridge: Cambridge University Press, 1998), 135–36.

79. Purkiss, *Witch in History*, 238.

80. The structure of the mort's tale supports the suggestion that the *Caveat* resembles a jest book despite Harman's claims to offer a true relation and the fact that his collection of tales has sometimes been taken as a reliable source of information about the vagrant poor. Linda Woodbridge, *Vagrancy, Homelessness, and English Renaissance Literature* (Urbana: University of Illinois Press, 2001), 47; see also Stephen Greenblatt, *Shakespearean Negotiations: The Circulation of Social Energy in Renaissance England* (Berkeley: University of California Press, 1988), 50.

81. Thomas Harman, *A Caveat for Commen Cursetors* (London, 1567), sig. F1r–v. I quote from the Borleian copy via EEBO. Arthur Kinney presents this text with modernized spelling and punctuation in *Rogues, Vagabonds and Sturdy Beggars: A New Gallery of Tudor and Early Stuart Rogue Literature* (Amherst: University of Massachusetts Press, 1990), 139–40. I similarly modernized the text in *The Taming of the Shrew: Texts and Contexts*, ed. Frances E. Dolan (Boston: Bedford, 1996), 320.

82. Greenblatt, *Shakespearean Negotiations*, 52.

83. Elizabeth Hanson, *Discovering the Subject in Renaissance England* (Cambridge: Cambridge University Press, 1998), 103. William C. Carroll also talks about Harman's paradoxically "voyeuristic moralism" and the ways the stories he "cajoles" out of women end up being, at some level, projections of his own fantasies, *Fat King, Lean Beggar: Representations of Poverty in the Age of Shakespeare* (Ithaca, N.Y.: Cornell University Press, 1996), 91–92. Fumerton emphasizes the economic ties between housed and unhoused women revealed by this story (*Unsettled*, 38–39). A. L. Beier emphasizes not Harman's prurience but his moral conservatism about marriage, adultery, and sexual predation, "New Historicism, Historical Context, and the Literature of Roguery: The Case of Thomas Harman Reopened," in *Rogues and Early Modern English Culture*, ed. Craig Dionne and Steve Mentz (Ann Arbor: University of Michigan Press, 2007), 98–119, esp. 102–5. Of the sources describing vagrants, Beier writes that "the greatest defect of the records is that they all are records of officials working to suppress vagrants, so that the voice of the vagrant is always transmuted," A. L. Beier, "Vagrants and the Social Order in Elizabethan England," *Past and Present* 64 (1974): 3–29, esp. 5. See also Jodi Mikalachki, "Women's Networks and the Female Vagrant: A Hard Case," in *Maids and Mistresses, Cousins and Queens: Women's Alliances in Early Modern England*, ed. Susan Frye and Karen Robertson (New York: Oxford University Press, 1999), 52–69.

84. Kinney, "Introduction," *Rogues*, 106. Kinney also states that, in the story of the walking mort, Harman "exposes himself, for he narrates a jest in which he played no part and for which he has no hard data" (106). The difficulty of collecting and fencing off a dispersed first person can also be seen in a very different text, Lady Mary Wroth's prose romance *Urania*. The editors of the second part of the romance comment that "There are several places where the beginning and ending of direct discourse is in doubt" and that "the line between speakers and the reflections of the omniscient narrator is sometimes blurred," *The Second Part of the Countess of Montgomery's Urania, by Lady Mary Wroth*, ed. Josephine A. Roberts, completed by Suzanne Gossett and Janel Mueller (Tempe: Renaissance English Text Society/Arizona Center for Medieval and Renaissance Studies, 1999), xli. On the indistinct relationship between first and third persons, narrators and characters, in *Urania*, see also Quilligan, *Incest and Agency*, 193; and Tiffany Jo Werth, *The Fabulous Dark Cloister: Romance in England After the Reformation* (Baltimore: Johns Hopkins University Press, 2011), 132–59.

85. Margreta de Grazia, "Sanctioning Voice: Quotation Marks, The Abolition of Torture, and the Fifth Amendment," in *The Construction of Authorship: Textual Appropriation in Law and Literature*, ed. Martha Woodmansee and Peter Jaszi (Durham, N.C.: Duke University Press, 1994), 281–302, esp. 287–88; de Grazia, "Shakespeare in Quotation Marks," in *The Appropriation of Shakespeare: Post-Renaissance Reconstructions of the Works and the Myth*, ed. Jean I. Marsden (Hertfordshire: Harvester Wheatsheaf, 1991), 57–71, esp. 66. De Grazia identifies, in the wake of widespread use of quotation marks, "a new preoccupation with *who spoke what*, with the proper attribution and the accurate reproduction of written materials" ("Shakespeare in Quotation Marks," 57).

86. In *The Voices of Morebath: Reformation and Rebellion in an English Village* (New Haven, Conn.: Yale University Press, 2001), Eamon Duffy mines the church warden's accounts kept by Sir Christopher Trychay, vicar of Morebath 1520–74, "the most vivid country clergyman of the English sixteenth century" (xiii), for voices and both does and does not find them. Duffy says both that "ruffling the pages of Sir Christopher's book we hear once again a chorus of forgotten but fascinating voices" (xv) and that "All the voices of Tudor Morebath are one voice, caught between the pages of a single book" (17). The claim that all the voices are one voice is the first and last sentence of a chapter called "The Voices of Morebath" (17–46).

87. O'Hara, *Courtship and Constraint:* , 8, 33–4. In a review of O'Hara's book, Eric Josef Carlson says that "she claims that what respondents say in depositions ought not to be believed, preferring to deconstruct the words so that subtler readings will reveal deeper and hidden meanings." He questions her interpretation of this particular deposition, arguing that "in the absence of any evidence it is hard to see why we ought to reject the more straightforward reading of the deposition"—which appears to be that Richards did not want to marry Coppyn and was not under any particular external pressures. Carlson contrasts straightforward reading to a postmodern approach, asserting that "one's personal feelings about postmodernism will determine how convincing one finds [O'Hara's] readings"

(*Albion* 33, 2 [2001]: 279–80). I want to challenge O'Hara's interpretation here as not "post-modern" or "literary" enough.

88. O'Hara is referring to Canterbury Cathedral Archives, Archdeaconry Court Deposition Volumes CCAL, MS. X/10/7, f. 134v, *Coppyn v. Richards* (1560).

89. I have identified this as Dennys's examination by reviewing all the depositions in this case as well as O'Hara's discussion of them scattered across her book. I was only able to locate and comprehend these records because of O'Hara's careful work with them.

90. O'Hara, quoting again from Dennys's examination, Canterbury Cathedral Archives, Archdeaconry Court Deposition Volumes CCAL, MS. X/10/7, f. 134v, *Coppyn v. Richards* (1560), on her page 115; see also 103–4 (re. CCAL, MS. X/10/7, f. 134v–5, 326v–7).

91. In a deposition included in *Depositions . . . from the Courts of Durham*, ed. Raine, undated but c. 1565–73, one William Bayker describes how he found Agnes Carr "wepinge and sore lammentyng" because her husband, who had been ordered to "use hir as he aught to doo," refused to allow her to spend the night with him (97–98). In this deposition too, a male deponent describes a woman as "lamenting."

92. Judith Butler, *Giving an Account of Oneself* (New York: Fordham University Press, 2005), 8, see also *Excitable Speech: A Politics of the Performative* (New York: Routledge, 1997), 25.

93. Gowing, *Domestic Dangers*, 58, 56.

94. Elizabeth A. Foyster, *Manhood in Early Modern England: Honour, Sex and Marriage* (Harlough, Essex: Longman, 1999), 14. Steve Hindle argues of one case that "The story was retold in ways that were plausible, that traded registers with the 'truth' of what was already 'known' or suspected" and that was shaped by knowledge of the law and familiarity with "literate culture." "The Shaming of Margaret Knowsley: Gossip, Gender and the Experience of Authority in Early Modern England," *Continuity and Change* 9, 3 (1994): 363–419, esp. 401, 396.

95. Catherine Richardson, *Domestic Life and Domestic Tragedy in Early Modern England: The Material Life of the Household* (Manchester: Manchester University Press, 2006), 30; Stretton, *Women Waging Law*, 208.

96. Walker, "Rereading Rape," and Gowing, *Common Bodies*, 83, 99.

97. Richardson, *Domestic Life*, 30.

98. Gowing, *Domestic Dangers*, 56.

99. Gaskill, *Crime and Mentalities*, 222. On the connections between depositions and print, see also Gaskill "Reporting Murder."

100. Griffiths, *Lost Londons*, 198.

101. Gaskill, *Crime and Mentalities*, 239. Rather than arguing for influence in either direction, Bernard Capp observes a parallel: "The scolding wife is a stock character in plays, satires, ballads, and sermons, and women railing at abusive or feckless husbands appear frequently in court records too" (Capp, *When Gossips Meet*, 87).

102. Bailey, *Unquiet Lives*, 23; see also her "Voices in Court," 396, 408.

103. Walker, "Just Stories," 99.

104. Gowing, *Domestic Dangers*, 47–48. Gowing says also that "the multilayered and multivalent shape of depositions, bound as they were with restrictions, left space for some

very personal tellings"; and "the written account bears many of the hallmarks of oral narrative" (239, 235). Flather picks up one of Gowing's phrases, arguing that, despite their mediation, many testimonies are "notably individual in content, vocabulary, and tone" (*Gender and Space*, 12). On details, see also Giese, *Courtships, Marriage Customs, and Shakespeare's Comedies*, 7; Stretton, *Women Waging Law*, 210; Richardson, *Domestic Life*, 31; and Catherine Richardson, " 'Having nothing upon hym saving onely his sherte': Event, Narrative and Material Culture in Early Modern England," in *Clothing Culture, 1350–1650*, ed. Catherine Richardson (Aldershot: Ashgate, 2004), 208–21, esp. 212.

105. Bailey, "Voices in Court," 393; Purkiss, *Witch in History*, 167; Gaskill, *Crime and Mentalities*, 27. "Expletives" might also prompt clerical interventions. Of a deposition in which one man tells another "you hath a wife of your own and she hath a good fat C," Gowing adds in a note, "He probably said cunt, and the 'C' is the clerk's" (*Common Bodies*, 215n45).

106. Orlin, *Locating Privacy*, 153. Discussing work on Bridewell courtbooks, Karen Newman argues that "the telling or titillating detail is rare indeed, and its citation by social historians and literary critics may tell us more about the narratives we are writing than about the general character of early modern prostitution" (*Cultural Capitals: Early Modern London and Paris* [Princeton, N.J.: Princeton University Press, 2007], 138).

107. Gallagher and Greenblatt, *Practicing New Historicism*, 51.

108. Loreen Giese, "The Evidence Against Joane Waters," in *Reading Early Modern Women*, ed. Ostovich and Sauer, 33–34; this deposition is also reproduced in *Women's Worlds in Seventeenth-Century England: A Sourcebook*, ed. Patricia Crawford and Laura Gowing (London: Routledge, 2000), 138–39.

109. Mary Blackstone, "The Star Chamber Deposition of Lady Elizabeth Vaux (1622)," in *Reading Early Modern Women*, ed. Ostovich and Sauer, 35–39, esp. 38–39.

110. J. H. Baker would call the peephole a "convention" rather than a legal fiction, which he defines strictly as those formulations that "allow the operation of the law to change while avoiding any outward alteration in the rules" (*The Law's Two Bodies: Some Evidential Problems in English Legal History* [Oxford: Oxford University Press, 2001], 33–57, esp. 35).

111. Paula Humfrey presents this deposition in a chapter on "what the servants knew" in Frith, ed., *Women and History*, 63.

112. Ingram, *Church Courts*, 245.

113. Ian W. Archer, *The Pursuit of Stability: Social Relations in Elizabethan London* (Cambridge: Cambridge University Press, 1991), 77; Gowing, *Domestic Dangers*, 71, 190, and *Common Bodies*, 106; Stone, *Road to Divorce*, 213–14; and David Underdown, who refers to "the usual convenient chink in the wall" in *Fire from Heaven: Life in an English Town in the Seventeenth Century* (New Haven, Conn.: Yale University Press, 1994), 70. John Ayliffe's *Parergon juris Canonici Anglicani: or, a commentary, by way of supplement to the canons and constitutions of the Church of England* (London, 1726) explains that, under canon law, it is difficult to secure proof of fornication and adultery "Because, though one should see a Man upon the very Body of a Woman, with her Coats up above her Middle, yet it

does not necessarily follow from thence, that carnal Copulation did intervene or ensue between them" (44). As a consequence, "presumptive Evidence alone, is sufficient Proof." Ayliffe's description of what constitutes presumptive evidence corresponds to the content of many church court depositions, although it is important to note that he is codifying these standards of evidence considerably later. "For the finding of a Man and a Woman together by themselves naked in a suspected Place, kissing and embracing each other, and in a very immodest Posture, and they being both suspected before of Incontinency; this, I say, will raise a vehement Suspicion, and make a presumptive Proof of their Guilt, these Things being the Preludes of Debauchery, and of a libidinous Conversation" (45). Ayliffe describes exactly what many witnesses "find" when they peer through keyholes.

114. Richardson, *Domestic Life*, 55, 56, 63n114.

115. George E. Haggerty, "Keyhole Testimony: Witnessing Sodomy in the Eighteenth Century," *Eighteenth Century* 44, 2/3 (2003): 167–82, 168. As Haggerty points out, when the depositions he discusses were published in the eighteenth century, they were presented in the first person (169).

116. Orlin, *Locating Privacy*, 188.

117. Ibid., 192, 189. On a perceived right to know and therefore to peep, see also Keith Thomas, *Religion and the Decline of Magic* (New York: Scribner's, 1971), 527.

118. Capp, "Life, Love and Litigation," 62, 63.

119. Crawford and Gowing, eds., *Women's Worlds*, 151–52, Bridewell Hospital Records, Guildhall BCB 4 (microfilm), fo. 23.

120. While Clement seems to challenge Michael with the rapier, one might also see the knife as a kind of courtship gift, since, however unlikely it may seem, knives were sometimes exchanged between lovers. On courtship gifts, see Giese, *Courtships, Marriage Customs, and Shakespeare's Comedies*, 81–97; and O'Hara, *Courtship and Constraint*, 57–98.

121. Newman, *Cultural Capitals*, 138–39.

122. Valerie Traub, "The Present Future of Lesbian Historiography," in *A Companion to Lesbian, Gay, Bisexual, Transgender, and Queer Studies*, ed. George Haggerty and Molly McGarry (Oxford: Blackwell, 2007), 124–45, esp. 137.

123. Alastair Bellany, *The Politics of Court Scandal in Early Modern England: News Culture and the Overbury Affair, 1603–1660* (Cambridge: Cambridge University Press, 2002), 18, 137, 91.

124. Cynthia B. Herrup, *A House in Gross Disorder: Sex, Law, and the 2nd Earl of Castlehaven* (New York: Oxford University Press, 1999), xvi, 6. Carlo Ginzburg similarly argues that historians working with legal records should not seek to arrive at a verdict but rather to achieve "the reconstruction of the *relationship* (about which we know so little) between individual lives and the contexts in which they unfold." Carlo Ginzburg. "Checking the Evidence: The Judge and the Historian," *Critical Inquiry* 18, 1 (1991): 79–92, 90.

CHAPTER 5. THE RULE OF RELATION:
DOMESTIC ADVICE LITERATURE AND ITS READERS

1. *A Pleasant Conceited Comedie, Wherein is shewed how a man may chuse a good Wife from a bad* (London, 1602), sig. L1r. Richard Rowland, *Thomas Heywood's Theatre, 1599– 1639: Locations, Translations, and Conflict* (Aldershot: Ashgate, 2010), points out that the play, which is often attributed to Thomas Heywood, was reprinted six times; none of the printings names an author. While some works of advice literature address the prospective wife's choice, such as Patrick Hannay, *A Happy Husband: Or Directions For a Maid to Chuse Her Mate* (London, 1622), Alexandra Shepard points out the disproportionate emphasis on the husband's duties, "with the implication that the burden of ensuring a successful marriage rested more with husbands than with wives." *The Meanings of Manhood in Early Modern England* (Oxford: Oxford University Press, 2003), 80.

2. Jeremy Lopez, *Theatrical Convention and Audience Response in Early Modern Drama* (Cambridge: Cambridge University Press, 2003), 188.

3. Natalie Davis, *Society and Culture in Early Modern France* (Stanford, Calif.: Stanford University Press, 1965), 192; Natalie Glaisyer and Sara Pennell, "Introduction," in *Didactic Literature in England, 1500–1800: Expertise Constructed,* ed. Natalie Glaisyer and Sara Pennell (Burlington, Vt.: Ashgate, 2003), 1–18, esp. 12, 13. See also Sara Pennell, "Perfecting Practice? Women, Manuscript Recipes and Knowledge in Early Modern England," in *Early Modern Women's Manuscript Writing,* ed. Victoria E. Burke and Jonathan Gibson (Aldershot: Ashgate, 2004), 237–58. For Anna Bryson, in contrast, the fact that didactic literature attempts to supplement or substitute for personal instruction, which she assumes to be the more typical mode of teaching, compromises its status as evidence. Anna Bryson, *From Courtesy to Civility: Changing Codes of Conduct in Early Modern England* (Oxford: Clarendon, 1998), 5.

4. Roland du Jardin, *A Discourse of the Married and Single Life* (London, 1621), sigs. A3r, A8v; Alexander Niccholes, *A Discourse of Marriage and Wiving* (London, 1615), sig. A4v.

5. Suzanne Hull, *Chaste, Silent and Obedient: English Books for Women 1475–1640* (San Marino, Calif.: Huntington Library, 1982), 48. On male readers, see also Anne McLaren, "Monogamy, Polygamy and the True State: James I's Rhetoric of Empire," *History of Political Thought* 25, 3 (2004): 446–80, esp. 459; and Gina Hausknecht, "'So many shipwracke for want of better knowledge': The Imaginary Husband in Stuart Marriage Advice," *Huntington Library Quarterly* 64, 1/2 (2001): 81–106.

6. See, among others, Michelle M. Dowd, *Women's Work in Early Modern English Literature and Culture* (New York: Palgrave Macmillan, 2009), 133–72; Catharine Gray, *Women Writers and Public Debate in Seventeenth-Century England* (Houndmills: Palgrave, 2007), 37–66; Megan Matchinske, *Women Writing History in Early Modern England* (Cambridge: Cambridge University Press, 2009); Kristen Poole, "'The Fittest Closet for All Goodness': Authorial Strategies of Jacobean Mothers' Manuals," *SEL: Studies in English Literature, 1500–1900* 35, 1 (1995): 69–88; and Wendy Wall, *Imprint of Gender: Authorship*

and Publication in the English Renaissance (Ithaca, N.Y.: Cornell University Press, 1993), 279–340.

7. Mary Beth Rose, *The Expense of Spirit: Love and Sexuality in English Renaissance Drama* (Ithaca, N.Y.: Cornell University Press, 1988), 119.

8. Louis B. Wright, *Middle-Class Culture in Elizabethan England* (Chapel Hill: University of North Carolina Press, 1935), 203.

9. Advice literature also includes guides to social mobility, as Frank Whigham in particular has explored. See *Ambition and Privilege: The Social Tropes of Elizabethan Courtesy Theory* (Berkeley: University of California Press, 1984).

10. Shepard, *Meanings of Manhood*, 71.

11. Tessa Watt, *Cheap Print and Popular Piety, 1550–1640* (Cambridge: Cambridge University Press, 1993), 227, 251.

12. Wright, *Middle-Class*, 226. According to Elizabeth Eisenstein, "there is simply no equivalent in scribal culture for the 'avalanche' of 'how-to' books which poured off the new presses," *The Printing Press as an Agent of Change* (Cambridge: Cambridge University Press, 1979), 88. Kathleen Davies also connects the increasing popularity of these books to "the publishing explosion of the sixteenth century and the growth of a middle-class lay reading public, rather than changes in attitudes to marriage itself." Kathleen M. Davies, "Continuity and Change in Literary Advice on Marriage," in *Marriage and Society: Studies in the Social History of Marriage*, ed. R. B. Outhwaite (New York: St. Martin's, 1981), 58–80, 61.

13. Alan B. Farmer and Zachary Lesser, "The Popularity of Playbooks Revisited," *Shakespeare Quarterly* 56, 1 (Spring 2005): 1–32.

14. Tessa Watt, " 'Godly tables for good householders'," *Cheap Print and Popular Piety*, 217–53.

15. Anthony Fletcher, review of *Conduct Literature for Women, 1: Early Modern, 1500–1640*, *Seventeenth Century* 20, 2 (2005): 294–98, esp. 294.

16. According to David Hall, "Throughout the seventeenth century the colonists depended upon imports for the bulk of their reading," David D. Hall, *Cultures of Print: Essays in the History of the Book* (Amherst: University of Massachusetts Press, 1996), 42n18, 90. As a consequence, colonists spoke "a borrowed language" purveyed to them from "London printers and booksellers," David D. Hall, *Worlds of Wonder, Days of Judgment: Popular Religious Belief in Early New England* (New York: Knopf, 1989), 71–72. See also Hugh Amory and David D. Hall, *The Colonial Book in the Atlantic World* (Worcester, Mass.: American Antiquarian Society, 2000).

17. Scott Cutler Shershow, *Puppets and "Popular" Culture* (Ithaca, N.Y.: Cornell University Press, 1995); and "New Life: Cultural Studies and the Problem of the 'Popular'," *Textual Practice* 12, 1 (1998): 23–47.

18. Wright, *Middle-Class*, 202.

19. Glaisyer and Pennell, "Introduction," 7.

20. Chilton Latham Powell, *English Domestic Relations, 1487–1653: A Study of Matrimony and Family Life in Theory and Practice as Revealed by the Literature, Law, and History of the Period* (New York: Columbia University Press, 1917), 139, 135.

21. Charles Whitney, *Early Responses to Renaissance Drama* (Cambridge: Cambridge University Press, 2006), 104.

22. As I have discussed in my introduction, many historians of reading emphasize the agency of the early modern reader. On didactic literature in particular, see Juanita Feros Ruys, "Introduction: Approaches to Didactic Literature—Meaning, Intent, Audience, Social Effect," in *What Nature Does Not Teach: Didactic Literature in the Medieval and Early-Modern Periods*, ed. Juanita Feros Ruys (Turnhout: Brepols, 2008), 1–38; and Randall Ingram, "Seventeenth-Century Didactic Readers, Their Literature and Ours," in *Didactic Literature in England, 1500–1800: Expertise Constructed*, ed. Natalie Glaisyer and Sara Pennell (Burlington, Vt.: Ashgate, 2003), 63–78.

23. Powell, *English Domestic Relations*, 140, 142.

24. Davies, "Continuity and Change," 59. On continuities in marriage advice, see also Margot Todd, *Christian Humanism and the Puritan Social Order* (Cambridge: Cambridge University Press, 1987); and Margaret J. M. Ezell, *The Patriarch's Wife: Literary Evidence and the History of the Family* (Chapel Hill: University of North Carolina Press, 1987), 7.

25. Garthine Walker, *Crime, Gender and Social Order in Early Modern England* (Cambridge: Cambridge University Press, 2003), 86. Other versions of this admonition can be found in Elizabeth A. Foyster, *Manhood in Early Modern England: Honour, Sex and Marriage* (Harlough, Essex: Longman, 1999), 2; Paul Griffiths, *Youth and Authority: Formative Experiences in England, 1560–1640* (Oxford: Clarendon Press, 1996), 290; Shepard, *Meanings of Manhood*, 72; and Phyllis Rackin, "Misogyny Is Everywhere," *A Feminist Companion to Shakespeare* (Oxford: Blackwell, 2000), 42–56, esp. 49.

26. Anthony Fletcher, *Gender, Sex, and Subordination in England, 1500–1800* (New Haven Conn.: Yale University Press, 1995), xxi.

27. Amy Louise Erickson, *Women and Property in Early Modern England* (London: Routledge, 1993), 8–9.

28. Susan Amussen, *An Ordered Society: Gender and Class in Early Modern England* (Oxford: Blackwell, 1988), 117; Bernard Capp, *When Gossips Meet: Women, Family, and Neighbourhood in Early Modern England* (Oxford: Oxford University Press, 2003), 27, 36. See also Alison Wall, *Power and Protest in England, 1525–1640* (London: Arnold, 2000), 95; Fletcher, *Gender, Sex, and Subordination*, 116–17; and Timothy Stretton, *Women Waging Law in Elizabethan England* (Cambridge: Cambridge University Press, 1998), 10.

29. Lena Cowen Orlin, *Locating Privacy in Tudor London* (Oxford: Oxford University Press, 2007), 153; Amussen, *Ordered Society*, 6.

30. Ralph A. Houlbrooke turns to "intimate documents," that is, letters and diaries, *The English Family, 1450–1700* (London: Longman, 1984), 103; Amy Erickson points to the value of wills (*Women and Property*, 93); Alison Wall looks at letters, "Elizabethan Precept and Feminine Practice: The Thynne Family of Longleat," *History* 75, 1 (1990): 23–38.

31. Keith Wrightson, *English Society, 1580–1680* (New Brunswick, N.J.: Rutgers University Press, 1982), 92.

32. Fletcher, *Gender, Sex and Subordination*, 114.

33. I quote from *The Norton Shakespeare*, ed. Stephen Greenblatt, Walter Cohen, Jean E. Howard, and Katharine Eisaman Maus (New York: Norton, 1997).

34. Davies, "Continuity and Change," 76–77, 78; William Gouge, *Of Domesticall Duties* (London, 1622), sig. R8r.

35. Lorna Hutson, *The Usurer's Daughter: Male Friendship and Fictions of Women in Sixteenth-Century England* (London and New York: Routledge, 1994), 23, 24, 21, 22. See also Lisa Jardine, *Reading Shakespeare Historically* (London: Routledge, 1996), 111–28.

36. On the functions of fictions about marital unity, see my *Marriage and Violence: The Early Modern Legacy* (Philadelphia: University of Pennsylvania Press, 2008).

37. Powell, *English Domestic Relations*, 128.

38. Wright, *Middle-Class*, 226.

39. Susan Cahn argues that repetition demonstrates consensus in *Industry of Devotion: The Transformation of Women's Work in England, 1500–1660* (New York: Columbia University Press, 1987), 187. For the argument that variety within and among these treatises suggests cultural conflicts, see Dolan, *Marriage and Violence*; Heather Dubrow, *A Happier Eden: The Politics of Marriage in the Stuart Epithalamium* (Ithaca, N.Y.: Cornell University Press, 1990), 12–13; Rebecca Ann Bach, *Shakespeare and Renaissance Literature Before Heterosexuality* (Houndmills: Palgrave, 2007); and Valerie Traub, *Renaissance of Lesbianism in Early Modern England* (Cambridge: Cambridge University Press, 2001).

40. Kathryn Schwarz, *What You Will: Gender, Contract, and Shakespearean Social Space* (Philadelphia: University of Pennsylvania Press, 2011), 7. Schwarz quotes Richard Rambuss, *Closet Devotions* (Durham, N.C.: Duke University Press, 1998), 1–2: "Too often interpretation desists" at the moment of determining conventionality, "as if the status of being conventional would make a discursive construct or a sentiment any less thick with significance."

41. Capp, *When Gossips Meet*, 20–25; Zachary Lesser, *Renaissance Drama and the Politics of Publication: Readings in the English Book Trade* (Cambridge: Cambridge University Press, 2004), 132; Tim Meldrum, *Domestic Service and Gender, 1660–1750: Life and Work in the London Household* (Harlow: Longman/Pearson, 2000), 40.

42. Capp, *When Gossips Meet*, 26.

43. Glaisyer and Pennell, "Introduction," 8. See also Lori Ann Ferrell, "How-To Books, Protestant Kinetics, and the Art of Theology," *Huntington Library Quarterly* 71, 4 (2008): 591–606, esp. 595; Eve Keller, *Generating Bodies and Gendered Selves: The Rhetoric of Reproduction in Early Modern England* (Seattle: University of Washington Press, 2007), 75; Sandra Sherman, "Printed Communities: Domestic Management Texts in the Eighteenth Century," *Journal for Early Modern Cultural Studies* 3, 2 (2003): 36–67; and Wendy Wall's discussion of the hands-on nature of literacy and "how to read a how-to book" in "Literacy and the Domestic Arts," *Huntington Library Quarterly* 73, 3 (2010): 383–412.

44. Compliance is also a form of practice and of power, as Kathryn Schwarz has shown, revealing the dependence of the social order on women's willing fulfillment of the role assigned to them in it (Schwarz, *What You Will*, 27). Similarly, Ann Rosalind Jones reminds us that women wrote "by appropriating positive prescriptions rather than immobilizing prohibitions." Ann Rosalind Jones, "Nets and Bridles: Early Modern Conduct Books

and Sixteenth-Century Women's Lyrics," in *The Ideology of Conduct: Essays in Literature and the History of Sexuality*, ed. Nancy Armstrong and Leonard Tennenhouse (New York: Methuen, 1987), 39–72, esp. 68.

45. Foyster, *Manhood*, 4. According to Tessa Watt, "The good householder was not only the product, but the market for the product" (*Cheap Print and Popular Piety*, 225). See also Wendy Wall, *Staging Domesticity: Household Work and English Identity in Early Modern Drama* (Cambridge: Cambridge University Press, 2002), 18, 58.

46. McLaren, "Monogamy, Polygamy and the True State," esp. 461, 459, 480, 479; Kathleen Brown, *Good Wives, Nasty Wenches, and Anxious Patriarchs: Gender, Race, and Power in Colonial Virginia* (Chapel Hill: University of North Carolina Press, 1996), 17.

47. Jennifer Mylander, "Early Modern 'How-To' Books: Impractical Manuals and the Construction of Englishness in the Atlantic World," *Journal for Early Modern Cultural Studies* 9, 1 (2009): 123–46. See also Brown, *Good Wives, Nasty Wenches*, 13–41.

48. William Whately, *A Bride-Bush. Or, A Direction for Married Persons* (London, 1623), sig. Dd2v.

49. Christopher Hill, *Society and Puritanism in Pre-Revolutionary England*, 2d ed. (New York: Schocken Books, 1967), 466. On the role of analogies between household and state in advice literature, see Amussen, *Ordered Society*; Lena Cowen Orlin, *Private Matters and Public Culture in Post-Reformation England* (Ithaca, N.Y.: Cornell University Press, 1994); Peter Stallybrass, "The World Turned Upside Down: Inversion, Gender, and the State," in *The Matter of Difference: Materialist Feminist Criticism of Shakespeare*, ed. Valerie Wayne (Ithaca, N.Y.: Cornell University Press, 1991), 201–20; and Rachel Weil, *Political Passions; Gender, the Family and Political Argument in England, 1680–1714* (Manchester: Manchester University Press, 1988).

50. McLaren, "Monogamy, Polygamy and the True State," 480.

51. *Revolutionary Prose of the English Civil War*, ed. Howard Erskine-Hill and Graham Storey (Cambridge: Cambridge University Press, 1983), 49.

52. John Milton, *Milton's Selected Poetry and Prose*, ed. Jason P. Rosenblatt (New York: Norton, 2011), 405.

53. Wendy Wall, *Staging Domesticity*, 8.

54. Sara Mendelson and Patricia Crawford, *Women in Early Modern England, 1550–1720* (Oxford: Clarendon, 1998), 128.

55. David Cressy, *Birth, Marriage, and Death: Ritual, Religion, and the Life-Cycle in Tudor and Stuart England* (Oxford: Oxford University Press, 1997), 7–8.

56. Natasha Korda, *Shakespeare's Domestic Economies: Gender and Property in Early Modern England* (Philadelphia: University of Pennsylvania Press, 2002), 7. Similarly, while Pamela Allen Brown distinguishes "popular" from "documentary" sources, she turns popular sources, such as jest books, into documents through an inventive reading practice. See Pamela Allen Brown, *Better a Shrew Than a Sheep: Women, Drama, and the Culture of Jest in Early Modern England* (Ithaca, N.Y.: Cornell University Press, 2003), 2 and passim.

57. Laura Gowing, *Domestic Dangers: Women, Words, and Sex in Early Modern London* (Oxford: Clarendon, 1996), 26, 27.

58. Shepard, *Meanings of Manhood*, 11.

59. Traub, *Renaissance of Lesbianism*, 21. In *The Family, Sex and Marriage in England, 1500–1800*, Lawrence Stone both oversimplified the relationship between women's interiority and prescription and charted a course for those who are still trying to figure out how to use advice literature to think about elusive historical subjects. Stone distinguishes "private reality" from "public rhetoric" yet also conflates the two when he claims that "the theoretical and legal doctrines of the time were especially insistent upon the subordination of women to men in general, and to their husbands in particular, and that many women accepted these ideas" and that "the sense of inferiority was fully internalized by most women." Stone slides from claiming that rhetoric, doctrines, and literature informed women's interiority to taking them as evidence therefore of that interiority. Although many scholars agree that women's subjectivities were constituted in part through advice literature, they tend to create more space for contesting and appropriating it than does Stone. Lawrence Stone, *The Family, Sex and Marriage in England, 1500–1800* (New York: Harper and Row, 1977), 199.

60. Although Alison Wall concedes some variety among the authors and their books, she claims that "Most of them were single when they proposed patterns for husbands and wives to follow, and celibate college communities had provided them with little experience of family life" (Wall, *Power and Protest*, 83). In contrast, William and Malleville Haller refer to the authors as "the preachers, themselves married men," William Haller and Malleville Haller, "The Puritan Art of Love," *Huntington Library Quarterly* 5 (1942): 235–72, 253; Alexandra Shepard writes that "most authors were in their late forties and had several years' personal experience of marital relations" by the time they wrote (Shepard, *Meanings of Manhood*, 71).

61. Whately, *A Bride-Bush*, sigs. G2r, E4r, G2v.

62. There were four more editions of *A Bride-Bush* in the eighteenth century. It was also reprinted by Methodist presses in the eighteenth and early nineteenth centuries as *Directions for Married Persons* (1753, 1768, 1790, 1794, 1804). Cotton Mather begins his character of the virtuous wife, in *Ornaments for the Daughters of Zion*, 3rd ed. (Boston, 1741), by referring to the fact that William Whately dedicated *A Bride-Bush* to his father-in-law and claiming that he too is inspired by the daily example of his own wife (86). On Whately, see Jacqueline Eales, "Gender Construction in Early Modern England and the Conduct Books of William Whately (1583–1639)," in *Gender and Christian Religion*, ed. R. N. Swanson (Woodbridge: Boydell, 1998), 163–74.

63. Daniel Cawdrey, *Family Reformation Promoted* (London, 1656), sigs. A2v–A3r. Powell dismisses *A Godly Forme* as long, derivative, and "poorly arranged" (*English Domestic Relations*, 133); Wright emphasizes its popularity (*Middle-Class*, 211–12).

64. Hutson, *Usurer's Daughter*, 17–51; Wendy Wall, *Staging Domesticity*, 18–58; Korda, *Shakespeare's Domestic Economies*, 15–51. See also Catherine Belsey, *Shakespeare and the Loss of Eden: The Construction of Family Values in Early Modern Culture* (New Brunswick, N.J.: Rutgers University Press, 1999), 55–83; and Sid Ray, " 'Those Whom God Hath Joined Together': Bondage Metaphors and Marital Advice in Early Modern England," *Domestic*

Arrangements in Early Modern England, ed. Kari Boyd McBride (Pittsburgh: Duquesne University Press, 2002), 15–47.

65. William St. Clair and Irmgard Maassen, "Introduction," in *Conduct Literature for Women, 1500–1640*, ed. William St. Clair and Irmgard Maassen, vol. 2 (London: Pickering & Chatto, 2000), 3; Haller and Haller, "Puritan Art of Love," 241–42.

66. Carrie E. Euler, "Heinrich Bullinger, Marriage, and the English Reformation: *The Christen State of Matrimonye* in England, 1540–53," *Sixteenth Century Journal* 34, 2 (2003): 367–93, esp. 379; David Daniell entry on Miles Coverdale in the *ODNB*.

67. Euler, "Heinrich Bullinger," 367.

68. Thomas Becon, *The Worckes of Thomas Becon*, 3 vols. (London, 1564), I, sig. Civ. Becon wrote his own "The Booke of Matrimony" including this same preface and published it in his works in 1564; this is not the same as Bullinger's book, although it has sometimes been taken as such. See Haller and Haller, "Puritan Art of Love," 240n1; Wright, *Middle-Class*, 207n7; and Powell, *English Domestic Relations*, 114n1.

69. Euler, "Heinrich Bullinger," 367n2.

70. The editors of a useful facsimile edition, William St. Clair and Irmgard Maassen, argue that Coverdale did so because he was more interested in "doctrinal questions" than in "the practical points of conduct" (William St. Clair and Irmgard Maassen, "Introduction," Heinrich Bullinger, *Christen State of Matrimonye* (Antwerp, 1541), *Conduct Literature for Women, 1500–1640*, ed. William St. Clair and Irmgard Maassen, vol. 2 (London: Pickering & Chatto, 2000), 3. Parenthetical citations are to this edition. Euler specifies that Coverdale's translation is "complete" and "accurate" with regard to chapters 1–18 and 25, that is, the chapters about Bullinger's marital theology that were of key importance to English reformers, but that the chapters regarding the conduct of marriage and family life (19–24) were shortened "significantly by leaving out many of Bullinger's examples" (Euler, 381, 382).

71. Despite these excisions, the book remained controversial and was banned in 1546.

72. Roland Mushat Frye, "The Teachings of Classical Puritanism on Conjugal Love," *Studies in the Renaissance* 2 (1955): 148–59, esp. 149; Haller and Haller, "Puritan Art of Love," 240; Wright, *Middle-Class*, 205. See also Powell, *English Domestic Relations*, 115, 119.

73. Powell, *English Domestic Relations*, 119, 115.

74. Karen Newman, *Fashioning Femininity and English Renaissance Drama* (Chicago: University of Chicago Press, 1991), 21, 23, 25. Susan Wabuda points out that Bullinger argued that "wedlock defiled no one and was forbidden to no one." "Sanctified by the Believing Spouse: Women, Men and the Marital Yoke in the Early Reformation," in *The Beginnings of English Protestantism*, ed. Peter Marshall and Alec Ryrie (Cambridge: Cambridge University Press, 2002), 111–28, esp. 121.

75. Euler, "Heinrich Bullinger," 379, 382.

76. Provoked by Jacques's prediction in *As You Like It* that Oliver Martext will join Audrey and Touchstone "together as they join wainscot; then one of you will prove a shrunk panel, and like green timber, warp, warp" (Norton 3.3.72–73), Patricia Parker explores the complex meanings of joinery in Shakespeare's plays and in the period more generally "as the figure for other kinds of joining," including the joining of words and bodies. Patricia

Parker, *Shakespeare from the Margins: Language, Culture, Context* (Chicago: University of Chicago Press, 1996), 88–89.

77. According to Euler, "Thomas Becon's contribution to the official *Book of Homilies* of 1547, 'An Homelie of Whoredome and Unclennesse,' contained material that could have been taken directly from Bullinger's book on marriage" ("Heinrich Bullinger," 389); as a consequence, "when pastors read Becon's homily from pulpits all over England, they reinforced the ideas found in the many copies of Coverdale's translation already in circulation at the time" (390).

78. Thomas Gataker, *A Good Wife Gods Gift: And, A Wife Indeed. Two Mariage Sermons* (London, 1623), sig. B3r.

79. Gouge, *Of Domesticall Duties.* Parenthetical citations throughout this chapter refer to this edition. Pages 191–96 are missing from the Folger copy available on EEBO. The content is available in the 1634 printing, sigs. N7v–O2v.

80. See, among others, Jeffrey Todd Knight, "Making Shakespeare's Books: Assembly and Intertextuality in the Archives," *Shakespeare Quarterly* 60, 3 (2009): 304–40; and Jeffrey Masten, "Material Cavendish: Paper, Performance, 'Sociable Virginity'," *Modern Language Quarterly* 65, 1 (March 2004): 49–68.

81. Fletcher praises *Of Domesticall Duties* as "the best" of the Puritan conduct books and as a best seller (Fletcher, *Gender, Sex, and Subordination,* 116, 158); Davies calls Gouge a "distinct bestseller" with three reprintings in ten years ("Continuity and Change," 80). In addition to the 1622 edition, "a handsome folio edition was brought out in 1626, followed by a third edition in quarto in 1634. Besides these, *Of Domesticall Duties* also appeared as a part of Gouge's *Workes* (1627), which went through three issues" (Wright, *Middle-Class,* 222).

82. The book is represented by an excerpt even in a series of facsimile editions such as *Conduct Literature for Women, 1: Early Modern, 1500–1640,* 6 vols. (London: Pickering and Chatto, 2000).

83. Haller and Haller, "Puritan Art of Love," 254.

84. Thomas Gouge describes his father's exegetical method as a matter of both association and application: first "opening the true literall sense of the text, then giving the *Logical Analysis* thereof, and then gathering such proper observations as did thence arise, and properly and pertinently applying the same." "A Narrative of the Life and Death of Doctor Gouge," prefix to William Gouge, *A Learned and Very Useful Commentary on the Whole Epistle to the Hebrewes* (London 1655), b1v.

85. *Milton's Selected Poetry and Prose,* 349.

86. Powell, *English Domestic Relations,* 138; Alison Wall, *Power and Protest,* 84, 85.

87. Thomas Gouge, "A Narrative," sig. a2r. Samuel Clarke reprints this biography with some additions and rephrasings in *A Collection of the Lives of Ten Eminent Divines* (London, 1662), claiming to do so at Thomas Gouge's request (sig. R3r).

88. Thomas Gouge, "Narrative," sigs. a2r, b2r.

89. Paul Griffiths recounts two instances in which Gouge extended his work as a governor of Bridewell Hospital into his house and his church, one in which he "caught three 'vagrants and suspicious nightwalkers' 'climbing over a yard' into his house in 1640"

and the other in which he "marched a cutpurse to Bridewell in 1633, who was 'taken in the act' of cutting a purse in a pew in his Blackfriars church as he boomed from the pulpit." Griffiths's anecdotes depict a vigilant Gouge, apprehending offenders wherever he finds them. Paul Griffiths, *Lost Londons: Change, Crime and Control in the Capital City, 1550–1660* (Cambridge: Cambridge University Press, 2008), 391.

90. Thomas Gouge, "Narrative," sig. a2r. Clarke's version intensifies this: "Having thus changed his condition, and entred into a married estate, that he might not be distracted, nor impeded in his studies by worldly business, he committed the whole care of his Family affairs to the management of his wife, and still applied himself wholly to his studies, and to the weighty businesses of his heavenly calling" (*Collection*, sig. O2v).

91. The earlier DNB entry mentions Elizabeth Gouge only as an afterthought.

92. Thomas Gouge, "Narrative," sig. a2v. See also William Jenkyn, *A Shock of Corn Coming in Its Season. A Sermon Preached at the Funeral of . . . William Gouge* (London, 1654), sig. F4v.

93. On parents instructing children and the duty of children to listen, see also sigs. Ee8v; Gg6v. On masters instructing their servants and servants' duty to listen, see sigs. S2v, Mm5v, Qq2v, Rr1r–v, Vv16r–v.

94. Thomas Gouge, "Narrative," sigs. c1r–v. Compare Jenkyn, *Shock*, sig. F4r.

95. Alison Wall, *Power and Protest*, 85. See Gouge's detailed instructions on catering to a pregnant wife, sigs. Cc8r–Dd1v.

96. Davies, "Continuity and Change," 63. See also Haller and Haller, "Puritan Art of Love," 248, among others.

97. Patrick Collinson, *The Birthpangs of Protestant England: Religious and Cultural Change in the Sixteenth and Seventeenth Centuries* (Houndmills: Palgrave Macmillan, 1988), 71; Margaret George, "From 'Goodwife' to 'Mistress': The Transformation of the Female in Bourgeois Culture", *Science and Society* 37, 2 (1973): 152–77, 168; Haller and Haller, "Puritan Art of Love," 249; Jennifer Panek, *Widows and Suitors in Early Modern English Comedy* (Cambridge: Cambridge University Press, 2004), 62–63; Alison Wall, *Power and Protest*, 86; Charles Whitney, *Early Responses to Renaissance Drama* (Cambridge: Cambridge University Press, 2006), 222; and Linda Woodbridge, *Women and the English Renaissance: Literature and the Nature of Womankind, 1540–1620* (Urbana: University of Illinois Press, 1984), 129–30.

98. Wright, *Middle-Class*, 204.

99. Fletcher, *Gender, Sex and Subordination*, 117; Alison Wall, *Power and Protest*, 69. Jacqueline Eales argues that while prescriptions for wifely subordination might not have applied to "city wives" they did apply to ministers' wives like Elizabeth Gouge. "There were no formal opportunities for a cleric's wife to share in his ministerial functions, and unlike many other wives, she could not continue his work if she were widowed. This point has previously been overlooked by historians, but it explains why clerical conduct book writers put such great stress on the division between the public duties of the husband and the private domestic duties of the wife." Jacqueline Eales, *Women in Early Modern England, 1500–1700* (London: UCL Press, 1998), 28.

100. Amussen, *Ordered Society*, 46. See also Constance Jordan, *Renaissance Feminism: Literary Texts and Political Models* (Ithaca, N.Y.: Cornell University Press, 1990), 291–92; Rose, *Expense of Spirit*, 128, 130–31. According to Louis B. Wright, "To mold the sort of wife who would have just the proper amount of obedience and humility and yet would possess the spirit and capacity to be a real helpmeet of her husband was the aim of many a book on domestic relations" (*Middle-Class*, 204).

101. Korda, *Shakespeare's Domestic Economies*, 46, 49, 45–46, 43. Gouge discusses wives' control of property at considerable length, including sigs. T8r–X2v.

102. *An Exposition of the Whole Fifth Chapter of S. Johns Gospell: Taken from the Mouth of Mr. William Gouge* (London, 1631), "Advertisement to the Reader." This text was printed in 1630 and 1631. Only the 1631 edition explains Pemble's role and qualifies Gouge's claims to authorship. The 1630 printing describes the text as "taken" but does not explain from whom or by whom. Parenthetical references are to the 1631 edition.

103. William Gouge, *A Recovery from Apostacy* (London, 1639), sigs. A3r–v. In this particular case, Gouge "contracted his matter" because time was short, so his printed version, like *A True and Perfect Relation*, which I discuss in chapter one, is authorized precisely because it is not what was delivered but rather what Gouge wishes he had been able to deliver (sig. A3v). On new note-taking strategies in the 1640s and 1650s that focused on grasping "the substance of the speech" rather than trying to transcribe it, see Ceri Sullivan, "The Art of Listening in the Seventeenth Century," *Modern Philology* 104, 1 (August 2006): 34–71, esp. 42.

104. Schwarz, *What You Will*, 82. She argues elsewhere that "When women theorize what should be practiced through and on them, meanings shift," Kathryn Schwarz, "A Tragedy of Good Intentions: Maternal Agency in *3 Henry VI* and *King John*," *Renaissance Drama* 32 (2003): 225–54, esp. 246. On the way that conduct literature "exists as a fragile, continuous negotiation between what is and what could be, between what it says and what it disavows," see also Kim Solga, *Violence Against Women in Early Modern Performance: Invisible Acts* (Houndmills: Palgrave, 2009), 76.

105. Shepard, *Meanings of Manhood*, 73 (she repeats this on 84), 86. See also Shepard, 11; and Foyster, *Manhood*, 66.

106. Gouge himself is unclear as to whether he directly addresses subordinates or talks to their superiors about them. He says for instance to children: "though thou maiest doe nothing against Gods will, yet thou oughtest to doe many things against thine owne will, it if be contrary to thy parents" but then immediately proceeds to discuss children in the third person: "They must labour to bring their judgement and will to the bent of their parents: to thinke that meet and convenient for them to doe which their parents will have them doe" (Gg8v).

107. Paul Seaver, *Wallington's World: A Puritan Artisan in Seventeenth-Century London* (Stanford, Calif.: Stanford University Press, 1985), 79.

108. Fletcher, *Gender, Sex, and Subordination*, 116; cf. 206.

109. Erica Longfellow, "Public, Private, and the Household in Early Seventeenth-Century England," *Journal of British Studies* 45 (2006): 313–34, esp. 325–26. These articles

can be seen in *The Notebooks of Nehemiah Wallington, 1618–1654: A Selection*, ed. David Booy (Aldershot: Ashgate, 1988), 271–72. Other readers left records of their engagement with Gouge as well. In his diary, the Reverend Henry Newcombe makes various references to consulting books about domestic relations including "I read a little in Dr. Gouge" and "studdyed in Dr Gouge and noted several thgs out of him about wives & husbands" and "read and noted in Dr Gouge"; see *The Diary of the Reverend Henry Newcome, from September 30 1661 to September 29 1663*, ed. Thomas Heywood, Chetham Society 18 (Manchester, 1840), 55, 56. William H. Sherman discusses Dorothy Clegge's copy of Gouge's *Of Domesticall Duties* (1634), now at the Huntington Library, which she signed in 1709 and inscribed with "cross-references to Gouge's other works" and a table of her family history. Clegge is, for Sherman, an excellent example of a reader who uses a book as "an official place for individual readers or groups of readers to take stock—of their families, their beliefs, their belongings, and their textual resources." William H. Sherman, *Used Books: Marking Readers in Renaissance England* (Philadelphia: University of Pennsylvania Press, 2008), 61.

110. Anne Kugler, "Constructing Wifely Identity: Prescription and Practice in the Life of Lady Sarah Cowper," *Journal of British Studies* 40 (July 2001): 291–323, esp. 292, 303. See also Anne Kugler, *Errant Plagiary: The Life and Writing of Lady Sarah Cowper, 1644–1720* (Stanford, Calif.: Stanford University Press, 2002). Of Lady Sarah's notebooks, Anthony Fletcher writes, "this unusual source . . . shows how subtle and free-wheeling the process of appropriation of texts could be" (Fletcher, *Gender, Sex, and Subordination*, 410); Elizabeth Foyster cites Cowper as a "case study of how prescription was shaped and altered in practice," *Marital Violence: An English Family History, 1660–1857* (Cambridge: Cambridge University Press, 2005), 93.

111. Thomas Gouge, "Narrative," sig. a2v. The parenthetical phrase is Clarke's (*Collection*, sig. O3v).

112. Fletcher, *Gender, Sex, and Subordination*, 116.

113. See Schwarz, *What You Will*, esp. 78–103, on the dependency on female volition and consent.

114. For your information, one should, according to Gouge, allow servants at least five but no more than seven hours of sleep.

115. See also "In this respect it is said (*Pro*. 18.22) *who so findeth a wife, findeth a good thing*, which by the rule of relation is true also, of an husband" (P1v; repeated at Q1r–v; R3v) and "That which *Salomon* expresseth of an husband, by the rule of relation must be applied to a wife" (P5r).

116. Many of the critics discussed here have linked the drama to advice literature, including Bach, Pamela Brown, Hutson, Korda, Rose, and Wendy Wall. I have done this myself, here and elsewhere. Others argue that advice literature lays the foundation for the novel. This is a vast bibliography but see, for example, J. Paul Hunter, *Before Novels: Cultural Contexts of Eighteenth Century Fiction* (New York: Norton, 1990); and Michael McKeon, *The Origins of the English Novel, 1600–1740* (Baltimore: Johns Hopkins University Press, 1987).

117. Wright, *Middle-Class Culture*, 224.

CHAPTER 6. RELATIONAL TRUTHS:
DRAMATIC EVIDENCE, *ALL IS TRUE*, AND *DOUBLE FALSEHOOD*

1. Tiffany Stern, *Documents of Performance in Early Modern England* (Cambridge: Cambridge University Press, 2009), 1.

2. On piecing together garments and identities out of disparate pieces, see Ann Rosalind Jones and Peter Stallybrass, *Renaissance Clothing and the Materials of Memory* (Cambridge: Cambridge University Press, 2000); and Will Fisher, *Materializing Gender in Early Modern English Literature and Culture* (Cambridge: Cambridge University Press, 2006).

3. Margaret Jane Kidnie, *Shakespeare and the Problem of Adaptation* (New York: Routledge, 2009), 2.

4. Natasha Korda, *Labors Lost: Women's Work and the Early Modern English Stage* (Philadelphia: University of Pennsylvania Press, 2011), 3, emphasis mine.

5. E. K. Chambers, *The Elizabethan Stage*, 4 vols. (Oxford: Clarendon Press, 1923); and Records of Early English Drama (REED), now moving into electronic formats, among many others.

6. On theater companies, see Mary Bly, *Queer Virgins and Virgin Queans on the Early Modern Stage* (Oxford: Oxford University Press, 2000); Andrew Gurr, *The Shakespeare Company, 1594–1642* (Cambridge: Cambridge University Press, 2004); Lucy Munro, *Children of the Queen's Revels: A Jacobean Theatre Repertory* (Cambridge: Cambridge University Press, 2005); Scott McMillin and Sally-Beth MacLean, *The Queen's Men and Their Plays* (Cambridge: Cambridge University Press, 1998); and Brian Walsh, *Shakespeare, The Queen's Men, and the Elizabethan Performance of History* (Cambridge: Cambridge University Press, 2009). On grouping plays by publisher, see Zachary Lesser, *Renaissance Drama and the Politics of Publication: Readings in the English Book Trade* (Cambridge: Cambridge University Press, 2004).

7. Simon Palfrey and Tiffany Stern, *Shakespeare in Parts* (Oxford: Oxford University Press, 2007), 9.

8. Peter Laslett, "The Wrong Way Through the Telescope: A Note on Literary Evidence in Sociology and in Historical Sociology," *British Journal of Sociology* 27, 3 (1976): 319–42, esp. 320, 325, 331.

9. Laslett uses this example in "The Wrong Way Through the Telescope" and elaborates on it in *The World We Have Lost—Further Explored: England Before the Industrial Age*, 3rd ed. (New York: Scribner's, 1984), 81.

10. Laslett, "Wrong Way," 324, 325.

11. Lawrence Stone, *The Family, Sex and Marriage in England, 1500–1800* (New York: Harper & Row, 1977), 102.

12. Elizabeth Foyster, *Manhood in Early Modern England: Honour, Sex and Marriage* (Harlough: Longman, 1999), 16. Throughout, Foyster draws heavily on the drama as valuable "fictional evidence," reading it in relation to other sources including ballads, court records, and advice literature (130).

13. Anthony Fletcher, *Gender, Sex, and Subordination in England, 1500–1800* (New Haven, Conn.: Yale University Press, 1995), xix, xxi.

14. David Cressy, *Agnes Bowker's Cat: Travesties and Transgressions in Tudor and Stuart England* (Oxford: Oxford University Press, 2000), 103–4. See also David Cressy, *Birth, Marriage, and Death: Ritual, Religion, and the Life Cycle in Tudor and Stuart England* (Oxford: Oxford University Press, 1997), 8.

15. Peter Lake, *The Antichrist's Lewd Hat: Protestants, Papists and Players in Post-Reformation England* (New Haven, Conn.: Yale University Press, 2002), xxiii, xxiv–xxv, 88.

16. Bernard Capp, "Life, Love and Litigation: Sileby in the 1630s," *Past and Present* 182 (February 2004): 55–83, esp. 81. See also Diana O'Hara, *Courtship and Constraint: Rethinking the Making of Marriage in Tudor England* (Manchester: Manchester University Press, 2000), 8, 31, 50n7.

17. Paul Griffiths, *Lost Londons: Change, Crime, and Control in the Capital City, 1550–1660* (Cambridge: Cambridge University Press, 2008), 291. See also 367.

18. Eric S. Mallin, *Inscribing the Time: Shakespeare and the End of Elizabethan England* (Berkeley: University of California Press, 1995), 16, 7.

19. Lynda E. Boose, "Scolding Brides and Bridling Scolds: Taming the Woman's Unruly Member," *Shakespeare Quarterly* 42 (1991): 179–213, esp. 198, 181.

20. Contrast David Underdown, "The Taming of the Scold: The Enforcement of Patriarchal Authority in Early Modern England," in *Order and Disorder in Early Modern England* (Cambridge: Cambridge University Press, 1985), 116–36; and Martin Ingram, "'Scolding women cucked or washed': A Crisis in Gender Relations in Early Modern England?" in *Women, Crime, and the Courts in Early Modern England*, ed. Jenny Kermode and Garthine Walker (London: University College London Press, 1994), 48–80.

21. Fredric Jameson, *The Political Unconscious: Narrative as a Socially Symbolic Act* (Ithaca, N.Y.: Cornell University Press, 1981), 81.

22. Walter Cohen, "Political Criticism of Shakespeare," in *Shakespeare Reproduced: The Text in History and Ideology*, ed. Jean E. Howard and Marion F. O'Connor (New York and London: Methuen, 1987), 18–46, esp. 34.

23. Julian Yates, "Accidental Shakespeare," *Shakespeare Studies* 34 (2006): 90–122, esp. 99.

24. For an example of the argument that Shakespeare's plays "reflect," see B. J. Sokol and Mary Sokol, *Shakespeare, Law, and Marriage* (Cambridge: Cambridge University Press, 2003), 12.

25. Michael Neill, *Putting History to the Question: Power, Politics, and Society in English Renaissance Drama* (New York: Columbia University Press, 2000), 3. For another important formulation of the relationship between Shakespeare's plays and history, see Lisa Jardine, *Reading Shakespeare Historically* (London: Routledge, 1996), 1, 17.

26. Lena Orlin, "Domestic Tragedy: Private Life on the Public Stage," in *A Companion to Renaissance Drama*, ed. Arthur F. Kinney (London: Blackwell, 2002), 367–83, esp. 368, 380, 369. On the relationship between church court depositions and plays, see also Loreen L. Giese, *Courtships, Marriage Customs, and Shakespeare's Comedies* (Houndmills: Palgrave Macmillan, 2006), 14.

27. Mallin, *Inscribing the Time*, 3, 13. According to Joel Altman, Shakespeare's

"dramaturgy begins and ends in figuration, in the collocations, intuitions, and tropes by means of which he composed his plays—and, in so doing, himself—out of the fragments of text to which he responded ingeniously." Altman, *The Improbability of Othello: Rhetorical Anthropology and Shakespearean Selfhood* (Chicago: University of Chicago Press, 2010), 235.

28. For a judicious discussion of "parallel developments" in the law and the theater, see Luke Wilson, *Theaters of Intention: Drama and the Law in Early Modern England* (Cambridge: Cambridge University Press, 2000), 4 and passim. Holger Schott Syme similarly explores "a profound structural homology" and "common structural logic" shared among "theatrical, legal, historiographical, and political modes of authorization," Holger Schott Syme, *Theatre and Testimony in Shakespeare's England: A Culture of Mediation* (Cambridge: Cambridge University Press, 2012), 5, 19, passim. Such formulations present neither the law nor the theater as marginalized by or oppositional to the rest of early modern culture but rather as deeply embedded.

29. Subha Mukherji, *Law and Representation in Early Modern Drama* (Cambridge: Cambridge University Press, 2006), 55–56, 67, 42–45.

30. For the phrase "conceptual ecologies," see Katherine Rowe, "Inconstancy: Changeable Affections in Stuart Dramas of Contract," in *Environment and Embodiment in Early Modern England*, ed. Mary Floyd-Wilson and Garrett A. Sullivan (New York: Palgrave, 2007), 90–102, esp. 100. On word play, see, among others, Patricia Parker, *Shakespeare from the Margins: Language, Culture, Context* (Chicago: University of Chicago Press, 1996), esp. 18. On the circulation of objects, see, among others, Jonathan Gil Harris and Natasha Korda, eds., *Staged Properties in Early Modern English Drama* (Cambridge: Cambridge University Press, 2002); Jonathan Gil Harris, *Untimely Matter in the Time of Shakespeare* (Philadelphia: University of Pennsylvania Press, 2009); Natasha Korda, *Shakespeare's Domestic Economies: Gender and Property in Early Modern England* (Philadelphia: University of Pennsylvania Press, 2002); and Andrew Sofer, *The Stage Life of Props* (Ann Arbor: University of Michigan Press, 2003).

31. Stephen Greenblatt, *Shakespearean Negotiations: The Circulation of Social Energy in Renaissance England* (Berkeley: University of California Press, 1989), 5. Building on Greenblatt's notion of circulation, Valerie Traub studies how desire in the plays exceeds that attached to particular characters to "anonymously circulate through the texts," Traub, *Desire and Anxiety: Circulations of Sexuality in Shakespearean Drama* (London: Routledge, 1992), 18 and passim.

32. For example, see Karen Cunningham, *Imaginary Betrayals: Subjectivity and the Discourses of Treason in Early Modern England* (Philadelphia: University of Pennsylvania Press, 2002), 5; Carol Thomas Neely, *Distracted Subjects: Madness and Gender in Shakespeare and Early Modern Culture* (Ithaca, N.Y.: Cornell University Press, 2004), 7; and Anthony B. Dawson and Paul Yachnin, *The Culture of Playgoing in Shakespeare's England: A Collaborative Debate* (Cambridge: Cambridge University Press, 2001), 6.

33. Harris, *Untimely Matter*, 9. See also Yates, "Accidental Shakespeare," and Henry S. Turner, "Lessons from Literature for the Historian of Science (and Vice Versa): Reflections on 'Form'," *Isis* 101 (2010): 578–89, esp. 588–89. All these critics rely on actor-network

theory. See Bruno Latour, *Reassembling the Social: An Introduction to Actor-Network Theory* (Oxford: Oxford University Press, 2005).

34. Richard Levin, "The Poetics and Politics of Bardicide," *PMLA* 105 (1990): 491–504.

35. Fletcher, *Gender, Sex, and Subordination*, xx.

36. Wendy Wall, *Staging Domesticity: Household Work and English Identity in Early Modern Drama* (Cambridge: Cambridge University Press, 2002), 15.

37. Mary Beth Rose, *The Expense of Spirit: Love and Sexuality in English Renaissance Drama* (Ithaca, N.Y.: Cornell University Press, 1988), 131. See also Orlin, "Domestic Tragedy," 369.

38. Carla Mazzio, *The Inarticulate Renaissance: Language Trouble in an Age of Eloquence* (Philadelphia: University of Pennsylvania Press, 2009), 17.

39. Katharine Eisaman Maus, *Inwardness and Theater in the English Renaissance* (Chicago: University of Chicago Press, 1995), 32. Parker points to "a theatrical problem shared by the law courts and other contestatory sites of epistemological or evidentiary certainty, of what might be reliably substituted for what could not be directly witnessed" (*Shakespeare from the Margins*, 259). See also William N. West, " 'But this will be a mere confusion': Real and Represented Confusions on the Elizabethan Stage," *Theatre Journal* 60 (2008): 217–33, on the burdens and opportunities of confusion for spectators. Whereas some scholars argue that plays trained their audiences, others argue that they can, in turn, be taken as evidence of what audiences liked or were learning to like. See Jeremy Lopez, *Theatrical Convention and Audience Response in Early Modern Drama* (Cambridge: Cambridge University Press, 2003), 7; and Matthew Steggle, *Laughing and Weeping in Early Modern Theatres* (Aldershot: Ashgate, 2007), 1.

40. Jean E. Howard, *The Theater of a City: The Places of London Comedy, 1598–1642* (Philadelphia: University of Pennsylvania Press, 2006), 12.

41. Jean E. Howard, "The Evidence of Fiction: Women's Relationship to Goods in London City Drama," in *Culture and Change: Attending to Early Modern Women*, ed. Margaret Mikesell and Adele Seeff (Newark: University of Delaware Press, 2003), 161–76, esp. 165, 171. Similarly, Lake argues that drama and popular print provided "contemporaries with a complex, interconnected and gendered web of narrative conventions, images and tropes that allowed them to confront and control, to scare themselves with and reassure themselves about, some of the most threatening aspects of their social, religious and political worlds" (Lake, *Antichrist's Lewd Hat*, xxvi). See also Michael O'Connell, *The Idolatrous Eye: Iconoclasm and Theater in Early-Modern England* (Oxford: Oxford University Press, 2000), 19.

42. Amanda Bailey, *Flaunting: Style and the Subversive Male Body in Renaissance England* (Toronto: University of Toronto Press, 2007), 18.

43. Many critics argue that, as Daniel Vitkus puts it, the theater "played a special role in adapting, articulating, and disseminating foreignness" because, through drama, "the different appearances, behaviors, and beliefs of other cultures were imported, distorted, mimicked and displayed." Daniel Vitkus, *Turning Turk: English Theatre and the Multicultural Mediterranean* (Houndmills: Palgrave, 2002), 29. See also Emily Bartels, *Spectacles of*

Strangeness: Imperialism, Alienation, and Marlowe (Philadelphia: University of Pennsylvania Press, 2003) and *Speaking of the Moor: From "Alcazar" to "Othello"* (Philadelphia: University of Pennsylvania Press, 2008); and Ania Loomba, *Shakespeare, Race, and Colonialism* (Oxford: Oxford University Press, 2002), 8. In contrast, Marjorie Rubright argues that rather than parading differences in the interests of codifying them and then defining Englishness against this spectacle of strangeness, representations of the Dutch, on the stage and elsewhere, explored the kinship between the English and Dutch. See "Going Dutch in London City Comedy: Economies of Sexual and Sacred Exchange in John Marston's *The Dutch Courtesan* (1605)," *English Literary Renaissance* 40, 1 (Winter 2010): 88–112. Despite their differences, all these critics argue that the stage played a crucial role in what Rubright calls "ethnicity in the making."

44. Dympna Callaghan, *Shakespeare Without Women: Representing Gender and Race on the Renaissance Stage* (London: Routledge, 2000), 7.

45. Lara Bovilsky, *Barbarous Play: Race on the Renaissance Stage* (Minneapolis: University of Minnesota Press, 2008), 19; Callaghan, *Shakespeare Without Women*; Barbara Fuchs, "Faithless Empires: Pirates, Renegadoes, and the English Nation," *English Literary History* 67 (Spring 2000): 45–69.

46. Dawson and Yachnin, *Culture of Playgoing*, 5; Lake, *Antichrist's Lewd Hat*, xxxi.

47. Henry S. Turner, *The English Renaissance Stage: Geometry, Poetics, and the Practical Spatial Arts, 1580–1630* (Oxford: Oxford University Press, 2006), 30.

48. Lorna Hutson, "Fortunate Travelers: Reading for the Plot in Sixteenth-Century England," *Representations* 41 (Winter 1993): 83–103; Martin Brückner and Kristen Poole, "The Plot Thickens: Surveying Manuals, Drama, and the Materiality of Narrative Form in Early Modern England," *English Literary History* 69 (2002): 617–48; Turner, *English Renaissance Stage*, 21, 24.

49. Greenblatt, *Shakespearean Negotiations*, 8.

50. Lake, *Antichrist's Lewd Hat*, xxx–xxxi, xxxiv.

51. David Schalkwyk, *Shakespeare, Love and Service* (Cambridge: Cambridge University Press, 2008), 36–37.

52. As Dympna Callaghan shows, Shakespeare often serves as evidence not of history but of aspects of the human condition that are outside history, Dympna Callaghan, "The Ideology of Romantic Love: The Case of *Romeo and Juliet*," in *The Weyward Sisters: Shakespeare and Feminist Politics*, by Dympna Callaghan, Lorraine Helms, and Jyotsna Singh (Cambridge, Mass: Blackwell, 1994), 59–101, 67–68.

53. See Kidnie, *Shakespeare and the Problem of Adaptation*; Harris, *Untimely Matter*; Linda Charnes, *Hamlet's Heirs: Shakespeare and the Politics of a New Millennium* (London: Routledge, 2006); and Madhavi Menon, *Unhistorical Shakespeare: Queer Theory in Shakespearean Literature and Film* (New York: Palgrave, 2008).

54. Leah S. Marcus, *Puzzling Shakespeare: Local Reading and Its Discontents* (Berkeley: University of California Press, 1988), xi–xii.

55. Bruce R. Smith, *Phenomenal Shakespeare* (Malden, Mass.: Wiley-Blackwell, 2010), 181, 182.

56. Kathryn Schwarz, *What You Will: Gender, Contract, and Shakespearean Social Space* (Philadelphia: University of Pennsylvania Press, 2011), 20.

57. Valerie Forman, *Tragicomic Redemptions: Global Economics and the Early Modern English Stage* (Philadelphia: University of Pennsylvania Press, 2008), 23.

58. David Glimp, *Increase and Multiply: Governing Cultural Reproduction in Early Modern England* (Minneapolis: University of Minnesota Press, 2003), 69. Although Tiffany Stern (*Documents of Performance*) argues that these parts of plays were probably not written by the author(s) of the rest of the play, this would not alter their status as reflections on the stage's relation to its audience.

59. These are what Wall calls "hypercharged dramatic moments" and "scenes that depict curiously heightened emotional expressions" (Wall, *Staging Domesticity*, 5, 11). See also Paul A. Kottman, *A Politics of the Scene* (Palo Alto, Calif.: Stanford University Press, 2007); Lori Humphrey Newcomb, *Reading Popular Romance in Early Modern England* (New York: Columbia University Press, 2002); and Jeffrey Dolven, *Scenes of Instruction in Renaissance Romance* (Chicago: University of Chicago Press, 2007).

60. Wendy Wall, "Just a Spoonful of Sugar: Syrup and Domesticity in Early Modern England," *Modern Philology* 104, 2 (2006): 149–72, esp. 155. Laslett concedes that "literary evidence is persuasive as to incidentals, especially of the material environment" (Laslett, "Wrong Way," 327).

61. Wall, "Just a Spoonful of Sugar," 172, 151.

62. Howard, "Evidence of Fiction," 165, and *Theater of a City*, 120. Richard Strier argues that "resistant structures" are "there" in Renaissance texts and that the appropriately modest critic attends to what is there, even what resists his or her own hypotheses, Strier, *Resistant Structures: Particularity, Radicalism, and Renaissance Texts* (Berkeley: University of California Press, 1995), 8. While I hope I am not advocating immodesty, I emphasize the importance of what is *not* there in texts and what interpretation requires the reader to supply to join what is there to what is not.

63. Schwarz, *What You Will*, 21.

64. Margreta de Grazia, *Hamlet Without Hamlet* (Cambridge: Cambridge University Press, 2007).

65. Lorna Hutson, *The Invention of Suspicion: Law and Mimesis in Shakespeare and Renaissance Drama* (Oxford: Oxford University Press, 2007), 68, 106, 1.

66. Gordon McMullan, "Introduction," in William Shakespeare and John Fletcher, *King Henry VIII*, Arden Shakespeare, Third Series (London: Thompson Learning, 2000), 63, 8. Throughout my discussion of the play, I rely on McMullan's introduction and edition.

67. Thomas Cogswell and Peter Lake, "Buckingham Does the Globe: *Henry VIII* and the Politics of Popularity in the 1620s," *Shakespeare Quarterly* 60, 3 (2009): 253–78, esp. 253. Focusing on this later performance, Cogswell and Lake remind us that plays can provide evidence of tastes and interests not only at the time they were first printed but when they were revived or reprinted. On this, see also Alan Farmer and Zachary Lesser, "Canons and Classics: Publishing Drama in Caroline England," in *Localizing Caroline Drama: Politics*

and Economics of the Early Modern English Stage, 1625–1642, ed. Alan Farmer and Adam Zucker (New York: Palgrave, 2006), 17–41.

68. The fire is remarkably well documented. See E. K. Chambers, *The Elizabethan Stage* (Oxford: Clarendon, 1923), 4 vols, 2: 419–22, esp. 420, for Wotton's letter. Dawson and Yachnin offer contrasting interpretations of Wotton's letter (*Culture of Playgoing*, 88–89, 119). For other accounts, see Maija Jansson Cole, "A New Account of the Burning of the Globe," *Shakespeare Quarterly* 32, 3 (1981), 352; and Adam Smyth, "A New Record of the 1613 Globe Fire During a Performance of Shakespeare's *King Henry VIII*," *Notes and Queries* 52 (June 2005): 214–16. McMullan also reproduces and discusses some of these accounts in his edition of *King Henry VIII*, 58–60.

69. Ellen MacKay, *Persecution, Plague and Fire: Fugitive Histories of the Stage in Early Modern England* (Chicago: University of Chicago Press, 2011), 5, 156.

70. Lee Bliss, "The Wheel of Fortune and the Maiden Phoenix of Shakespeare's *King Henry VIII*," *English Literary History* 42, 1 (1975): 1–25, esp. 2, 3. Bliss responded to and revised earlier work that assumed that the play has "a pervasive providential cast," as Howard Felperin put it. See Howard Felperin, *Shakespearean Romance* (Princeton, N.J.: Princeton University Press, 1972), 197, 209; and David Scott Kastan, *Shakespeare and the Shapes of Time* (Hanover, N.H.: University Press of New England, 1982), 133–40, esp. 139.

71. Judith Anderson, *Biographical Truth: The Representation of Historical Persons in Tudor-Stuart Writing* (New Haven, Conn.: Yale University Press, 1984), 126, 124. The argument that the play is skeptical about truth claims has reached a kind of consensus. See Ivo Kamps, "Possible Pasts: Historiography and Legitimation in *Henry VIII*," *College English* 58, 2 (1996): 192–215; Thomas Healy, "History and Judgement in *Henry VIII*," in *Shakespeare's Late Plays: New Readings*, ed. Jennifer Richards and James Knowles (Edinburgh: Edinburgh University Press, 1999), 158–75; Zenón Luis-Martinez, " 'Maimed Narrations': Shakespeare's *Henry VIII* and the Task of the Historian," *Explorations in Renaissance Culture* 27, 2 (Winter 2001): 205–43; Madhavi Menon, *Wanton Words: Rhetoric and Sexuality in English Renaissance Drama* (Toronto: University of Toronto Press, 2004), 168; and Peter L. Rudnytsky, "*Henry VIII* and the Deconstruction of History," in *Shakespeare and Politics*, ed. Catherine M. S. Alexander (Cambridge: Cambridge University Press, 2004), 44–66. I find particularly helpful Barbara Kreps, "When All Is True: Law, History and Problems of Knowledge in *Henry VIII*," *Shakespeare Survey* 52 (1999): 166–82, as will be evident in my engagement with her below.

72. McMullan, "Introduction," 105. See also Dennis Kezar, "Law/Form/History: Shakespeare's Verdict in *All Is True*," *Modern Language Quarterly* 63, 1 (2002): 1–30, esp. 14, 30.

73. McMullan, "Introduction," 9–10.

74. Kreps, "When All Is True," 181. See also Frank V. Cespedes, " 'We are one in fortunes': The Sense of History in *Henry VIII*," *English Literary Renaissance* 10, 3 (1980): 413–38, esp. 416; and Jonathan Baldo, "Forgetting Elizabeth in *Henry VIII*," in *Resurrecting Elizabeth I in Seventeenth-Century England*, ed. Elizabeth H. Hageman and Katherine Conway (Madison, N.J.: Fairleigh Dickinson University Press, 2007), 132–48.

75. Chris R. Kyle, "*Henry VIII, or All Is True*: Shakespeare's 'Favourite' Play," in *How to Do Things with Shakespeare: New Approaches, New Essays*, ed. Laurie Maguire (Malden, Mass.: Blackwell, 2008), 82–100, esp. 86.

76. Stuart M. Kurland. "*Henry VIII* and James I: Shakespeare and Jacobean Politics," *Shakespeare Studies* 19 (1987): 203–17; William M. Baillie, "*Henry VIII*: A Jacobean History," *Shakespeare Studies* 12 (1979): 247–66. See also Anston Bosman, "Seeing Tears: Truth and Sense in *All Is True*," *Shakespeare Quarterly* 50, 4 (1999): 459–76.

77. Susan Frye, "Anne of Denmark and the Historical Contextualisation of Shakespeare and Fletcher's *Henry VIII*," in *Women and Politics in Early Modern England, 1450–1700*, ed. James Daybell (Aldershot: Ashgate, 2004), 181–93, esp. 184. The queens, like the favorites with whom they compete, are also figures for the subject's relation to the king. On queens in the play, see also Kim H. Noling, "Grubbing Up the Stock: Dramatizing Queens in *Henry VIII*," *Shakespeare Quarterly* 39 (1988): 291–306; Jo Eldridge Carney, "Queenship in Shakespeare's *Henry VIII*: The Issue of Issue," in *Political Rhetoric, Power, and Renaissance Women*, ed. Carole Levin and Patricia A. Sullivan (Albany: State University of New York Press, 1995), 189–202; Phyllis Rackin, *Stages of History: Shakespeare's English Chronicles* (Ithaca, N.Y.: Cornell University Press, 1990), 164–66, 176, 194; and Ruth Vanita, "Mariological Memory in *The Winter's Tale* and *Henry VIII*," *Studies in English Literature* 40, 2 (2000): 311–37, esp. 328. On the ways in which the play troubles reproduction and succession, see Steven Bruhm, "The Unbearable Sex of Henry VIII," in *Shakesqueer: A Queer Companion to the Complete Works of Shakespeare*, ed. Madhavi Menon (Durham, N.C.: Duke University Press, 2011), 28–38; Glimp, *Increase and Multiply*; and Menon, *Wanton Words*.

78. Kezar, "Law/Form/History," 28.

79. Frye, "Anne of Denmark," 428.

80. McMullan, "Introduction," 95, 92. In his emphasis on the play's cyclical structure, McMullan follows Clifford Leech, "The Structure of the Last Plays," *Shakespeare Studies* 2 (1958): 19–30.

81. *Henry VIII* Prologue 25–27; Syme, *Theatre and Testimony*, 239, 240.

82. Julia M. Walker, "Reading the Tombs of Elizabeth I," *English Literary Renaissance* 26 (1996): 510–30.

83. Cogswell and Lake, "Buckingham Does the Globe," 255, 258, 270. Another example of a performance supposedly commissioned for political ends, and requiring viewers to grasp relations between the history dramatized and the present moment, would be the much-discussed staging of a play about Richard II on the eve of the Essex rebellion. For a survey of and intervention in the debate, see Paul E. J. Hammer, "Shakespeare's *Richard II*, the Play of 7 February 1601, and the Essex Rising," *Shakespeare Quarterly* 59 (2008): 1–35. Several critics have argued that relating the drama to politics intensified in the decade leading up to the closing of the theaters and thereafter. See Martin Butler, *Theatre and Crisis, 1632–1642* (Cambridge: Cambridge University Press, 1984), 271; and Susan Wiseman, *Drama and Politics in the English Civil War* (Cambridge: Cambridge University Press, 1998), 16.

84. Cogswell and Lake, "Buckingham Does the Globe," 257.

85. Ibid., 258, 278.

86. Ibid., 271, 272, 278.

87. Mario DiGangi, *Sexual Types: Embodiment, Agency, and Dramatic Character from Shakespeare to Shirley* (Philadelphia: University of Pennsylvania Press, 2011), 7; see also 223–24. On the "monstrous favorite" more generally, see DiGangi, 192–220; and Curtis Perry, *Literature and Favoritism in Early Modern England* (Cambridge: Cambridge University Press, 2006). For other studies of the complex operations of types, see Valerie Traub, *The Renaissance of Lesbianism in Early Modern England* (Cambridge: Cambridge University Press, 2002); Jennifer Panek, *Widows and Suitors in Early Modern English Comedy* (Cambridge: Cambridge University Press, 2004); and Pamela Allen Brown, *Better a Shrew Than a Sheep: Women, Drama, and the Culture of Jest in Early Modern England* (Ithaca, N.Y.: Cornell University Press, 2003).

88. Ian Hacking, *The Social Construction of What?* (Cambridge, Mass.: Harvard University Press, 1999), 34.

89. Valerie Traub, "The Present Future of Lesbian Historiography," in *A Companion to Lesbian, Gay, Bisexual, Transgender, and Queer Studies*, ed. George Haggerty and Molly McGarry (Oxford: Blackwell, 2007), 124–45, esp. 127.

90. Chilton Latham Powell, *English Domestic Relations, 1487–1653* (New York: Columbia University Press, 1917), 219. On the text's authorship, see Henry Ansgar Kelly, *The Matrimonial Trials of Henry VIII* (Stanford, Calif.: Stanford University Press, 1976), 123, 198. EEBO presents Henry VIII as the author of this text. It appears to have been printed twice in the same year.

91. J. Christopher Warner, *Henry VIII's Divorce: Literature and the Politics of the Printing Press* (Woodbridge: Boydell, 1998), 40–41.

92. On the legal fiction that a child born in wedlock is legitimate, see Bradin Cormack, *A Power to Do Justice: Jurisdiction, English Literature, and the Rise of Common Law, 1509–1625* (Chicago: University of Chicago Press, 2007), 291–329.

93. On the testimony about the consummation of the marriage, compare Edward Herbert's *Life and Raigne of King Henry the Eight* (London, 1649), which includes statements from male deponents repeating Arthur's boast and testifying that they themselves had been able to "carnally know and use" at Arthur's age (Hh2r–v), to Thomas Baily's, *The Life and Death of That Renowned John Fisher, Bishop of Rochester . . . with a full relation of Qu: Katherines Divorce* (London, 1655), which presents Doctor Ridley dismissing the "frolic or jest" about being in Spain as "meere conjectures and presumptions" that should not be allowed "to stand in competition with so great a testimony" as the queen's "attestation" (G1v).

94. Kreps, "When All Is True," 169.

95. Eric Ives, *The Life and Death of Anne Boleyn* (London: Blackwell, 2004), 201.

96. Cunningham, *Imaginary Betrayals*, 8–9. See also Ives, *Life and Death of Anne Boleyn*, 344–45 and passim.

97. Wegemer points out that the phrase "All Is True" only appears in *The Winter's*

Tale, where Leontes insists that all is true "as he perceives it": "All's true that is mistrusted" (2.1.50). Gerald Wegemer, "Henry VIII on Trial: Confronting Malice and Conscience in Shakespeare's *All Is True*," *Renascence* 52, 2 (2000): 111–30, esp. 126.

98. Syme, *Theatre and Testimony*, 239.

99. Bliss, "Wheel of Fortune," 3, 4. On this opening exchange, see also A. Lynne Magnusson, "The Rhetoric of Politeness and *Henry VIII*," *Shakespeare Quarterly* 43, 4 (1992): 391–409, esp. 392, 406. On the reliability of testimony, see also Camille Wells Slights, "The Politics of Conscience in *All Is True* (or *Henry VIII*)," *Shakespeare Survey* 43 (1991): 59–68; and Susannah Brietz Monta, " 'Thou fall'st a blessed martyr': Shakespeare's *Henry VIII* and the Polemics of Conscience," *English Literary Renaissance* 30, 2 (2000): 262–83.

100. Kreps points out that the play does not directly tackle the question of whether Katherine's marriage to Arthur was consummated (178–79).

101. Powell, *English Domestic Relations*, 114n1; Heinrich Bullinger, *Christen State of Matrimonye* (Antwerp, 1541), facsimile in *Conduct Literature for Women, 1500–1640*, ed. William St. Clair and Irmgard Maassen, vol. 2 (London: Pickering & Chatto, 2000), sigs. I8r–v.

102. Louis B. Wright, *Middle-Class Culture in Elizabethan England* (Chapel Hill: The University of North Carolina Press, 1935), 203. More recent critics of *Henry VIII* or *All Is True* have argued that the play's subject matter links it to other discussions of marriage. See Vanita, "Mariological Memory," 323, and Kezar, "Law/Form/History," 30.

103. William Gouge, *Of Domesticall Duties* (London, 1622), sigs. R4v–R5r. Gouge similarly enjoins children (sig. Hh4v) and servants (Qq4r–Qq5r; Ss2v–Ss3r) against spreading or hearkening to "relations" about their parents and employers. While he warns that servants who are tale-bearers "are even as treacherous spies, the most dangerous enemies that can be" (Ss3r), he makes the telling exception that servants should alert one spouse of the other's sinful or criminal intentions (sig. Ss5r).

104. Annabel Patterson denigrates Fletcher's potential as a collaborator in " 'All Is True': Negotiating the Past in *Henry VIII*," in *Elizabethan Theater: Essays in Honor of S. Schoenbaum*, ed. R. B. Parker and S. P. Zitner (Newark: University of Delaware Press, 1996), 147–66, esp. 153.

105. Jeffrey Masten, *Textual Intercourse: Collaboration, Authorship, and Sexualities in Renaissance Drama* (Cambridge: Cambridge University Press, 1997); Brian Vickers, *Shakespeare, Co-Author* (Oxford: Oxford University Press, 2002); and Heather Anne Hirschfeld, *Joint Enterprises: Collaborative Drama and the Institutionalization of the English Renaissance Theater* (Amherst: University of Massachusetts Press, 2004). For a challenge to what he calls a "new orthodoxy," see Jeffrey Knapp, *Shakespeare Only* (Chicago: University of Chicago Press, 2009).

106. Tiffany Stern, " 'The Forgery of some modern Author'? Theobald's Shakespeare and Cardenio's *Double Falsehood*," *Shakespeare Quarterly* 62, 4 (2012): 555–93, esp. 568.

107. Lewis Theobald, *Double Falshood; or, The Distrest Lovers. A Play. . . . Written Originally by W. Shakespeare; And now Revised and Adapted to the Stage by Mr. Theobald* (London, 1728), sigs. A3r, A3v–A4r, A5r–A5v.

108. As Howard Marchitello argues, we are always finding *Cardenio* and then losing it again. Marchitello, "Finding *Cardenio*," *English Literary History* 74 (2007): 957–87.

109. *Double Falsehood*, ed. Brean Hammond (London: A & C Black, 2010), 1–3. Subsequent references to Hammond's introduction and to the play refer to this edition and appear in parentheses. *The Norton Shakespeare*, following the *Oxford Shakespeare*, includes a one-page discussion of *Cardenio* and *Double Falsehood* by the Oxford editors, concluding that, while *Double Falsehood* "deserved its limited success, it is now no more than an interesting curiosity" (3109).

110. John Freehafer, "*Cardenio*, by Shakespeare and Fletcher," *PMLA* 84, 3 (1969): 501–13, esp. 501.

111. Philip Lorenz, "Absonant Desire: The Question of *Cardenio*," in *Shakesqueer: A Queer Companion to the Complete Works of Shakespeare*, ed. Madhavi Menon (Durham, N.C.: Duke University Press, 2011), 62–71, esp. 69.

112. Theobald, *Double Falshood*, sig. A4v.

113. Jennifer Richards and James Knowles, "Introduction: Shakespeare's Late Plays," in *Shakespeare's Late Plays: New Readings*, ed. Jennifer Richards and James Knowles (Edinburgh: Edinburgh University Press, 1999), 1–21, esp. 18–19; Stern, "Forgery," 592.

114. See the Oxford University Press online description of *The Quest for Cardenio: Shakespeare, Fletcher, Cervantes, and the Lost Play*, ed. David Carnegie and Gary Taylor (Oxford: Oxford University Press, 2012).

115. Julia Briggs, "Tears at the Wedding: Shakespeare's Last Phase," in *Shakespeare's Late Plays: New Readings*, ed. Richards and Knowles, 210–27, esp. 222. Interestingly, the Eighteenth-Century Collections Online database suggests in a note attached to the full citations for the four printings of the play it includes that it was "Probably written originally by James Shirley."

116. Stern, "Forgery," 577.

117. Barbara Fuchs, "Beyond the Missing *Cardenio*: Anglo-Spanish Relations in Early Modern Drama," *Journal of Medieval and Early Modern Studies* 39, 1 (Winter 2009): 143–59, 145.

118. Richard Wilson, *Secret Shakespeare: Studies in Theatre, Religion, and Resistance* (Manchester: Manchester University Press, 2004), 235–36. Compare this to Wilson's "Unseasonable Laughter: The Context of *Cardenio*," in *Shakespeare's Late Plays: New Readings*, ed. Richards and Knowles, 193–209, esp. 199.

119. Wilson, *Secret Shakespeare*, 240, 238, 236, 242, 239.

120. Fuchs, "Beyond the Missing *Cardenio*," 149, 155, 156, 143 (cf. 151), 146.

Index

Acknowledgments

In some ways, this project began a long time ago at the Newberry Library, when Robyn Muncy and I spent a summer working as interns for John Tedeschi. Our assignment was to find out all we could about names and titles on the Index of Prohibited Books. Burrowing through the stacks in a library closed for renovation, I got hands-on training in research, training of a sort most graduate students in English do not get. I made a friend for life, and I learned early on to think in relation to historians and their discipline. Much later, a National Endowment for the Humanities/Newberry Library Fellowship enabled me to conduct some of the research that would lead to this book, while I was also working on another project. In short, I have long-standing debts to the Newberry as the place where I learned the pleasures of sleuthing and interdisciplinarity.

I wrote this book largely while I have been on the faculty at the University of California at Davis, which has been, for me, a most congenial environment. Two chairs, Margaret Ferguson and Scott Simmon, helped me find the time and resources I needed in a variety of ways. In the years I was working on the book, my dean, Jessie Ann Owens, helped to arrange a Faculty Development Award, a Henry A. Young Dean's Society Fellowship, and publication subvention to support my work. Two colleagues, Alessa Johns and Gregory Dobbins, nominated me for awards; these were time-consuming processes for them, and I deeply appreciate their votes of confidence and their efforts on my behalf.

I am grateful for two fellowships without which I would not have been able to finish the book. One from the John Simon Guggenheim Memorial Foundation enabled me to complete a draft. I am grateful to Patricia Fumerton, Linda Woodbridge, Carol Neely, and Margaret Ferguson for writing in support of my application. A Fletcher Jones Foundation Distinguished Fellowship at the Huntington Library enabled me to revise and finish the book. I am grateful to Robert C. Ritchie for appointing me to the fellowship and to Steve Hindle for so ably directing research during my tenure. Juan Gomez offered help and kindness. My fellows at the Huntington, especially Elizabeth Allen, Lisa Cody, Heidi Brayman-Hackel, Sarah Easterby-Smith, Elizabeth Eger, Ann R. Jones, Heather Keenleyside, Rachel Klein, Peter Stallybrass, Harry Stout, Will West, Bob Westman, Kariann Yokota, and Carla Zecher made my time there enjoyable as well as productive.

Dympna Callaghan, Ray Clemens, Karen Cunningham, Christopher Kyle, Lowell Gallagher, Jean Howard, Ethan Shagan, and Richard Strier all extended invitations—some of them quite long ago—that prompted me to write my way toward and through this book. Audiences at the Clark, Folger, Huntington, and Newberry libraries, University of Arizona, Indiana University, New York University, Columbia University, Northwestern University, University of Chicago, University of California at Berkeley, and Washington State University all offered helpful comments and questions. Of the many people I have conversed with in various places, I remain mindful of Susan Amussen, John Archer, Meg Lota Brown, Todd Butler, Thomas Cogswell, Vanessa Corredera, Kari Boyd McBride, Will Fisher, Julia Fleming, Patricia Fumerton, Constance Furey, Tyler Fyotek, Ernst Gilman, John Guillory, William Hamlin, Deborah Harkness, Cyndi Headley, Carmen Ortiz Henley, Amy Hollywood, David Kastan, Rebecca Lemon, Julia Lupton, Ellen Mackay, Arthur Marotti, Jeffrey Masten, Edward Muir, Linda Levy Peck, Kyle Pivetti, Lyndal Roper, Marjorie Rubright, Laurie Shannon, James Shapiro, Deborah Shuger, Michael Slater, Regina Schwartz, Valerie Traub, and Wendy Wall.

Gina Bloom, Margaret Ferguson, Lowell Gallagher, Jessica Murphy, Kathryn Schwarz, Laura M. Stevens, and William N. West all read chapters in draft and offered invaluable comments. I am very lucky to have Gina and Margie as my colleagues at Davis. I am also grateful to two anonymous readers for the press, who read the whole manuscript in a longer version and offered both encouragement and helpful suggestions for improvement. While I have no one to blame but myself, I am deeply grateful to these readers for their counsel. At the University of Pennsylvania Press, Jerome Singerman expressed interest in the project early on, encouraged me to get it done and send it out, and supported it right up to the finish line. He is a pleasure to work with. I am also grateful for the help of Caroline Winschel and Alison Anderson at the press and to Mary Lou Bertucci for her copyediting, Alex Trotter for the index preparation, and John Hubbard for the cover design.

Three of the chapters have appeared in earlier forms. They have all been reframed and revised. Chapter 1 first appeared as "True and Perfect Relations: Or, Identifying Henry Garnet and Leticia Wigington by Their Confessions,"

ACKNOWLEDGMENTS 331

in *Redrawing the Map of Early Modern English Catholicism*, ed. Lowell Gallagher (Toronto: University of Toronto Press, 2012), 52-83. I am grateful to
the press for permission to reprint it here. I first grappled with the ideas and
materials in Chapter 2 in "'Ridiculous Fictions': Making Distinctions in the
Discourses of Witchcraft," *differences: A Journal of Feminist Cultural Studies* 7,
2 (1995): 82-110. Stuart Clark acknowledged this article as "one of the first attempts to look at the role of narrative conventions in deciding matters of truth
and fact in witchcraft cases"; see Clark, "Introduction," in *Languages of Witchcraft: Narrative, Ideology and Meaning in Early Modern Culture* (Houndmills:
Macmillan, 2001), 1-18, esp. 11. I have dramatically revised, expanded, and reframed my analysis to engage the scholarship that has been done since. While
the chapter has been reconceived so substantially as to be unrecognizable, I remain grateful to the journal for a formative process of revision at its inception
and for allowing me to publish it in its final form. Chapter 3 began as "Ashes
and 'the Archive': The London Fire of 1666, Partisanship, and Proof," *Journal
of Medieval and Early Modern Studies* 31, 2 (2001): 379-408. I am grateful to the
journal for allowing me to reprint the essay in revised form here.

In the process of finding materials, securing permissions, and identifying
illustrations, I have incurred debts to Mario Corral, Alisa Monheim, Jaeda
Snow, Stephen Tabor, Catherine Wehrey, and Jennifer Watts at the Hunting-
ton Library; to Megan Dunmall, archivist at the Canterbury Cathedral Ar-
chives; Andrew George, Kevin Briggs, and Joanne Peck at the Lichfield Record
Office; and Caitriona McCabe at Tower Bridge. I would also like to thank
Claire Dawkins, Natalie Giannini, Tara Pedersen, Anna Pruitt, and Vanessa
Rapatz for research assistance and Kelly Neil for help proofreading.

Robyn Muncy has sustained, amused, and counseled me in the weekly
conversations through which we've assessed and managed life and work in the
thirty years since we met at the Newberry. I "love the limbo," too, as long as
we're in it together. Deborah Harkness and Karen Haltunnen found room on
busy schedules and set a place at the table, and made me laugh and think. Wit,
whole grains, and wine; histories, stories, and the relations between the two. It
was more than I could have hoped for. Thank you. Scott Shershow was completely present even during my absences, flexible, supportive, and nourishing
in every sense. He is woven into my work process and the reward at the end of
the day. How did I get so lucky?